A PURE DROP'

A PURE DROP'
The Life Of **Jeff Buckley**

A Biography by **Jeff Apter**

OMNIBUS PRESS

London/New York/Los Angeles/Paris/Copenhagen/Madrid/Berlin/Sydney/Tokyo

Exclusive Distributors
Music Sales Limited,
14/15 Berners Street,
London, W1T 3LJ.

Music Sales Corporation,
257 Park Avenue South,
New York, NY 10010, USA.

Macmillan Distribution Services,
53 Park West Drive,
Derrimut, Vic 3030,
Australia.

Every effort has been made to trace the copyright holders of the photographs in this book but one or
two were unreachable. We would be grateful if the photographers concerned would contact us.

Typeset by Phoenix Photosetting, Chatham, Kent
Printed by Gutenberg Press Ltd, Malta

A catalogue record for this book is available from the British Library.

Visit Omnibus Press on the web at www.omnibuspress.com

Contents

For Christian

'Jeff Buckley was a pure drop in an ocean of noise.' – Bono

Introduction

I've written books where the subject has been willing to have their life turned inside out, and other books where the subject has been more elusive than Spiderman. There's a vast difference between someone not wanting to speak in their own defence, and someone not being able to do so, as is the case with Jeff Buckley. The writer Susan Orlean once compared this type of quest to being 'a little like studying animal tracks and concluding everything from the impression that it has left behind.' That's exactly how I felt as this book came together: what remains of Jeff Buckley is a handful of songs, some finished, some merely sketches, and the vivid memories he left behind. That's not a whole lot to go on, really.

Jeff Scott Buckley lived any number of lives: suburban loner, music school misfit, west coast headbanger, New York troubadour, rock and roll gypsy, Memphis dreamer, lover, poet, boozer, schemer, band leader, dog stalker. And he also got close to hundreds of people, although it's questionable whether many of them were allowed to get too close in return. There's no doubting that he was damaged goods – anyone whose father jumps the family ship *even before you're born* is bound to carry some heavy emotional baggage. So there was some dark meat on this bird, but he was also a goof, a professional 'doofus', in the words of one friend, a guy who could seamlessly segue from a heart-breaking ballad to an impression of Robert Plant – at 78rpm, no less – all in the time it would take to reach the bar, buy a drink and return to your seat. The commonly held perception of Buckley as some darkly romantic brooder is about as accurate as saying John Lennon was all about bed-ins for peace: it's really only one chapter of a long and wayward story, and it doesn't do the guy justice. There were so many sides to Buckley he was almost round.

So how do you accurately capture the life of a guy that, as one insider told me, only revealed itself with any clarity after his tragic death? 'There was a woman in England, someone in France, a woman in Canada, things I only found out after he died,' a friend of his told me, 'but at the time he made you feel like you were one of the most important people in his life.'

My solution was to let his friends, peers, enemies, lovers, collaborators and others tell their tales and let the story grow from there. Everyone I spoke with had a Jeff Buckley story, be it the tour manager who had to explain to the desk clerk how both beds in his Sydney hotel room came to be wrecked – a crime of passion, as it turned out – or a friend of Jeff's father who, after meeting the son for the first time, exclaimed: 'Tim died and sent us an angel.' Then there was a Buckley buddy from the early days, when he was a struggling guitarist in LA, who told me how socially inept he could be. '[Jeff would] 'always [be] picking up weird shit and running up to you like a five year old and sticking it in your face,' he recalled. Another insider described Jeff as having an 'emotional feral-ness' about him. Others just loved his voice. Some simply loved him.

As incomplete as his life was – he took his fateful dip in the Mississippi literally hours before starting rehearsals on his latest attempt to record a follow-up to 1994's remarkable *Grace* – Buckley lived an incredibly full 30 years. Some even felt that he had a sense of his future. 'I think he was trying to shove a lot of stuff into his short life, to get as much experience as he could,' I was told. Yet another friend told me that any suggestion he had a death wish was way off the mark. 'The next asshole who walks up to me and says that shit... it brings out that really South Central side of me that wants to knock someone the fuck out.' I've drawn no radical new conclusions about his death; it was a misadventure, a poorly timed and badly executed swim that was typical of the freewheeling, often reckless side of his nature. The fact that he was wailing 'Whole Lotta Love' at the time, one of his favourite songs from one of his favourite bands, only makes his demise more poignant and somehow pointless at the same time.

As I write this, more than 10 years have slipped away since Buckley did likewise. But he's impossible to avoid: his take on 'Hallelujah' – a cover of a cover, as it turns out – appears to be the go-to song whenever a TV show or film needs some emotional set dressing. Nowadays almost every other band with a widescreen flair and a worthy singer, not least such critical and commercial giants as Radiohead and Coldplay, readily confess to Buckley's influence on their craft. It's no small achievement for a guy who has had way more music released since he died than while he walked amongst us, and who freely admitted that he didn't exactly have a 'reservoir of songs' to draw from. Tunes came to him infrequently, but when they did, they hit him hard and fast.

In the end, though, it all boils down to a singular tragedy that brought about the demise of a still-developing talent, the poignancy of his life and death only heightened by the echoes of his own father's life and equally premature end. Like father like son indeed, as much as Jeff Buckley would have been uncomfortable with the connection.

Prologue

St Ann's Church, Brooklyn Heights, New York, April 26, 1991
'Greetings from Tim Buckley' Tribute Concert

The kid sure did look familiar. Even such veterans as Hal Willner, the event's producer, and Herb Cohen, the guy who suggested inviting him in the first place, were shaking their heads in disbelief. And these were seasoned campaigners who in their various roles as dilettante, manager, insider and confidant hadn't just seen everything, but met everyone, too. Lou Reed and Frank Zappa, to name just two, ranked among their associates. Yet the kid, who had asked to be billed for tonight's tribute as 'Jeff Scott Buckley', with his tousled mane of hair and what he disdainfully referred to as his 'unibrow' – an unfortunate union of his two eyebrows, somewhere over the bridge of his nose – simply had to be the son of the late Tim Buckley, the evening's star-in-absentia. He just looked too much like his long-gone father to be mistaken for anyone else. And then, when the kid finally took the stage, alongside New York guitarist and one-time Captain Beefheart consort Gary Lucas, and opened his mouth to begin singing his father's 'I Never Asked To Be Your Mountain', a cop out of a song actually written about Jeff and his mother Mary Guibert, and their strange, brief role in Tim's life, there was clearly no mistake: this was a Buckley. His voice packed the same sense of grandeur, the type of other-worldliness that made his father's recordings from the 1960s and '70s so unique. This bird could sing.

Greetings From Tim Buckley was part of the annual 'Arts at St Ann's' series of shows, put on by Willner, a fabulously well-connected New York tastemaker, and Janine Nichols, the St Ann's program director. Together they'd presented such previous nights as *Songs for Drella*, Lou Reed and John Cale's nod to their Factory mentor Andy Warhol. This year's event opened on a lighthearted note, with a Public Service Announcement voiced by Tim, talking up the US Army Reserve, crackling over the PA. (Jeff had unearthed the tape amongst his collection of his father's things, back at home on the west coast.) But then the night got serious, as jazz guys, keyboard player Anthony Coleman and guitarist Elliott Sharp, re-interpreted 'Strange Feelin'' for the downtown set. Shelley Hirsch, later to join Buckley on stage, then delivered 'Café', followed by 'Come Here Woman'. Buckley buddy Eric Andersen gave a downbeat interpretation of 'Song for Janie', before Syd Straw came on stage and worked herself into a Tim Buckley-worthy lather during 'The Earth Is Broken' and, later on, 'Pleasant Street'. Punk vet Richard Hell growled his way through 'Moulin Rouge', before throwing the curve-ball that was 'Chinese Rocks', definitely not a Tim Buckley song, belted out in honour of hard-living New York Dolls' guitarist Johnny Thunders, who'd OD'd and died a few days before in New Orleans. (Given that Tim Buckley had also OD'd, back in 1975, this was an act of questionable tact, but Hell, ever the maverick, carried on regardless.)

Most of the 21 pieces in the tribute were played by members drawn from an ensemble that included Coleman, Sharon Freeman (French horn and piano), cellist Hank Roberts, and one (or more) of five guitarists, whose numbers included Robert Quine, who'd worked with Lou Reed, and GE Smith, the sometimes bandleader on *Saturday Night Live,* whose impressive CV also included stints with touring bands backing Bob Dylan, Mick Jagger and David Bowie. Many of the night's performances were taken from *Starsailor*, the album thought to be both Buckley's best and most challenging, and those on the bill were to be applauded for not heading straight to the obvious – 'Song To The Siren', for instance, which had been posthumously turned into an alt-rock anthem of longing and loss by gloomy Goths This Mortal Coil. But nothing, as yet, had grabbed the attentive, yet slightly distracted crowd by their short hairs, as Buckley himself so often did in concert.

Then Jeff Buckley and Lucas quietly took their turn on stage, and the mood in the stately St Ann's hall changed. As Lucas unleashed a firestorm of guitar effects and sonic ambience – a sort of revamped take on the Beatles' 'Tomorrow Never Knows', minus Ringo's legendary backwards drum loops – Jeff inhabited 'I Never Asked To Be Your Mountain', swooping and wailing in a style not too far from that of *qawwali*, the musical mantras of his beloved Nusrat Fateh Ali Khan. Although he constantly downplayed his relationship with his father, whom he'd met only a handful of times, Buckley understood 'Mountain' deeply; he recognised the role that he and his mother, Mary Guibert, played in the song. He revealed this to *Interview* magazine in 1994. '["Mountain"] was about him having to take the gypsy life over a regular one,' he explained. 'I both admired it and hated it, so that's why I sang it.'[1]

In fact, the startled reaction of the gathering was as much a response to the dramatic use of lighting – halfway through the song, a switch was flicked, throwing the younger Buckley's stark silhouette against the back wall of St Ann's – as it was to the undeniable similarities in the Buckleys' octave-leaping voices. (According to David Browne, biographer of the Buckleys, Jeff wasn't too thrilled by the lighting 'moment'. He phoned a friend afterwards and said it was 'like the fucking Second Coming.') But Jeff also put his own spin on 'Mountain', adding a new verse that he'd written only moments before he went onstage. 'My love is the flower that lies among the graves', he half-sang, half-swooned, 'spread my ash along the way.' Anyone with a passing knowledge of the original – and that would include virtually everyone gathered in St Ann's on this April night – would have duly noted this new and deeply personal twist. And with a simple, muffled 'thanks a lot', Jeff Buckley was gone, at least for the time being, and a well-intentioned tribute night was now officially an event. The one question repeatedly asked as Julia Heyward took his place on stage and tackled 'The River', was pretty damned simple: 'Where the hell had the kid been hiding?'

In fact, Buckley's arrival in New York was almost as low-key as his down-played position on the *Greetings From Tim Buckley* bill, or his muddled self-penned bio in the event's program, which read, in part: 'I got my first electric guitar at 13. Left home for LA at 17, spent some time in a so-called music school, went on the road with some reggae acts... My life is now complete and utter chaos.'[2] On the strength of Cohen's tip and an unfocused demo tape (known as *The Babylon Dungeon Sessions*) that Buckley sent to the organisers at St Ann's, he'd received an invitation from Janine Nichols, who was unsure what role Buckley would pay in his father's tribute night, but felt it appropriate to reach out to him nonetheless.

At first, Buckley was unsure; after all, both he and his mother had been left off the invitation list to his father's 1975 funeral; 16 years down the line, he admitted that 'it still kind of gnawed at me'.[3]* Yet it dawned on him that this

---

* It must be said that Buckley's anger was misdirected: it wasn't as though his father had any control over who was invited to his funeral, after all. 'His anger was justified,' wrote Lee Underwood, a colleague and close friend of Jeff's father, '[but] how could he be angry at Tim?'

would be a chance to pay his respects to his father, and then he 'could be done with it', and move on with his life.[4] After arriving just before 8.30pm on April 20, six days before the show, Buckley headed straight to the church from the airport; I mean, where else did he have to go? Armed with a guitar and a small bag and wearing a green pea coat that had once belonged to his father, and had been handed down to him by Daniella Sapriel, one of the many friends and associates of Tim who'd watched out for Jeff over the years, he drifted into St Ann's, a raggedy kid who could have walked straight off the pages of Dickens' *Great Expectations*. The church was as imposing to Jeff as New York, a city he knew – he'd been there the year before with a band called Shinehead, staying for several months – but was still coming to understand. Located on Montague Street, Brooklyn Heights' equivalent of a high street, the church, built in 1855, had such striking features as the first stained glass windows to be made in America, and no less than six chandeliers, which hung from its 60-foot high ceiling. On-stage, the image of highly regarded New York punk poet Richard Hell, who was roaring his way through a dry run of Tim Buckley's 'Moulin Rouge', was almost as intimidating as St Ann's decor. After some cursory introductions, Buckley the younger took respite in one of the back pews, unsure if he actually belonged with such an assured group of players, artists and scenesters.

But within a week, his situation had improved; after spending some time with Gary Lucas, and getting close to Rebecca Moore, a woman who would drift in and out of Buckley's orbit for the rest of his wild life, Buckley had a sense that New York might just be the city for him. Maybe. (Soon after, Buckley admitted that New York, a city he described as a 'fucking majestic cesspool', was 'where I blossomed'.[5]) And now, once more with stringman Lucas in tow, Buckley reclaimed the St Ann's stage and reconfigured 'Sefronia – The King's Chain', singing the dense, wordy lyric as if his life depended on every word, sometimes rolling them around in his mouth, almost as if he was tasting them. Buckley then handed over the stage, first to Loren Mazzacane, then Shelley Hirsch and Barry Reynolds, who jammed the sensual 'Love From Room 109 At The Islander (On The Pacific Coast Highway)'. But there was an unmistakeable sense that the gathering was now waiting for the return of the son, as imaginative and respectful as these other Buckley admirers had been.

He duly returned for 'Phantasmagoria In Two', a second selection from his old man's *Goodbye And Hello* LP (which, like everything else in his father's nine-album catalogue, suffered the curse of being a favourite of the critics and a stranger to the charts). This time he was helped out by harmonisers Hirsch and Julia Heyward, allowing Jeff to scat the oblique lyric, jazz-singer style. Then it was time for the finale, and everyone left the stage except for Jeff. On the raw bootleg recording of the show, you can sense his nervousness, as he attempts an introduction, of sorts, for his father's solemn, sadly beautiful 'Once I Was'. 'Uh, a long time ago,' he said, 'when I was a little kid, my mother sat on a bed and she put this record on. And, uh, it was like the first song where I ever heard my father's voice. I must have been, oohh, six. I was bored.' Here he stopped to share in the laughter of the crowd, who were now hanging on his every stumbling utterance as if he were delivering the sermon from the singer/songwriter mount. 'I was bored,' he repeated. 'I'm sorry. But you know, what can you expect from a cat who's into *Sesame Street* at the time?'[6]

He'd said enough. With that he exhaled deeply and launched himself into another of his father's melodramatic, lyrically opaque ballads, losing himself in its madrigal-like ebb and flow. 'Once I was a soldier,' he sang, 'fought on foreign shores for you,' strumming gently as he prepared himself for the anthemic build, scouring the song for the personal connection that was missing from his brief, unsatisfying relationship with his father. But then, just before the last chorus, Jeff snapped a string on his acoustic guitar (an instrument that would henceforth be shelved by Buckley, in favour of a far sexier Fender Telecaster), and so he sang the final, heartfelt lines: 'Sometimes, I wonder for a while/Do you ever remember me?', sans accompaniment. Clearly rising to the moment, his voice soared heavensward on the word 'me', just as his father's did so often back in the day. And that was it. A quick bow, a mumbled 'thanks', and Jeff Scott Buckley was gone, and the night was over.

But this was really just a beginning; the son who could count on one hand the number of times he'd actually been alone with his father, who'd spent his first 24 years sidestepping the prickly issue of the Buckley legend and his musical bloodline, who insisted that he'd only sung his father's songs in the shower and was unsure about even appearing at St Ann's until they offered to pay his air fare out from the west coast, had emerged from Californian obscurity and made a New York debut that stirred even the most jaded punter. He may have been massively under-prepared; he'd only met accompanist Gary Lucas six days earlier. And his performance could have been better; the *New York Times*, in their review, only mentioned him briefly, and then simply to report how he had 'delivered his first public performances of several of his father's songs in a high droning voice that echoed his father's keening timbre.' But the New York music cognoscenti knew that they'd witnessed something truly special. 'It was very spooky, but impressive,' said one onlooker, Nichols Hill, a DJ from WFMU-FM, a station that would become a second home to Buckley. 'The buzz was pretty immediate after that.'[7] Regardless of his ambivalence towards the star-making machinery that had chewed up his father, Jeff Buckley's life would never be the same.

Notes

1.   Rogers, Ray: 'Jeff Buckley, Singer-Songwriter'; Interview, February 1, 1994
2.   Anon: Concert bill, 'Greetings from Tim Buckley'
3.   Browne, David: 'The Unmade Star'; *New York Times*, October 24, 1993
4.   See note 3
5.   See note 3
6.   Transcript, live recording 'Greetings from Tim Buckley', April 26, 1991
7.   See note 3

Chapter One

'Hello/Goodbye'

The Golden Bear, Huntington Beach, California, March 1975

Even in this room, surrounded by ageing beatniks and finger-popping fusion nuts, the kid still looked way out of place. For one thing, he was the only eight year old in a house full of adults, many of them pleasantly stoned out of their gourds. Those who weren't were wondering to themselves, how did the kid get in here? And was this music really suitable for such an innocent-looking youngster, with his trusting face and wide-open eyes? The intense guy on stage, who wasn't so much singing as channelling some kind of crazy spirit, part cosmic folkie, part jazz-rock adventurer, was surrounded by diligent, furrowed-brow muso types, deeply immersed in their playing. And the music itself – a very strange, slightly over-heated brew of rock, soul, psychedelia and sex – was as far out there as the guy singing. And yet the kid, perched in the front row, was bouncing wildly in his chair, finding it impossible to keep still. His face was lit up like a Christmas tree, absolutely beaming with joy. He seemed to be truly digging the freeform, avant-garde sounds emerging from the serious things on stage, which was very odd, considering that most children his age were mad for more kid-friendly acts like The Muppets and The Flintstones.

The kid looking on with such rapture was Jeffrey Scott Buckley – simply 'Scotty' to every one who knew him, or Scotty Moorhead according to the rolls of the many schools he'd attended so far in his short life. The guy on stage was his biological father, Tim Buckley, space-folkie, jazz-rock fusionist, one of the rarer musical talents of the Woodstock era, a guy with a voice that could scale the kind of heights usually reserved for opera divas or freaks of nature. He'd just turned 28. But theirs was hardly a typical father-son relationship: since 'Scotty' was born on November 17, 1966 – just two days before positive notices began appearing for his father's self-titled debut long player – they'd spent precious little time together. Buckley had left Jeff's mother, Mary Guibert, well before his child was born, barely a year after they married, and she moved back with her family in California's Orange County, while he continued touring and recording, eventually settling in Malibu with a woman named Jane Goldstein. In the autumn of 1968, mother and son visited Tim in Malibu, yet since then, apart from a monthly alimony cheque for $80, they had very little to do with each other. There were no Christmas cards, no catch-up calls, no postcards from the road. Nothing.

In 1969, when 'Scotty' was two, Mary had met mechanic Ron Moorhead, who, despite a strong interest in rock music, dwelt in a world entirely different from that of Tim Buckley: he was a solid-state citizen, dependable, hard working, drug free. That might have been the very reason why he and Mary Guibert married in December 1969: Moorhead seemed to offer considerably more stability than Buckley, and the one thing that 'Scotty' needed right now was a solid base, for already he and his mother had fallen into an almost gypsy-like existence, shifting base whenever she sniffed out a new job or had a falling out with her parents, which was often.

By 1975, life for Mary and her son was unstable yet again. Despite having a child, Corey James Moorhead, who was born in March 1972, Guibert and Moorhead had split in 1973. In early 1975, Guibert was flicking through a local newspaper when she noticed that her former husband was playing in Huntington Beach, at The Golden Bear, a legendary venue located at 306 Pacific Coast Highway. The Golden Bear was the type of place where comic Steve Martin could have been spotted opening for the Nitty Gritty Dirt Band, or the Ramones would plug in and make eardrums bleed.* Maybe Guibert was even kicking around the idea of a reunion, as unlikely as that seemed. Yet Tim Buckley's life – or at least his career – was at a similar lowpoint to Guibert's. For the first time since 1966's *Tim Buckley* he was sans manager and record label, while *Look At The Fool*, his ninth LP, had been panned by *Rolling Stone* (who had pretty much ignored all his earlier releases), who described its mix of 'hyper-speedy funk and … octave-spanning howls all but unbearable.' Most other reviews were just as harsh.

---

* Nowadays The Golden Bear is buried under yet another bland urban redevelopment.

(Years later, even his son weighed in, questioning whether Buckley was unsure if he was emulating Tom Jones or Al Green, 'and the two mixed together don't really sound that great.'[1]) But his estranged son felt differently on this night in 1975, bouncing wildly in his seat, first to the band and then to his father playing solo, his straggly blond hair falling into his eyes as he lost himself in the music with almost the same intensity as the guy on stage.

When asked about this now legendary meeting between father and son, Guibert swore she witnessed an exchange between the two Buckleys while Tim was playing. '[Tim's] eyes were closed, and he'd open them a little bit to see Scotty in the second row, and Scotty was grooving. I was watching the two of them and I thought, "This is really going to be amazing".' At the end of the first set Guibert asked her son if he wanted to go and talk with his father. He had agreed even before she'd finished her sentence.

There was the usual crowd of hangers-on and legit visitors backstage, along with such Buckley consorts as guitarist Lee Underwood. Guibert, at first, couldn't spot her former husband; it didn't help that he'd recently cut his typically unruly halo of air. But then she heard a voice call out: 'Jeffrey.' Although no-one called him by this name, he immediately responded to his father's voice, racing across the room and jumping into his arms, as if it was the most natural thing on earth. As Guibert recalled, 'He was sitting on his lap and chattering a mile a minute. He said things like, "My dog's name is King, he's white" and he was telling [Tim] everything he could think about himself to tell his father. The scene was the most heartrending sight I'd seen in my life.' Guibert could see her ex-husband's face from where she was standing, and tears were rolling down his cheeks, clearly a mixture of joy at reuniting with his firstborn, and guilt at having been out of his life for so long. Guibert quietly returned to her seat stage front, leaving them together. She didn't want to spoil the moment. 'I literally watched my son fall in love with his father,' she'd later confess.[2]

Within minutes, Buckley's wife Judy returned with 'Scotty', who was still charged from his brief meeting – 'sparks were coming out of his eyes,' Guibert recalled.[3] Judy took a deep breath and asked Guibert if there was any chance that he could come home with them, just for a few days, sometime soon. Her initial instinct was to say no, but when she saw the look of sheer bliss on her son's face, Guibert knew she didn't have a choice. But within a few months of that reunion, which took place soon after the Huntington Beach gig, his father, her former husband, died from a lethal drug cocktail. Yet that one chance experience at The Golden Bear set the guy who would eventually be known as Jeff Buckley down a similar musical road to this father: both were seekers, sonic explorers, with voices that

3

had been touched by a higher force. And they were both destined to fade away far too quickly.

It would be a massive understatement to describe Mary Guibert's heritage as complicated; it's be like saying her son had a reasonable grasp of how to milk every last drop of adulation from his swooning audience, or that Tim didn't rate with the best fathers on the planet. The Guibert bloodline had more tributaries than the Mississippi, while the Buckley family history was equally complex.

'Jeff's cultural background is pretty varied,' she once said on-line. 'My mother is Greek and my father is part French, part Panamanian. Both my parents were born and raised in Panama; I was born there, and we all immigrated [to the USA] when I was three. So there was a very strong Central American family culture.'[4] Clearly, Jeff Buckley was a man of conflicting parts: he may have been cursed with the Buckley 'unibrow' but he was blessed with a golden voice, while his darkly romantic side could be traced back to his mother's exotic roots. (A fascination with the French side of her family inspired Guibert to study the language, which led to her first close encounter with Tim Buckley. But more on that later.)

Mary's father, George Peter Guibert (pronounced with a hard G, as in *Ghee*-bert), was a little rough around the edges. Born in September 1923, and raised in the western Panamanian city of Boquete, he didn't study beyond the sixth grade, couldn't write or speak English, and despite having a solid job as an aircraft mechanic, had a fondness for pot, not exactly the pastime of choice back then. George Sr, his long-absent father, was an American, living in Pittsburgh, who'd made a habit out of heading south to Panama and having unprotected sex before high-tailing it back to the States (hence his two Panamanian sons). 'My father was the illegitimate son of a French-American merchant marine who abandoned him, his mother and brother,'[4a] Mary Guibert explained. In 1943, a guilty George Sr returned to Panama and tracked down his two children: he found Mary's father working in what was known as the 'Canal Zone' (*Zona del Canal de Panama*), a 553 square mile territory inside Panama that, at the time, was US-controlled and was used mainly for military purposes. US presidential hopeful John McCain was actually born in the Canal Zone, not long before Guibert started working there.

It was only through this meeting with his father that George Jr learned that he could become an American citizen, which he promptly did. The benefits were immediate: he graduated from a 'silver roll' pay rate (which was strictly for Panamanians working in the Canal Zone) to the 'gold roll', which applied only to Americans. It was a sort of unofficial caste system that operated there; being on the 'gold roll' meant that your pay was three times higher than the locals, more than sufficient incentive for George Jr to change his nationality.

George Jr met Anna Smiroses, a beautiful Panamanian woman, at a wedding in 1944. Her grandfather was a Greek named John Payablas, while her father, Costas Smiros, was also of Greek extraction. Anna, one of five Smiros children, was born in February 1924. Costas met an early and grisly demise; while in New York, painting houses as a second job so that he could raise much-needed extra cash, he fell off a ladder. The injury to his leg became gangrenous and he died. Although he had managed to extricate a few of his children from Panama and relocate them to the US, at the time of his death, his wife was still in Panama City, barely getting by, with Anna and two other remaining daughters.

Fluent in English, Anna left school at 15 and scored a job in the Canal Zone. Although pot-smoking George Jr seemed an unlikely partner at first, his upgrade to the 'gold roll' came with a newfound desirability, especially to someone in such dire circumstances as Anna. George Jr was equally smitten with her; he'd sometimes roll up to her bedroom window at night, guitar in hand, and croon Spanish folk songs.* Now a citizen, George had been drafted into the US Army, but received an honorable discharge soon after WWII ended. He and Anna were married in a Catholic ceremony on January 10, 1946. Although a bout of pneumatic fever as a child meant that bearing children could be risky, staunch Catholic Anna put in a prayer to the Virgin Mary and when her daughter was born, she named her Mary Ivette in the virgin's honour.

George Guibert shared two things with Mary's grandfather: he was a hothead, inclined to dishing out rough justice on his kids, and he knew that a move Stateside was the best way to improve their circumstances. By September 1950, when Mary was two-and-a-half, the family relocated to Long Island in New York State, where George scored a job as a sheetmetal worker. Two more children were born: George Peter III, in 1951, and Peggy, in October 1953.† Although the family's financial state was improving –

---

* Music was very clearly a Buckley/Guibert family tradition. When asked about his Panamanian roots in 1995, and its link to his love of music, Jeff Buckley stated how 'everybody [in the family] sang, everybody had songs all the time – and they loved music.'[5]
† Peggy would become a key person in the life of Jeff Scott Buckley; many feel that she was as much a mother to him as Mary Guibert, maybe even more so.

they bought their first home in Massapequa, for $10,000 – the deadly chill of American winters was too much for Mary's mother, who was used to the temperate climes of Panama, and the family shifted west, to California. They rolled up in the Guibert family Plymouth, in early June 1954, optimistic about their new life on the west coast.

Their optimism was well founded, too: if one part of America typified the country's newfound, post-war prosperity, it was Orange County, and the Guiberts chose Anaheim as their destination. It wasn't a part of the world that excited Jeff Buckley very much – when asked about his Orange County youth, he scathingly referred to living life 'surrounded by the Disneyland Nazi youth of Anaheim, California'[6] – but there was no question that to his mother's family, it was truly a 'Magic Kingdom'.

Anaheim was the 10th largest city in California, but until July 17, 1955, when Disneyland opened its front gates for the first time, remained a relatively sleepy outpost, some 40 miles out of smoggy, seedy Los Angeles. Although the troubled kids from *The OC* might have suggested that this part of California was forever young, cashed-up and prosperous, that wasn't always the case. Founded in 1847 by German farmers and vintners – its name a mix of 'Ana', from the nearby Ana River, and 'heim', the German word for home – it was first planned as a wine-growing region, but when that failed it became renowned for its many types of orange.

The city's population reflected its slow growth: in 1876, when Anaheim was incorporated, only 881 hardy folk dwelled there. The population increased to 5,000 in 1920, and to 14,556 by 1950, just before the Guiberts settled there. But then Anaheim was hit by a one-man cultural explosion detonated by Walter Elias Disney, and the city would be forever changed. Since establishing the Disney Burbank Studio in 1940, after the runaway success of such animated features as *Snow White And The Seven Dwarfs*, Disney had been planning a large-scale family theme park, inspired, in part, by the inadequate public facilities he'd encountered when he played in local parks with his daughters. Disney was no fool; he also recognised the money-making potential of this dream theme park.

Disney's plan typified the conservative, crew-cut, *Leave It To Beaver* mindset that gripped America during the prosperous post-war era: he envisaged a return to simpler times, where families could fish, ride a carousel, relax at a bandstand and stroll up and down Main Street – his own spin on Anaheim's Center Street – while all the time surrounded by Goofy, Mickey, Minnie and the myriad other characters of Disney's undeniably fertile, if somewhat naïve, imagination. It also helped Disney's plans that the recently completed Interstate 5 went right through the heart of Anaheim; no longer a backwoods-y, orange-growing distant outpost of LA, Anaheim was now a breezy 45 minute drive from the big smoke. Visitors to the park could hang their hat in the city, check out the Hollywood studios and then drive south for their Disney experience. Every inch the entrepreneur, Disney struck up a deal with TV network ABC, who would hand over $500,000 and also guaranteed $4.5 million in construction costs for Disneyland; Disney, in exchange, would produce a weekly, hour-long TV show for the network. All things considered, it was a quantum leap from Disney's original plan of a 10-acre lot backed by a budget of $10,000.

During the first week of Disneyland business, its visitors included the Guiberts, who had recently settled in Greenacre Avenue on the fringe of the city. Their tract home set them back all of $11,000. Mary's father George, meanwhile, found work as a foreman, handing out orders to an all-female assembly line at an electronics plant. The mind-and-body-numbing winters of Long Island must have seemed like some weird, distant memory to the family, as they settled into life in balmy California behind the so-called 'Orange Curtain'. By January 1960, the Guiberts' lot in life improved yet again when they shifted to a larger house, in Anaheim's Archer Street. Though hardly palatial, it offered three bedrooms, separate living and dining rooms, a laundry, even a backyard. And it was a steal at just under $20,000. As Anna Guibert told biographer David Browne, 'We thought we were such hot stuff.'[7]

Life for the Buckley family, however, was not quite as upbeat. Just like the Guiberts, the Buckleys had first settled in New York. But whereas the Guiberts were escaping the limited opportunities of life in the 'Canal Zone', the Buckleys had their own cross to bear: like many of their countrymen they sailed the Atlantic to avoid the Penal Laws, which were introduced in Ireland by the British to discriminate against Protestant non-conformists and Roman Catholics. Under the original Penal Laws, Irish Catholics were denied their rights to vote, own land, practise law, attend school, serve an apprenticeship, possess weapons or practise their religion. No wonder so many of them jumped on the first boat to Ellis Island; this might also explain the moody, melancholic streak that gripped such troubadours as Tim Buckley.

Originally from County Cork, the first America-bound Buckley was Timothy Charles Buckley, who, along with his wife Charlotte, had, by the early 20th century, settled in Amsterdam, a small industrial centre about 20 miles out of Albany, in New York State. Populated mainly by immigrants – Poles, Russians, Germans, Italians and, of course, the Irish – Amsterdam was

perched on the banks of the Mohawk River. Priding itself on its manufac-
ture of carpets, the population of Amsterdam had swollen to more than
33,000 by 1920. What it didn't pride itself upon was the fact that one of its
better-known natives, the congressman Benedict Arnold, had been named
after the man who was perhaps America's most notorious traitor. Kirk
Douglas – better known to Amsterdammers as one Issur Danielovich – was
also born there, in 1916.

The Buckleys were an itinerant clan, moving to different houses within
the city pretty much every year. Timothy Charles Buckley Jr, their first
child, later known simply as 'Buck', was born in November 1916. By the
mid 1930s, Tim Sr was tending bar, and the family was living on the poetically named Mechanic Street (somewhat ironically named, too, given that
Buckley had just lost his savings in a failed auto repair enterprise).

Although they never met, Jeff Buckley had a strong impression of his
paternal grandfather 'Buck', based on facts he steadily acquired during his
own short life. Writing in his journal in August 1995, Buckley commented
upon his grandpa's 'beautiful voice... Irish tenor... beautiful.'[8] But Buckley
was also fully aware of his grandfather's emotional coldness, an unfortunate
trait that may have even contributed to the dreadfully fractured relationship
Jeff had with his own father. Maybe Tim was so shit-scared to find out that
he shared Buck's venomous mean streak that he couldn't face being a parent. As Lee Underwood wrote in his Tim Buckley memoir *Blue Melody*, and
later confirmed with me, 'Buck was not so much a loving parent as he was
a powerful force. Ironically, and in a very different way, Tim passed the
father-suffering onto his own son, Jeff. Tim and Jeff both grew up desperately yearning for love and respect and emotional nourishment from fathers
who simply were not able to fulfill these primal needs. Deep psychological
wounds seemed to pass from one generation to the next.'[9]

Much of Buck's wayward behaviour stemmed from his service in WWII.
At the age of 21, in December 1937, he'd enlisted in the National Guard
and began active duty in mid-October 1940. In late May 1942 he was
drafted and posted to the 101st Airborne, the so-called 'Screaming Eagles',
a unit trained principally for air assault operations. When the unit was 'acti-
vated' on August 15, 1942, its first commander, Major General William C
Lee, announced, in a statement that must have scared the hell out of his new
recruits, that the 101st had a 'rendezvous with destiny'. The US military
General Order Number Five spelled out the 101st's mission statement just
as ominously: 'Due to the nature of our armament, and the tactics in which
we shall perfect ourselves, we shall be called upon to carry out operations of
far-reaching military importance and we shall habitually go into action

8

when the need is immediate and extreme.' It didn't take long for Timothy Buckley to grasp the significance of this; after leaving the US in September 1943, he was involved with campaigns in the Rhineland, Normandy, northern France and elsewhere, during which time up to 25% of his comrades were killed in action. Officially referred to as sergeant, Buckley was responsible for blowing up bridges, buildings, railway lines and other forms of transport and communication.

After more than two years of overseas service, Buckley returned home on Christmas Day 1945, bringing with him a chest-full of medals – a Bronze Star, a Distinguished Unit Badge, even a Purple Heart – and, quite literally, a head full of ghosts. While in Europe, he'd been injured by a landmine explosion, and needed to have a steel plate inserted in his skull. Initially, he seemed to adjust relatively smoothly to civilian life, marrying Elaine Doris Scalia (his second wife), a woman with a genuine passion for music, a constant in both the Buckley and Guibert bloodlines. Their first child – Timothy Charles Buckley III, the best known of the many Tim Buckleys – was born in Washington DC on February 14, 1947. Although over the ensuing years his father's demons gradually began to emerge and do irreparable damage to the family, Tim Buckley did give due credit to the role Tim Sr and Elaine played in his musical development. 'My parents listened to [jazzmen] Miles Davis and Coltrane, Gerry Mulligan, Stan Kenton and the big bands,' he recalled in a 1973 interview. 'In America, if you are brought up here, you grow up with music whether you like it or not. You know about country music and all the ethnic music and although I was born in Washington I travelled around a lot hearing all kinds of things.'[10]

Within days of his birth, the Buckleys returned to Amsterdam, where Tim's father found work, first with General Electric and then American Locomotive. But when their son was in second grade, they felt a similar longing to the Guiberts, and began to look west. The paths of Tim Buckley and Mary Guibert were soon to intersect.

Back in Anaheim, the Guiberts had spotted a fast-developing musical talent in their daughter Mary, which they actively encouraged, buying an upright piano from a neighbour. 'I studied piano from the age of nine through my late teens,' said Guibert. 'The cello was an instrument I picked up in Junior High and played in school orchestras through high school.'[11] Further down the line, Guibert studied privately, playing cello in the Orange County Youth Symphony Orchestra (first chair), the Cal State Long Beach Symphony Orchestra (third chair) and was fourth chair in the La Mirada Symphony Orchestra. (Jeff Buckley also tried his hand at the cello, for one

9

year in junior high, but the lure of the guitar was far too irresistible.) By the age of 12, Guibert envisaged a Broadway career, having got a taste for the stage by appearing in a local production of *South Pacific*. But her plans were bent out of shape when she met Tim Buckley.

By 1958, the Buckleys had laid roots in Bell Gardens, a roughneck town seemingly a million miles from Anaheim, the land of milk and Disney (only a short drive of 18 miles separated them, in reality). Despite a rich Indian heritage dating back thousands of years, and a strong history of agriculture, during this post-war period Bell Gardens was best known as the chosen place for relocated Okies, fresh from the Midwest Dustbowl. Aside from a proliferation of churches, Bell Gardens was dotted with defence plants, which helped add some economic stability to the area; many homes and schools were built there, as munitions workers moved into the neighbour- hood. Among these new residents was Eddie Cochran, straight out of Minnesota, who, in his Bell Gardens garage, grabbed hold of the zeitgeist and cranked out teen rock anthems 'Twenty Flight Rock' and 'Summertime Blues'.* When the Buckleys bought a home not far from Bell Gardens' hobo camps, Elaine had just given birth to their second child, Tim's sister Kathleen.

Before being gripped by the folk music boom, Tim Buckley was a rela- tively well-adjusted teenager. He spent three years as the quarterback on Bell Gardens' Junior High School football team, was actively involved in the Letterman's Club and the school newspaper, and was the student body pres- ident for a time. Clean-cut and smartly turned out, it was almost impossible to associate this Tim Buckley with the cult figure with the white-man's Afro whose legion of admirers included New York punk poet Patti Smith and her confidant, maverick photographer Robert Mapplethorpe. As recently as 2007, Smith admitted to a colleague of mine how 'I loved Tim Buckley and listened to him all the time.'[11a]

Just like his son many years later, Tim Buckley was a musical sponge; while the charts may have been clogged with easy-listening crooners and starlets like Pat Boone, Connie Francis and Bobby Vee – this was the pre-Beatles era, of course – Buckley looked elsewhere for musical sensations. Country music was a particular passion; he was a huge admirer of such stars as Johnny Cash and Hank Williams. 'In 1960 when I started thinking about music,' he explained many years later, 'there was rock and roll and jazz and some folk

---

* Nowadays, Bell Gardens' claim to fame is that it's one of only five cities in Los Angeles County that permit casino gambling; it's also the home of NHRA drag racing champ John Force.

stuff to look at. Folk and country-blues were the first things I learned to play well, and then as you progress you get into more complex things.'[11b] Accordingly, he regarded jazzman Miles Davis as nothing less than a God; during early interviews he stuck to the unlikely boast that he first realised music was his calling when he heard one of his mother's Miles Davis albums – he figured that he was five at the time. 'Among the Americans, I like Lead Belly, Robert Johnson, Hoagy Carmichael, Louis Armstrong and Ray Charles,' Buckley added during the same 1973 interview. Buckley's tastes were eclectic and colour-blind, which would eventually shine through in his own recordings (and his own band, too; African/American percussionist Carter Collins was a key Buckley sidekick for years).

Well before he set out on his own freeform sonic journey, Buckley's musical skills were somewhat more pastoral – he knew how to play the banjo, having been given one as a gift by his mother when he was 11. Both this skill and his mother's top-shelf tastes were talked up like a mantra in one of Buckley's earliest press releases, which stated that, 'Tim's mother listened to Sinatra, Damone, and Garland, and Tim listened to Flatt & Scruggs, Bill Monroe, and Johnny Cash. When he was in the ninth grade at school he taught himself to play the banjo – and that was the beginning.' It was around this time that Buckley also began to stretch his tenor voice, an octave-jumping wonder that critic Andy Childs would soon rate as one of 'the two most expressive, versatile, and controlled voices in contemporary music'[12] (The other belonged to Van Morrison.) Or, as writer Ian Penman would declare, as late as 1994, 'Contemporaries like Lennon and Morrison, Jagger and Joplin may have been good rock singers, but that is after all a very limited boast, which doesn't necessarily mean you are *a good singer* – not in the realm of the Eternal Singer, which was undoubtedly Buckley's pitch and path.'[13]

Buckley's first foray was in a short-lived duo with Bell Gardens' High classmate Corby Alsbrook on guitar. He then performed as part of the Cobblestone Three alongside two other Bell Gardens buddies, Dan Gordon and Larry Boren. Their repertoire barely hinted at the freewheeling, mind- and audience-fucking direction Buckley would eventually head; playing local clubs and school assemblies, they'd end their sets with a cover of 'Lonesome Traveller', a fearfully earnest number made famous by the Pete Seeger-led Weavers. As conservative as his folkie aspirations appeared to be, music, nonetheless, had overtaken Buckley's interest in sport by the time he enrolled at Bell Gardens High School in 1962. Nevertheless, despite his mother's strong musical inclinations, she wasn't actively encouraging a career in music for her son; she hoped that he'd become a dentist, which now seemed about as likely as Tim getting back on the football field.

At home, Tim's father 'Buck' was gradually coming undone. A workplace accident, in which he fell off a roof and cracked the back of his head, marked the end of a relatively serene time at Buckley HQ. As Jeff Buckley would note, many years later, 'he was never the same' after his fall, and clearly Buck used Tim as a whipping post. 'His life was hell,' Jeff Buckley once said of his father.[14] Tim would discourage his school friends from visiting his house, as his father's behaviour took a turn towards the bizarre. 'After the war, he wasn't right anymore,' Jeff's grandmother Elaine Buckley told Lee Underwood in *Blue Melody*. 'And after he took that fall in the factory, things got progressively worse.' When Elaine took him to see a psychiatrist, he stopped at the door and refused to enter. 'I'm not the one who's crazy,' he snapped at Elaine, 'you are.' Soon after he and Tim came to blows in the family garage, and then he threatened Elaine with a gun.[15] Fortunately, Tim Buckley had an outlet – folk music – and a new hero, an electric-haired Midwestern poet going by the name Bob Dylan, whose lyrically potent anthem 'Blowin' In The Wind' had become a massive hit for airbrushed, family-friendly folkies Peter, Paul & Mary.

It was Dylan's on- and off-stage partner Joan Baez who'd provide the version of the old chestnut 'Geordie' that Buckley performed at the 1964 Loara High School hootenanny. (The Buckleys had recently, finally, gotten the hell out of Bell Gardens and relocated to the far mellower climes of Gilbuck Street, Anaheim, hence Tim's shift to Loara High.) Looking on were two 16-year-olds, Jim Fielder and Larry Beckett. Like Buckley, Beckett was a recent Anaheim transplant; he shifted there with his father, a teacher of English and speech, and his mother, who ran a career counselling business, when he was 10. Fielder, who was born in Denton, Texas, was yet another wanderer who'd finally settled in the land of Disney. Playing from the age of seven, he had been tutored on bass by Ralph Pena, Frank Sinatra's bassman, so his credentials were strong. Of all the crooners from the pre-rock era, the Chairman of the Board ranked the highest, at least to Tim Buckley.

Both were gobsmacked by Buckley's talent, especially his voice, and wasted no time in forming a musical team with the intense, gaunt dude in the sports jacket, who, at the time, bore a passing resemblance to folk legend Woody Guthrie. As Beckett gushed in the liner notes for *Morning Glory: The Tim Buckley Anthology*, the impact was immediate. 'We'd sit there and go, "Oh my God! I've never heard anything as beautiful as this voice".'[16] Fielder was equally impressed – and almost as effusive as Beckett. 'One hesitates to get flowery but [I'd use] the words "gift from God",' he told writer Martin Aston. 'He had an incredible range of four octaves, always in tune, with a great vibrato he had complete control over. You don't normally hear that stuff from a 17-year-old.'[17] Fielder, Beckett and Buckley shared the same gym class, and that was where their friendship began. 'I don't remember his dad, maybe he'd already gone insane,' Beckett said of Buckley. '[But] his mom was a sweetheart, with great music lying around, Johnny Cash, Frank Sinatra, Ray Charles, Pete Seeger.'

But 1964 was also a banner year for Tim Buckley the romantic, especially when he spotted a dark-skinned, doe-eyed, if slightly uptight beauty in French class at Loara High. In many ways Mary Guibert was the anti-Tim Buckley: she was studious and diligent, a self-confessed teacher's pet, who was already harbouring dreams of a Broadway career. Buckley, meanwhile, was wild-eyed and adventurous – a wearer of turtlenecks, no less – and a completely different guy to the over-achieving quarterback of a few years back. And just like his rapidly deteriorating father, Buckley had developed a taste for booze, something the church-going Guibert frowned upon. Buckley wasn't much of a student, either. As Beckett recalled, while he and Fielding were chasing straight As in honours classes, 'Tim was barely making it to school.' Beckett was actually Loara High's vice president and the president of the Honors Society, with vague plans of becoming a mathematical physicist, but clearly found Buckley's rebellious streak as seductive as Guibert eventually would. He'd also fallen hard for the beat poetry of Allen Ginsberg. '[Tim] dressed like a man, not a boy,' Beckett told an interviewer in 2000, '[He] had sex in the backs of cars, and was happy-go-lucky and contemptuous of all institutions. When he sang, you thought you were sitting around with fucking Caruso.'[17a]

Meanwhile, in Loara High's French class, a note was passed to Mary Guibert. It was a love poem, written and signed by Buckley, that went into some heavy-breathing detail about 'what fires he knew lurked inside' this beautiful, buttoned-up teenager. She was both attracted and appalled by this come-on, but soon began dating Buckley, who was one year older than her. Though she didn't realise it at the time, with this gesture she'd kissed her artistic aspirations goodbye. As they'd discover, both shared disruptive home lives; Mary's father prohibited her from shaving her legs or using make-up and would lose his temper at the slightest disturbance. 'Buck' Buckley, meanwhile, had checked into a Veterans Administration hospital, as his downward mental spiral continued.

Buckley's musical ambition remained unaffected by whatever negativity and ugliness might have been happening around him. He'd switched from the banjo to an acoustic six-string, and when he wasn't listening closely to such crooners as Nat King Cole and Johnny Mathis, he'd scream at buses and mimic the sound of trumpets, stretching his voice like a rubber band.

As you do. As for Beckett, the self-confessed 'perfect though increasingly arrogant schoolboy' was fast turning into a rebel, hugely inspired by his new buddy Buckley. Their bond was formed in 1965 when Buckley came to his defence after Beckett was suspended for three days for arranging a 'sit-in' demonstration, prompted by Loara High's vice-principal, who'd torn down some posters designed by Beckett. (One read: 'Drink Up', alongside the image of a huge cocktail; another cryptically said: 'Keep a Cool Tool'.) Buckley and Beckett celebrated by taking their prom night dates (most likely not Guibert) to the legendary Cocoanut Grove, where jazz chanteuse Nancy Wilson headed the bill. 'Tim showed me how to let my natural rebellion out,' Beckett admitted in 2000. 'We'd play hooky and drive to Hollywood, to go through La Cienaga Boulevard art galleries.'

Inspired by the songwriting success of The Beatles' John Lennon and Paul McCartney, he suggested that Buckley start writing his own songs, while he'd supply the lyrics. Buckley readily agreed. Beckett had also begun drumming; when combined with Fielder's bass playing, the Bohemians were born. (During 1964, Buckley also appeared with a country band going by the name Princess Ramona & the Cherokee Riders, decked out in a yellow hummingbird shirt and turquoise hat. *Or at least he said he did*; like his son, Tim had a liking for seeing just how far he could embellish his past and pass it off as the truth.) Beckett's writing influences were hardly typical So-Cal teen fare: he cited Ginsberg, Shakespeare, Yeats and James Joyce as his idols, and also listed Bob Dylan, Donovan and Fred Neil as key figures. The records shared by Buckley, Fielder and Beckett were equally diverse, as Beckett related: 'Our music started with the Beatles and Dylan and so-called folk rock, and then fanned out to include Indian raga, Miles Davis, Bulgarian folk music, Villa-Lobos, Erik Satie, Peggy Lee, B. B. King, Ramblin' Jack Elliott, Bach. We listened to all of this, day and night.' The Band would become firm favourites, too; Beckett once shared a Venice duplex with Buckley's guitarist Lee Underwood and Buckley christened it Big Pink, in honour of the band's immortal debut LP. Throughout his short, fast life, Jeff Buckley would emphatically downplay his father's role in shaping his destiny, but it's indisputable that they shared a natural musical curiosity. Jeff's tastes would closely parallel those of his father. Merri Cyr, Jeff Buckley's 'official' photographer, was one of many who noted this. 'He had such difficulty dealing with his father's memory,' she told me. 'Yet I think, more than anything, he compared himself to what his father did.'

The Bohemians were intent on capturing some momentum from the cultural tsunami that had recently hit the USA, courtesy of The Beatles. Many decades down the line, it's still hard to grasp just how significant this shift

was: only a year before The Beatles held three of the Top 10 LP chart plac-
ings Stateside (and also picked up the Grammy for 1964's Best New Act), the
charts still welcomed such mainstream martini-sippers as Dean Martin or
novelty country acts like Roger Miller. But the British Invasion, as it became
known, was overwhelming, as The Beatles opened the chart doors for countrymen The Rolling Stones, The Kinks, The Animals and The Dave Clark
Five, who all scored big in North America. At their commercial peak, The
Beatles shifted a million copies of *A Hard Day's Night* in just four days, had
30 tracks in the US singles chart in 1964, including six chart-toppers, and in
April of that year famously held down the top five places in the singles chart.
US authorities reacted with customary short-sightedness, drastically cutting
the number of work permits handed out to UK groups, thereby allowing
such obvious Limey knock-offs as Gary Lewis & The Playboys and The Beau
Brummels to have their few minutes in the spotlight. So maybe the time was
right for the so-called Orange County Three, as well.

Yet the Bohemians – who also moonlighted in folk clubs as Harlequins
3, a more loose-knit combo who'd sing, read poetry and perform comic
skits – stood apart from their peers: it's unlikely that Beach Boy Brian
Wilson had even heard of WB Yeats, let alone aspired to reach his lofty
lyrical heights in song. And Buckley had already shown signs of his fast-
developing interest in improvisation. As Beckett explained in a 2004 interview with Carson Arnold, their vastly different personalities probably had a
great deal to do with their songwriting synchronicity; even at this early
stage they sensed an unusual musical chemistry. 'I was very intellectual and
disciplined and [Tim] was very loose and passionate. I think actually that
was part of the secret, that obscurely we sensed we each had what the other
person needed – the whole human being, the whole artist. If he would try
to write a song it would just drift aimlessly. But if I had these overly rigor-
ous lyrics in place, then it would give a structure for him to work with. He
would infuse my too-tight songwriting with his passion, and loosen it up. It
was a kind of magical formula. And it worked in life and it worked in art.
We sensed that, I don't think we really understood it at the time, though.'
(Jeff Buckley also co-wrote much of his music, possibly for similar reasons.)

As Buckley's musical relationship with Beckett went from strength to
strength, he continued to date Mary Guibert. She'd scored a job at
Disneyland, at the Mexican eatery Casa de Fritos, and Buckley could often
be spotted there, sitting at the counter, waiting for her to finish another
shift. He also held down a job in fast food, working at Taco Bell during the
day, while playing at various LA venues by night. Buckley enrolled at college – either Ventura or Fullerton, no-one is really sure – but dropped out

after two weeks, sensing that a formal education didn't suit his plans. As Guibert admitted to biographer David Browne, it was around this time that she lost her virginity to Buckley, at the apartment of his friend Dan Gordon. '[It] was the closest thing we had that might have resembled sex,' said Guibert. However, the respite that their relationship offered them from their shared domestic unrest was soon shattered. In August 1965, Mary missed her period. Not long afterwards, Anna Guibert found herself shaking hands with Mary's musician boyfriend, but it was hardly the introduction that could have been hoping for. Buckley told Anna that he loved her daughter and wanted to marry her – Mary has said that even before she missed her period, they'd planned to wed when she was 18 and no longer in high school – and arrangements were hastily made for their wedding.

The not-entirely-happy event took place on October 23, 1965, in the Guibert family church in Anaheim, St Michael's Episcopal. Barely two dozen family members and friends were spread amongst the chapel's dozen rows. Mary's father was a no-show. Allegedly, prior to taking his vows, Buckley turned to his best man Beckett and said that he didn't want to go through with it. He may have genuinely loved Mary, at least for a time, but everything was happening way too fast for Buckley, who sensed his musical career was slipping away from him, replaced by a life of suburban humdrum. Afterwards, the newlyweds spent their wedding night at an anonymous Laguna Beach hotel, where they slept on the floor because the vibrating bed wouldn't stop shaking. As unfortunate metaphors go, that first night pretty much summed up what lay ahead for Buckley and Guibert.

The Buckleys rented an apartment in Anaheim, not far from the home of Mary's parents, and Mary, now shunned, dropped out of Loara High and signed up for typing classes. The Bohemians continued to play their usual round of gigs in and around Orange County, with the occasional road trip to LA, where they'd perform at open-mic nights at The Troubadour. Then, inspired by Bob Dylan's legendary show at the Hollywood Bowl – a gig cited by many as almost as significant as his electric 'coming out', polka-dot shirt, shades and all, at the 1965 Newport Folk Festival – Bohemians Fielder, Beckett and Buckley decided to get some music down on tape. They pooled their cash and cut their first demo, of sorts, at a shop just outside of Anaheim that provided a rudimentary recording service, and all for six bucks an hour. 'It's kinda cool,' Beckett said in 2004.

Included amongst the dozen songs they cut that day was 'She Is', a Beckett/Buckley co-write that would turn up on his self-titled debut the next year. And the tape wasn't simply comprised of Dylan-like strums. According to Beckett, it included 'some hard-rockers – you never hear it until much later in his career like "Honey Man", but when we first started out [Tim] would do a song like "Please Be My Woman" and was rocking like Elvis. I don't know where he got that from either.'[18] As Buckley biographer Browne succinctly stated, 'The Bohemians sounded like exactly what they were: a scruffy little folk-rock bar band, albeit one with a secret musical weapon: a powerful, emotive singer who could slide from a falsetto to a gritty grunt, who could ooze vulnerability and tenderness one moment, petulance the next.'[19] Browne may well have been describing the work of Jeff Buckley at the same time.

Meanwhile, the Buckleys' domestic situation was falling apart. Buckley would later suggest to a New York journalist that Guibert used her classical training as a way of undermining his music – something she emphatically denied. Others have suggested to me that Mary was a control freak, and that she drove Tim away. It's also been said, fairly enough, that they were both simply too young to be married in the first place. Regardless of the reason, if a date was needed to mark the beginning of the end it was January 1966. On New Year's Eve Mary was rushed to hospital after waking up to find their sheets soaked in blood; three days later she felt her waters break and returned to hospital, only to learn that she hadn't, in fact, been pregnant in the first place: she was suffering from a so-called 'hysterical' or 'phantom' pregnancy (*pseudocyesis* in medical terms). Hippocrates had recorded a dozen different cases of women with the disorder as early as 300BC, and Mary Tudor, Queen of England during the 16th century, also suffered from the complaint, but it is a relatively rare condition – typically, only a couple of cases are reported each year. It's actually more common in dogs and mice than it is in humans. 'Phantom' pregnancies are an odd mix of legitimate physical signs of being 'with child' – morning sickness, breast tenderness, weight gain, even abdominal swelling, which is caused by the build-up of fat, gas, etc – combined with a stone-cold conviction on the part of the woman that she is pregnant. It's obviously more an emotional condition than a physical one.

It seemed that for every step forward Buckley would take with his nascent musical career, his and Guibert's life would slide several steps in the opposite direction. Jeff Buckley documented what lay ahead when he came clean during an on-air session in 1994, at Philadelphia station WXPN. 'He split before I was born,' Buckley said, 'and didn't really keep contact with me and my mum. He decided not to be my father.'[20] Buckley's first step in detaching himself from Guibert was to travel to New York.

His father's fateful trip to Manhattan actually began in a Sunset Strip club called – very much in the parlance of the time – 'It's Boss'. It was there, in early 1966, that Buckley, Fielder and Beckett spoke with Jimmy Carl Black, a Native American who, when he wasn't drumming for Frank Zappa's Mothers of Invention, gave lessons at the same Anaheim music store where Fielder taught young Orange County guitar hopefuls. Black arranged a meeting with Herb 'Herbie' Cohen, the manager of Frank Zappa and the Mothers and as colourful a character as any who impacted on the lives of either Buckley. Cohen, a native New Yorker then in his mid 30s, had ended up in Los Angeles after a stint in the army; it was in LA that he became connected with the music biz, organising shows for folkies Pete Seeger and Odetta, both early favourites of Tim Buckley. During the late 1950s and early 1960s, even before Sunset Strip became the place to be heard and seen, Cohen ran coffee bars Cosmo Alley, the Purple Onion and the Unicorn. 'Herbie' was a notoriously hard man, who was known to keep a loaded gun handy in case trouble broke out at his clubs, and was also rumoured to have dabbled in gun-running. He was like a character lifted directly from Warren Zevon's 'Roland The Headless Thompson Gunner'. Buckley was impressed by Cohen's cut-the-crap approach when they first spoke, even though he thought he resembled a 'dope smuggler or someone out of *Che!*'[21]

Cohen's next venture was more legitimate, though still fraught with danger: artist management. He handled the careers of belter Judy Henske, the highly regarded Modern Folk Quartet and musical maverick Zappa, possibly the most bent character never to actually use the mind-enhancing drugs so prevalent at the time. Zappa was also one of the few people not overly intimidated by the man handling his business affairs; close examination of the cover of his wildly satirical 1966 LP *Freak Out!* reveals that Cohen is listed under the credit: 'These People Have Contributed Materially In Many Ways To Make Our Music What It Is. Please Do Not Hold It Against Them'. Cohen would be credited with contributing 'cash register noises' on Zappa's *Absolutely Free* album, another less-than-subtle dig by Zappa towards the role of his and Buckley's boss. He was the suit, the money guy.

Not long after their first meeting, Cohen signed Buckley to a publishing deal. Far too 'arty' to show any interest in the business end of things, Buckley raised no objection when Cohen suggested the Bohemians disassemble, although it was agreed that he'd keep writing with Beckett and Fielder would play on his recordings. (Fielder would score work with the Cohen-managed Mothers of Invention and Judy Henske, before moving on to 'serious' mainstream acclaim with Blood, Sweat & Tears, so there was an upside to the Bohemians' split. The ever-contrary Zappa, however, deleted Fielder's credits from the *Absolutely Free* album, because he'd jumped ship

18

and moved on to Buffalo Springfield.[22] Cohen, whose future clients included Tom Waits and mid-western shock-rockers Alice Cooper, also came up with a new strategy for Buckley's domestic arrangements, suggesting that he move in with Fielder, while Mary relocate to the Cohen compound, where she could help look after his daughter Lisa. Cohen has denied that the intention was to end the marriage in deference to Buckley's musical career, but you'd have to imagine that was in the back of his mind somewhere.

It wasn't long after this arrangement was set in place that Buckley met LA scenester Jane Goldstein and began a new relationship. Speaking with David Browne, Goldstein made an observation that would ring as loudly for Jeff as it would for his estranged father, Tim. '[Tim] was sad because of his father,' she said. 'He really missed having a father.'[23]

Occasionally, Tim would spend time at the Cohens' home with Mary, but in spring 1966, acting on a tip regarding a New York record label, Buckley and Goldstein began their fateful trip to the east coast, the journey that would effectively derail the already wobbly Buckley/Guibert relationship. Danny Fields, a legendary music industry figure who'd soon become Tim's publicist and friend, and much later on a close confidant of Jeff Buckley, agreed that it wasn't just the lure of a label that drove Tim to head east. 'She [Guibert] was one of the reasons Timmy fled to New York. I could only have imagined what it was like. The possessiveness... that must have driven Timmy to insanity and heroin.' It was the start of what Jeff Buckley would refer to as his father's 'gypsy life', deftly chronicled in Tim's song 'I Never Asked To Be Your Mountain', a deeply-felt outpouring that was also one of the biggest cop-outs in modern music. (In the song, Buckley quotes Guibert's description of him as Jeff's 'scoundrel father', while a reference to 'barren breasts' could be Buckley's dig at Guibert's phantom pregnancy. It's a catfight either way.) 'It's a beautiful song,' Jeff once said of the epic, but it was also a song he equally loved and loathed.[24]

The New York label that Tim Buckley sought out was Elektra. As unlikely as it seems on the surface, and as much as Jeff Buckley hated being likened to his absent father – one of his friends went as far as to say 'it would have made him puke' – there was more than one similarity between Tim Buckley's signing with Elektra and his son's record deal with Columbia. While both labels recognised the need for acts that kept cash registers ticking over, they were also on the lookout for credible, serious artists, whom Columbia would one day nobly refer to as 'heritage' acts. When Jeff Buckley signed his deal, those 'artistes' included Bruce Springsteen, Bob Dylan and the late Miles Davis. When Tim Buckley signed up in 1966, Elektra's roster included protest singers Phil Ochs, Tom Paxton, David Blue and Judy Collins, along with more cutting-edge acts from the burgeoning psyche-delic rock scene, including LA's Love and The Doors, plus – two years later – Detroit noisemakers The Stooges and MC5, and also the revered Paul Butterfield Blues Band. Both Columbia and Elektra were doing their best to juggle art and commerce. Yet the word humble doesn't do justice to Elektra's origins; like Rick Rubin's Def Jam label many years later, it came into existence in a dorm room. Founder Jac Holzman and his business part-ner Paul Rickholt sank a hefty $300 into establishing the enterprise in 1950. The label's name was a twist on the Greek mythological heroine Electra – as Holzman famously explained, 'I gave her the "K" that I lacked.'

Holzman's response to Buckley's new demo – six songs he'd recently cut in LA with Fielder – was as immediate as Cohen's, as he revealed in a 1995 story that ran in *Mojo* magazine. 'I must have listened to it twice a day for a week,' Holzman said. 'Whenever anything was getting me down, I'd run for Buckley.' The Elektra boss could sense that this Dylan lookalike, with his heaven-sent voice and genre-jumping sound, represented precisely what his label needed. 'He was exactly the kind of artist with whom we wanted to grow – young and in the process of developing,' Holzman said. It's eerie how similar his take was to that of Columbia's Steve Berkowitz, on seeing Jeff Buckley perform in the early 1990s. 'Frankly,' Berkowitz stated in the BBC documentary *Everybody Here Wants You*, 'I thought that Jeff would make 25 records, and I think Columbia and Sony thought it went: Dylan, Springsteen, Buckley.'

Buckley and Goldstein, meanwhile, drank in New York. During one of his many visits there, Buckley befriended similarly gifted singer-songwriter Fred Neil, another Cohen client, the writer of such era-defining songs as 'Everybody's Talkin'' and 'Dolphins'. He was a huge influence on tune-smith-under-development Buckley, who covered 'Dolphins', and beauti-fully. He also crossed paths with Cambridge-based folkie Eric Andersen, who, weirdly enough, would feature alongside Jeff Buckley years later at the *Greetings From Tim Buckley* tribute. 'I saw Tim frequently,' Andersen told me in 2007. 'His interests were more jazz meets psychedelia, a weird intersec-tion that he arrived at. I was more interested in the lyrical content; I liked jazz but my roots weren't in psychedelia. He had one foot in Indian raga music. He played with some very good players; people respected him, he was on his own adventure.'

Once back on the west coast, however, everything rapidly came apart. According to Jim Fielder, 'The marriage was a disaster [even though] Mary was full of talent and life, a classical pianist and Tim's equal.'[25] In August

1966, Buckley had returned to LA to cut his debut LP, with the help of, amongst others, recently recruited guitarist, and longtime sidekick, Lee Underwood, producer Paul Rothchild (soon to score critical and commercial acclaim with The Doors), and Hollywood arranger and provocateur Van Dyke Parks (a richly gifted and immensely charming musical all-rounder, once described to me as the 'gayest straight man on the planet'). Throughout this self-titled debut, Buckley made his domestic confusion abundantly clear, especially in tracks such as 'Valentine Melody' – even though the lyrics were Beckett's – and 'It Happens Every Time'. Buckley brazenly celebrated his new lady love and his infidelities in 'Song for Jainie', the song performed by Andersen in 1991 at the Buckley tribute – even the misspelling of Goldstein's Christian name didn't make it any less of a slap in Guibert's face.

As if their situation couldn't be any more complicated, Guibert had delivered some heavy news to her free-love-embracing, wandering minstrel husband: she was expecting his baby, and this time it was no 'phantom' pregnancy. He recommended that she return to her family in Anaheim, and consider an abortion. (There remains some confusion whether Buckley actually knew of her pregnancy before leaving for New York; it's been documented that Guibert actually came clean to Buckley's mother.) Deep in denial, Guibert thought there was some remote possibility that Buckley would return to her, until, finally, a mutual friend filled her in on his relationship with Goldstein. As Jim Fielder recalled, 'The pregnancy made it [their marriage] go sour, as neither of them was ready for it. To Tim it was draining his creative force, and Mary wasn't willing to take the chance on his career, putting it to him like, "Settle down and raise a baby or we're through", that kind of showdown.'[26] Lee Underwood had a slightly harder take on the clearly hopeless situation. 'Tim had to decide whether to follow his musical calling or stay at home with Mary and work in the local Taco Bell. Tim left not because he didn't care about his soon-to-be-born child, but because his musical life was just beginning,' he wrote in a letter from 1998. 'And, in addition, he couldn't stand Mary. He did not abandon Jeff, he abandoned Mary.' (To Tim Buckley's credit, he did send money whenever he could.)

Several unfortunate confrontations later, Mary reluctantly accepted that their marriage was over and filed divorce papers, with only a couple of months remaining until the baby was due. It must be said, though, that Buckley's situation was hardly uncommon, as Danny Fields pointed out to me in mid 2007: 'As for kids, well, everyone had a few lying around if you were cute and living in Los Angeles in the late 1960s; I think there were very few young men who weren't fathers. But he certainly wasn't domestic and I think he had no intention of staying with her.' Jeff Buckley wasn't exaggerating, years later, when he was asked about his biological father and replied: 'I never knew him.' When Mary went into labour on the morning of Thursday, November 17, 1966, and was driven by her mother to Anaheim's Martin Luther Hospital, Tim Buckley was nowhere to be found. It would be several years before father and son spent more than a few hours in each other's company.

Notes

1. Diehl, Matt: The Son Also Rises... *Rolling Stone*, October 20, 1994
2. Koha, Nui Te: Love from the Grave, *Herald-Sun*, April 30, 1998
2. Browne, David: *Dream Brother, The Lives and Music of Jeff and Tim Buckley*, Fourth Estate 2001
3. Anon: *Q&A with Mary Guibert*, www.homestead.com/dawnsjeffbuckley page/mary.html
4. Guibert, Mary: on-line interview
4a. See note 4
5. Courtney, Kevin: Grace and Danger, *Irish Times*, June 7, 1997
6. Jellie, Dugald: Buckley's Burden, *The Age*, February 23, 1996
7. Rogers, Ray: Jeff Buckley, Singer-Songwriter, Interview, February 1, 1994
8. See note 2
9. Underwood, Lee: Blue Melody: *Tim Buckley Remembered*, Backbeat Books, 2002
10. Charlesworth, Chris: Tim Buckley, Digging Deeper to the Roots, *Melody Maker*, 1973
11. See note 10
11a. Sariban, Mark: unpublished interview with Patti Smith, 2007
11b. See note 10
12. Childs, Andy: A Happy Sad Starsailor from Washington DC, *ZigZag*, October 1974
13. Penman, Ian: T.B. Sheets: In Praise of Tim Buckley, *The Wire*, April 1994
14. Browne, David: The Unmade Star, *New York Times*, 24 October 1993
15. See note 9
16. Alfonso, Barry: Liner notes for *Morning Glory: The Tim Buckley Anthology* (Elektra/rhino)
17. Aston, Martin: Tim Buckley, *Mojo*, July 1995
17a. www.willybrauch.de/In_Their_Own_Words/larrybeckett.htm (Larry Beckett interview, April 2000)
18. Arnold, Carson: *Reflections from a Shadow*, January 2004 (unpublished)

19. See note 2
20. WXPN bootleg
21. See note 9
22. Callow, David: Jim Fielder interview, 10/99;
    www.rdrop.com/users/rickert/fielder.html
23. See note 2
24. See note 2
25. See note 18
26. See note 18

Chapter Two

The White-Trashville-Disneyland-Nazi-Blues

As if Jeff Buckley's life wasn't already complicated enough, thanks to his missing-in-action father, there was also the slight complication of his name. Soon after he was born, just before 11pm on Thursday, November 17, 1966, Mary named him Jeffrey Scott – 'Jeffrey' in a nod to Mary's previous boyfriend before Tim Buckley, and 'Scott' as a mark of respect towards a family friend, John Scott Jr. 'John "Scotty" Scott was our next door neighbour and childhood hero,' Guibert explained, 'who'd been killed in an accidental fall the year before my son was born.'[1] She'd entertained the idea of calling her son Scotty, but felt, simply enough, that 'Scott Jeffrey didn't sound as good as Jeffrey Scott. So we just called him "Scotty", anyway.'[2] It may not have been the best choice, because her son copped the usual round of nicknames when he started school: Scotty, Potty, Snotty. (This didn't stop when he adopted his birth father's surname: Snotty was now called Jeff Fuckley or Jeff Butt Lick. Kids can be cruel.)

Regardless, his name was set in stone when he was baptised at St Michael's soon after leaving hospital. In keeping with his high spirits, even at this early stage of his life, Buckley farted during the baptism ceremony, seemingly unconcerned about the sombre proceedings going on around him. As public debuts go, this wasn't bad.

Years later, when his studio debut *Grace* was released, Jeff Buckley boasted – in a sort of 'too cool for school' way – of his deprived roots, as if he had walked straight off the pages of a John Steinbeck novel, albeit one set in the relatively comfortable Orange County in the late 1960s and early 1970s. As

Buckley recalled, he was 'rootless trailer trash born in Southern California'.[3] He'd say it often enough to convince himself it was true, because he'd repeat it in the Columbia-generated bio for *Grace*: it quickly became part of the Jeff Buckley mythology. Even though he didn't quite lead the So-Cal dream of many kids growing up behind the so-called Orange Curtain, to describe himself as 'trailer trash' was still something of a stretch, but mythologising was a favourite pastime of Buckley's, an honours student of rock and roll history. However, many of Buckley's closest friends told me that he suffered a lot as a kid, and his parents were to blame. 'He had a hideous childhood,' said one insider. 'He was always being uprooted. His mother was very young when Tim split. Knowing her, I could understand why: she's a control freak.'

His father's monthly alimony cheque was typically gone within days, and an illness forced Mary to move back in with her family soon after her divorce with Buckley became final, on August 29, 1967. Yet any refuge she might have found there was short-lived; by Christmas of that year, after her father's latest outburst, Mary grabbed her son and headed for the door, taking their few possessions with them. This marked the beginning of a period in their life that did justify his 'rootless' description. 'I didn't even have any luggage,' he recalled. Whenever they relocated, he simply 'put my stuff into paper bags' and moved on.[4] As he related years later, their domestic situation hinged upon 'what job she had, what man she was with and the state of her finances. It gave me strength, insight, resolve and at the same time it depleted my understanding of what it's like to have a home, or even a dog, for more than a year.'[5] He'd repeat this often, both to journalists and those that crossed the line between the personal and professional, such as photographer Merri Cyr, who mentioned the 'paper bag' story when we spoke in 2007. 'He told me that when he was a kid he never lived in one place for too long, so being settled in a home was not natural for him,' she said. Another close friend of Buckley's, who knew him for most of his adult life, had a similar, if less kind, take on his rootless life with Mary. 'If you want to see the real Mary, rent *The Cable Guy*,' he said. 'I believe the Jim Carrey character in that film is a good mirror for how Jeff was really raised: "Mommy is going to happy hour; maybe I'll find you a new daddy", that kind of thing.'

Mary found a place to live in North Hollywood, where she stayed during the week, leaving Jeff with her parents (their rocky relationship with her clearly didn't extend to their grandson). Mary would spend the weekends back in Anaheim with her son. His father's appearances in Jeff's life were cameos at best: one visit took place at Mary's apartment, another in Anaheim. Yet Tim Buckley hadn't completely erased his son from his memory, because he mentioned 'the kid' during an interview with New Yorker

Izzy Young, referring to him as 'Jeffrey', as his career momentum increased with the release of his second album, *Goodbye And Hello*, in late September 1967. Buckley went on to say that he was prevented from visiting both his son and ex-wife, insisting that the Guiberts barred him from their home – a claim Guibert has refuted – and that Mary was living on welfare. Clearly willing to purge, he also revealed 'that my father's doing a mental thing in some hospital'. Compassion wasn't necessarily his strong point.

With *Goodbye And Hello*, Buckley had reached the career 'high' of having his image plastered on a billboard that hovered above Sunset Strip like some kind of message from the marketing gods: thou shalt buy Tim Buckley records, it seemed to scream. Elektra's Jac Holzman went as far as to say that Buckley was the new voice of his generation (a poisoned chalice if ever there was one). 'As we got deeper into 1967 and Vietnam,' Holzman said, 'the combined effect of his words, his music, his passion, his persona, struck a particular resonance. To some extent he was the bright side of people's tortured souls.'[6] It was also around this time that Buckley met, was photographed by, and some suggest had a brief relationship with, New York photographer Linda Eastman (later McCartney). 'I think Linda was in love with Tim, maybe only for a brief while, especially when you look at those pictures,' said Danny Fields, Buckley's Elektra publicist and close friend.*

It would be more than a little unfair, however, to suggest that Tim Buckley's life was guilt-free. As flawed as it was, 'I Never Asked To Be Your Mountain', the album's centrepiece, showed that Buckley hadn't filed his son and former wife into the 'never to be mentioned again' pile. His cry of pain – 'Baby, pleeeeeaaaaeeeesse' – during the song's climax was as much a comment on his troubled state of mind as the rest of the song's clever, faintly veiled wordplay. No wonder Jeff Buckley had such mixed emotions about the song; what could be worse than the knowledge that you're a burden on your biological father?

Father and son were briefly reunited in the autumn of 1968, when Mary and Jeff visited Tim at home in Malibu, at 9550 Pacific Coast Highway, just prior to his first European tour. In a letter that he wrote years later, Jeff vaguely recalled the encounter, writing how 'we all three had a big blanket around us. Just sitting there saying nothing.'[7] But these family reunions were rare.

While Tim pursued his musical ambitions, Jeff sought respite in a manner not uncommon for a kid his age, growing up at that time: he watched

---

* Many years later, Fields would introduce the McCartneys to Jeff Buckley and admitted to falling for the younger Buckley himself, 'though not necessarily in a romantic way. [But] "Jeffy" left a trail of broken hearts, including mine.'

television with an intensity that he would soon bring to his music. An early favourite show of his was *The Muppets*. And it was probably through TV that he had his first musical experience, of sorts. 'I saw the harmonium on *Mister Rogers' Neighborhood*,' he said in 1994, 'and that's how I learned about it.'[8]⋆

Jeff also began attending Montessori school in Anaheim at the age of two, which hinted at his knack for over-achieving. Montessori schools employed both a methodology and educational philosophy that discourage the traditional measurements of achievements, such as grades and tests. Instead, the Montessori method encouraged independence and freedom of thought and expression. It seemed the perfect outlet for the younger Buckley, who was already showing signs of being a fast learner, despite the problems of his early years. Yet his Montessori school experience encouraged development in an unexpected way: it was the beginning of Jeff Buckley the mimic (or the 'human jukebox', as he'd refer to himself).

His teacher there was a Sri Lankan woman, with a pronounced sub-continental accent, and, according to Guibert, her boy 'had her accent down a T'. He'd come home from class and pull off note-perfect imitations of his teacher, leaving Guibert and others doubled up with laughter. '[He] had us in stiches,' she said.[9] At the same time he began learning 'little songs and poems in Spanish'. Step by baby step, he was moving in a musical direction.[10]

Like the Buckleys and the Guiberts before him, Ron Moorhead and his family had moved to the west coast – in his case from Pennsylvania in 1960 – seeking out some Californian sunshine and all the possibilities that came with it. Like the man whose place he took in the life of Jeff Buckley, Moorhead was a music obsessive – 'a record junkie', according to Jeff – but that was pretty much all he shared with Tim Buckley. His runaway muttonchop sidelevers might have suggested a wild streak, but Moorhead was a reliable citizen, a mechanic whose love of Led Zeppelin almost matched his mania for cars.

His relationship with Guibert developed faster than a hotted-up Camaro, and the two were wed at the Anaheim Unity Wedding Chapel in December 1969, with Jeff ably performing the duties of ring boy. The Moorheads set up home in a nice-enough house on Pritchard Street in Fullerton, a suburb of Anaheim. Even though they hadn't chosen the quietest of locales to live – their property backed onto a factory, while the Fullerton Municipal Airport and the train line were a few noisy blocks away – life in the Moorhead

---

⋆ Hosted by one Reverend Frederick McFeely Rogers, *Mister Rogers' Neighborhood* was a thoroughly wholesome kids' show that ran from 1968 to 2001, that unintentionally provided older kids – and adults – with an ironic kick.

household was relatively serene. Guibert set up a fashion line, named Elegant Funk, which she operated out of the garage, comprising 'weird clothing she would make', as Buckley told Australian DJ Richard Kingsmill in 1995.[11] Every time Buckley heard Diana Ross' 'Ain't No Mountain High Enough', he'd think of this time in his life, for reasons only he fully understood. Nearby, Moorhead opened a VW repair shop called the Bug Inn, which provided ample time for him to be a far more attentive and involved parent than Tim Buckley. Although Jeff was never formally adopted, he'd insist that Ron Moorhead was his father, not Tim Buckley. He made his feeling perfectly clear in the BBC2 documentary *Everybody Here Wants You*. 'I don't hate my [biological] father,' Buckley admitted, 'and I don't resent him existing. [But] he really wasn't my father; my father was Ron Moorhead.'[12]

Meanwhile, the man who wasn't really Jeff's father, Tim Buckley, was undergoing a few changes of his own. *Goodbye And Hello*, his acclaimed second album, was hardly a commercial smash, peaking at a relatively dismal #171 in the *Billboard* charts. During autumn 1968, his word-man Larry Beckett was drafted into the army. With Beckett out of action for a year – 'mostly in jail,' he admitted – he and Buckley missed the chance to pen the theme song for the John Schlesinger film *Midnight Cowboy*, after the director had rejected Dylan's 'Lay Lady Lay' and approached Herb Cohen, looking for a substitute. 'I was in the army, and absolutely out of communication with everybody,' Beckett said in 2000, 'and Tim said, "I don't wanna do it by myself."'[13] The plum gig went to another of Cohen's clients, Fred Neil, whose 'Everybody's Talkin'' was a career-maker for singer Harry Nilsson, and a handy little earner for everyone concerned.

By late 1969, a time when Buckley learned that Moorhead was considering relocating his new wife and stepson to Australia, where he had family, matters had improved for Buckley. In mid-March, he'd headlined a gig at the prestigious New York Philharmonic Hall, while the *Happy/Sad* album – though not quite the crossover hit that his manager or label were banking on – further established his reputation for musical genre-jumping. As the *Rolling Stone Album Guide* declared (well after its release, admittedly), 'the songs soared past any verse-chorus-verse structure; this was abstract expressionism of a rare bravery.' Sadly, bravery rarely runs hand in hand with sales; instead the record-buying public gravitated towards the swampy sounds of Creedence Clearwater Revival, a revitalised Elvis Presley, whose 'In the Ghetto' marked an unlikely career rebirth, and the power rock of *Tommy*, by The Who, the British band whose breathtaking stage show made them the stars of Woodstock. Pot and acid may have freed half a million minds at Woodstock, but middle America wasn't quite willing to fork over their hard-earned for an album that featured such marathon headtrips as 'Love From Room 109 At The Islander (On Pacific Coast Highway)'. Buckley remained a critic's favourite, inspiring renowned New York-based Australian rock writer Lillian Roxon to engage overdrive as early as 1968. 'There is no name yet for the places he and his voice can go,' she declared.[14]

To Buckley's eternal credit, he was finding his own way in the world, often quite publicly. He was handpicked by pre-fab popsters the Monkees to appear on their last-ever TV show, and Buckley seized the moment in his own mercurial way, as Beckett would recall. 'Now here he is, he's going to be on national TV, millions and millions of people are going to hear him sing, and he'll have a much wider audience than [ever before]. They say, "You can sing whatever you want." So what does he do? Does he do one of the singles that were released through the years? Anything that could promote his product? No. He does "Song To The Siren", a song which was the growing edge, the latest and most experimental piece we had. That's what he sat down and sang because... that's who he was. Nobody quite heard songs that beautiful.'[15]* Again, it was the type of willfulness that his son also embraced during his career; he may have signed with multi-national Columbia, and assumed all the commercial baggage that came with it, but Jeff Buckley would still find a place in his set for a 15-minute sonic and emotional assault like Big Star's 'Kanga Roo', when another *Grace* track might have done just fine.

While the Moorheads shelved their relocation plans, Buckley's artistic purple patch continued; during 1970 he released no less than three almost-impossible-to-categorise albums (*Blue Afternoon* in January; *Lorca* in May; and *Starsailor* during the first week of November). He'd also remarried, tying the knot with Judy Sutcliffe, who had a seven-year-old son called Taylor, and settled down – as much as the restless Buckley ever could – at Laguna Beach.

While his birth father was undergoing a creative evolution, the boy still known as Scotty was in the midst of his own musical awakening. Moorhead's tastes, though clearly influenced by the FM radio hits of the day, still showed discernment: he'd turn his stepson onto such acts as smooth harmonizers Crosby, Stills & Nash, suburban headbangers Grand Funk Railroad, melodic minstrel Cat Stevens and cosmically-inclined Englishmen the Moody Blues. But of all the music Moorhead introduced to his stepson, it was the bloozepower blitzkrieg of Led Zeppelin that Jeff embraced like no other. Throughout his short career, Buckley would never

---

* This starkly beautiful take is the final track on 2001's sterling *Morning Glory: The Tim Buckley Anthology* and was covered by many artists, including Jeff Buckley's hero, Robert Plant.

miss a chance to talk them up with an evangelical fervour. (Jimmy Page would repay the kudos in spades, too, but we'll get to that eventually.)

Led Zeppelin was a huge influence on Jeff's sonic stance; the sheer earth-quaking wallop heard in many of *Grace's* standouts, especially when played live, owed a hefty debt to his love of Led Zep. A formidable blend of bluescraft, metal bombast and million-dollar pop hooks, Zeppelin – the quietly sinister master-guitarist and all round tactician Jimmy Page, Adonis-haired wailer Robert Plant, a singer Buckley claimed as 'my man', experienced all-rounder John Paul Jones and mad-dog demolition drummer John 'Bonzo' Bonham – were a band that, over the course of 10 albums and hundreds of life-changing live shows, proved it was possible to flex both brawn and brain. Zeppelin might have been British but America was their spiritual home, especially California, where the sunshine and the girls who tanned beneath it offered inspiration by the goblet load. The *Rolling Stone Encyclopedia of Rock & Roll* deftly summed up the group's musical legacy thus: 'It wasn't just Led Zeppelin's thunderous volume, sledge-hammer beat and edge-of-mayhem arrangements that made it the most influential and successful heavy-metal pioneers, it was their finesse.' He mightn't have even reached his teens, and his musical career was some way off, but the youthful Buckley listened hard and learned plenty. 'Led Zeppelin was... my favourite music when I was growing up,' he told *Mojo* in August 1994, as he drew a link between their best work and his album *Grace*. 'The thing about Led Zeppelin... is that they carried with them this unexplainable thing, this spirit. They let their deepest eccentricities be the music itself. Everything I love and have heard about music – I want to leave it all behind and go some place else. There are so many more ways of saying, "I love you" or "where the hell do I fit in?" And it's nothing arty, nothing lofty, just fucking different.'[16]

The first album that he claimed as his own was a vinyl copy of *Physical Graffiti*, Zep's cover-all-musical-bases career highwater mark from 1975, a double-album set that would shift a handy four million copies in its lifetime. It was a gift from Moorhead.* Yet as much as he loved Led Zep, they were

---

* Years later, one of most prized Buckley bootlegs – and there are many – was a collection of New York-recorded rarities. Amongst them was his thunderstruck cover of Zep's 'When The Levee Breaks', from Led Zeppelin's untitled fourth album, where he takes lascivious joy in the lyric 'going down', rolling it around in his mouth as if he's tasting the words. He'd also jam Led Zep songs during rehearsals for the band Gods And Monsters, ably copying Bonham's 'hammer of the gods' drum parts, during his brief stint with the group in the early 1990s. And yet again, during the early, exploratory sessions with his *Grace*-era band, he used Zeppelin songs as a way of connecting with the rest of the group. One of many Buckley friends, Irishman Glen Hansard, witnessed this in a New York rehearsal studio. 'All they played was Led Zeppelin,' Hansard said. 'It was amazing.'

but one of the many musical flavours that spiced up his early listening life. As Chris Dowd, the garrulous, straight-shooting former keyboardist of Fishbone, and one of Buckley's closest allies, told me, 'Jeff was such an amalgamation of everything that was wonderful growing up the kid of hippies; [he grew up] listening to a really eclectic amount of music.' Or, as Buckley somewhat more poetically described, music was everywhere. 'There was my mother's breast, then there was music. [It would become] my friend, my ally, my teacher, my tormentor.'[17] It also provided a handy escape when things turned sour at home.

Albeit accidentally, Ron Moorhead also did his bit to steer his stepson in a pop direction. In October 1992, Buckley revealed to WFUM DJ Nichols Hill that he mastered plenty of Elton John songs while sitting around 'waiting for my stepfather to come pick me up for the weekends'. Such songs as John's 'Curtains' and 'We All Fall in Love Sometimes' meant so much to Buckley that he'd willingly throw them into his early sets, during his 'human jukebox' phase, long after Moorhead and his VW ceased to feature in his life.

But if anything, it was the hours that he spent in the passenger seat of the family car, especially when his mother was driving, that shaped his pop instincts. He'd take over the car radio and lose himself in the hits of the day, including such easy-listening fluff as Seals & Crofts' 'Summer Breeze', an unstoppable force on mainstream radio in 1973. Guibert, no musical slouch herself, would join him in a full-throated singalong, as they motored around Orange County. 'I just always sang,' he said in 1994. 'My mum and I would always listen to the radio while driving to school. "Summer Breeze" would come on, and she would sing the second harmony and I would sing the third harmony. Music was like my first real toy.'[18]

Guibert agreed. Amongst her treasured personal possessions are photos of her son, as a 'toddler, singing little ditties and nursery rhymes'. Buckley would assume the position on the raised hearth of the fireplace at their home, which became his 'little stage'. It was here, Guibert recalled, 'where he would sing and recite poems.'[19] With their relationship almost as fractured as that of Jeff and his father, this was probably the closest that mother and son would ever get. 'Who wants the father who wasn't there and the mother who was the party girl?' said Chris Dowd. But Guibert also introduced her son to the music of his father. One day, when Jeff was five, with Moorhead safely out of the house, she cracked open a copy of Tim's *Goodbye And Hello*, and played her son 'Once I Was', an emotionally potent, if somewhat turgid, few minutes of trademark Buckley cosmic folk music. He was enthralled, and memorised the song on the spot, a handy habit that the musically curious Buckley had acquired. In fact, this ability to hear a song – or even a few bars of music – and commit it forever to memory was a Jeff Buckley trait that would fascinate and amuse many of his friends from later years, including Dowd.

'One thing that blew my mind about Jeff was this mimic thing; he was freakish,' Dowd said to me in mid 2007. 'You'd write like a melody or hook and forget it and he'd remember the entire lick, exactly how you played – and your inflections, anything. I heard him play "Giant Steps" on the guitar once and he was exactly like John Coltrane solo. My God.' Another witness to his amazing copycat ability was Antony Fine, from the New York band Glim, who'd share a number of bills with Buckley in the days before Columbia spotted him and set to work on creating the next Bob Dylan. Riding a train back to the city together, the morning after a benefit show in upstate New York, Fine discovered just how closely Buckley had listened to the radio while riding with his mother, back in the early 1970s. 'He could jump into The O'Jays or Stevie Wonder, KC & The Sunshine Band or Joni Mitchell, with equal ease,' said Fine, who recalled sharing a few verses of 'Love Rollercoaster' with Buckley on that train ride, a 1975 chart monster for the Ohio Players. 'He was a wonderful, funny mimic, and had an encyclopedic grasp of all kinds of music.'[20] Andrew Gold's 'Lonely Boy' was another favourite of Buckley's, a song that he felt typified ''70s cheese pop, the good stuff,' which he loved.[21]*

It seemed only natural, of course, for Buckley to start searching out a musical instrument, from a very young age. 'He was from this environment where he was very much pushed towards music,' said Merri Cyr. 'From the time he was born, not only did he have obvious natural gifts, but they were developed from the time he was a very young child, by his mum and others.' There was a piano at home – Guibert still played, opening up her son to the music of Bach and Chopin – and he'd sometimes 'plink around on it', but that didn't really fill any holes in his soul. Aged six, he picked up his grandmother's unused guitar and immediately felt comfortable, strumming along to the radio. 'I loved the thing,' admitted Buckley in the brief bio he wrote for the program of the 1991 *Greetings From Tim Buckley* show. 'I think that she'd gotten it in the hope that one of her children would start to play,' Buckley added during *The Making of Grace* EPK. 'But it just sat there until

---

* Jack McKeever, another friend of Buckley's, related the story of a night they spent on a couch in New York venue The Fez, singing Prince songs to each other. 'We challenged each other to see who knew the third verse of each song,' he laughed.

they became adults and then I found it. I strummed on it, although mostly I put my marbles on it.' It would be a few years before he actually owned an axe, but he'd found his weapon of choice, even if it did initially serve more than one purpose.

The escape that music provided would prove handy, too, because his mother's second marriage was coming apart at the seams, despite the birth of their son, Jeff's stepbrother, Corey James Moorhead, in March 1972. Ron Moorhead, Guibert learned, had begun a relationship with another woman. This infidelity, combined with the failure of his VW repair shop, and his unwillingness to encourage Mary's planned return to a musical career, signalled the end for their marriage. She and Moorhead separated in early 1973, although this time around she came away with some material things (a car, the house, two kids). Ron Moorhead, the man Jeff Buckley called his 'real father', was now out of his life. As Buckley archly recalled, again in the *Greetings* program, 'The auto-mechanic eventually found the woman he loved and he and my Mom divorced.' (Guibert would eventually marry twice again but all these marriages failed, too.)

At the same time, Guibert's first husband – or, at least, his music – was never too far away. Herb Cohen stayed in touch with Guibert, sending her Tim's albums. When Mary let him know that her first-born had started playing the guitar, Cohen's managerial radar went into overdrive and he began calling Guibert more regularly, with a simple query: 'Has he written songs yet?' The inevitable and unavoidable connection with his father had already begun. 'I knew there would be [comparisons] from [when] I was a small child,' Buckley once said, 'from the time that his manager started calling the house. So I've been doing the maths in my head about inevitable comparisons all my life.'[22] However, despite Cohen's overtures, it would still be a few more years before Buckley actually wrote his first song, 'something stupid about a break-up,' as he remembered.[23]

Tim Buckley's career, meanwhile, had taken a nosedive, much like his former wife's love life. After the creative high that was signalled by *Goodbye And Hello* and *Happy/Sad* – the album that included the song 'Dream Letter', another ode to his 'lost' son – his desire to chart unexplored sonic territory alienated him from his label (he'd been dropped by Elektra and signed to Frank Zappa's Straight Records, a sort of halfway home for wayward talents such as Buckley), his bandmates (guitarist Underwood left in 1971) and a good chunk of his audience, who'd moved on to a whole new generation of singer/strummers, including the touchy-feely James Taylor, John Lennon's running buddy Harry Nilsson, confessional queen Carole King and Neil Young, a relocated Canadian run aground, literally and emotionally, in

California. Buckley was simply too 'weird', too out-there, to register commercially with this new audience. It must have crushed Buckley's spirit just
that little bit more as he watched such peers as Linda Ronstadt, and Jackson
Browne, a fellow Orange County singer/songwriter, rise up the charts. 'He
was never going to sell records,' said Danny Fields, 'which I thought was a
pity. I think [Elektra] should have given him a hit single; they didn't give him
anything very much.'

Tim Buckley was always up for improvisation and seeing 'where the song
led' well before his split with Holzman and Elektra. He was also a contrary
character, whose sheer wilfulness and distrust of the 'biz', perhaps increased
by Cohen's urging to write some hits, created plenty of tension both on-
and off-stage. On one occasion, he walked off the set of a New York TV
show in disgust after being instructed to lip-synch the vocals to 'Pleasant
Street', a song that, amongst its many themes, dealt with the destructive
force of mind-expanders. Frequently he'd drift on stage without a set list,
barely noticing the band behind him, and launch himself into another 15-
minute epic of improvisation. 'You're supposed to move on artistically,' Tim
said in an interview from the time, 'but the way the business is... you're supposed to repeat what you did before. It's very hard to progress.'[24] It was yet
another side of Buckley that somehow seemed to be spliced directly into his
son's DNA, who, according to more than one person I spoke with for this
book, seemed to be at odds, if not at all-out war, with Columbia virtually
from the moment he signed up, despite the best intentions of A&R man
Steve Berkowitz. In words that very much echoed those of his father, Jeff
Buckley, just after inking his deal – a time when most acts are awash with
the largesse typically served up by the 'majors' – was asked about life with
Sony. He baulked, saying that it was best not to get too deeply into it, as it
brought out the cynic in him. It might have been possible to count in hours
the time that father and son had spent together, but clearly this apple, in
many ways, hadn't fallen too far from the family tree.

Jeff Buckley would one day find his escape from the hassles of the music
industry in drink, drugs and random sex – 'There was a woman in England,
someone in France, a woman in Canada, things I only found out after he
died,' Merri Cyr told me, echoing similar tales of carnal pursuit that were
attributed to his father. Tim also briefly looked beyond music; for a time he
was convinced that his future lay in cinema. In 1969 he'd scored a little-seen
film called *Changes*, and there was talk of him playing a character by the
name of, erm, 'Fender Guitar' in an unrealised project entitled *Wild Orange*.
He finally did make a film, during 1970, when he appeared in an avant-
garde piece called *Why?*, shot for $150,000 and notable for an appearance

34

from gridiron hero (and later alleged murderer) OJ Simpson. It was never released, possibly for reasons of quality control as much as anything else. In his role as the drummer Glen, Buckley contributed one noteworthy monologue, where he spilled his guts, moaning about the pain that his parents' frequent spats caused him. He talked about his father's fall, first from a ladder and then from the world around him, ending in his stint in a VA hospital. Somewhere during Buckley's monologue, the line between fact and fiction had become disturbingly blurred.

There were more Tim Buckley albums: 1970's groundbreaking though largely overlooked *Starsailor; Greetings from LA* in 1972; 1973's *Sefronia*. Then there was 1975's *Look At The Fool*, a defeated-sounding album, both musically and spiritually. The painting of Buckley on the album's cover said plenty: he looked tired and old, his eyes as empty as the faux-rock and roll he was attempting to create on the record. *Rolling Stone* panned *Fool*, calling it 'desperate'. Hal Willner, who'd produce the *Greetings From Tim Buckley* show that would introduce Jeff Scott Buckley to the downtown New York crowd in 1991, felt those 'rock' albums suffered because of the compromise Buckley decided that he needed to make to reach a wider audience. 'He felt forced to endure the pitifully pedestrian, inadequate and unfulfilling R&B context [of those songs],' Willner wrote in the *Greetings* program.[25] A bad idea, in short.

It wasn't too long after *Fool's* release that Guibert put in her fateful call to Buckley, asking if she could bring his son to his upcoming Golden Bear show. By this time, Mary and her two sons were living in Riverside, an hour's drive out of Anaheim. Since the end of her marriage to Moorhead, she'd worked in various jobs, including the aforementioned clothing business, but that had failed. Her latest partner was a recently divorced plumbing-supplies salesman by the name of George Vandergrift, who Guibert had met through work. He had helped her establish a sideline in potted plants, sold out of a small greenhouse.

Even though her life with Vandergrift at their home on 12th Street was as stable as anything she'd experienced before, it's possible that Mary was entertaining the seemingly impossible notion of reconciliation with Tim, hence her trip to Huntington Beach. However, she'd insist the connection was made because 'I began to think it's really sad that this boy hasn't had any contact with his father: no birthday cards, no Christmas cards.'[26] Guibert and Buckley hadn't been in the same room for six years. Of course it didn't play out quite as Guibert envisaged, even though she would describe it as 'an amazing reunion'. Instead it was her son who'd reconciled with Tim, and it was he who was invited to spend some time with Buckley and his new wife. In fact, the reunion with his father left such a deep impression that when her nine-year-old son was signing up for his new school at Riverside, he asked to be enrolled as Scotty Buckley, not Moorhead.

The Buckley family reunion, of sorts, took place in early April 1975, at Tim and Judy's latest home, in Santa Monica, at a building called the Ocean Air Terrace. The time Jeff spent with his father wasn't as memorable as the Golden Bear gig; father and son shared some random small talk and a little cable TV, and Tim bought Jeff a model airplane during one of their few trips outside the apartment. But in the main Tim stayed in his bedroom, working on new music; he and Larry Beckett were tinkering with the idea of a musical adaptation of Joseph Conrad's *An Outcast Of The Islands*, a huge intellectual step forward from the sleazy bump and grind of *Look At The Fool*. Also during his stay Jeff hooked up with his stepbrother Taylor, who Tim had recently adopted, and wasted a day hanging around a construction site, passing the time by scaring Taylor's pet rabbit. It was hardly the dream catch-up for which Jeff had hoped. After a week passed, Judy and Tim put him on a bus home from Fullerton, with Tim's phone number scrawled on a box of matches stuffed in his pocket. It was the last time he'd ever see his father.

Just under three months later, on June 29, the day after a gig in Dallas, Tim Buckley stopped in at the house of a friend, Richard Keeling, on the way back to Santa Monica. While there, Tim snorted a particularly potent foil of smack – he'd been avoiding hard drugs and his system was relatively clean – and drifted in and out of consciousness as Keeling drove him back to his apartment. (According to one report, Keeling had pushed the drugs in front of Tim, 'challenging' him to hoover the lot, which he promptly did.) Judy was home, but thinking that Tim was simply drunk, she put him to bed, returning to the room in the early evening to watch TV. After an hour or so, she turned Tim over and saw that he'd turned blue. After unsuccessful attempts at reviving him, Tim was raced by ambulance to Santa Monica Emergency, but it was all too late. He was pronounced dead at 9.42 pm, at the not-so-ripe-old-age of 28. The next day, Herb Cohen got in touch with Guibert, telling her what had happened and advising that she let Jeff know, too. She drove to Moorhead's house, where Jeff was spending the weekend, and broke the news. Although he cried, Jeff didn't seem too overwhelmed, allegedly telling his mother, 'Well, I guess it'll just go back to being the way it was before.'[27]

Jeff was massively conflicted by the death of his father and was scarred for the rest of his life. It didn't help any that he wasn't mentioned in the hopelessly inaccurate Associated Press obituary that appeared soon after – Tim's

OD death was referred to as a heart attack – or that he and Mary weren't asked to attend Tim's funeral. Jeff was more at ease with the concept of his father while he was alive; at least he knew he was out there somewhere, living hard, making music. But in death it was as though Jeff had been totally erased from his father's life. It was a crushing blow for anyone, let alone an estranged eight-year-old whose world was unstable, to say the least. Not being asked to the funeral 'kind of gnawed at me', Jeff stated in 1994, almost 20 years after his father's passing. Clearly the emotional wound was deep and as permanent as a tattoo. 'It was cruel,' Mary Guibert said of Tim's death. 'Jeff was ripped away from the possibility of ever knowing him.'[28] His father, 'whom he barely knew and bailed out on him more or less at birth', as a friend of Buckley's told me, was gone.*

Jeff Buckley never really resolved his mixed emotions towards his father. It was only in the later part of his life, when he started seeing a Freudian therapist and went through a process known as 're-nurturing', that he came close to dealing with the pain of rejection. 'The conflict was in him,' said Merri Cyr. 'If someone asked an innocuous question about his father, he made it into a big deal because that conflict was inside him. If he had resolved some of those emotions that wouldn't have been a big deal at all. He was always comparing himself to Tim all the time. I remember him saying to me, "By the ripe old age of 26, Tim had made 10 records [sic], he'd slept with the most beautiful women in the world, I can never catch up, I can never compete with that".' The Pretenders' Chrissie Hynde, who befriended both Buckleys as their stars rose, agreed that there was a massive tug-of-war within Jeff towards his father, made even more confusing when Jeff came to respect the far-reaching music that Tim spread over nine studio albums. 'He obviously had unresolved feelings about a man who abandoned him,' she said, '[but] he really knew and loved his father's music. He never talked about him, but I think he was really proud of his father.'[29]

Of course one possible solution to his emotional quandary would have been not to follow in his father's freeform footsteps, but the need to express himself musically was hotwired into Jeff Buckley's DNA. However, one thing that Jeff did take away from his father's sordid demise was a conviction that he wouldn't die such a clichéd death. He said this bluntly to many people, including Glim's Antony Fine, who wrote that 'Jeff said he disapproved

---

* A few years after his death, Jeff's aunt, Peggy Hagberg, took him to see *The Rose*, a turgid melodrama starring Bette Midler, about a drug-addled star on a fast-track to death. 'He ended up getting freaked out, crying, and ran out of the movie,' I was told. Clearly he saw a connection between the Midler character and his dead father.

of the way his father had done himself in.'[30] Buckley's west coast buddy Chris Dowd – who, like Buckley, was raised by his mother – spelled it out even more precisely. 'When it came to his own legacy, he very much didn't want to go out like his father. He didn't want to do anything stupid. Suicide? Jeff? It's preposterous. He had too much of an ego towards things like living, a healthy respect for life.'

Yet, as Dowd admitted, Jeff's contradictory nature led to him experimenting with most types of drugs, despite knowing the damage it did to his father. But, then again, it wasn't as though he was the first musician to use. 'I know he dabbled in all sorts of stuff but never to a point where it'd fuck him up. He didn't know that I knew certain shit about what was going on with him, dabbling in dope and shit like that; I knew about that, I just never busted his chops on it.' Dowd was quite the authority on the subject, too; he'd once been dubbed the 'Black Belushi' and spent time running wild with such near-terminal junkies as Jane's Addiction singer Perry Farrell and Red Hot Chili Pepper John Frusciante. He also moved in the same circles as Hillel Slovak, the Red Hot Chili Peppers' original guitarist, who died of a smack overdose in 1988, and Alice in Chains' singer Layne Staley, who also OD'd and died, from a drug 'speedball', in 2002.

But this chronic double standard was in Jeff Scott Buckley's future. As the dust started to settle in the wake of his father's death, he sought out a musical education. The first step, weirdly enough, was to fall in love with the curse of the 1970s: arena rock. And although it wasn't done with the same awareness of some of his later actions, Jeff couldn't have chosen a genre less connected to the quasi-intellectual, philosophically-searching, genre-bending music of his father.

It may seem unlikely, but there was a direct link between the British Invasion heyday of the mid 1960s and the almost cancerous spread of arena rock a decade later. After The Beatles' legendary August 1965 Shea Stadium gig – widely regarded as the first-ever 'arena rock' concert – bands felt the need to play the type of music that could fill such large venues (and in the process pocket increasingly large sums of cash). It was all about *projection*, man. Legendary acts like The Who and Led Zeppelin worked their way up to arena status and in the process opened the doors for such lesser acts as Foreigner, Yes, Journey, Heart, Boston, Styx, Queen and REO Speedwagon, the band with possibly the dodgiest name in the history of rock and roll, who struck out for a sonic middle ground that blended solid-gold pop hooks with arena-filling metal bombast. And the gradual improvement in recording facilities meant that all these acts could add a radio-friendly sheen to their records, spawning such FM radio monsters as 'More Than a Feeling', 'Cold As Ice', 'Crazy for You', 'Keep on Loving You' and many more. These were songs that typified arena rock and also foreshadowed the birth of an even cheesier musical movement, hair metal. But let's not go there.

At the same time, more musically competent acts like Canadian power trio Rush sniffed out a way of combining arena rock's sonic overkill with potent musical chops, high IQed lyrics that drew inspiration from such unlikely sources as author Ayn Rand (whom Jeff also read), and upscale concepts, resulting in albums like *2112* and *A Farewell To Kings*. Their 1978 LP *Hemispheres* was a particular favourite of Buckley's. 'Prog rock' bands, with their 'no such thing as too much' outlook, and questionable fashion sense, all held an undeniable appeal for a young Jeff Buckley. He was also a massive fan of Peter Gabriel-led Genesis (whose 'Back In NYC' he'd cover in 1997) and Buggles-era Yes: their much-maligned LP *Drama* was another Buckley fave. He'd tap back into his past when he befriended Tripp Lamkins of Memphis band The Grifters; clearly he'd never lost his love of all things prog. 'Yes, King Crimson and Genesis were the holy trinity of prog rock, in our eyes,' Lamkins wrote in an email. 'Even though we were only a couple of weeks apart in age I was very comforted when he told me, "Don't ever take any shit for liking Yes".' Another time, after smoking a little too much weed, Buckley and Lamkins tried and failed to play Rush's *2112* in its entirety, a serious challenge when straight, let alone stoned.

Prog and arena rock was a handy escape from the 'Disneyland Nazi youth' of Anaheim that left Buckley in 'complete misery every day of my life' (as he confessed in a 1994 KCRW radio interview). Buckley simply had to flick the switch on his radio to hear everyone from Grand Funk Railroad to Jethro Tull, Styx and Queen. These bands were gaining as much exposure as the res-olutely bland, mainstream sounds of Bread, John Denver and Captain & Tennille. No wonder his father's albums sank like a stone; where the hell did they fit amidst such saccharine and bluster? Even the most astute musicologist would struggle to find a link between 'Bohemian Rhapsody' and anything on *Look At The Fool*, let alone 'Phantasmagoria in Two', for Christ's sake.

And then there was Kiss. Before Buckley fell deeply for Led Zeppelin's *Physical Graffiti*, and the devilish double act of Robert Plant's lemon-squeezing vocals and the guitar heroics of Jimmy Page, he, like millions of other sub-urban American teens, was lured to rock and roll's dark side by four rock and roll hedonists straight outta Nowheresville, New York. How could Buckley resist? Kiss offered the ultimate in low-brow entertainment, a cash-register-friendly mix of cartoonish mystery (what did they look like under-neath all that greasepaint?) and circus-like flash (fire-eating, blood-drooling, out-of-this-world outfits), all set to a soundtrack of dumbed-down anthems like 'Rock And Roll All Nite' and such mawkish power ballads as 'Beth'. Jeff Buckley may have resembled a hippie kid, with his long hair and open-minded mother – both Guibert and her partner Vandergrift liked to 'party' – but he was hooked on these rockin' reprobates, turning his schoolfriend Willie Osborn on to *Kiss Alive!* and *Destroyer*. The smash hit single 'Detroit Rock City' was a particular favourite.*

As late as 1996, Jeff would still rate Kiss amongst his all-time faves, along-side more 'credible' acts like Sun Ra, Lou Reed, Patti Smith, The Grifters, Tom Waits and the ubiquitous Led Zep. Clearly, the impression that Kiss left was long-lasting. And there was always a hint of arena-rock's overkill in Buckley's later work, particularly when he assembled a band and trans-formed the intimacy of *Grace* into a much larger, louder spectacle. Duncan Sheik, an American singer/songwriter and peer who'd write one of many posthumous odes to Jeff Buckley (the sadly beautiful 'A Body Goes Down'), sensed the classic rocker trapped inside the troubadour's body. According to Sheik, it was Buckley's voice, especially as it disappeared into the higher register, that hinted at his suburban rock past. 'It reminded me of things from the '70s,' Sheik told me when we spoke in mid 2007. 'It made me think of Yes and prog rock that I'd listened to as a teenager. But God for-bid you ever said to Jeff that you liked him *and* Journey.'

Jeff Buckley's immersion in all things rock coincided with another unfor-tunate downturn on the domestic front. At first, George Vandergrift seemed to be the perfect match: he respected Mary Guibert's artistic bent, and encouraged her business pursuits, but the failure of the latter created a rift that in 1979 ended their relationship. Jeff was never as close to Vandergrift as he was to Ron Moorhead; it said a lot that he'd always refer to Moorhead as his father, not Tim Buckley or Vandergrift. (Despite their divorce, Moorhead still featured in Jeff's life, slipping him that all-important copy of *Physical Graffiti* when he was 12.)

By the time he finally got his hands on his own guitar, Jeff, Guibert and Corey had moved, yet again. This time they settled in Riverside, an Orange County suburb of several hundred thousand, distinguishable only for a University Of California campus and Fairmont Park, an 'urban oasis' that greets you as you entered Riverside from Route 60. Riverside didn't impress the increasingly alienated Buckley; he'd describe the suburb as 'a

* In a truly perverse twist of fate, on the day of Buckley's death in 1997, a press release trumpeted the arrival of the Kiss Visa card. Weird but true.

modest hell'. Even at this early stage in his life he was beginning to sense that his true home lay several thousand miles on the other side of the country. 'I never fit in California,' he said in the bio that accompanied *Grace*, 'even though my roots are there.'[31] Sometimes, when asked where he was from, Buckley would simply reply: 'Nowhere.'

Amongst the gifts that he received on Christmas Day, 1980, when he was 14, was a guitar. It was the one thing that Jeff had been craving for years, ever since he brushed the cobwebs off his grandmother's six-string. It was an impressive axe, too, a Gibson Les Paul, the weapon of choice for Zep's Jimmy Page, Paul Stanley of Kiss and Rush's Alex Lifeson. Underwhelmed by the world outside his window, Buckley would barricade himself inside his bedroom, playing along to his favourite records. The first song he mastered was the Knack's 'My Sharona'. 'What I remember most,' said Mary Guibert, 'is that he'd play different artists' albums incessantly and play along with them until one couldn't tell whether it was Jeff or the stereo playing.'[32] In particular, he flogged *Physical Graffiti* 'until the grooves were gone'. It was around this time that Buckley made a declaration: he wanted to be a guitar player, not a singer. 'He was going to be a guitar god and that was all,' Guibert said in the BBC's *Everybody Here Wants You*. 'And he had the best teachers: he studied Led Zeppelin, he played them until his fingers were raw.'[33]

Despite some rudimentary lessons in high school, where he studied the cello for one unsatisfying year, Buckley remained self-taught, at least until he signed up at LA's Musician's Institute. Regardless, his friend Chris Dowd wasn't alone in sensing that Buckley could have cut it purely as a guitar player, if he'd chosen that path. 'His understanding of chord progressions, how things worked together, I've never witnessed anything like that in my life. And I've played with Hillel [Slovak] and so many other of my contemporaries, but Jeff was uncanny,' said Dowd. 'He could have easily played guitar and people would have said he was amazing. If he put his mind to being the next [jazz guitarists] Peter Bernstein or Wes Montgomery, and never sung, he would have been a bad motherfucker, no question.'

Whether this choice to simply shut up and play his guitar was a reaction to his growing understanding of what happened to Tim Buckley, doomed singer, is unclear. According to Guibert, 'I don't know if he was resisting being a replica of his father, [but] that *might* have stopped him stepping up front.'[34] Many of the West Coast-based musicians he'd encounter in the following years, including friends and bandmates such as Carla Azar, later of Ednaswap, as well as Dowd, had no idea that he could sing. In fact, in Dowd's case, it would take a couple of years of tight friendship with

Buckley before making the startling discovery. Indeed, they shared a house for something like 18 months, got wasted together, hung out constantly, and yet Buckley never sang in Dowd's company and certainly didn't mention his father. Kathryn Grimm, leader of hard rockers Group Therapy, with whom Jeff would briefly play, had a similar experience. 'In my mind he was a guitar player,' Grimm said in the same BBC documentary. 'I'd never heard him sing.'[35]

As he developed his playing skills, Buckley turned further and further inwards, becoming something of a cliché: the guitar-loving loner. His reclusive nature became part of his 'official' story, and he took every chance to talk it up. 'I never travelled in packs,' Buckley said in 1994. 'I've never needed a pack of people around me to feel secure. I've always been alone – nothing has changed since high school.'[36] In another interview from the same time, he figured that being an only child – at least until Corey came along in 1972 – strengthened his 'loner' status. 'I was alone a lot of the time,' he said, 'and I liked it.'[37] Although he didn't say it out loud, it's quite likely that Guibert's absence, be it during the days she spent at work or the nights she devoted to socialising, only heightened his feelings of isolation. Lost in daydreams, his Gibson nearby, Buckley was, in many ways, the classic American teenager: the victim of a broken home, in love with rock and roll, aware of the endless possibilities of life but totally unsure how to go about improving his lot. He definitely didn't fit the mould of the archetypal Californian: for one thing, he disliked going to the beach, as he explained in 1996. 'I'd love to learn how to surf; I'm a Californian boy. But I never went to the beach. I hated it. I loved the sand and the water but the beach-goers irked me. Boneheads. Kids in cliques.'[38]

Numerous key events occurred in Buckley's life during 1981: he witnessed his first arena-rock spectacle (the bill featured soon-to-be-huge Def Leppard and eminently forgettable southern rockers Blackfoot) and he and Guibert moved back to Orange County. The perennial loner now found himself becoming, in his own words, 'the man of the house'. 'It was a dislocated childhood,' he once said, 'moving from place to place, making friends, letting them go.' Buckley would take some steps to fit in, such as trying out for school plays, but even if he got lucky and scored a part, he'd come home and 'find out that evening that we had to leave'. (Paying the rent wasn't always Guibert's strong point.) 'It made me grow up more quickly; I feel I was born old.'[39]

Something did work in his favour when they returned to Anaheim, however. He was able to enroll at Loara High, the school that both Tim and Mary had attended. Loara was regarded as one of the best schools located behind the so-called 'Orange Curtain', with a strong focus on the arts. It suited the wannabe guitar hero – who was now toying with the idea of calling himself 'Jeff Buck', in honour of his latest idol, erstwhile Yardbird and fusion fanatic Jeff Beck – right down to the ground.

Loara High opened on November 1, 1962, with its then 400-odd students decked out in school colours of red, gold and white ('red, white, and gold we honour,' declared the school song, ''til our dying day'). The school quickly became renowned, at least throughout California, for its marching band, 'the Show Band of the Western States'. It was also known for the many musicians who would spend their formative years in its liberal, student-friendly surrounds. Former student Mike Miller, who'd become a No Doubt insider, recalled with a laugh how he was surrounded by future idols while attending Loara. 'When we went to high school, I was the only one from our lunchtime crew that didn't become a rock star. We'd sit around and there was Gwen and Eric [Stefani], Jeff Buckley, T Bone [aka singer Jeff 'T Bone' Gerard], and drum'n'bass guy Q.'

As open-minded and tolerant as Loara High undoubtedly was, it still didn't fill any holes in Jeff Buckley's soul. One of his classmates, Deborah Reed, recalled how Buckley remained the archetypal outsider. 'He was removed from the usual high school activities,' she told me, '[but] I really enjoyed his company. He was a sensitive soul with a tough exterior. He was witty and fun and very bright. His humour was realistic, sometimes biting, but good.' Buckley, she said, wasn't much for the usual lunchtime chitchat, 'but he was very open and honest with me.' One topic that was off limits, however, was his family: 'He never spoke of home life or life away from school,' Reed said. 'I never really pushed it.' (Another friend of Buckley's, who preferred not to be named, was less empathetic, referring to Guibert as 'quite crazy… a nutty hippie', adding that Jeff drifted away from his mother in years to come.)

In an on-line posting from 1998, a Loara High classmate of Buckley's related the events of a party that she attended with Jeff, where they made out briefly, and she slept on the couch of the apartment that he and Guibert shared. 'In the morning he made pancakes for us,' she wrote, 'and showed me one of his father's albums.' Apparently Tim Buckley wasn't totally off-limits. She also hinted very strongly that some of the lyrics for 'So Real', a song from *Grace*, was based on the events of this night. '[It's] one of the most peaceful yet powerful memories I have: under a dark blue starry sky, the intensity of two people who are clinging to each other not for sex, but in pure understanding of the unhappiness of our lives, and the happiness of simply being with each other.'

With the exception of what Deborah Reed called his 'Ric Ocasek hairdo' – referred to as 'a funny, fluffy, Bay City Rollers-style' cut by another classmate – the high school Buckley slouched around like a typical teen rocker, favouring jeans and a variety of T-shirts emblazoned with the logo of his current band of choice. Away from music, he only really came alive in senior year literature class, presided over by a Mr Roberts.* 'I thought he was brilliant,' said Reed. 'I am pretty left-brained but he could interpret the literature so well. He obviously was very good with words and finding hidden meanings in all kinds of literature. I did consider him pretty artsy. You could tell high school wasn't easy for him,' she added. 'It was so sad that he finally found his way in the world only to die when it was all starting for him.' Reed's brother, another Loara High alumnus, was more closely involved with the school's music scene 'and thought highly' of Buckley. But it seemed as though he didn't form any strong bonds in his years at Loara.

Other classmates, including Theresa Johnson, recalled seeing Buckley in the school band room, which was his sanctuary. 'He was at school because he had to be,' Johnson said many years after graduating from Loara. 'He had to be there only to do what he had to so he could move on to what he wanted. You could see how much talent he had even then. He was special.'[40] Buckley summed up his time at Loara with his cut-the-crap entry in the senior yearbook. 'My only goal,' he wrote, 'is to fulfill my abilities with music. That's what I'm about.'[41] Michael 'Bear' Schwartz was another Loara classmate – and fellow big band member, playing the trumpet – who recognised that music was an obsession for Buckley. 'He could never stop playing,' he said. Even when the director of the big band, Bill Schroeder, was illustrating a point, Buckley would continue to noodle away on his guitar. Even though the volume on his amp was turned way down, the sound of Buckley plucking on his strings was very audible. 'So, he'd get scolded,' said Schwartz. Although he felt that Buckley was 'respectful' of what the big band was doing, he could see he wasn't always in agreement with Schroeder. (Buckley and Schwartz were the only members of the band to master the blues scales in all 12 keys.) Buckley summed it up with another pithy yearbook entry: 'Well, it looks like the years ahead are stinking with band offers, and I hope you come out smelling like a skunk.' 'Sometimes his humour was a little different,' Schwartz admitted, 'but I appreciated it.'

This was one goal he set in motion while at Loara High. While doing time in a section of the school orchestra that was strictly for jazz devotees, he met Jason Hamel, a bassist, a 'short kid with long curly blond hair,' according to Schwartz. ('Hey, it was the '80s,' he added. 'Hair bands were the thing.') Hamel, in turn, introduced Jeff to Robin Horry, a junior who led a

---

* This was during the same year that Gwen Stefani enrolled at Loara as a freshman.

local combo called Powerage, that specialised in covers of Def Leppard, Jimi Hendrix and, not surprisingly, given their name, AC/DC. Tim Marse played the drums. Using chunks of their surnames, the group soon morphed into an outfit called Mahre Bukham, which gave Jeff the chance to impress with his note-perfect covers of such prog-rock standards as Yes' 'Long Distance Turnaround'. Although he'd willingly take the piss out of the otherworldly, heliumated vocals of Jon Anderson, Buckley still had no plans of going vocal: he was a guitarist and that was it.

Though short-lived, Mahre Bukham never failed to leave an impression. They graduated from the garage to the stage on September 21, 1982, when they played to a few curious friends and family at an Anaheim metal club called the Woodstock Concert Theater, Buckley prancing about in a pair of spandex ball-huggers purchased especially for the occasion. They may have preferred the complexity of prog rock, but the flash of hair metal – or at least its grotesque fashion sense – wasn't completely lost on the hard-rocking foursome. Rare footage from around this time, unearthed for the *Everybody Here Wants You* documentary, shows the band stomping through an amped-up take on the Police's 'Roxanne', with far more hair on stage than absolutely necessary. Buoyed by her son's experience, Guibert bought him his first amp, a Roland Jazz Chorus, a 16th birthday gift. It was the perfect companion for his second guitar, a cream Ovation Viper.

Mahre Bukham played the grand total of four gigs, the most memorable of which was probably a concert at a military base in Tustin where Buckley's smart-ass attitude led to a punch-up with some Marines. He also scored his first press coverage, in Loara High's school newspaper, the *Saxon Shield*, saying, rather wisely, that the band was hoping for 'a good slow climb to the top', with their immediate goal being to write some originals. (One of their few non-covers, written by Hamel, was called 'Murder In Ojai'.) But soon after the interview Mahre Bukham had run their course. As Robin Horry recalled in *Everybody Here Wants You*, it's likely that Buckley had outgrown his bandmates. 'It was the '80s, Eddie van Halen and all that guitar wizardry,' he said. 'He laughed at that kind of stuff; [instead] he was playing Al Di Meola, Jeff Beck, all those jazz guys. When we would jam we'd go from Zeppelin songs to UFO, AC/DC to The Police, you know, everything.'[42]

Although he could have used a little more stability on the home front, musically speaking, Buckley just wanted to keep on moving. He was heading into a period where he'd play in as many bands as humanly possible. 'They were proving grounds and fact-gathering expeditions,' said his soon-to-be-roommate John Humphrey. But first, Jeff Buckley had to go to music school.

Notes

1. Guibert, Mary: on-line interview
2. See note 1
3. Sony Records: Grace biography
4. Diehl, Matt: The Son Also Rises... *Rolling Stone*, October 20, 1994
5. Smith, Alex Duval: Cult Rock Singer Jeff Buckley Feared Drowned; *The Guardian*, June 2, 1997
6. Aston, Martin: Tim Buckley, *Mojo*, July 1995 283
7. Browne, David: Dream Brother, *The Lives and Music of Jeff and Tim Buckley*, Fourth Estate 2001
8. Rogers, Ray: Jeff Buckley, Singer-Songwriter, Interview, February 1, 1994
9. See note 1
10. See note 1
11. Kingsmill, Richard: Jeff Buckley's High 5, *Triple J FM* August 29, 1995, transcript
12. BBC 2, *Everybody Here Loves You* documentary
13. Arnold, Carson: *Reflections from a Shadow*, January 2004 (unpublished?)
14. See note 11
15. See note 13
16. Houghton, Mick: Jeff Buckley: Grace, *Mojo*, September 1994
17. Taylor, Sam: Inherited Torment, Just Like His Dad, *The Observer*, June 8, 1997
18. See note 1
19. Koha, Nui Te: Love from the Grave, *Herald-Sun*, April 30, 1998
20. Fine, Antony: *Jeff Buckley Drowns* (unpublished)
21. See note 11
22. Scatena, Dino: The Last Goodbye; *Daily Telegraph,* June 6, 1997
23. Simpson, Dave: Grace Under Fire; *The Guardian*, May 1, 1998
24. Anon, St Ann's program, *Greetings From Tim Buckley*, 1991
25. See note 25
26. See note 19
27. See note 7
28. See note 19
29. See note 17
30. See note 20
31. See note 3
32. See note 1
33. See note 12
34. See note 12
35. See note 12
36. Creswell, Toby: Grace Under Fire, *Juice Magazine*, February, 1996
37. See note 1
38. See note 11
39. See note 17
40. Wener, Ben: Dead Ringer for Drake's Legacy? Buckley May Be; *Orange County Register*, June 13, 1997
41. See note 40
42. See note 12

Chapter Three

The Guitar-Loving Monks of Cherokee Street

With its 30-odd thousand feet of floor space and row upon row of 'labs', where hopeful guitar heroes could jam with such shit-hot players as Scott Henderson, LA's Musician's Institute must have seemed like nirvana for someone like Jeff Buckley, trapped as he was behind the Orange Curtain. According to his buddy Chris Dowd, that's exactly why Buckley enrolled there, arriving just before autumn, 1984, bankrolled by $4000 that Mary managed to squeeze from a Tim Buckley trust fund. 'Among musicians, in a certain way, that's where fucking hacks go to spend Mummy and Daddy's money, you know what I mean?' Dowd said of the Institute. 'It helps wannabe rock stars. That's the reputation to someone like me and Flea and Anthony [Kiedis], who grew up in LA, guys on the edge. To the average kid like Jeff, from Anaheim, it seemed like a chance, to get out from behind that Iron Curtain. Jazz guys came out of there, but to the rock guys that I know they just seemed like noodlers, with all their fucking tricks and technical bullshit. From what Carla [Azar, another MI student] told me about Jeff, before he met her, he was going down that road. I believe it because he's sort of like a sponge.'

Originally known as the Guitar Institute, which in itself says plenty, the school was opened in February 1977. Drawing on the educational philosophy of journeyman guitarist Howard Roberts, it was co-founded and managed by Los Angeles music businessman Pat Hicks, 'a real shyster opportunist', in the words of Tom Chang, an expat Canadian who would become very tight with Jeff Buckley during their two years at the Institute.

In 1978, the Bass Institute was opened, followed by the Percussion Institute two years later. Despite Hicks' questionable business ethics – amongst other things, he'd hire students as cheap labour to do essential maintenance work on the building, which led to Buckley being hired as an electrician's assistant soon after graduating – he did manage to persuade well-regarded players and bands to lecture, and play alongside, the hopefuls who'd enrolled there. The Bass Institute's first director, Chuck Rainey, had kept it deep and funky for Aretha Franklin, Marvin Gaye and Stevie Wonder and was also bassist of choice for Steely Dan's Donald Fagen and Walter Becker, while jazz pianist Carl Schroeder, one of MI's most popular teachers during Buckley's stint, had played with Sarah Vaughan and John Lee Hooker. The three original instructors at the Institute were Joe Diorio, one of the most gainfully employed jazz guitarists of the 1960s and '70s; Ron Eschete, whose list of jazz credits was equally credible; and Don Mock, who produced recordings by jazzman Tommy Tedesco and put in many hours of session time.

'That was part of the appeal,' said Chang, who'd become Buckley's roommate and would remain a life-long friend. 'I remember one time [Weather Report bassist] Jaco Pastorius showed up, right out of the blue. And Rush came by once. Jeff was very much into all that, Rush and Led Zeppelin, as well as Weather Report and a lot of jazz. He would listen to a lot of stuff; at the time he was right into people like [guitarist] Steve Morse – and everybody was big on Scott Henderson, because he was a teacher there.'* Chang had a slightly different perspective to Chris Dowd. 'Back then it was known as a player's school,' he told me. 'What I'd heard from past students is that you could interact with all these great teachers on a personal level, rather than in, say, an academic-type situation. And when I went there it was all about that; I don't think I went to any classes. I wanted to pursue a career in professional music and wanted training in live-playing situations. There were other schools that offered some of that, but I wanted an environment that was strictly geared towards guitar.' Chang agreed that it offered Buckley an escape from Anaheim, but felt there were other reasons behind Jeff's enrolment. 'A lot of it was that he had this passion for music. It definitely afforded him the opportunity to get away, but he was hell-bent on becoming a guitarist, a musician.'

Chang's first meeting with Buckley typified just how 'lost in music' he was at the time. Drummer Randall Stoll, another expat Canadian studying

---

* Henderson was a former student, enrolling at the Guitar Institute in 1980.

there, invited Chang to meet a new friend of his, who was living in the run-down apartment block across the street. 'So we went over to this building,' Chang recalled, 'and there's this party going on; all these heavy metal guys, real '80s types with big rooster haircuts, walking around with these jagged guitars under their arms. So Randall says, "I gotta find Buckley" – and there he was, in the middle of the party, with his headphones on, nursing his guitar, transcribing this really difficult Steve Morse guitar solo while this party was going on around him.' Apart from his total immersion in music and his enviable ability to shut himself off from the rest of the world, the one thing that left its mark on Chang was Buckley's odd speaking tone: 'He had this really high-pitched voice. It was bizarre.'

John Humphrey, a Musician's Institute instructor and future Buckley friend, agreed that the school offered Buckley a chance to move ahead as a player. 'I think that, amongst other factors, it introduced him to the notion of being a "professional" musician,' said Humphrey. 'There certainly was a lot of talk about that around the school in those days. There were quite a few paying gigs around.' But Humphrey also recognised the more idealistic side of Buckley, even during these early days: he recalled how they both read Ayn Rand's *The Romantic Manifesto*. (Sharing new sensations, and accumulating a remarkable number of friends from all over, was one of Buckley's many traits; he'd reminisce how he made some 'lifelong' friends while at the Musician's Institute, which is clearly true.) 'Jeff was a romantic person,' Humphrey insisted. '[But] the less romantic side of Jeff was looking to make his living playing guitar. He was evolving a set of skills, and at the same time, building his self-confidence. [However], like a lot of us, I think he discovered that getting paid didn't make a gig worth doing.'*

Buckley spent most of his time in a tight-knit group that comprised Chang, Stoll and bassist Tony Maryatt, another Canadian. Buckley was christened 'an honorary Canuck'. Mary Guibert appeared infrequently, if at all. 'I remember a few times, when Jeff was living on Sycamore, and she'd turn up,' recalls Chang. 'But my feeling was that she was all over the place. Sometimes she'd be there, camped out for a week, sometimes two, at his place, which was odd. She seemed to be flying by the seat of her pants.' At the time, according to one source, Guibert was taking acting lessons – 'headshot and all' – while holding down various office jobs in and around

---

* Humphrey himself found a few gigs worth doing, playing bass alongside teacher Scott Henderson in the Blues Trio and working with singing/songwriting legend Carole King.

49

Orange County. (Guibert would also spend two weeks, at Buckley's request, at the LA apartment of Chris Dowd, when he was on the road, which suggests that Chang's assessment of her doing it tough is pretty accurate.) As for Tim Buckley, he was never mentioned, certainly not to Chang's recollection. In fact, he'd only learn about his friend's 'famous' father through a friendship with Tamurlaine Adams, the daughter of Herb Cohen. 'Jeff was very private about certain things; he never really discussed his family life at all. And he was very reserved to begin with. He completely blocked out the past, and that was cool, because a lot of our interaction was about music, not whatever personal hang-ups we had. But it became pretty clear that there were problems, that he came from something of a broken home, and he became pretty reclusive. It was apparent that something was amiss.'

The year before he enrolled at the Institute, Buckley had grown tired of his mother's peripatetic lifestyle and moved in with his maternal grandmother on Archer Street in Anaheim. Anna Guibert handed down the Tim Buckley albums that Mary had kept, and a few notes from the time Tim was wooing Mary back in their Loara High days, feeding her grandson's interest in his long-gone father. It was also around this time that he met Roy Rallo, who'd turn him onto a recording of Benjamin Britten's 'Corpus Christi Carol', later to become one of the many highlights of *Grace*. And this time spent apart from Mary also helped develop Buckley's skills at self-sufficiency, which would come to prove incredibly handy.

Alleged 'shyster' Pat Hicks enticed many wide-eyed students to the Institute on the basis that it was located in the heart of Hollywood, which promised a tantalising, close-up glimpse of the LA high life. Chang admits that he was seduced by the idea. 'It certainly fooled me. I thought, wow, Hollywood; it's going to be glamorous. Well, *kind of*.' The reality of life there was something else altogether: the building was located in a broken-down part of town that many described as the 'armpit' of Hollywood. Most of the students, including Buckley and his Canadian crew, lived on Cherokee Street, a thriving marketplace for the two of the biggest local industries: gangs and drugs. 'Where the school was situated was a pigsty, practically a ghetto,' Chang said. 'There were a lot of Mexican gangs, drugs, all kinds of shit. It was Cherokee hell.' The next building over from the Institute housed possibly as many as 100 gang members at a time, and there was an agreement that no-one would leave the school by themselves. If anyone needed to go outside, they'd travel in groups of four or five to avoid the inevitable muggers. 'Every night I recall helicopters flying over, trying to get somebody,' Chang added. 'It was like a war zone, really bad. I was 17, Jeff was 17, we were right out of high school; I think one of the reasons we endured it was because we were so young and didn't know better.'

But in some ways, the perils of gangland worked to Buckley's advantage: he and other students such as Chang and Stoll lived a monk-like existence, spending as much as 10, sometimes 12 hours a day at the Institute. They'd only return to their Cherokee flophouse when they needed sleep or food. And despite the proximity of LA's many rock clubs, they never ventured out, at least not until after they graduated. 'With all the bad shit that was associated with the school – the bad living conditions and everything,' said Chang, 'it was a great place to meet people and play. It was all there, our whole world. Jeff was there all the time.' Buckley was surviving on the money eked out of his trust fund, so he was able to concentrate totally on his guitar. Initially, he dutifully attended as many formal classes as he could, but quickly learned that the curriculum was pretty informal, at best. Unlike more academically-inclined schools, there was no formal testing; students simply had to show up and log a certain number of hours attendance.

'You'd get a schedule which would break it down that you had to go to Ear Training or Reading, Harmony, Fingerboard Harmony, stuff like that,' Chang recalled, 'but the school was very loose. They didn't care; it wasn't like someone was taking attendance. You pretty much set up your own schedule. Jeff at first was going to a lot of classes but then spent most of his time at the live-playing workshops.'

Along with unannounced cameos from such rock bands as Rush, those workshops were one of the school's biggest drawcards, although Buckley was still too reserved to step up and play. Jazz and the dreaded 'fusion' might have been Buckley's obsession at the time, but he still preferred to stand back and watch. Buckley was 'painfully' shy, according to Chang, 'and he was no ladies' man, although that changed later.' Having said that, during this time Buckley would become emotionally entangled with Tamurlaine Adams, which led to things 'getting pretty twisted' with Randall Stoll, who was also romancing Adams at the time. 'There was a lot of energy in that relationship [with Adams], whatever it was,' said one source. Given that she was the daughter of his father's former manager just made it that little bit weirder. And this wasn't Buckley's last 'bizarre love triangle' while trying to find his way in La-La Land, either; a few years later he'd have to deal with his unrequited love for another Institute alumnus, Carla Azar.

Despite his 'painful' shyness, Buckley was a regular at the workshops run by jazz pianist Schroeder, essential events for most students at the time. 'I think he lacked a lot of confidence as far as his jazz playing goes,' Chang said, 'even though I know that's what he was into at the time. He was very reserved, and not aggressive at all.' Instead, Buckley felt more comfortable hanging out in the 'labs', rabbit–warren–like rooms that seemingly stretched forever. A couple of amps were set up in each, which had just enough space to fit a few students and whichever teacher happened to be in attendance. It was the perfect way for a player-under-development such as Buckley to develop his chops. 'You'd find people like Scott Henderson [in the labs],' Chang recalled, 'and you could jam with them for hours on end. It was about playing and being in a real playing situation. [The school] really wasn't about being in a classroom.'

In another part of the Institute, rehearsal stages were set up to simulate a live playing environment. Again, Buckley didn't feel ready to step up and cut loose with his Ovation guitar, but he was willing to flex his stand-up skills. Chang and others were astounded by the 'human jukebox'; one minute Buckley would be a wallflower, head-down in yet another transcription of a tricky Steve Morse guitar part, then suddenly he'd be pulling off note-perfect impersonations of some *Saturday Night Live* regular. 'He was this incredible mimic,' recalled Chang. 'He'd get up and do a vaudeville or comic routine, sending up a comic, whatever, and people would die laughing, because he had it down.' Chris Dowd, who'd befriend Buckley soon after, agreed that he was 'funny as hell', but also found Buckley 'completely socially awkward at times; he would say any shit. You know, like, "Jeff, this may not be the time to say that one, dog." He was always picking up weird shit and running up to you like a five year old and sticking it in your face. It was like, "Jesus, Jeff, come on, man." '*

Another contradictory aspect of Jeff Buckley the student was that while he may have been willing and able to sing all the drum and bass parts of a song – note perfect, naturally – he would never actually sing a song. When he went on to become probably the finest voice of generation alt-rock – 'a chanteuse', by his own description – Buckley's classmates couldn't believe it was the same guy. 'That's the amazing thing,' said Chang, 'he never once sang. I didn't even *know* he could sing.' Yet in spite of his humility and awkwardness, many of his fellow Institute hopefuls sensed that Buckley had the right stuff, but figured that he'd become a guitar-slinger, the archetypal sideman. 'He was really developing,' Chang said. 'He wasn't the player that he became, but he had a lot of natural ability. Most people knew it, too; they

---

* Many years later, during an interview on Sydney's Triple J radio station, Buckley admitted his social hopelessness. 'I'm used to being a fool,' he said. 'I'm a horrible clown, doing the funny shit that falls flat. I'm the poster boy for saying the wrong thing at the wrong time.'

figured it would just be a matter of time before this guy became the next big thing. He could pick things up so quickly; he had perfect pitch and natural musicality.' Even in his early days at the school, Buckley tackled jazz standards, a discipline 'that takes a long time to develop,' according to Chang. What Buckley lacked in 'front' he clearly made up for in ambition.

That was proved, in spades, by Buckley's graduation performance, which was played out on September 15, 1985, at a venue called the Odyssey in Granada Hills. While the sonic crush and enviable chops of Rush and Led Zeppelin still rocked the world of this Orange County teen, Buckley had also developed a real taste for such 'noodlers' as Weather Report. And if there was one band that would appeal to the type of music snob that Buckley was in danger of becoming, this was it. The group was essentially a loose-knit ensemble built around saxophonist Wayne Shorter and keyboardist Joe Zawinul. Both were former Miles Davis sidekicks, Shorter playing a key role in the revered Davis Quintet of the 1960s and Zawinul leaving his stamp on Davis' *In A Silent Way*, the precursor to the era-defining *Bitches Brew* LP. They formed Weather Report in New York in 1970, bringing together influences from all over the musical shop: Zawinul was raised on the Gypsy folk music of his family and studied classical piano as a pre-teen living in Nazi-occupied Vienna; Shorter was a New Yorker who'd done time with Art Blakey's Jazz Messengers before working with Davis. When Zawinul heard the Shorter composition 'Nefertiti', which Davis recorded, he knew they should join forces (for a time they played together in Davis' band).

The sky was starting to cloud over, though, for Weather Report – whose madly eclectic sounds were described by *Rolling Stone* as possessing 'the drive of rock, the harmonic sophistication of jazz, the formal ingenuity of classical music and hints of Brazilian, African and Oriental traditions' – when Buckley discovered them. (They'd break up in 1987.) But they'd made their mark, recording such albums as 1973's *Streetnighter*, with its pioneering use of synths, and their biggest success, 1977's *Heavy Weather*, which shifted over 500,000 units, great numbers for such a steadfastly 'serious' band of players who mainly peddled instrumentals and paid little heed to the formulas of mainstream pop music. During its 17-year run, the ensemble's numbers included bassist (and Institute guest star) Jaco Pastorius, plus Alphonso Johnson and numerous other A-list players.

The number chosen by Buckley for graduation was their 'D Flat Waltz' (not 'Pearl On The Half-Shell', as documented elsewhere, which they'd performed at a previous event), a typically complicated few minutes of Weather

Report neo-fusion – a 'really cool piece, very involved', according to Tom Chang – and a standout from their 1983 set *Domino Theory*. But Buckley, accompanied by Stoll on drums and Maryatt on bass, didn't just play the piece, he also wrote the individual parts out beforehand for the band. According to Chang, 'Jeff transcribed everything: the keyboard part, which he arranged for guitar, which was really difficult, not just to transcribe but to actually play. And he transcribed the bass part; I remember Tony was having a real hard time playing it [in rehearsal] so Jeff would play it for him.' 'The trio was kind of obsessed with "D Flat Waltz",' added Randall Stoll, 'and I suspect some of the other students may have become nauseated from hearing us play it so much. I found the piece both challenging and joyful to play, and obviously the other guys did, too.'

As recalled by those in attendance at the Odyssey, including teacher Scott Henderson and jazz guitarist Joe Pass, there was a heavy mix of electricity and anticipation in the room. Chang said how all of the night's performances up to that point 'was just bullshit, pretty lame', so Buckley and co had plenty to prove. Fortunately, the trio erased the memory of all that came before as soon as they plugged in and started playing. 'Right from the get-go,' said Chang, 'everyone perked up. It was incredible stuff.' Duly impressed, Scott Henderson turned to the students around him and stated: 'This *is* Weather Report.' Pass was equally taken, seeking Buckley out afterwards and shaking his hand.

Typically, Buckley had to deal with his own insecurities before this musical 'coming out'; the high regard with which his fellow students regarded his playing probably increased his intense nervousness and performance anxiety. 'It was hard for him to do that,' recalled Chang, 'playing in front of his peers and all those shit-hot players. [In hindsight] it was hilarious, though not to him.' Yet still Buckley refused to sing, and with the exception of such fusion instrumentals as 'Black Tattoo', a Frank Zappa-inspired piece that he'd tried out in rehearsal with Maryatt and Stoll, he was very much a songwriter-under-development. But there's no denying how, in the words of his friend Chang, Buckley's stint at the Institute was both 'important and formative'.

Much has been made of Buckley's devotion at this time in his life to such fusionists as Weather Report, but his love of rock and roll maverick composer Frank Zappa was never far from the surface either. According to Danny Fields, who'd take Buckley under his wing when he moved to New York in the early 1990s, 'Frank was like a father-figure to him.' Buckley also formed a bond with Zappa's daughter Moon Unit that Fields described as 'like brother and sister'. Randall Stoll recalled receiving a late-night visit from a fellow student, who complained about not having enough time to complete a complex Zappa transcribe. 'Jeff agreed to help him and stayed up the whole night transcribing it. Let's just say Jeff was a seriously enthusiastic creature when it came to music,' Stoll laughed.

Despite his crippling shyness, Buckley had grown substantially as a musician and as a player, while his experiences in 'Cherokee Hell' meant that there'd be very few domestic situations that he couldn't handle. Once you've survived Mexican gangs and drug wars, any big city would seem like sleepy Anaheim by comparison. Yet beneath his nervous exterior, there was an aura surrounding Buckley; those close to him felt that even at this early stage in his musical growth, he knew he had something magical going on. Chris Dowd was one of many who sensed this. 'While I wouldn't call him vain, Jeff knew he was the fucking man, you know what I'm saying? We all laboured in our levels of insecurity, you know what I mean? But he knew he was badass.' And in such people as Chang and Stoll, and soon after, John Humphrey, Buckley found rock-solid friends who'd watch his back, no matter how far he was sucked into the star-making machinery. Buckley didn't feel quite the same compassion towards the Institute, however; he later denounced it as a 'so-called music school'. But his most immediate concern, now that he had a graduate's certificate amongst his few belongings, was quite simple: where to next?

It would be an exaggeration to suggest that Buckley's high-flying Institute finale opened any real doors for him for him in the later months of 1985. His first move was to find another apartment, so he and Maryatt moved into a run-down one-bedder located at 7000 Hawthorn. Though it was slightly removed from the battleground that was Cherokee – it overlooked Hollywood High, the school that had produced singer and heartthrob Ricky Nelson, comic Carol Burnett and superstar Judy Garland, whom Buckley would later do his best to emulate – Hawthorn by night wasn't that different to Cherokee hell, as gangs conducted their nocturnal business nearby, while the lights of patrolling police helicopters sometimes lit up their apartment like a Christmas tree. By day, Buckley got a harsh reality check about a musician's life, as he ran cable and performed running repairs as an electrician's sidekick (actually working in the Musician's Institute building), while during his free hours he practised guitar with all the fervour and single-minded devotion of a monk. As for his Canadian buddies, now that the common ground of the school was no longer part of their lives, their bond started to fall apart. Stoll found work in a Top 40 covers band; Maryatt left to study at Berklee College of Music in Boston, as did

Chang soon after (although all their paths would intersect with Buckley's over the next decade or so, mainly in and around New York). 'It was tough for all of us,' surmised Chang, 'because the school was such a central part of our lives, and we lost some focus once we finished there.' This left Buckley alone in LA, unsure whether to continue his formal guitar training. For a time he seriously considered studying under Joe Diorio, a highly-regarded jazz player who'd done time in the music scenes in Chicago and Florida before signing on as a teacher at the Institute.*

This was a period in Buckley's life when he tried his hand in a seemingly endless array of LA bands, whose styles were as diverse as their merit. It was best summed up by his close friend John Humphrey, who said that Buckley was 'evolving a set of skills and at the same time building his self-confidence'. Humphrey felt these bands gave Buckley the chance to gather experience and prove himself. Record producer Michael Clouse, soon to work with Buckley, agreed with this, when he spoke on the *Everybody Here Wants You* documentary. 'He would play in a funk or ska band, he'd play rock, hair metal, that goofy nonsense, but you always knew that Jeff was looking for something that was his.'[1]

The first of these bands was a jazz combo named B#, which didn't last much longer than their name. Then he signed on as guitarist in the AKB Band, a reggae group led by saxman Al Kirk. His most high-profile gig with them was backing singer Judy Mowatt, a one-time sidekick of Bob Marley, at Long Beach Arena, as part of the Bob Marley Day Celebration festival. Curiously, Buckley struggled with reggae, as uncluttered as it seemed by contrast with his fusion-centric studies. 'He told me that no matter how hard he tried, those guys would give him a hard time,' said Tom Chang. 'He said that it was so hard to play that music, it was so hard for him to get laid-back. They were so diametrically opposed to what he was doing, but he was like a musicologist, interested in so many different forms.'

Buckley's job soldering wires and trying his best not to electrocute himself at his former school didn't last long. Along with a move to Hollywood Hills – he lived at 3270 Oakshire, the apartment he shared with Humphrey from September 1987 through the spring of '88 – Buckley found work at the poetically-named Magic Hotel (aka the Magic Castle Hotel), located at 7025 Franklin Avenue in Hollywood. Earning the princely sum of $7.50

---

* Interestingly, Diorio cited Indian sitar master Ravi Shankar as a major influence on his life and work; not long after this Buckley would also look to the East, where he discovered revered Pakistani qawwali singer Nusrat Fateh Ali Khan, who he'd claim as 'my Elvis'.

per hour, Buckley manned the front desk, as wannabe actors, writers and rock stars drifted in and out of the kind of on-the-edge hotel that truly belonged in Hollywood. While toiling there, Buckley befriended video director Drew Carolan, who was holed up editing a pair of videos for Hollywood band-on-the-rise, the Red Hot Chili Peppers, 'Knock Me Down' and 'Higher Ground'. (The latter featured cameos from two of Chris Dowd's Fishbone brothers, Angelo Moore and Fish, while Carolan's friend Ernie Fritz would go on to direct the Sony promo EPK for *Grace*.) 'I knew Jeff pretty well in those days before he got his due,' said Carolan. 'Just little things but sweet nonetheless. He gave me a demo tape with a lot of his first tracks on it and called it "Jeffmusic for Drew".'

That demo contained a trio of Buckley-penned instrumentals – 'Gravestone Man', 'Promise Ring' and 'Aigeedhe' – that he compiled on a tape actually named *Whiteboy Music*, the name he used for his song publishing company. As first recorded outings go, these three slices of indulgent, derivative fusion were hardly life-changing, but its recording did provide Buckley with a useful leg up. They were cut at the home studio of his friend James Morrison, who'd soon mention Buckley's name to Michael Clouse (aka Michael J Clouse III, no less).

To a suburban drifter such as Buckley, the Boston-born Clouse's back story must have read like something straight out of a John Le Carre page-turner. Born in 1955, he graduated from Massachusetts' Framingham North High School, and received a degree from the American College Of Greece while playing top-level basketball in Europe. Clouse then travelled extensively, soaking up diverse styles of music like a human sponge, with a view to returning to the States and finding his place in the 'biz'. In the mid 1980s he did return to the US, setting up a studio just outside of Hollywood, where he cut demos for local up-and-comers. He was doing some sessions with Morrison when he heard a whisper about some hot new 'guitarslinger' that they were hoping to use on the session. The skinny white kid who strolled into Clouse's studio was the absolute antithesis of the guy Clouse expected to meet: for one thing, he was white; and for another, he was barely out of his teens. But when Buckley added a funky guitar part that was perfect for the track that Morrison and band were cutting, a piece called 'Lift Them Up', Clouse didn't care a lick that Buckley wasn't the studio vet he was expecting.

Clouse could sniff out a talented player, and he also detected that Buckley was equally hungry to find his way in the music industry, so they joined forces in an informal coalition known as 'The X-Factor'. They were essentially record-makers for hire, backing up various wannabes, no-hopers and soundalikes. While Buckley figured out arrangements and played numerous instruments and parts, Clouse engineered and mixed the finished product. During their time together, Buckley and Clouse worked for anyone with cash: a Janet Jackson clone, a Tom Waits-styled growler. In one demo, a hair-metal shrieker called 'Snowblind', Buckley actually sang, which was definitely a first. But this was truly a one-off, born from necessity: as far as Buckley was concerned, he was a guitar player.

While studio-bound with Clouse, Buckley continued moonlighting with a variety of bands, including a brief fling with John Humphrey's group Wild Blue Yonder.* Humphrey had been making a living, of sorts, as a bassist, but had always been writing songs. He fronted Wild Blue Yonder, because, as he explained, 'the previous couple of bands I'd tried to put together always fell prey to the whims of singers.'[2] Buckley would be involved from the time he moved in with Humphrey in September 1987, until he decided to move on in mid 1989. Drummer Danny Carey, later of prog-metal outfit Tool, played with Wild Blue Yonder during Buckley's brief tenure, which must have generated some serious sparks in the rehearsal room.

Buckley was the band's first guitarist, and was a constant presence in that rehearsal room early on, as Humphrey tried to find both the right line-up and pursue an unexpected sound he was hearing in his songs. 'I'd always been a fan of roots music,' Humphrey said, 'but the "twang" caught me off guard. I decided to go with it because it felt so comfortable and the songs were just flowing.' (This was clearly a fusion-free zone.) Yet Buckley would only play one gig with Wild Blue Yonder. It was evident to both Buckley and Humphrey that 'he was destined to do his own thing and he left gracefully to do so', although Buckley was never anything less than generous with his time and opinions. 'He was great to bounce things off,' said Humphrey, whose ongoing friendship with Buckley was based, amongst many things, on a shared interest in psychology. 'You would certainly see how someone with Jeff's temperament would be fascinated with the process of individuation,' Humphrey wrote to me. 'All the stuff bubbling under the surface.'[†]

---

* Rare snaps of Buckley with the band can be seen at www.johnhumphrey.com.
† Around the time of his involvement with Wild Blue Yonder, Buckley developed what one friend described as a 'mutual crush thing' with singer Abby Travis. 'I'm really leaning against talking about a dead friend,' Travis said in an email, when I requested an interview.

But it was in the company of another woman, husky-voiced, spandex-clad, big-haired screamer Kathryn Grimm, that Buckley found his next musical port of call, while he continued to tinker away in the studio with Clouse in his spare time. Seattle-born Grimm, another Musician's Institute graduate, led a metal outfit going by the name Group Therapy, comprising Buckley, drummer Jack Cook and bassist Mark Frere, who also wrote many of their songs (and who brought Buckley into the band).

Grimm had met Buckley while they were both at school, and recalled him drifting into one of the music 'labs' while she was jamming. 'He walked into a rehearsal room with a Rod Stewart shag haircut, and we happened to be playing a Rod Stewart song, which he knew,' she said. 'I remember thinking at the time, "This guy is really good." I saw him a few years later when someone was talking about this guitar player, who came to one of our shows. I said, "Oh, I know you" and he said that he wanted to join.'

As for Group Therapy, they weren't strictly a hard-rock band, although they played at most of the metal clubs in Hollywood. 'We were playing kind of rock with a lot of blues and R&B. Metal was prevalent but it wasn't the only music that was going on in LA,' said Grimm. Their live centrepiece, and set closer, was a bluesy little vamp going by the name 'Hot Date With Buzz', which was pitched somewhere between Stevie Ray Vaughan and Spinal Tap. 'It was the showstopper, for sure,' Grimm said. 'Mark wrote that; I don't know what he was thinking.' During 'Buzz', Buckley would go slide-crazy on his fretboard with a vibrator, before handing the female plea-sure toy to Grimm, who'd duly sing to it. The punchy lyrics summed up this ode to onanism: 'Ten inches of plastic/And hard as rock/She kept him in a drawer/wrapped in a sock/He was always prepared/Her ideal man.' A demo version of 'Buzz' that can be found at the MySpace site of Mark Frere fea-tures a bizarre ad-libbing outro from Buckley, where he drops into a pass-able Elvis Presley mumble, stating: 'C'mon baby/Lemme out of that sock.' Classy stuff.*

Again, just as he'd done with the Wild Blue Yonder, Buckley was a gui-tarist first and foremost while with Group Therapy, although Grimm did encourage him to sing 'parts'. 'But he wasn't comfortable with that, he was the guitar dude,' Grimm said. 'In my mind he was a guitar player; I'd never heard him sing until he joined my band.' And his playing was the highlight

---

* Of all Buckley's LA crowd, Grimm was probably the only one to get especially tight with Mary Guibert. 'They were close for some years,' said one source. Whether Guibert was comfortable with Grimm's on-stage rapport with her son and 'Buzz' remains unclear.

of such numbers as the mid-tempo, Fleetwood Mac-ish 'Money Talks' and the pedestrian rocker 'Don't Make Me Beg'. Nonetheless, Buckley's axe grinding left its mark on the Hollywood kids and metalheads who'd front at such clubs as The Whisky and The Shamrock, to see Group Therapy strut and strum. 'I don't think anyone is aware of what an amazing guitar player he was,' Grimm added. 'He was a shredder in my band. Guys would stand at the side of the stage and gawk at him.' And the quirky songwriting of Frere, who died in 2007, had an influence on Buckley, who apparently told him: 'You are my biggest songwriting influence.' According to Grimm, Buckley learned plenty from Frere, who'd 'write a song a day'. She could also see that Buckley was incredibly ambitious; even at this early stage he was definitely shooting for stardom. 'He wanted to be big. [But] I'm not sure he was feeling the same way once that happened. We had a couple of personal conversations about that.'

Buckley's metal makeover dovetailed neatly with his latest musical transformation: rediscovering the teenage kicks that he'd enjoyed listening to Led Zeppelin. Fusion be damned. One night, an excited Buckley put in a call to Tom Chang, explaining his new direction. 'He told me that he'd got back into Led Zeppelin and was singing, but he didn't say to what extent,' Chang said. 'I always knew him a guitar player. He was really developing; he wasn't the player that he became but he had a lot of natural ability. Most people knew it, too.'

But Led Zep wasn't his only new sensation. Buckley had also been blown away by the new wave of English bands that he was hearing on LA's KROQ, including The Cocteau Twins – he'd later have a brief affair with singer Elizabeth Fraser – The Cure, and The Smiths. Especially the Smiths. In their tortured leader Morrissey and guitar wizard Johnny Marr, the Manchester group had a creative sparkle that made them the bedsit brigade's very own Lennon & McCartney, a fine antidote to Thatcher's Britain for all those who felt repressed by her much loathed right-wing crusade. Buckley was as drawn to Morrissey's arch lyrical outpourings as he was to the jangly, upbeat melodies supplied by Marr. He'd often cover their songs live; one time, in 1995, at a Manchester University show, he even adopted a faux English accent during a cover of 'I Know It's Over', for better or worse. And he'd defend The Smiths to the death: during an on-stage tirade at Chicago's Cabaret Metro in May 1995, he derided the entire musical decade of the 1980s as shit, 'except the Smiths'.

Despite some very marketable qualities – banshee Grimm, Buckley's 'shredding' skills, Frere's quirky tunes, Cook's rock-steady drumming – and some interest from EMI, Group Therapy didn't really fulfil their potential.

'Our goal, like everyone else at the time, was to get signed,' Grimm said. 'But the people that make these decisions aren't knowledgeable about music. People have to tell them that music is good, hit them over the head.' However, as Grimm told me in 2007, they did record about a dozen tunes, all featuring Buckley on guitar, which she hopes to release at some point as a sort of memorial, especially for Frere. 'They're mastered. They're the real deal,' she said. 'We did an album's worth, at two different studios. It was a blast. With this band there was no drama, no tension, no egos.'

Although Buckley was the junior member of the band by several years, Grimm felt that he was the one opening minds within the group. 'Jeff, literally, listened to everything, from opera to punk,' she said. 'He really liked Joni Mitchell; he loved Zeppelin, whereas I was into The Pretenders and other rock. And it seemed like he was born with a guitar in his hands.' Grimm, like so many others, was stunned by Buckley's skills as a mimic. 'He could have been an actor,' Grimm figured. 'There were many sides to Jeff: he had a very serious side, and a really good sense of humour, which he brought out with people he knew. On stage his happy side would come out. He lived to play.'

Buckley might have derived some easy kicks rocking out with Group Therapy, but his real obsession was the demos that he cut with Clouse, which he'd name *The Babylon Dungeon Sessions* in honour of the bunker in which they were recorded, Eurosound studio in the San Fernando Valley. *Babylon* was finally completed in September 1990. Buckley packaged the tape with a Xeroxed picture of Jodie Foster in *Taxi Driver* on the cover. His friends and peers might have spotted Buckley's potential back at the Institute, but, as John Humphrey saw it, they weren't quite ready for what they heard on these rough-as-guts originals.

'I think everyone who knew Jeff knew he was talented, but it actually wasn't until after he finished the *Babylon Dungeon* tapes that we realised the scope and depth of his talents,' said Humphrey. '*Babylon Dungeon* seemed to me like his manifesto, and that MI, and the various bands he played in up until then, were proving grounds and fact-gathering expeditions. The *Babylon Dungeon* tapes seemed a little bit to come out of nowhere – even those of us who were quite close to him at the time were shocked and amazed.' Kathryn Grimm was especially thrilled by 'Last Goodbye', which Buckley wrote one night on her couch. 'He was very secretive about writing, but when he played me that, I went: "That's the first song you ever wrote? Wow." It was incredible.'

Given that Buckley, just like Jimi Hendrix and Tupac Shakur, has released more music dead than alive, it's surprising that the *Babylon Dungeon Sessions* hasn't been put out at some point in the years that have passed since his death – it is, however, widely bootlegged. As the portrait of an artist under development, a creative coming out, it's very similar to the *Pocketwatch* cassette that Dave Grohl would quietly piece together a few years later in the wake of Nirvana's bloody demise.

'Unforgiven' (aka 'Last Goodbye') opened with a twinkle of bells, a cascading bass line and a shimmering, snake-like guitar riff that owed a massive debt to The Cure; Buckley's Britpop obsession was on full and frank display. And any song that began with the line 'this is our last goodbye' would surely have appealed to Robert Smith. The song's tempo was significantly swifter than the 'finished' version that appeared on *Grace* (although it's a stretch to call any Buckley recording the final or definitive version; his songs were in a constant state of metamorphosis). But even at this early stage, Buckley's voice was the standout: it was pure and crystal-clean, surprisingly soulful for some kid straight outta Anaheim. He hadn't quite polished the lyric – during one take, when he sang 'kiss me not just because of desire/but consolation' it's obvious he wasn't entirely happy with the result. He wasn't and it would soon change.

'Radio' was Buckley's nod to DC hardcorists Bad Brains. The song may have opened with a 'Copacabana'-like rumble of percussion, but it exploded into a punkish rant, Buckley spitting out words and riffing himself into submission. Underneath it all was some kind of mainstream-sucks, anti-corporate rant that the Brains' HR would have deemed acceptable, but it was hard to make out Buckley's message amidst the full metal racket that's on the demo. ('Radio/Why are you so lame?' is about as clear as he gets.) It may have been clear-cut evidence that white boys can't rap, but it was a lot of fun – and it would have been a killer live, if he'd ever gotten the chance to try it out on an audience. Buckley even let out a punk-rock yodel a few minutes in. 'Radio' would become a favourite of Gary Lucas.

The prototype version of 'Eternal Life' followed. While not quite as tumultuous as what would be heard on *Grace*, or the many showstopping live variations that Buckley and band would pull off while touring the album, there was a certain grandeur to this then-instrumental hard-rock groove, powered by rudimentary drums, some nimble bass and more shimmery, Cocteau Twins-like guitar from Buckley. All the track needed was a lyric and a vocal and it was good to go. As for 'Strawberry Street', this was clearly influenced by Buckley's stint as guitarist for hard-rockers Group Therapy: it was a well-executed dirty boogie. Buckley's innuendo-heavy vocal comes on like Perry Farrell with a better range, and he riffs and solos with an energy and imagination that suggested he'd been tuning into the fretwork of Farrell's Jane's Addiction bandmate, Dave Navarro. It's not much of a song – really, it's little more than a hard rock bump and grind, Buckley adding the requisite leer to the line 'strawberry/what you gonna do for me?' – but his playing and singing were a cut above, something that wasn't lost on John Humphrey and others. Buckley must have felt some attachment to 'Strawberry Street', though, because he resurrected it during sessions just prior to recording *Grace* and it ended up on the Legacy edition of that album, released in 2004. It was also one of the first originals he played for future bassist Mick Grondahl: Buckley told him that it targeted the Hollywood casting couch policy and how the entertainment biz turned people into commodities. Maybe there was a little of the Tim Buckley story hidden away in the lyric, too.

The actual recording of *Babylon* typified Buckley's occasional good fortune. Herb Cohen saw him shaking it with Group Therapy, tracked him down (he was in New York at the time) and offered to put up the cash. And throughout his brief life, Jeff Buckley developed a knack for not just meeting, impressing and frequently seducing people, but for befriending them under peculiar circumstances. Take East Village performance artist Penny Arcade, an earth mother-type who'd fill a hole in his life left by the rarely seen Mary Guibert. Buckley was introduced to her backstage, as she readied herself for yet another runthrough of her way-off Broadway hit, *Bitch! Dyke! Faghag! Whore!*, as scantily clad dancers drifted in and out of her dressing room. Buckley didn't know which way to look.

Chris Dowd, who'd play a crucial role in Buckley's life, especially during his *Babylon Dungeon* days – Buckley lived with him for roughly 18 months, in Dowd's loft on South Lake Street – had an even more bizarre introduction to the geeky Orange County wunderkind. Their first encounter came via Dowd's then-girlfriend, Carla Azar, the former Musician's Institute student, over a long night's journey into day that featured a very dark, possibly even suicidal Dowd, a torrential rainstorm, and an open car window. It was around the time that Buckley was living with John Humphrey, just prior to recording his *Babylon* tape.

'One night she called me and said she was going for a ride, and her friend Jeff was in the car,' Dowd recalled. 'I was going through a weird kind of depression at the time. I was burned out from touring. I was trying to find my way and I was depressed: "What does all this shit mean? Who are all these famous actors I'm hanging out with, this arsehole and that arsehole? Are the Chili Peppers going to be bigger than my band?" Complete wackadoo shit, typical band nonsense: "You fucked my girlfriend", that kind of

shit. Anyway, Carla came out to my house to rescue me because I was trying to drink myself to death with tequila,' Dowd continued, 'and Jeff was in
the back of her Jeep. I was as drunk as shit, it was raining, I had my head out
the window and it rained all over Jeff in the back. He just sat there quietly,
didn't say shit, and I was so caught up in my depression that I didn't even
notice.'

The next day, Dowd got a call from his less-than-impressed girlfriend.
'Carla told me to call Jeff and apologise for getting him so wet. I did, and we
became friends.' It was a strange bond, formed, as much as anything else, on
their shared neuroses. 'The same kind of insecurities that I was going
through with my playing he was going through with trying to find himself,'
Dowd explained. Buckley was in awe of Dowd, a member of one of his
favourite bands at the time, a freaked-out combo that was described by one
astute observer as a 'junkyard ska, punk, funk metal outfit from South
Central'. And they had a record deal with heavyweight Columbia, no less.
All up, it made for a slightly imbalanced relationship. 'I was in his favourite
band,' Dowd said of his new best friend. 'I was *Chris out of Fishbone*.'*

As for his Fishbone bandmates, they found the odd union of a dread-
locked African-American and a rail-thin, sweetly nerdy kid from the OC a
bit hard to digest. 'They just thought Jeff was my weird friend,' Dowd
laughed. 'They'd ask me: "What's up with this weird goofy white guy?"
They even thought he was gay. I was like, yeah, whatever.' Buckley silenced
them one night when he jumped on stage and jammed with Dowd, Alice
in Chains' Layne Staley and Fishbone drummer John Steward. 'Then they
figured it out,' Dowd laughed.

At this stage, certainly for Dowd, his band's success wasn't giving him any
satisfaction. Their differences were usually settled with fistfights, and he'd
started to distance himself from the rest of the group. 'It was a bunch of guys
with dominant personalities,' he said. 'We came from the fucking hood, and
the way you deal with your differences is to fight, literally. We were fed up
with each other, and that's when Jeff and Carla emerged in my life. They
were friends who watched my back.'

The one useful connection that Dowd (and, by association, Buckley)
would take away from his Fishbone days was meeting Columbia's Steve

* Dowd had met Azar in equally strained circumstances: after playing what he
  considered the best Fishbone show of his life, at the Jon Ford Anson Theatre in
  1988, he and Azar locked eyes at the after-party. 'My girlfriend at the time was like,
  "Who's that fucking bitch staring at you?"'

Berkowitz, later to become Jeff Buckley's A&R man and key cheerleader at Sony. Dowd, however, may not have given Berkowitz the respect he deserved when they were working together on the first four Fishbone LPs: their self-titled debut, 1986's *In Your Face*, 1988's *Truth and Soul* and their masterwork, 1991's *The Reality of My Surroundings*. (The latter's standout was the brilliant 'Everyday Sunshine', a song Dowd admits he spent two years crafting.) 'Motherfuckers in the band – me included – used to give Steve shit,' said Dowd. 'But let me tell you, there's no perfect anything, as far as A&R guys are concerned. I didn't realise this until after quitting the band, but Steve is like a serious buffer. I didn't really become good friends with Steve until he was Jeff's A&R person.'

In the second half of the 1980s, ecstasy had taken over from cocaine and/or smack as the drug of choice, having really kicked in at Manchester's Hacienda nightclub and then swiftly crossed the Atlantic. It became a useful tool in the fast-developing relationship between Dowd and Buckley, with Buckley initiating its use amongst them. One night he approached Dowd with some pills and said, 'OK, let's all try this thing. What will it make us do?' 'That's how we all ended up taking ecstasy,' said Dowd. 'Sometimes that shit, speaking for me, can get out of hand, but he was never the type. With ecstasy, some people go to raves and burn their brains out, for us it was like a social lubricant,' he added. 'That's what it was; it wasn't like we were popping Es, going out every night and Jeff was over in the corner babbling, that kind of dramatic bullshit.'

The only downside for the trio was an incident that took place when Buckley was high one night. Ecstasy does have a tendency to loosen lips and in the spirit of 'full disclosure', Buckley came clean, admitting that he saw Azar as more than a friend – a feeling she didn't reciprocate. 'This awkward thing came out that nobody wanted to acknowledge,' said Dowd. 'It was not easy for him to admit he had feelings for his best friend's girlfriend; that's how it was.' Looking back, Dowd now understands the attraction. 'Every guy at that time was in love with Carla: she played drums, she was pretty, she was the coolest girl you ever met in your entire life. Carla was the perfect girlfriend.'*

As was so typical of Jeff Buckley in the days before he headed east, he didn't let either of his two new best friends know that he could sing – not

---

* Azar's musical CV included stints with Prince cohorts Wendy and Lisa, proof that her multi-instrumental skills were highly regarded.

even when he was pilled to the gills – nor did he discuss his 'famous' father. To Dowd, Buckley was simply an 'awesome housemate', a nerdy, funny 'dude' with whom he could be 'open and honest, talking for hours'. 'I knew him as a guitar player only,' Dowd added. 'I had no idea he could even sing.' He thought that Buckley was a good enough guitarist, however, to mention his name to Berkowitz, who'd sometimes prod Dowd about the musical development of his housemate. (It's been documented that Berkowitz wasn't aware of Buckley until he started his Sin-E residency, but this clearly isn't true.) 'When Jeff and I lived together,' Dowd said, 'Steve would ask me: "What's Jeff doing?" I'd say, I dunno, don't worry about it. This was before the New York thing happened. I guess he knew Tim Buckley's songs; a lot of people knew about him.' Berkowitz *was* a Tim Buckley fan.

As Buckley paid many years' worth of dues in go-nowhere bands, he looked and learned as Azar and Dowd, especially, struggled with their own musical careers. But Buckley couldn't help but envy the pair. 'Carla and I probably represented like the arbiters of cool, if you will,' figured Dowd. 'Carla had played with Wendy and Lisa, done some big session work, played with some serious motherfuckers. And he got to watch our mistakes – mostly mine. And he watched *everything*, you know? I think the one lucky thing with Jeff was that he got to be around my ass and watch something really cool implode, so when it came time for him to do his shit he knew.'

Azar actually got to hear Buckley sing well before Dowd – she overheard him playing his father's 'I Never Asked To Be Your Mountain', of all things, in her apartment – and was less than impressed by what she heard. As Dowd recalled, Azar 'talked shit about Jeff's voice; she said it was all high and shrill, and she said my voice was better. But I think she was saying that because we were going out together.' When Dowd did eventually hear Buckley sing, he was amazed, and let Azar know that she was way off the mark. ' "You're bugging!", he told her. '*He can't sing*? No way.'

Apart from being Buckley's 'arbiters of cool', Azar and Dowd also set out to 'deprogram' Buckley's Institute training and introduce him to a whole new planet of sound. Buckley was just as diligent now that he was living with Dowd, and would noodle away on his guitar for eight, maybe 10 hours a day, but Dowd had reservations about his housemate's musical vocabulary. 'Jeff was never really funky. He knew about Al Green but he didn't know why it was cool. And he liked the blues but he didn't really know blues albums.'

Dowd, who'd learned plenty from such people as producer and future Columbia exec David Kahne – who'd worked on the first four Fishbone albums, and also produced records for everyone from Romeo Void to the

Bangles and Dick Dale – took it upon himself to do more than widen Buckley's musical horizons. He turned Buckley on to The Last Poets, a group of politically active rhymers who joined forces on the anniversary of Malcolm X's birthday, in 1969 in East Harlem, and have been cited by many as one of the earliest and most crucial influences for rap music. So did Buckley fully comprehend what he was hearing? 'He loved that shit,' Dowd said. 'How could you not get it? He's white, I'm black, and every culture has their thing.'

Dowd recalls that Jeff paid his rent with his father's royalties; in 1987, Tim's widow Judy had tracked Jeff down to pass along some cheques. As she recalled in the BBC's *Everybody Here Wants You*, their first get-together combined pure theatre on Buckley's part, and a mixture of shock and awe for Judy. When she stopped her car, she saw him leaning against her building, in the exact same pose – even down to the jacket flung jauntily over his shoulder – that his father struck on the cover of the *Tim Buckley* album. 'I had a cigarette and sat there and watched him for a long time,' she said. '[I was thinking] now it begins.' Buckley was fully aware of the picture he was painting, too, because when Judy honked the horn, he came over and asked: 'What do you think, do I look like him?'[3] (She did, saying so in a conversation soon after.) Amongst other things, they discussed his favourite Tim Buckley LPs: Jeff said that they were, in no special order, *Goodbye And Hello*, *Starsailor* and *Sefronia*. But he didn't have copies of the albums, so his half-brother Taylor agreed to tape them for him.

It was the first time they'd seen each other since those few shared days together back in Easter 1975, just months before Tim Buckley OD'd and died. During their meeting, Judy handed over an old pea coat owned by Tim, which swiftly became the choice item amongst his few possessions. In a conversation soon after, she described Jeff as 'fragile, delicate, really bright... a bit distant and quiet', and also commented upon his anti-smoking and drinking stance, and the fact that he drove an old Chevy Impala, the same model as his father once drove. (Buckley didn't know this, apparently.)

Soon after he also met with Lee Underwood, his father's long-time guitarist and champion (even to this day). In a letter dated 1990, Buckley explained why he sought out Underwood. 'I wanted to know about my father, Tim' he wrote, 'what he was like, what did he think, why did he do what he did, stuff like that. I figured – flawless logic on my part, I gots [sic] to say,' Buckley continued, 'that since Lee was involved with some very seminal albums, had toured with him, that the relationship would have been the basic... music/spiritual type.' His father's guitarist and friend was just as shocked as Judy when he first laid eyes on the younger Buckley, partly because he adopted exactly the same pose for Underwood. 'When I opened the door I gasped,' he told the BBC. 'He had the same hair, eyebrows, high cheekbones, the mouth, the pose was the same. [Then] he said, "OK, *how did he die?* Phew. I said, "You go for the jugular, don't you?"' They spoke for two hours; at one point, Underwood told Jeff that his father truly loved him. 'He did not!' he spat back. Underwood pointed him in the direction of 'Dream Letter' and also revealed that Tim had every intention of reaching out to his son when he got older. 'His departure before your birth had nothing to do with you,' Underwood said. 'He said he didn't know Mary was pregnant... when he split for New York. He did not leave you, he left your mother.'[4]

Two days later, Buckley – who'd describe their first encounter as a 'pretty heavy evening' – returned to talk again with Underwood. In the interim he'd shaved one half of his hair right back to the scalp. 'It was as if he was defiantly and belligerently presenting himself as an ugly stupid two-bit sleazy grunge-rock street-rat,' Underwood wrote. Underwood ignored Jeff's Mohawk makeover and continued answering all of his questions about Tim. Yet Underwood didn't get a clear sense of the degree of rage Jeff felt towards his father, which he'd eventually reveal during interviews. 'I thought he would welcome hearing the truth about his father,' Underwood stated in *Blue Melody*. 'Otherwise, why did he contact me?' (Underwood was deeply offended later on by Jeff's many public attacks on his father. 'Jeff wasn't just putting down his father, which was bad enough. He was also putting down my best friend, which was upsetting and offensive to me personally.')

Tim Buckley's old friend Dan Gordon was equally shaken up by meeting Jeff. 'He moved like Tim, he sat like Tim, his posture was Tim's, his gestures were Tim's,' Gordon told the BBC. 'It was Tim, sitting opposite me.'[5] Meanwhile, another of Tim's old friends, Daniella Sapriell, hosted a 24th birthday party for Jeff: the guests included members of the Guibert and Buckley family, as well as Ron Moorhead and Judy and Jeff's stepbrother Taylor. These were all steps along the way to 'discovering' Tim Buckley, a quest he would maintain for the rest of his life, as much as he'd downplay that in public.

It was just before this birthday bash that Buckley took his first journey east. Buckley had actually been eyeing off New York since he was a teenager, and had spent several months there in early 1990, ostensibly to play some shows as part of the backing band for reggae toaster Shinehead. However, he first had to quit Group Therapy. As Kathryn Grimm recalled, Buckley 'had a fixation about New York,' even though he'd never been outside of LA. 'I went by the Magic Hotel and he said that he was making serious plans to go to New York and that he'd have to leave the band,' she said. 'But he suffered in New York worse than he ever had in LA.'

Buckley wrote about the experience in 1991. 'Escaped to NYC in '90 for about seven months, got into hardcore and Robert Johnson.' While there he also discovered legendary qawwali singer Nusrat Fateh Ali Khan, the man he'd label 'my Elvis', and fell heavily for Bad Brains, DC's leading hardcore punk act. 'Re-Ignition', a standout from their 1986 LP *I Against I*, was a particular favourite. He'd describe the track as 'my introduction to New York. HR is the man, is the man. *Is the man*.'[6]

But he stayed beyond those few Shinehead dates, bouncing between shared apartments, initially in Harlem with a Musician's Institute acquaintance, and then on West 89th Street with actress Brooke Smith, whom he'd met during his stint at the Magic Hotel. Grimm and Mark Frere of Group Therapy caught up with him when they went to Flushing in Queens to clean out the apartment of Frere's parents, who'd both recently died. 'Mark hired Jeff to help him move stuff, so he'd come over and stay for a while. He was thinking about taking the apartment – he was living with Brooke at the time, so we offered him the apartment, which he didn't end up taking. He was just trying to get by. He might have been dabbling with writing with some people, but he was just so broke, his focus was on feeding himself.'

While in New York, Buckley wrote several letters to Louie Dula, a compulsive Tim Buckley collector, in an effort to try and locate his grandmother and aunt. (He wasn't so keen on finding out if his grandfather was still alive, though. 'Because,' as he wrote to Dula, 'the guy's got this fucking LEGEND behind him of apocalyptic violence and hellish dementia. Nice family.') Lee Underwood had put them in touch. In a letter dated April 23, 1990, Buckley sent Dula a photo of himself in his apartment – 'Monkey Boy King', read the caption – and itemised his belongings: 'My guitars, my clothes (got my Jimi Hendrix shirt on) and my saxophone case with all my tapes inside.' He also thanked Dula for turning him onto long-dead Brit folkie Nick Drake. 'I've been hearing about Nick Drake ever since I started reading those rock 'n' roll biographies about Led Zep and Jimi and The Doors,' he wrote, 'I'd always think, "So who's fucking Nick Drake?" Now I'll be looking out for the box set in the future.'

Around this time he also sent a letter to Underwood. Writing in a vivid upper case, Buckley said that speaking with Dula 'was like breaking a flimsy membrane releasing thousands of tons of crashing water right on my head'. He rhapsodised about 'THE BOX', which Dula had sent to him, top-heavy with Tim Buckley material. 'The box had everything,' Buckley wrote, 'clippings, photos, articles, posters, cassettes, a videotape with two performances dubbed repeatedly, over and over again. It was quite an experience.' He'd keep this Tim Buckley collection close at all times. Then Buckley adds, poignantly: 'It's obvious that Tim was loved and respected, now missed, by many and with good reason. And if he were still around maybe there would be at least one guy who had something real to say – some exist, but there would at least be one more... If he was alive, I would have liked to have kissed him and told him that everything was OK; everything he'd done was cool, there's no reason not to go on living, no magic spell, that I thought he was beautiful, that I thought he was a fool for even believing for a second that art comes from pain, that I would've laughed in his face and hugged him if he really believed for a second that he thought he loved death more than he loved me. I'm done looking for him.' *Take care, Jeff.*

While in New York, Buckley learned that the romantic notion of busking in the subway didn't even cover the cost of a bagel, let alone the cream cheese to go with it. So he took odd jobs, working at an answering service for such A-list thespians as Denzel Washington and F Murray Abraham, and folding clothes and manning the counter at a Banana Republic store around the corner from Smith's apartment. This gig ended badly, when Buckley was accused of stealing. In tears, he went to see his buddy Tom Chang, who was now living in New York. 'That was fucked up,' Chang recalled. 'After it happened, he looked at me and said: "Me?" He was one of the most honest people I've ever met, he'd go out of his way to be courteous to people. He was just floored when they accused him of that.' Grimm, who described the experience as 'disastrous' for Buckley, received a similar call. 'He was crying over the phone. He told us that he'd been accused of stealing and they were asking him to sign some papers saying he did it or they'd call the cops. It freaked him out. He was a very honest kind of guy. He didn't lie, he didn't play games. He was shocked.'

This first stab at New York ended in September 1990 with the call from Herb Cohen, summoning him back to LA to work on the aforementioned *Babylon Dungeon Sessions* demos. This may have been an unbeatable opportunity, but it did come with its dangers: by hitching his star to Cohen he was replicating some of the career moves of his father. And Buckley didn't actually have any songs written at that point. When he returned to LA, he stayed with Grimm, who recalled him sitting on her couch, trying to write, right up until the night before he was due in the studio. 'He was pressured to write once his dad's manager got in touch with him. He sat down on our couch and wrote "Last Goodbye".'

It was inevitable that the turbulent trio of Dowd, Azar and Buckley would form some kind of band, given their collective backgrounds and super-tight bond. Dowd dubbed them the Insouciant Inbreds: he sang and played keys,

Azar drummed and Buckley played guitar. Other players would sit in, too, including Chris Bruce, a friend of Dowd's, and Todd Hoffman, the bassist of Hollywood college rockers Lions & Ghosts. *Rolling Stone's* David Fricke, in LA to write a Fishbone piece, actually chanced upon the band rehearsing in early 1991, and got very interested when he learned the identity of this skinny-arsed guitarist's father. He recalled the meeting in the liner notes to *So Real: Songs From Jeff Buckley*. 'The music was rough and hard,' Fricke wrote, 'actually, a lot like the long, frenzied passages of serrated riff-and-feedback improvisation that would be a closing feature of Buckley's shows in a couple of years. And when we spoke briefly, mostly about music, it was clear that he had an explorer's heart. And his search was just beginning.'[7]

That's an understatement; despite Dowd's desire to ditch Fishbone, The Inbreds were destined never to leave the rehearsal space. And Buckley's unrequited feelings for Azar created what could only be termed a bizarre love triangle, hardly the best emotional climate for a band-under-development. According to Dowd, Buckley and Azar would 'mess around' once, soon after the release of *Grace* and long after he and Azar split. Reluctantly, Buckley came clean to his friend. 'He was very weird about telling me,' Dowd recalled, 'and I said, "Dog, at this point in time I could so not give a fuck." I was more pissed off that he had to keep something from me in a way that could ruin our relationship.'

The Inbreds really came undone when Dowd, Buckley and Azar had, in Dowd's words, gotten 'into a huge row about music. That's why Jeff went to New York [in 1991]. I didn't want to leave Fishbone, because I was so insecure and Carla was ready to move on and join a band – and she did.'* Clearly, what Dowd described as the 'dysfunctional shit' that existed between him and Azar, and Buckley's unrequited affection for her, was more than enough to convince him that heading east was the perfect escape, although he didn't need much convincing after a fateful night, spelled out in more detail elsewhere, with Irish musician Glen Hansard.

In early April 1991, Buckley got a call from Janine Nichols, the program director at St Ann's Church in Brooklyn. She'd been speaking with fellow New Yorker Hal Willner about organising a tribute show, as part of the annual 'Arts at St Ann's' series of shows, celebrating the music of Tim Buckley. As Nichols explained to me, neither she nor Willner knew that Buckley had a son, until they started doing photo research, of all things. 'Hal

---

* She drummed for the original version of Ednaswap, whose song 'Torn' became a massive hit for doe-eyed Oz popstress Natalie Imbruglia.

had the idea to do the show about Tim and we were doing our research, you know, Who should we get?, that kind of thing. And I was looking for a photograph of Tim and someone said that I had to call Herb Cohen, who managed Tim and Frank Zappa, both of whom wanted him dead, from my understanding. So I got his number and told him what we were doing and he said, "You know Tim had a son who can sing his ass off? He's a good-looking kid who lives out here on the west coast."

'So I got his number and called him up. Simple. I told him about me and the show and I remember how little and soft his voice was on the phone. The whole thing took him aback. But he knew who Willner was – it was like destiny calling. He needed a couple of days to think about it because he'd never done those songs before. But we hadn't heard a note and didn't ask to hear a note. He showed up, fell in love, and turned the whole world on its head. It was an amazing thing.'

Notes

1. BBC2: *Everybody Here Wants You*, BBC documentary
2. www.johnhumphrey.com
3. See note 1
4. Underwood, Lee: *Blue Melody: Tim Buckley Remembered*, Backbeat Books, 2002
5. See note 1
6. Kingsmill, Richard: Jeff Buckley's High 5, *Triple J FM* August 29, 1995, transcript
7. Fricke, David: Liner Notes, *So Real: Songs From Jeff Buckley*, Columbia 2007

Chapter Four

'Dude, I'm fucking home. This is it.'

March 1991 wasn't especially the best month of Penny Arcade's life. Barely had the dust settled on the AIDS killing spree of the 1980s when her friend Doc Pomus died from cancer. Towards the end of the month she was squeezed into the back of a limo, returning from the funeral for the legendary Brill Building songwriter, so you'd hardly describe her mood as upbeat. Seated in front of her was fellow New Yorker Hal Willner, a guy whose role as a music biz scenester was just as lively and as attention-grabbing as the confrontational performance pieces that made Arcade an icon for sexual misfits. Arcade was drifting in and out of the conversation when she heard Willner mention the name 'Jeff Buckley'. She knew of Tim Buckley, sure, but who, exactly, was Jeff Buckley? Actually, Arcade's first thought was this: 'I hated Tim Buckley's music – I wonder if this other Buckley sucks as badly?' What she didn't know was that within months she'd begin playing any number of roles in Buckley's life: confidante, advisor, inspiration, romance counsellor, friend – and surrogate mother.

Several years older than Jeff Buckley, Arcade was living out a classic American story of rebellion: she'd come to New York – in her case from sleepy New Britain, Connecticut – to reinvent herself. Her father had left when she was four, and she was raised by her mother in a scenario very familiar to Buckley. The first step was to change her name from Susana Carmen Ventura to something more rock and roll; although it was almost as colourful as her *nom de plume*, her real name positively reeked of her Italian roots, and it was forever banished to her pre-Manhattan past. (Except, however, in the case of the psychologist that both she and Buckley saw, a Mrs Williams, who insisted on addressing her as 'Ms Ventura'.) Arcade's next move was to locate the epicentre of 1960s' New York weirdness and make it her new home. She soon found her place amongst the freaks, geniuses, tragedies-in-waiting and lost souls that populated Andy Warhol's Factory, and starred in the Warhol extravaganza *Women In Revolt*. She also dropped plenty of acid – her name change came to her while under its influence, at the ripe old age of 17, in the company of her mentor, gay photographer-slash-actor Jaimie Andrews.

And it was while he was on acid that Danny Fields, Elektra's proudly gay publicist, who would also play an important role in Jeff Buckley's life, had a revelatory close encounter with Penny Arcade in 1969. 'I was sitting in the front row of a show she was doing and her tits were jumping up and down in my face,' Fields recalled. 'Now, I don't like girls and anything they have on them, but I was so exhilarated by her tits. Later in the night I was at Max's [Kansas City] and I went up to her and said, "I couldn't take my eyes off your tits. Who are you?" That's how we met.' Bonded by acid and boobs, a friendship was formed between the pair, one that still exists today. And they'd both as good as adopt Jeff Buckley once he moved east.

However, soon after her starring role in *Revolt*, Arcade found the atmosphere at the Factory a little too stifling, and spent the best part of the following decade in Europe. Somewhere along the way she also had an affair with eccentric, droll singer/songwriter Loudon Wainwright III, which later placed her in an unusual position playing den mother to both Jeff Buckley and Wainwright's son Rufus. (Loudon Wainwright 'presented' his son to Arcade, when Rufus came out as a teenager.)

Once she'd resettled in New York in the early 1980s, Arcade really went to work, writing four full-length shows, including her autobiographical trilogy: *Based on A True Story, Invitation to The Beginning Of The End Of The World* and *La Miseria*. And in 1990, just before she met Buckley, she created her most famous work, the long-running and frequently namechecked *Bitch!Dyke!Faghag!Whore!*, a potent blend of political humanism, freedom of expression and erotic dancing. Peter Milne, an Australian photographer and occasional journalist, summed up the sensory overload that was *Bitch! Dyke!* when he documented the show for Australian *Rolling Stone*. 'I would rather eat sandpaper than use terms like "life affirming" or "transcendental" but I cannot pretend that this show didn't move me or that I wasn't entranced by Penny Arcade.'[1] (Jeff Buckley clearly agreed; after connecting with Arcade he sat through her show dozens of times, totally enthralled.)

As for Hal Willner, at the time of Pomus' funeral he was trying to piece together his latest sonic jigsaw puzzle, a tribute to Charlie Mingus (which, in its own circuitous way, would bring Sony's Steve Berkowitz into Jeff Buckley's life). During business hours, Willner paid the bills with a high-profile gig as music supervisor at *Saturday Night Live*, a job he landed in 1981, after serving an 'apprenticeship' under Grammy-winning record producer Joel Dorn. But Willner truly found his place in the musical world when he started compiling tribute albums: he's even been cited as the 'father' of the modern tribute record. His first was *Amarcord Nino Rota*, a nod to the Italian composer best known for his work with director Federico Fellini. Tributes to jazz giant Thelonious Monk and Kurt Weill followed; then he somehow managed to entice Michael Stipe, Ringo Starr and Sun Ra to pay homage to Mickey Mouse's creator in *Stay Awake: Interpretations of Vintage Disney Films*. And he'd seen Tim Buckley play several times, including a set at the Main Point in Philadelphia that he considered 'one of those "the greatest thing I've ever seen" live experiences'.

Willner had friends in high places. Shane Doyle, who co-owned Sin-E, the East Village coffee-shop-cum-surrogate Irish embassy that would soon be linked with Jeff Buckley's rise, told me that it wasn't out of character for Willner to walk into Sin-E alongside Marianne Faithfull or Allen Ginsberg. 'He knew lot of people; he was totally connected.' Willner was also an advocate of Brooklyn's stately St Ann's Church: Its acoustics may not have ranked with Carnegie Hall, but the place had atmosphere. Marianne Faithfull's *Blazing Away* LP, which he produced, was recorded live there in 1989, while Lou Reed and John Cale chose St Ann's for the premiere of their Andy Warhol tribute, *Songs For Drella*.

St Ann's was the church-cum-cathedral-of-sound that Willner planned to use for the upcoming *Greetings From Tim Buckley* tribute night, although that wasn't the original plan, as Willner noted in the program. He'd set out to produce a special for *Night Music*, another network show he was involved with, that would feature an hour-long set of interpretations of Buckley's music by various peers and admirers. 'Anyway, it didn't happen,' he wrote. What did happen was that Janine Nichols, another *Saturday Night Live* veteran, caught wind of Willner's aborted show, just as she was kicking around ideas for her second 'Arts At St Ann's' series. Nicholls suggested they use the church instead, and Willner was sold. 'For some reason,' he wrote, 'I thought that Buckley's music, in this type of multi-artist situation, would work better live than on LP. I agreed to it thinking it would never happen. It happened.'[2]

Over several marathon listening sessions, Willner and Nichols compiled a wishlist of songs and performers: some were fans of Buckley's music – including guitarist GE Smith, sidekick to Bob Dylan and Hall & Oates, and folkie Eric Andersen, the only act on the bill who was amongst Buckley's peers – while others simply seemed to be interesting choices. 'We included music from every aspect of Buckley's career,' Nichols wrote in the *Greetings* program, 'including the experimental and more emotionally exposed music, which we really like, that cost him most of his audience.'[2a]

Nichols was in for a very timely surprise when she caught up with Herb Cohen, who gave her the unexpected news about Tim's musical son. And despite his initial reluctance, Jeff Buckley clearly wanted in on what was shaping up as the latest 'Hal Willner extravaganza', in the words of another invitee, New York guitarist Gary Lucas. Soon after Nichols' speculative call, Buckley called Willner at home, and they talked through songs that he could possibly play – apparently nothing was beyond his reach, so he'd obviously been doing his homework. The name 'Jeff Scott Buckley' was quickly added to the *Greetings* program, alongside what Lucas called the 'many disparate folk [from] the so-called downtown New York scene, which fundamentally is an experimental music scene.'[2b] For a geeky, guitar-loving kid raised on fusion and prog rock, who was dealing with the aftermath of an unrequited love, the St Ann's gig, set down for April 26, 1991, may as well have been taking place on the moon. This was another world altogether. According to Penny Arcade: 'He came into a scene that was totally different from what he thought the entertainment business was.'

But as soon as Buckley reached New York on April 20, 1991 – draped in his father's pea coat, for maximum effect – he found the city thrilling, if a little scary. 'He was so excited [by New York],' added his buddy Tom Chang, now finding his own way in the downtown jazz world. 'He'd say, "Man, it's fucking amazing." He was floored by it, the energy, he was just going off, he couldn't get enough. He just said that LA was nowhere, and this was where he had to be.'

The Willner/Nichols-produced *Greetings From Tim Buckley* wouldn't just be remembered as the New York debut of Jeff Buckley; in a twist of fate that is rarely seen this side of Charles Dickens, almost all of the characters who would feature in the early chapters of Buckley's New York life – Willner, Lucas, Fields, Arcade and numerous others – were either in attendance or somehow connected to the show. Also in the house was Rebecca Moore, who, in the deftly-chosen words of Chris Dowd, may not have been the love of Buckley's life, but was 'the first person that loved Jeff and he loved her back'.

Her background was as impressive as anyone else's that started to gather for rehearsals at St Ann's a couple of days before the event. The 22 year old was the daughter of Peter Moore, the lensman-of-repute for the Fluxus art movement, whose advocates had included Yoko Ono, in her pre-'bed-in-for-peace, she-broke-up-the-Beatles' days. This early 1960s underground art group played just as prominent a role in the Moore household on West 30th Street as the more traditional child-rearing aspects such as, well, school: Moore truly was a child of Fluxus. She was also a close friend of Penny Arcade, who cast Moore in one of her productions, in the role of 'Theresa The Little Flower', reciting a 'romantically erotic' monologue taken from the Song Of Solomon. Moore had volunteered to help out at the *Greetings* show and was taken by Buckley straight away, despite their vastly different backgrounds. Arcade detected a 'special vibe' when she first saw Buckley and Moore together, and Gary Lucas thought they were 'a very attractive couple'.

As for Gary Lucas, he was the guitarist-of-choice within the cool-school downtown music scene. 'We love Gary,' said Danny Fields. 'If there's anything Gary likes, it's got to be good.' He'd first made his mark as a guitarist-for-hire in the early 1980s incarnation of Captain Beefheart's Magic Band, before establishing a residency at New York venue the Knitting Factory. He also produced albums for The Woodentops and Adrian Sherwood, and was dubbed 'guitarist of 1000 ideas' by the *New York Times*. But not everyone was totally sold on his unique style, a dazzling maze of effects and mind-fucking soundscapes, quite possibly influenced by the copious amounts of pot that Lucas admitted to smoking, sometimes with Buckley. 'I never got it about him,' said Tom Chang. 'Nothing struck me as genius. I remember hearing him play at a rehearsal space next door to us and one of the guys said: "Hey, that's Gary Lucas" and I went so what? I know his big claim to fame was playing with Captain Beefheart, but what I heard of Gary was that he was into all these gadgets and making certain sounds, and I think that was his appeal, this guy who could create all these textures. But at the time I was listening to Bill Frisell and he was doing that and so much more.'*

Hal Willner didn't have any such qualms about Gary Lucas. Soon after speaking with Jeff Buckley, Lucas had approached the producer and asked whether he could perform Tim Buckley's 'Sefronia' on the night. It was also a song on Jeff Buckley's shortlist, so Willner had a brainwave: 'Why not put him and the Buckley kid together?' It was a shrewd move: at the rehearsals, the pair bonded over such diverse musical flavours as Led Zeppelin, The

---

* In an ironic footnote, Frisell would be tapped by Mary Guibert to add some overdubs to a pair of songs on *Songs To No-One*, one of many posthumous Jeff Buckley releases, a collection of demos and live performances cut with Lucas over six months, from late 1991 to early 1992.

Doors and English mopers The Smiths. (In fact, as their musical relationship developed, Lucas suggested that they take the sonic stance of these acts that they loved and update it for the 1990s.) 'We were immediately simpatico musically,' said Lucas, who was also drawn to Buckley's boundless enthusiasm. 'He was this longhaired kid just bursting out of his skin, making faces like he was going to explode. I was immediately attracted to that energy; I really felt he had charisma.'[3] Post rehearsal, Lucas invited Buckley back to his apartment, where they clicked, eventually writing a song called 'Bluebird Blues' and also working out an arrangement of Tim's 'Sefronia'. 'I created a loop with an Eastern sound,' Lucas said, 'and played some chords behind it. Jeff just started singing over this – it was overwhelming.'[4]

Clearly, it did Gary Lucas' stop-start career no harm that he'd soon be associated with a musician who, in the words of future Buckley friend and admirer Dave Shouse, 'was channelling something way hotter than I'd ever dreamed of'. Danny Fields described Lucas' subsequent role as Buckley's 'sort-of benevolent patron. He introduced [Jeff] into New York society.' Interestingly, while most of Buckley's new crowd saw him as 'green' and naive, especially amongst such lofty company, Fields didn't agree. 'I don't think he was so wide-eyed. He was a generation Hollywood person: how long could he pretend to be green before people say, "Hello, Hollywood and New York are the same city"? You get moved into the right circles very quickly if you go from one to the other. It's the first thing you do.'

But on the night of the *Greetings* gig, Fields had a more important task to fulfil than passing judgements on Jeff Buckley's character: he'd been delegated by close friend Linda McCartney, who was in town with her Beatle husband Paul but unable to attend, to personally deliver a note to Buckley. There was one catch – Fields had no idea who he should be looking out for. As he recalled, 'I said to the woman in front of me, "I'm so embarrassed. His father was one of my best friends – he lived with me – so what if he comes out and says hello? I won't know who he is." She said that she'd never seen him either. Linda wrote a note that was delivered to my office, saying he she loved his father so much, so sorry she couldn't be there, blah, blah, blah; it was very nice. This gave me an excuse to go backstage and seek him out.

'So the lights went out and it was dark and then a single super spotlight fell on the stage and hit this ray of light on this guy – I saw the cheekbones and the profile and went: "AHHH!" It was loud enough to attract attention, I kid you not. Why did I ever wonder? This was him. Later I gave him the letter and he told me that Linda's picture of his father was his favourite, and that he always kept it with him.' Fields and Buckley soon fell into a conversation about his father that was as frank as any he'd have at *Greetings*. According to Fields, 'I asked, "Did you know him?" and he said that he met him once as a baby and then met him once again after and that was the only time they spent together. He said he remembered that but not the first time.'

The bond between Fields and Buckley was forged that night, as was Buckley's relationships with Lucas, Rebecca Moore, even the McCartneys. Co-producer Janine Nichols was another convert; soon after the show she loaned Buckley her white Fender Telecaster guitar, which he would guard with his life for many years. (Buckley's old Ovation guitar had been stolen when Dowd's apartment was ransacked, thereby removing any material ties Buckley had with LA. 'Crackheads visited my pad and stole my guitar,' Buckley declared during a later visit to the St Ann's stage.) Looking back, Nichols laughs at how much historical significance has been attached to this pricy chunk of wood and wires. 'He was a babysitter for me and that was how the guitar thing happened. I had this infant, I was nursing, so I said, "You take the guitar and go play." I figured at some point he'd make enough money to buy another and give that back to me. That was the deal. But every six months or so he'd go, "I'm kind of building my sound around it; can I hang onto it a little longer?" It wasn't a special guitar or anything; it was a classic Tele that I just bought off the rack from Rudy's [Music Shop] on 48th Street. It had a good sound; it was pretty new, it wasn't broken in. It was loved.'*

Just like Fields, Nichols could almost smell Buckley's rare talent the moment he shuffled on stage at the *Greetings* show. 'He had a heart-stopping thing. Literally as soon as he opened his mouth everyone just stopped. The quality of the room tone shifted. Only a handful of times have I been in a room and thought, "Wow – rocket to stardom." That performance had that quality. Afterwards, everyone was handing him their cards and I thought, "Blood in the water. Blood in the water." ' Nichols eventually steered Buckley in the direction of George Stein, an attorney from the Madison Avenue law firm Zissu, Stein & Mosher, who became his manager. (A close acquaintance of Buckley's, however, wasn't convinced Stein was the right man for the job. 'I clearly recall Jeff telling me that Stein said he could be "as important an artist as John Cougar Mellencamp". How dumb is that?')

Nicholas Hill, from New Jersey radio station WFMU, also signed on as a Jeff Buckley devotee after witnessing his spot at the *Greetings* tribute. 'I was

---

* Nichols still has the guitar and refuses to take it outside of her New York apartment.

a huge fan of Jeff's from the first time I saw him, he just blew my mind,' Hill said. Buckley, either solo or with Lucas and, later on, out front of his *Grace*-era band, would take full advantage of Hill's offer of free air time at WFMU. 'He wasn't a gracious guest,' Hill admitted. 'He very much used the airwaves.'

Also backstage (and sometimes on-stage, as well) at the Tim Buckley tribute was Eric Andersen, an east coast folkie who encountered Buckley many times during the 1960s. Jeff Buckley knew who had 'the information' and made a beeline for Andersen as soon as the show was over. And he was right: Andersen was the one person amongst this curious mix of bohemians, artisans and scenesters who might be able to help the son learn more about the father he never knew. His curiosity about Tim was insatiable, which was fair enough, given that he'd just played a big part in an event celebrating his music.

The amiable Andersen still chuckles about how forthright Buckley was on the night of *Greetings*. 'He sat me down and grilled me: "What about this? What about that?" All Jeff wanted to know about was his father, and I was probably the only one around there on the scene that knew Tim. We talked for a long time,' he recalled, 'about how I'd seen him at the Tin Angel and on the streets and in the cafes, in the Village, watching him play. He just lapped up every word. I really liked him; he was the spitting image of his dad, and it was like seeing a ghost: The hair, everything.' Like virtually everyone else there on the night, Anderson was awestruck by Buckley's performance: 'He was very good.' He also recalled that the audience was both curious and 'very respectful' once Buckley took the stage.

'It's a double-edged sword, being the offspring of a singer and appearing at a tribute,' he added. 'On one hand you're rooting for him, on the other you're wondering if he was as good as his dad. But I think people just adored him. He was so honest and open and sweet, so beautiful. I think that's how he was.' Buckley's endless questioning, however, did place Andersen in a strange tug-of-love backstage. The area was tiny, made up of just a few folding chairs, and he found himself sitting with Buckley on one side, asking about his father, and guitarist GE Smith on the other, professing his love for Andersen's music and telling him how Bob Dylan – Smith had featured in his band for several years – had often played Andersen's songs during soundchecks. ('Blue River' and 'Thirsty Boots' evidently being particular favourites.) 'So I was stuck between GE and Jeff,' laughed Andersen, 'and that was the whole backstage area. We were just sitting around, talking. It was pretty wild.' As impressed as he was by Buckley both as a person and a fellow performer, Andersen sensed a sad spirit underneath the restless, eager surface. 'He probably didn't know Tim at all. He was asking

Jeff Buckley, 1966-1997: 'He was wide-eyed, a real goober, you know?,' said Merri Cyr, who first photographed Buckley in 1991. 'He didn't want to be a Chris Isaak lookalike. He was this fucking goofball.' (© 1992 JACK VARTOOGIAN/FRONTROWPHOTOS)

His father, troubadour Tim Buckley: Jeff would insist that his step-father, Ron Moorhead, was his 'real father', but there was no doubt that Tim's music left a deep impression on him. (HENRY DILTZ/CORBIS)

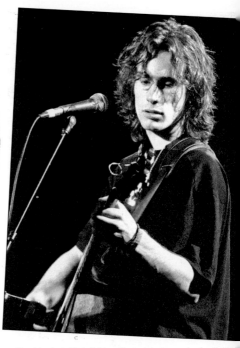

Buckley's 'official' New York debut was in April 199... when he played at the Greetings From Tim Buckle... tribute. Having not been invited to his father's funer... he felt it offered a chance to say farewell. It also kickstarted his career. (© 1991 JACK VARTOOGIAN/FRONTROWPHOT...

At one stage of the Greetings show, a spotlight hit Buckley like a thunderbolt. He phoned a friend afterwards, unimpressed, and said: 'It was like the fucking second coming.' (© 1991 JACK VARTOOGIAN/FRONTROWPHOTOS)

arla Azar, Buckley's one-time bandmate and fellow
ll student. Buckley's friend Chris Dowd insists that
he was the inspiration for at least one of his songs.
Last Goodbye" is for Carla, especially that line "kiss
me out of desire not consolation".' (ROBB D. COHEN/RETNA)

Fishbone keyboardist Chris Dowd was very
tight with Buckley, especially before he headed east.
When asked about his friend's death, he replied:
'There was no fucking romantic shit; it was a horrible
accident and that's it.' (PAUL NATKIN/WIREIMAGE.COM)

Buckley with New York guitarist Gary Lucas,
s bandmate and co-writer in Gods And Monsters:
'He was this longhaired kid just bursting out of
s skin. I was immediately attracted to that energy;
I really felt he had charisma,' said Lucas.
(© 1992 JACK VARTOOGIAN/FRONTROWPHOTOS)

'So here's what I look like,' Buckley wrote in
a note with this photo from April 1990. 'I've got the
ol' fuzz-head happening.' (COURTESY OF LEE UNDERWOOD)

Buckley in the New York apartment he shared with Brooke Smith. (COURTESY OF LEE UNDERWOOD)

When Buckley arrived to perform at the estate of Sony boss Donny Ienner, the skies opened.
Mariah Carey (far left) looked on as Buckley performed Led Zeppelin's 'Rain Song'. According to a witness,
'It was one of the most incredible musical moments I've ever witnessed.' (COURTESY OF LEAH REID)

Buckley in March 1992: He left Gods And Monsters just as they started to peak, soon after pulling what Lucas referred to as a 'ruthless power move' and insisting that the band's rhythm section be fired. (LARRY BUSACCA/RETNA)

Buckley at New York venue Sin-E: During one of his earliest sets there, alongside Frames' leader Glen Hansard, Buckley filled an empty venue within minutes. 'People were coming in off the street, pressing themselves against the glass,' said Hansard. (MERRI CYR/WWW.MERRICYR.COM)

Buckley had planned to name his debut EP in honour of the Joni Mitchell song, 'Café Days', at least until it crossed the desk of Sony boss Donny Ienner, who renamed it *Live At Sin-E*. This is the original mock-up. (COURTESY OF LEAH REID)

Buckley on the streets of New York: He and girlfriend Rebecca Moore shared a downtown apartment with a glimpse of the Brooklyn Bridge. 'It was a happy, goofy, wonderful and innocent time,' said Moore. (MERRI CYR/WWW.MERRICYR.COM)

Buckley at New York venue Wetlands, 1993: 'The crowd was almost ignoring Jeff,' said Columbia's Mike Webb. 'He started in on what sounded like a Buddhist chant and then it was silence, except for Jeff. He knew how to take the temperature of a room.' (STEVE EICHNER/RETNA)

Few instruments were beyond Buckley's reach: 'During breaks he'd start playing Led Zeppelin son on the drums and then grab my bass and keep goir said Gods And Monster's Tony Maimone. 'He was amazing, you know.' (BENJAMIN OLIVER/RETNA)

Buckley with the *Grace*-era band: Michael Tighe, Mick Grondahl and Matt Johnson (from left). 'I was dying to be with the band, dying for the relationship. You know, the chemistry, people, warm bodies, male, female, whatever.' **(CORBIS SYGMA)**

...aken from the *Grace* LP cover shoot: 'The record company didn't like what he was wearing, that it didn't fit the ...age they had in mind for him,' said Merri Cyr. '[But] he was in conflict with them all the time, about everything.'
(MERRI CYR/WWW.MERRICYR.COM)

Another Merri Cyr shoot: According to the photographer, Buckley was torn. 'He wanted to be on this major label and get all this worldwide exposure but he wanted to act like he was on an indie label.' (MERRI CYR/WWW.MERRICYR.COM)

everything about his dad: it just broke your heart. And he seemed much younger than 24.'

As far as the public record was concerned, Jeff Buckley had come to *Greetings* to 'pay his respects' to his father and move on, and there's no doubting that this particular mission had been accomplished. He'd done so well, in fact, that he extended his New York stay beyond his planned departure date of April 30, with the St Ann's folk picking up the tab. He and Gary Lucas had plans, as did Danny Fields, who, at Buckley's request, organised a lunch where he could get to know more about his father. *Greetings* may have been his 'formal' farewell to his father, but Buckley was still intent on learning everything he could from those who knew his dad. Fields brought along Donald Lyons, a classical scholar and film and theatre critic, who was another of Tim Buckley's New York crew back in the heady, folky 1960s. Lucas also sat in.

'He wanted to meet friends of his father's who he never knew,' said Fields. 'I thought that was very touching. I went through that with Cass Elliott's daughter as well. They never really knew their parents. So we had lunch at this Indian restaurant. Jeff asked, "What was my Dad interested in?" Donald said that Timmy was interested in politics. Now, I didn't know that. Afterwards, Donald said this: "Timmy has gone to heaven and sent us an angel." ' This touching assessment would stick with Fields throughout his relationship with Buckley.

Lucas' plans with Buckley were more forward-looking. He set up some meetings with various labels, hoping to sniff out a development deal that would enable him and Buckley to get into a studio and bottle some of the magic that he felt existed between them. Their April 29 meeting with Columbia, with whom Lucas had been signed until recently, didn't pan out so well. Buckley had heard enough from Chris Dowd to naively think that this label was the devil's work, and refused to shake the hand of David Kahne, the exec who had 'ruined' Fishbone, leaving Lucas red-faced outside his office.

Just before he'd left for New York, Buckley had a revelation for Chris Dowd: he finally told him about his 'famous' father, and how he'd been invited to a tribute night. It was the first his buddy had ever heard about Tim. 'The first thing that came out of my mouth was, "Who the hell was your dad?",' said Dowd. When Buckley returned to LA in mid May 1991, he had another surprise for Dowd. He was accompanied by Rebecca Moore, his new girlfriend, who stayed on the west coast for a couple of weeks while Buckley sorted out a way to return to New York. Writing via email from her home in Manhattan, Moore attempted to explain to me her bond with Buckley. 'I really loved Jeff,' she wrote. 'He was pretty much my first really deep connection and friendship, and it was a revelation when we met. It taught me that there was happiness and support out there. He was so unbelievably funny; he had such a supreme grasp of the comic and the tragic. It was a surreal and magical few years in my life.'

Dowd was less than impressed by Moore. 'She complained a lot about everything,' he recalled, while another Buckley confidante referred to Moore as 'wound very tightly; she's very dramatic, all she could talk about was the pain, the pain.' At the same time, when Buckley approached Dowd for some romantic advice, he didn't want to disappoint. 'I would not classify that relationship as profound as [future girlfriend] Joan [Wasser] and Jeff, for instance; that was an entirely different relationship. I'm not saying she wasn't special or important, but she wasn't the love of his life. But I [said to him], "Man, be honest; I'm not going to let you live a lie. If you love someone, go for it, love them by all means, life is too fucking short." That's one of the reasons he and I were so close.' Suitably reassured, Buckley started searching out a way to head back east: he was mad keen to eat up everything the Big Apple had to offer and see just where his relationships with Moore and Lucas would lead.

Around the same time that *Rolling Stone's* David Fricke dropped into SIR studios in LA, where The Inbreds rehearsed, Buckley made another fortuitous connection. The studio was also being used by The Commitments touring band, as they knocked themselves into shape for a high-impact two-week US tour, promoting the hit film with a series of live shows in LA, Chicago and New York. Among The Commitments' members was Glen Hansard, an amiable, cut-the-crap Irishman who'd go on to lead The Frames, a sort of homespun version of U2. As Hansard recalled, The Inbreds were hired to back up lead Commitment Andrew Strong and play a few tunes with him during each of these shows. (Dowd actually didn't play the shows, as he was on the road with Fishbone; his spot was taken by two of his friends, Bob Duhan and Kenneth Crouchl.) Buckley was hired as guitar-tech-cum-roadie for the main Commitments band, who'd end each gig jamming with soul legend Wilson Pickett, something they were unable to achieve in the film.

'So Jeff was doubling as the session guy for his band and the backline guy for The Commitments,' said Hansard. 'And he was fixing strings, making sure the amps were working. I didn't know who he was, but we ended up talking. The first night we hung out in LA we bonded over Dylan: I guess we somehow gravitated towards each other and Dylan was the common ground. Jeff had worked out most of the guitar tunings for *Blood On The Tracks* and was showing them to me, and we were jamming. I was really impressed by all this.'

By the time the roadshow reached Chicago, the two were firm friends, joined at the hip by his Bobness. What Hansard didn't realise was his new pal's connection to Tim Buckley, whose work he also admired enormously. That all changed during an interminable soundcheck in the Windy City, when Hansard innocently began strumming the chords to 'Once I Was', only to get a firm nudge from Maria Doyle, another member of the band. 'She said, "Did you know Tim was Jeff's dad?" Jeff was like, "Yeah, he was my dad, but I never really knew him. That's a really good song, isn't it?" I just went, that's fucking amazing, I was blown away. I just didn't know. He had this big 12-string guitar like his dad's, too, at the time.'

The Commitments' tour had barely settled in New York when Hansard's hotel room phone rang. It was Shane Doyle, the owner of Sin-E, who had a request. 'Do you think you could get The Commitments to come down and play?' As Hansard recalled, 'They had us on this heavy fucking press schedule: Andrew was doing *Letterman*, the girls were doing something else. Anyway, I was in the hotel room with Jeff and said that he and I could come down. To us, it was like, fucking hell, playing the Village, just like Dylan: it was our dream, you know?'

Doyle gave Hansard the midnight spot, but even though he was the 'star', of sorts, it was his mysterious friend who stole the show. 'I played a few songs, and was really into it,' Hansard recalled. 'Jeff got up while I was singing Van Morrison's "Sweet Thing". I did the first verse, which I guess takes about a minute and a half to sing, and Jeff did the second verse and took about 15 minutes to finish it! He just went off on this vocal trip. And by the end of the second verse of the song, the room was full. People were coming in off the street, pressing themselves against the glass. Sin-E was tiny; 100 people in there was insane, but people were in every corner, looking in. I did the third verse, which again took a minute and a half and Jeff went off again. It was great.'

Buckley left a massive impression on everyone at Sin-E, including Doyle, who accepted his offer to help out as a dishwasher and invited him to their regular open-mic nights. And the waitresses 'all fancied him', according to the envious Hansard. At the end of the night, an overwhelmed Buckley turned to Hansard and declared: 'Dude, I'm fucking home. This is it. I'm where I want to be.'

Interestingly, Doyle remembers the events of that night slightly differently. He says he was invited to The Commitments' 'proper' gig in another downtown venue called Heartbreak, and approached the 'LA guys in suits' who accompanied them to see if the band could play later on at Sin-E. Although he got an official knockback, at the end of the night the band came to Sin-E and played regardless. Twice, in fact. And to Doyle's recollection, Buckley had played in Sin-E prior to his cameo with Glen Hansard.

Also amongst the throng that fateful night at Sin-E was Hal Willner, who was friends with the venue's owners, Shane Doyle and Karl Geary, who lived in the same building as the Irish entrepreneur. Hansard had no idea who Willner was, but Buckley certainly did; when his friend asked about this bespectacled, slightly dumpy 40-something, Buckley turned to him and said: 'He's fucking huge, trust me.' At the end of the set, Willner invited Buckley and Hansard to his apartment in nearby Tompkins Square Park, where he played them old jazz records and talked a lot. Hansard was nobody's fool – he could tell that Willner, who'd sampled Buckley's magic at St Ann's, was only interested in serenading Jeff. 'I was tagging along,' Hansard admitted, 'but I was really enjoying it. It was my first time in New York – I was over the moon.'*

In the space of one wild night in New York, Jeff Buckley had scored a job, made an accidental debut in a venue that would soon make him famous, impressed plenty of women and strengthened his bond with Hal Willner. It was one hell of a night on the town. With the benefit of hindsight, Hansard has recognised his historical role, even though he admits that at the time, 'it was one of the minor events of the tour. But as history sees it, it was a very major event. I got to see history take place.' It's a story he dines out on, too. 'When people ask me about The Commitments experience, I tell them the Jeff Buckley story,' he laughed. 'I met this guy who was destined for great things.'

New York's East Village may not have been the safest place on the planet in the early 1990s – Irish singer/songwriter Mark Geary, another friend of Buckley's, whose brother was the co-owner of Sin-E, described the neighbourhood as 'pretty hairy... it really felt like *Taxi Driver*' – but it was no more dangerous than Buckley's experiences at LA's Musician's Institute, where police choppers swooped down on Mexican gangs dealing dope. The East

---

* Sin-E owner Shane Doyle had undergone a similarly enlightening musical experience one night at Willner's apartment. 'You'd be at his house,' he recalled, 'and after 30 seconds he'd go, "Now listen to this" and he'd go rummaging around and pull something else out. You could spend all night listening to stuff and there'd be a whole theme to it.'

Village was also incredibly affordable. It may seem unfathomable now, but you could rent an apartment for $300 to $400 a month, and, as Sin-E's Shane Doyle recalled, 'there'd be lots of people staying in those apartments'. There was also a thriving artistic community of writers, musicians, actors and wannabes, many of whom flopped in the 20 or 30 downtown buildings that were recognised as squats.

'When I opened Sin-E [in 1989],' said Doyle, 'the Anarchist Bookstore was down the street and there were people living in tents in Tompkins Square Park. All the kids that came into town were directed towards... the squats.' There was a communal spirit there, as down-rent and squalid as the block would appear to outsiders. 'After a while you developed this New York radar,' said Mark Geary, 'where one day no-one knows you and then suddenly you develop this sense of community. Because you didn't cook at home, everything happened in the cafes or on the stoops – that was your family, your community.' The centre of this, at least for the thousands of Irish shifting base to New York City, was Sin-E, the city's unofficial Irish embassy and the perfect place for a guy like Jeff Buckley to transform himself into a human jukebox.

Buckley took more away from his last couple of years on the west coast than a romantic infatuation and a taste for ecstasy; he left LA with a note-book of songs-under-development. One of these, entitled 'Dream Brother', would be misinterpreted as some strange, sad lament for his long-gone father – his response to Tim's 'Dream Letter' – when it was actually a poem about a crisis of Dowd's that he related to his 'weird' buddy Buckley during another all-night 'truth session'. Before he met Azar, Dowd impregnated a woman but was seriously considering breaking up with her, regardless. It would take several years for Buckley to finally match his heartfelt poem to the perfect melody. To make the point perfectly clear, and kill off yet another possible Tim Buckley link, he'd often dedicate the song to Dowd from the stage, usually accompanied by the comment 'because I fucking love him'.

Another song from the same period that was misinterpreted was 'Unforgiven' which Buckley was still tinkering with when he packed his few possessions and headed for New York and the *Greetings* show. Soon to be renamed 'Last Goodbye', 'Unforgiven' was a song from his *Babylon Dungeon Sessions* tape which eventually made its mark on *Grace*, and was misconstrued as a heavy-hearted valentine for Rebecca Moore, his soon-to-be New York girlfriend. ' "Last Goodbye" is for Carla,' Dowd insisted. 'Rebecca? Fuck no. It's about Carla, especially that line "kiss me out of desire not consolation".' Kathryn Grimm, who watched Buckley write the song on her couch, believes differently, mainly because Buckley told her the song's history. 'I'd met the person it was written about,' she told me. 'It's not about Carla or Rebecca. He told me that it was about someone he was dating. I don't know her name. She was a nurse, and she was quite a bit older than him. Jeff told me personally that it wasn't about Carla. I remember the exact conversation. She was very nice, she came to my place, came to some [Group Therapy] gigs. But I don't even know if she knows.'

All this confusion, however, was a while off for Jeff Buckley: he was now in a new city, with a woman who loved him back and some real musical possibilities. Life had never been better.

Buckley was just what Gary Lucas knew that he needed to make his band Gods And Monsters more than the darlings of the downtown set with a recently terminated record deal. And Lucas, who was born in Syracuse, New York, in 1952, was now staring down the barrel of rock 'n' roll middle age, not necessarily the most comfortable or rewarding time of many musicians' careers: this could well be his last chance for 'real' success. But initiative and musicality was something Lucas had in plentiful supply, as he'd demonstrated when he'd scored his prized gig with Captain Beefheart's Magic Band in the early 1980s after what he called a 'pilgrimage' to meet his musical hero, Don van Vliet. He spent five years working with Beefheart – he even co-managed the notoriously recalcitrant growler – and received due respect for his ability to interpret the Captain's often difficult and challenging tunes. A writer at *Esquire* mag was so impressed by his playing on the track 'Evening Bell' that he declared: 'Gary Lucas apparently grew extra fingers to negotiate his way through it.' In 1988 he performed his first solo shows at New York's Knitting Factory and Gods And Monsters – named after a line from the 1935 flick *The Bride of Frankenstein* – followed soon after. When Lucas joined forces with the youthful Buckley at St Ann's, his fellow Monsters were bassist Jared Nickerson and drummer Tony Lewis, although they wouldn't last too long, at least not in this incarnation of the ever-evolving rock band.

In the wake of their apartment jam back in April, songs came freely to Lucas and Buckley, and the Gods And Monsters quartet finally got together in a studio – New York's Krypton Studios – on August 17, 1991, and thrashed out this trio of Lucas/Buckley co-writes. 'Mojo Pin' – which Lucas had called 'And You Will' in its instrumental form – was similar in many ways to the 'finished' version on *Grace*: it had that same stately, hushed ambience. There was more of a bluesy quality to Lucas' fingerpicked guitar, while the jerky, stop-start arrangement gave bassist Nickerson and drummer

Lewis the chance to lock into a juicy groove during the song's chorus. Nevertheless, the 'freak out' finale was a miscalculation that did little more than drag the song on for a few more minutes than was absolutely necessary. While Buckley wasn't quite ready to see just where his voice would lead him, he did attempt a few of the gymnastics that would make 'Mojo Pin' one of many Buckley benchmarks for wannabe vocalists.

Opinions are divided on exactly what Buckley was singing about. 'Mojo Pin' could have been a statement about an inter-racial romance, as he sometimes stated, or an anti-drug song built around a term best known to junkies, another explanation also offered by Buckley at times. (A syringe full of smack was sometimes known as a mojo pin.) Another time he simply introduced 'Mojo Pin' as 'a song about a dream'. The closest he came to a definitive explanation of the lyric was from the London Astoria stage in January 1995. 'This is a song about obsession,' Buckley said. 'You you have to have her, you start watching her TV shows all night, you start buying her all the things she needs, you start drinking her drinks, you start smoking her bad cigarettes... this is called "Mojo Pin".'

The demo of 'Grace' (basically Lucas' 'Rise Up To Be' with Buckley's lyrics – they would rarely write together in the same room) was a close cousin to the better-known album version, and this time Lucas' busy guitar work complements the song perfectly. The same could not be said for the savage, startling blasts of harmonica that punctuate the track, that didn't make the *Grace* LP version. Even more than he did on 'Mojo Pin', Buckley inched closer to the dazzling vocal pyrotechnics that he'd pull off when he recorded the 'proper' version in Woodstock some time down the road.*

The explanation of this Buckley lyric was just as ambiguous as that for 'Mojo Pin'. The most common read was that he was spelling out his sorrow at being briefly separated from Moore, but Buckley loved to mess with his audience – at various times he'd introduce 'Grace' as 'a song about my death, but not fearing it' and, during an early Gods And Monsters show, as '[my] usual obsession of death and dying'. While playing at Sin-E he'd declare it to be 'a song about not feeling so bad about your own mortality when you have true love'. Buckley seemed to have even less of a clue of its true meaning at a Chicago show in 1995 when he went into the following rant before playing the song. 'Shit's happening now,' he said. 'It's all about now, now, now. Bigger, faster, sweatier, whiter, blacker, *gracer*.' Lucas wrote both songs as 'inspirational messages' for himself and Buckley.

---

* His future A&R man would dub them 'the flying Buckleys'.

The third and final track they cut that day, 'Bluebird Blues', was the first original that Lucas and Buckley wrote, during an April afternoon in Lucas' New York apartment, prior to the *Greetings* show. There's a good reason why 'Bluebird' didn't progress far beyond the demo stage: it wasn't much of a song. Buckley overdid the Screamin' Jay Hawkins growl, and huffed and puffed on a blues harp with such force that you feared he might swallow the thing. At one point the song simply broke down, drew breath and then tried to keep going. Lucas' pickin' was swift and efficient, and there was a certain naïve charm at play when Buckley rapped about 'my friend/his name is Gary/if he doesn't get his stuff two times a day he gets crazy', but the thing sounded half cooked, very much a work in progress. It wasn't really much more than some electrified talking-blues pastiche. It would, however, help flesh out upcoming Gods And Monsters live sets.

As far as Lucas was concerned, these Krypton Studio demos were ample proof that Buckley had what he needed to move Gods And Monsters back into the majors. 'I just heard magic happen,' he exclaimed. 'He surpassed my wildest expectations. I felt it could shake the world.' At the end of the session, as Lucas, Buckley, Nickerson and Lewis were packing up their gear, some jazz players stopped to hear what had just been recorded. 'I remember the look on their faces,' Lucas said afterwards. 'Wow. *What the fuck is that?*'[5]

On Lucas' invitation, Buckley was now a fully-fledged member of Gods And Monsters, even though it's unlikely this was the musical destiny he had planned, a fact confirmed by future members of the band and friends of Buckley. Not long after the Krypton session the group played with Buckley out front for three songs on November 1 at the Knitting Factory, Lucas' regular downtown venue. This was no ordinary gig; it was part of the CMJ music free-for-all, New York's attempt to match Austin's legendary South By Southwest festival. Interested onlookers in the crowd included Nick Cave and John Cale, proof that word was out on Lucas and Buckley. As high profile as the show undoubtedly was, Buckley was in a restless mood; when the band played 'Bluebird Blues', he changed the opening lyric from 'I have an angel/her eyes are the ocean blue' to the far more downbeat 'I am a stone cold loner'. And after his few songs he tried to abruptly end the set.

Nine days later Lucas and Buckley drove to New Jersey, where they played a set on *The Music Faucet*, a WFMU radio show hosted by Nicholas Hill, another early Jeff Buckley 'booster', who'd witnessed his 'coming out' at Greetings. The pair roared through four tracks, with a wild cover of Dylan's 'Farewell Angelina' added to the three tunes they'd cut in Krypton. Hill was dumbstruck by what he witnessed, and tried to get Buckley on air whenever he could.

Lucas, meanwhile, had started shopping their demo to various labels, including Imago Records, whose acts included Aimee Mann, creator of high-grade alt-pop; tortured punk self-flagellator, Henry Rollins, songbird Paula Cole and Oz rockers The Baby Animals. With a roster that diverse, there was no reason why they shouldn't be interested in a left-field guitarist and a nervy-looking kid with a soaring voice.

However, even though Imago's Kate Hyman would offer them $10,000 as part of a 'development' deal, basically to fund some additional recordings, the arrangement may have been cursed from the very beginning. Lucas' prodigious pot habit probably didn't help the situation, either: according to a source, he smoked some 'killer ganja, deadly chronic'. 'The stuff he smoked, man, if I smoked it I couldn't play, and Gary was smoking it all the time.'

'I've known Gary for maybe 30 years; we're neighbours, we see each other in the gym, at the supermarket; we sometimes have a drink together. There may be this chasm in his life but I didn't know about it,' Danny Fields said. When pushed, he blamed something else altogether for the tension that probably existed between Lucas and Buckley from the beginning of their musical mateship. 'I'm sure that Jeff was extremely difficult to work with. And I'm sure that Gary, as an extremely talented musician, is demanding. If you told me that this is a story without friction I'd say it'd be *non-friction*. That's what happens when these type of people come together: sparks fly.'

It was evident that Gods And Monsters, at least in its late 1991/early 1992 manifestation, wasn't long for this earth, but the romantic side of Buckley's life was definitely on the improve. By the end of the year he'd moved into Rebecca Moore's downtown apartment, at the intersection of Allen and Stanton Streets, with the Brooklyn Bridge just visible from the living room window. It set the happy loving couple back a princely $400 a month. Their domestic life was based around living on the cheap – they dined on omelettes and clothes-shopped at thrift stores – and a daily viewing of game show *The Price Is Right*. They even gave each other nicknames: Moore was 'Butterfly', Buckley 'Scratchy'.*

'She seemed like the mirror image of Jeff, kind of shy, laid-back,' said Chang, who saw them often. Moore looked back on this time in her life as nothing short of magical. 'We both seemed to support each other really

---

* 'Thank you, Butterfly,' Buckley wrote in the credits for his *Live At Sin-E* EP. 'I love you supremely.'

equally,' she wrote in an email. 'I am extremely grateful for having known him, and for getting to share what was a really happy, goofy, wonderful and innocent time, with such a great, unique person.'

Buckley would spend some of his spare time walking the streets of New York, quite a novelty for a guy raised in car-crazy California. He'd often drop into St Ann's and talk with Janine Nichols, to whom he felt close in this city of relative strangers. He'd even babysit her child, taking trips to the local playground.* According to Nichols, Buckley developed a strange habit during his long walks around New York. 'He used to follow dogs around. He has a half brother Corey, who rescues greyhounds, so he had a thing for dogs. He'd befriend dogs on the street and he'd relate to the dog, not the owner. So he'd follow the dog but the owner thought he was following him. He was like a dog stalker.' Nichols sometimes drove Buckley around the city and the two would sing along to whatever was on the radio; it must have felt incredibly similar to the time he spent as a kid harmonising with his mother. 'Jeff's enjoyment of his voice was palpable,' Nichols said in 2007. 'I've started singing in the past couple of years; part of that is because Jeff and I used to drive around in the car singing, and he'd say to me: "Why aren't you singing?" He loved to feel the wind in his throat. It was clear to other people that singing for him was fun.'

Another habit Buckley developed was buying cassettes on the street and pulling the contents apart, both physically and critically. 'He'd come by and play something he thought was bad and then he'd be pulling the tape out of the case and jumping up and down, screaming "How could they? How could they?",' Nichols recalled. 'He was so serious about being in service to the muse; anyone who wandered off the track, he was worried about them.'

It was around this time that Rebecca Moore decided Buckley was ready to meet Penny Arcade, her close friend and mentor. Arcade was a woman who liked to shock, and her first sit-down with Buckley made that pretty clear. Rather than co-ordinate a get-together at some bar or a cosy restaurant, Moore 'delivered' Buckley backstage, as Arcade applied her warpaint and readied herself for another performance of her long-running show *Bitch! Dyke! Faghag! Whore!* Then Moore left them alone. As blunt as a smack to the head, Arcade told him that the children of famous singers didn't interest her – she'd already been delegated the onerous task of

---

* A few years later he'd also connect strongly with the children of Mark Naficy, his sound guy throughout the Grace tour. He'd visit Naficy in Seattle simply to hang out with his kids.

helping with Rufus Wainwright's homosexuality – and added that she was no Tim Buckley fan. This didn't faze Buckley at all; in fact, he admired her bluntness. They spent 90 minutes together backstage, their getting-to-know-you session finally interrupted by a stagehand informing Arcade it was show time.

Arcade's performance also left a sizeable impression on Buckley; he'd never witnessed anything like it – she was exactly the same on- and off-stage. He was used to witnessing 'events', where the performer was way larger than life. Arcade, however, kept it very real, and Buckley looked and learned. He saw how a performer could connect with an audience by simply allowing their personality to shine through. From then on he referred to Arcade as a 'real rocker'. 'Penny,' he'd often tell her, 'you are a real rock chick.' Although Arcade sensed that a little bit of Anaheim stayed with Buckley – something she'd refer to as an 'emotional feral-ness' – she recognised a kindred spirit, someone who was seeking their place in the world. 'Jeff wanted a life of discovery and adventure; he was a sponge,' she said. 'His personality was like that of a displaced person; he had no sense of place. Jeff had a natural, unschooled intellect, enormous curiosity.' ('Personally, I didn't feel like he was trying to find a surrogate mother,' said Leah Reid, who worked very closely with Buckley at Columbia. 'I think he just related better to women than he did to men.')

Despite his growing unease with the Lucas partnership, Buckley continued to record and write with him in the wake of the Krypton Studio session. In October 1991 they demoed another song in Lucas' apartment, entitled 'Song To No One', then in January they cut another pair of co-writes, 'She Is Free' and 'Harem Man', and in February they worked on a cover of 'Hymne A l'Amour', an Edith Piaf standard of love and loss, which they transformed into a truly psychedelic 10-minute-plus soundscape, Buckley's voice drifting off into the ether while Lucas added loops and licks and all kind of sonic set dressing. The song didn't really reach any kind of emotional or musical climax, but it was a heady trip nonetheless.

There were other promising songs in this new batch of work-under-construction (which would eventually find a home in 2002's *Songs To No-One*, a compilation that was dreamed up by Lucas, produced by Hal Willner and co-ordinated by Mary Guibert). 'Song To No One' was a crisp backporch strum, a song in which it is possible to get a sense of Buckley discovering what he can do with his voice as he bends (and occasionally misses) notes just to see where they go. Lucas, meanwhile, was all over the fretboard, picking sweet notes seemingly at random. It was a gently charming tune, every bit as mellow as The Grateful Dead during their *Workingman's Dead/American Beauty* heyday. 'She Is Free' was in a similar vein with a discernible country-blues flavour in Lucas' playing, while Buckley's vocal was an aural caress. Indeed, these songs offer compelling evidence that he found his voice while the demos were being made.* 'Harem Man' could be filed alongside 'Bluebird Blues', Buckley sliding back into his Screamin' Jay voice while Lucas bent and stretched notes in all directions. But it simply didn't gel, even though Buckley was having some fun half-crooning, half-growling the horn-dog lyrics. When he sang, 'Oh pussycat/Rake your nails over me', you could almost hear him choke back a chuckle. The 'oh shit' that Buckley yelped when the song abruptly ended was probably its best moment.

Yet in spite of this one less-than-spectacular track, there was some real potential in these Buckley/Lucas collabs. There were also more Gods And Monsters shows in the works, including a return to Brooklyn's St Ann's church on March 13. It was now almost a year since Buckley had made his stunning debut there. Not long before this high-profile show, however, Buckley pulled what Lucas called a 'ruthless power move' and told him to fire Nickerson and Lewis and hire drummer Anton Fier and bassman Tony Maimone, the engine room of 'supergroup' The Golden Palominos. Maimone had a particularly impressive CV, having played a key role in Pere Ubu, Cleveland's answer to the Velvet Underground, and keeping a solid bottom end in They Might Be Giants. He'd also been part of the touring band of Bob Mould, the former leader of Husker Du. Fier had also played in Mould's band, and was an early member of The Lounge Lizards and The Feelies. This was a rhythm section with some serious underground cred, which may have been the attraction for Buckley.

Maimone, however, knew nothing of the sackings when he got a call from Fier – in fact, it was only during the interview for this book that he finally learned the full story. But he did have a history with Lucas. While he greatly admired his anything-goes guitar work, he'd had some trouble with him while touring Europe as part of another band, which resulted in Lucas suffering a broken arm and returning to New York alone. Nonetheless, Maimone did know and appreciate the music of Tim Buckley, so he was naturally curious to work with his son. And they clicked almost immediately; during a few days of rehearsals in a space on W28th Street, they discovered a mutual musical love. 'During breaks he'd start playing Led

---

* The 2002 version of the song would come with a soulful yet understated brass arrangement, courtesy of New York five-piece Sex Mob.

Zeppelin songs on the drums and then grab my bass and keep going. He was amazing, you know. I really liked the guy's energy.'

Throughout the brief time they spent together, Maimone learned just how charismatic and seductive Buckley was becoming, simply by accompanying him on walks around the East Village. 'Jeff was such a dynamic personality, here in New York people just glommed onto him. People would follow that cat around. He had a real personal magnetism and a big heart and was very, very generous with his time, but people would always want more.'* One afternoon, during rehearsals, they stopped for a drink, and Buckley took the chance to speak his mind. He told Maimone that he didn't think Gods And Monsters was the band for him. 'I think Jeff was nervous already by the time I got on the scene. I think he got nervous feeling that Gary was trying to manipulate him,' said Maimone. So was Lucas trying to control the situation with Buckley? 'Totally,' according to Maimone. 'Jeff had told me that he couldn't go on. I had no vested interest, trying to make a project or anything. [But] I loved playing with him, Anton and Jeff, it was a killer band. It's a pity we didn't get a chance to make a proper recording. My involvement with Jeff was short but sweet, you know.

'I've never met anyone who can sing like Jeff,' he added. 'Jeff was just one of a kind, man. Where do you find someone who can belt it like that, and then go up into those angelic ranges? Nowhere. Aside from chops, the guy was such an amazing poet, in the way that maybe a Robert Johnson is a poet. It's going to be a while before someone like that comes along again. He was so special.'

Yet in spite of the building tension within Gods And Monsters, their final shows did generate some real sparks. Who knows, maybe the existing friction actually drove the band to an exciting place; it wouldn't be the first time that a fractured relationship has resulted in some sonic thrills. And while a rift the size of the Grand Canyon may have been brewing between Buckley and Lucas, Jeff certainly didn't let it show, nor did Lucas sense it. Between songs he was the ultimate goof, throwing in impromptu covers, impersonations and dopey asides. For a man dealing with some heavy shit, he sure seemed to be having a whole lot of fun.

If what Lucas said from the St Ann's stage on March 13, 1992 was any gauge, then he certainly felt there was some life left in Gods And Monsters.

---

* Merri Cyr also witnessed this first hand. 'I remember walking around with him in the East Village, he'd walk down the street and everyone would recognise him, it was really tough to get down the street. I remember seeing girls, and some guys, too, see him and not be able to speak.'

'First thing,' he declared, before beginning their lengthy, well received set, 'is to dispel an impression that people might get if they see the sign outside that says "Gary Lucas' Gods And Monsters featuring Jeff Scott Buckley". This sign was constructed about six months ago and the band is very much a collab arrangement now. And we've co-oped Tony Maimone and Anton Fier to join us in this thing.' And then there were off, Buckley groaning 'yeah' as they ripped into 'Cruel', an emphatic Lucas/Buckley co-write, a bluesy growler pitched somewhere between Led Zeppelin and Hank Williams. The Imago Records reps in the crowd – the show was ostensibly a showcase for the label – were blown backwards in their pews.

Another indicator that there was at least some brief creative momentum in 'this thing', as Lucas put it, was that they didn't depend too heavily on covers. There were enough originals on display to show that they meant business. These included 'Grace', stunning even in its prototype form; a red-hot 'Harem Man', where Buckley pulled off a note-perfect Robert Plant wail; the breezily melodic 'She Is Free'; the incendiary 'No One Must Find You Here' and a set-closing 'Mojo Pin'. 'It was profoundly easy, in a way,' Lucas said of his songwriting with Buckley, in a 2007 interview. 'I would first come up with fully realised instrumental compositions – motifs, chord structures, rhythms intact, all there – mail them or play them directly to Jeff [and] he'd go away, sometimes for months, usually just weeks... and damned if he didn't always come back with perfect lyrics and a perfect melody line that sinuously entwined/enshrined itself inside the matrix of my instrumental, for all time.' (Buckley only ever suggested one minor tweak, asking Lucas to repeat a section of 'Mojo Pin' for added impact.)[6]

And they chose their covers judiciously, including such tunes as Piaf's 'Hymne A l'Amour' (a song from a 'dead French woman named Edith,' according to Buckley); the country lament 'Satisfied Mind', which Buckley dedicated to Michael Tighe, a friend and future bandmate, who was looking on at St Ann's; the traditional 'Dink's Song' (which Buckley thought was a Dylan tune); Van Morrison's 'Sweet Thing' – Lucas' wife's favourite song – and 'How Long Will It Take'. Lucas' space-raga instrumental 'Dream Of A Russian Princess' was also included.

Early in the St Ann's set, Buckley enigmatically introduced 'No Soul' by referring to 'page 13' in his lyric book. 'I came up with a love poem that kind of expresses the mood herein,' he said while flicking the pages, with Lucas adding quickly and firmly that the song was also known as 'Malign Fiesta'. If anyone was looking for signs of creative tension between the two, a Buckley lyric that basically insisted 'you got no soul' might have contained a few clues. (The presence of his notebook on stage suggested strongly that the band could have used a few more rehearsals.) Buckley always had a good instinct for 'reading' a room or maintaining a gag, because soon after he announced 'I want you to all turn to your books' like some pedantic school teacher, as he filled in the blanks while he sought out the lyrics for 'Distortion'.

Buckley the entertainer was starting to emerge, and his transition to one-man band at Sin-E seemed a natural progression. By then, thankfully, he'd ditched the dopey white-boy-meets-rude-boy patois that he used to introduce 'How Long Will It Take', which wasn't likely to build any bridges between black and white ska fans. Elsewhere, his beatboxing at the start of 'Hymne' – 'Gods And Monsters *styleeeee*' – was only marginally more tasteful, and was definitely lost on the downtown crowd. Bandmates Maimone and Fier, however, would chuckle at his light-heartedness. 'The dude was funny, he was always clowning around,' Maimone said. 'It reminded Gary and Anton and I that he was much younger than us. He was just a kid.' During another show, Fier almost fell off his drum stool when Buckley launched into an impromptu reading of Nirvana's 'Smells Like Teen Spirit', howling 'Grammy! Grammy! Grammy!' in a passable Kurt Cobain wail.

Throughout this brace of final shows – St Ann's, then a Knitting Factory set nine days later, which was broadcast by WFMU, and three more shows in April as a duo – it was clear why Lucas, especially, was hoping for something special and long-lasting to emerge from this incarnation of Gods And Monsters. There were some genuine thrills to be found in the interplay of Buckley's golden voice and Lucas' dazzling, fleet-fingered stringwork. The engine room of Maimone and Fier had some real propulsion, too, truly coming to the fore on 'Harem Man', a standout that raised the St Ann's roof. During moments like this they definitely had the feel of a real band, even if the physical contrast between handsome punk Buckley and the heavier-set, slightly shop-soiled Lucas, his wild hair defiled by an extremely wide centre part, was pretty damned stark.

The cruellest blow of all for Gods And Monsters – apart from a luke-warm *New York Times* review of the St Ann's gig – was the appearance of a story in the April 16 issue of *Rolling Stone*, where the Buckley-fronted version of Gods And Monsters was profiled in the mag's New Faces section. 'Lucas and Buckley,' the story announced, 'churn out music that runs the gamut of rock's family tree – swirling energy that is a schizophrenic mix of psychedelic spinning, jazz improvisation and raw-blues rambling.'[7] The irony was double-edged: Beefheart survivor and avant-garde veteran Lucas was hardly a new face, and within a week of the issue hitting the streets, Buckley would play his last dates with Lucas, at New York's Roulette Club on April 22 and soon after at CBGBs and Tramps. They were essentially unplugged and usually seated sets, with Lucas on guitar and Buckley singing and tapping away at whatever percussion was handy.

During a post-gig post-mortem, Buckley had mentioned to Lucas that when The Rolling Stones played live, Keith Richards always stayed a few steps behind Mick Jagger, but 'I noticed you were right up front with me'. Lucas replied that Gods And Monsters had been his band for several years and that he wasn't inclined to take a back seat to Buckley.' He wrote it off as a typical case of musician's egos, and certainly didn't expect to receive Buckley's resignation within days. He actually quit after the St. Ann's gig but Lucas coaxed him into playing the final shows.

Buckley wasn't really sure where his future lay, but he couldn't get off the stage at Tramps – where they played their final gig – fast enough to find out. (Although he did take the time to end their short final set with a reading of Dylan's 'Farewell Angelina', a wildly cheeky kiss-off to his fellow Gods And Monsters.) Lucas was 'deeply depressed' when Buckley told him he wanted out. Pushed for an explanation, Buckley was evasive. 'There was an issue as to whether I could play guitar,' he told *Rolling Stone* in 1994. 'So I disbanded it to go on my own.'[8] Yet in typical Buckley style, he made a point of paying Lucas back, a very public act of contrition, asking him to cameo on *Grace* and occasionally inviting him on stage to jam. Lucas even played at one of Buckley's final New York shows, in February 1997, at a time when Buckley was seeking him out to contribute new music for his second studio album. Buckley told him his career was 'total shit'.

One thing Buckley did know was that he didn't want to be part of a band again, at least not until he'd truly learned what direction he wanted to take. 'He was ethereal, man,' Maimone said. 'I remember when we were doing those Knitting Factory shows, and we stopped at this coffee shop on the corner of 14 and 6th Avenues, walking through the Village together, and he said, "You know, man, I just don't know how much more of this I can do." He meant the band, getting signed and stuff like that. He seemed to me to be so, like, light at that moment. I know that the rock star trappings, at least in the beginning when we spent some time together, the idea was uncomfortable for him. I think of all these people who front in music, who talk such a huge game, but Jeff was the real deal. He could bring a rowdy room to silence, he just had that gift.' What Buckley didn't really know was that the perfect place for him to fully develop that gift was only a few blocks away from the venue where he'd sign off from Gods And Monsters. The human jukebox was about to plug in.

Notes

1. Milne, Peter: Penny Arcade: Step Right Up; *Australian Rolling Stone* 1995
2. Anon: *Greetings From Tim Buckley*, St Ann's Church, program
2a. See note 2
2b. BBC2 *Everybody Here Wants You* documentary
3. Diehl, Matt: The Son Also Rises... *Rolling Stone* October 20, 1994
4. Irvin, Jim: It's Never Over, *Mojo*, August 1997
5. See note 4
6. Bloom, Michael: Rock Gods and Famous Monsters; Gary Lucas Interview, www.scrammagazine.com; March 5, 2007
7. Anon: New Faces, Gary Lucas and Jeff Buckley, *Rolling Stone*, April 16, 1992
8. See note 3

Chapter Five

Café Days

A few years before Jeff Buckley took one look at Sin-E and announced, 'Dude, I'm fucking home', there'd been some big changes taking place in that beaten-up, downtown slice of New York City, especially amongst the expat Irish population. A severe recession back home in the early 1980s had driven thousands of Irish abroad. But these weren't the great unwashed that had been settling in America since the time of Jeff Buckley's great grand-father; a large proportion of this 'new wave' of Irish were skilled profes-sionals: accountants, engineers, nurses and others. Lacking Green Cards, they formed a close-knit subculture, especially in New York, bonded by a fear of deportation. By the mid 1980s, an estimated 50,000 'undocumented' Irish lived in America.

Their lot improved substantially when an amendment was attached to the Immigration Act in 1986, which provided for 40,000 US visas to be issued over the following three years (these were known as 'Donnelly' visas, named in honour the congressman who introduced the act). The word spread quickly and some 16,000 of these visas were issued to Irish residents alone. Shane Doyle, the co-owner of Sin-E, was among these transplanted Irish. He'd come to New York in 1983 and had witnessed the influx of Irish into the city, and it seemed as though everyone with a Donnelly visa grav-itated towards the venue he'd open on the site of a former art gallery (now a kosher deli) at 122 St Mark's Place in the East Village, during 1989.

'They cleared the decks for the Irish,' Doyle told me. 'All the Irish com-ing to town were a lot better educated than previously. And they weren't going to hide out; they were coming to do their own thing. They were get-ting legitimised.' Doyle, by his own admission, was no businessman. He might have taken out a lease on the Sin-E site, but he had no idea as to the type of business he was going to open there. 'There was no such thing as building permits or any of those things' – Doyle and co-owner Karl Geary possessed neither Green Cards or a liquor licence at the time – 'so we literally opened the door. I had no money. A guy from Ecuador, who liked the place, did all the electrical work. People would stop in and say, "What's it going to be?" I'd say, "I don't know – what do you think?" I tried to be inclusive.'

Gradually, this tiny coffee shop-cum-music venue became a must-visit for every Irish musician playing New York. On more than one occasion, Doyle would be stopped in the street and asked whether, say, the Hothouse Flowers would be playing Sin-E that night. He'd admit that he had no idea – and why were they asking? 'I saw them at the airport and they said so,' he was told. 'Well, I guess they are,' Doyle would reply, and the band would duly turn up and play. Such A-list Irish acts as U2 and Sinead O'Connor would always frequent Sin-E when they were in town; sometimes they'd get up and sing, usually on Doyle's encouragement. 'I really just facilitated things,' Doyle said. 'I'd never go near a microphone, I'd just be floating around all the time. And if I saw someone show up, I'd go out of my way to get them to do something.'

Even as the venue's reputation grew, Doyle and Geary didn't know how to capitalise on it, and weren't too sure that they actually wanted to. They were doing their best to stick with their original plan: that Sin-E would simply be a cool place to hang out. According to Mark Geary, one of the Sin-E faithful, a good friend of Jeff Buckley's, and the brother of the venue's co-owner, Doyle had created a venue to purely suit his own interests. 'It was a place to hang, especially for a guy [like Doyle] who wasn't a drinker and wasn't into clubbing. Where could I go? What could I do? Live music at a coffee shop with an intimate vibe was the answer.' Doyle, however, started to get a sense of the broader interest in the place when one of his regulars, a guy who was frequently scribbling in a notebook, and who always seemed intent on squeezing the very last drop from his one morning tea bag, introduced himself. He was Harold Goldberg, a reporter who was keen to write a story on Sin-E. He then asked Doyle, 'Do you know who's here?' and pointed out the editor of *Sassy* magazine and the photo editor from *Rolling Stone*. 'I was flabbergasted,' admitted Doyle. 'I didn't know about them.'*

---

* Buckley joked about this in a 1992 radio interview. 'The owners are a couple of great Irish gentlemen,' he said. 'Shane is very tall and Karl is very pretty; all the girls go crazy for Karl. You've probably seen him in Sassy magazine. *Sassy!*'

Once writers started to profile this downbeat hole-in-the-wall, Doyle found himself selling more Sin-E T-shirts than coffees. 'That kept me alive,' he said. Only as the venue's star began to rise did Doyle investigate some kind of alcohol licence. 'I'd sell these two dollar cappucinos – and this was way before Starbucks – and no food. The Irish musicians who'd come and play there would buy a cappuccino, but they wouldn't touch it.' At the end of the night – and that could be as late (or as early) as five in the morning – Doyle would roll down the shutters, walk inside, and discover that the floor was littered with empty vodka bottles and half pints of whisky, which probably explained how all the players managed to get drunk on an untouched cup of coffee. 'The hustle,' said Mark Geary, 'was that you'd put whiskey in your coffee, and that's an Irish coffee. That's not liquor, you give that to kids.'

But even when Sin-E became a licenced joint, Doyle opted only for a beer and wine licence – and even then he'd only stock Rolling Rock, one of the cheapest and nastiest brews known to man. 'I didn't want to be serving six double vodkas or something and have to deal with it,' he said. 'People would come to the counter and order a vodka and orange, a vodka and cranberry and a Heineken, and I'd take the lid off three Rolling Rocks. That's the way it was.' In short, this deliberately understated yet incredibly vibrant slice of no-bullshit Irish culture was the ideal place for Jeff Buckley to work on his solo career. There's no doubt that his Irish roots – and his taste for alcohol – made assimilation that much easier, while he clearly identified with the spirit of rebirth that existed in New York at the time. 'That part of the American dream was still alive,' said Mark Geary. 'You can get off the plane in New York and go, "I'm a ventriloquist, I'm a pipefitter", whatever. And the beautiful thing about New York, and Jeff was included in this, was that it's a city of immigrants, and you're bonded by that.'

Another big attraction for Buckley was the bohemian spirit and tolerance that in 1989 could still be found in the East Village (even though it's now long gone, displaced by horrific real estate prices and what Doyle called the 'gentrification' of the city). Doyle recalled receiving an early morning visit from a disgruntled St Mark's Place neighbour, still in his pyjamas, who walked into Sin-E and pleaded with him to keep the noise down because he was due at work in a few hours. 'I said, "I'm sorry, I've got [the Pogues'] Shane MacGowan here." He said, "Is that him over there?" So he came in wearing his dressing gown, sat down and didn't go to work that day. That was the kind of people who were around then.' This was a place of writers, musicians, hustlers and actors. Some, like Buckley, were well on their way, and others were simply trying to get started. 'Everyone was learning when we got in there, Jeff included,' said Geary. 'Sin-E, in a way, was a bit like

Sesame Street: you always knew who was going to be in there, there was always someone to chat to. And there were lots of insane nights, people like [Bruce] Springsteen turning up and playing because they'd heard about the place. It was a club like no other.'

St Mark's Place also hosted what could only be termed 'colourful local identities'. Sin-E's best known was Tree Man, so named for the strips of bark that he shoved down the front of his shirt and wore like some environmental badge of honour. He developed an interesting ongoing relationship with Buckley and the many other players who squeezed onto the area of floor that passed for a stage at Sin-E. Geary has vivid memories of Tree Man. 'He didn't consider himself homeless, as far as he was concerned he was a street carnival guy,' said Geary. 'He'd show up in the middle of the gig and ruin it for you, because he'd be bumming for change and at Sin-E you played for tips. It was tough to win the audience back after the fucker left.'* Jeff Buckley, as dutiful as ever, thanked Tree Man in the liner notes for *Live at Sin-E*. 'You'll never walk alone,' he drolly noted.[†]

Various theories exist explaining how Jeff Buckley began his Monday night residency at Sin-E in April 1992. One notion is that he was steered towards the venue by Daniel Harnett, a musician friend of Rebecca Moore's, who played in the band Glim. Buckley backed this up in an early WFMU interview, and also mentioned that Dorothy Scott, a regular performer at Sin-E, 'put in a good word for me'. (Buckley had dropped a copy of his *Babylon Dungeon* demo tape into Sin-E, but it's unlikely that Doyle played it. He tended to ask hopefuls to play something on the spot, completely impromptu, rather than endure demos.) Doyle, however, believes that it was Hal Willner, a Sin-E regular, who suggested to Buckley that he return to play at the venue he'd turned on its head during that one night with the Commitments' Glen Hansard. 'I guess Hal took a liking to the place because it was a little odd,' Doyle figured. 'It was Hal who suggested Jeff play there. Hal knew Jeff.' On one occasion, Willner brought Marianne Faithfull into the venue and she liked it so much she played there on three consecutive Thursdays. 'He knew lots of people,' Doyle understated.

Regardless of the circumstances, Buckley warmed to Sin-E immediately, even if it took some time for his following to build there. Buckley, however,

---

* 'Passing the pitcher' was how the entertainment was paid at Sin-E; Shane Doyle distinctly recalled Sinead O'Connor pocketing the $20 sitting in the pitcher after singing a few songs one night.

[†] The rumour is that Tree Man is now a millionaire, enjoying his retirement in Florida, living out the American dream.

shied away from playing too many originals during his two-hour slots, not that he had many to choose from, admittedly. Instead he peppered his sets with covers from Dylan ('Just Like A Woman', 'I Shall Be Released'), Van Morrison ('Sweet Thing', 'The Way Young Lovers Do'), Led Zeppelin, and such haunted songbirds as Edith Piaf ('Je N'en Connais Pas La Fin') and Billie Holiday, along with one-offs like his version of the haunting track 'Calling You' from the film *Baghdad Café* (a cover suggested by Rebecca Moore) and his own impressive take on the devotional chanting of his 'Elvis', Pakistani legend Nusrat Fateh Ali Khan. Buckley needed to be a fast learner to fill out his sets, but, as Janine Nichols revealed, he 'had a photographic memory for music'. He'd hear a song, and if he liked it, it was committed to memory almost immediately. 'After he broke up with Gary and started performing solo, he didn't perform any of his own material at all, for at least a year,' said Nicholas Hill. 'He was inhabiting other people's songs. He was finding his own voice within the music of others.'

And it was just prior to another Sin-E set that he was introduced to Leonard Cohen's stately, profound 'Hallelujah'; but it wasn't the Cohen original that Buckley soon worked into his set. He was taken by the John Cale version that appeared on the Cohen tribute *I'm Your Fan*. What grabbed him immediately was not the ballad's delicacy but its subtle profanity and its undeniable wisdom. 'Whoever listens closely to "Hallelujah" will discover that it is a song about sex, about love, about life on earth,' he once said. 'The hallelujah is not a homage to a worshipped person, idol or god, but the hallelujah of the orgasm. It's an ode to life and love.'[1] Over the next few years, and after hundreds of performances of 'Hallelujah', Buckley, in his typically verbose way, fleshed out his explanation of the haunting ballad. 'It's not the bottle, it's not the pills, it's not the face of strangers who will offer you their lines and hot needles,' he stated on stage in Germany in 1995. 'It's not from the Bible, it's not from angels. It's for people who have been lovers. You are at last somewhere. Until then it's hallelujah.'[2] Regardless of his understanding of its message, the song would become irreversibly joined at the hip to Buckley, both during his life and for many years after.*

---

* According to St Ann's Janine Nichols, Buckley's recording of the song has become the stopgap for any screenwriter having trouble getting to the emotional heart of a scene. '"Hallelujah" has become the go-to ending for anything on TV that isn't working,' she said, something a cursory Google search will confirm. As of late 2007, the song has turned up on *The West Wing*, *Crossing Jordan*, *Third Watch*, *Scrubs*, *Without a Trace*, *The O.C.* and *LAX*.

But Buckley's lengthy Sin-E sets were as much about his witty asides and interplay with the few locals spread amongst the four or five tables, as it was the vast and varied collection of personal favourites (and the occasional original) he was singing. Wired on too many cups of coffee – he'd joke how friends dubbed him the 'William S Burroughs of caffeine' – and the occasional slug of wine, Buckley rambled at length about anything that crossed his mind, be it his musical heroes, the challenging acoustics in the venue, or his taste for Guinness, which he celebrated in a scat-based take on Van Morrison's 'Moondance'. ('It's a fabulous time for a Guinness/with the booze all about in your brain/the browwwwn liquor'.) Always up for improvisation, he quickly perfected an imitation of Sin-E's cappuccino machine, which became as much a part of his act as regular visitor Tree Man.

Sin-E, however, wasn't the easiest of gigs, as Mark Geary explained. 'In a subtle way, that was a very intimidating room,' he told me, 'because you were on the audience's level. Your job is twice as hard as playing a big club, with a PA and lights, where it's a show, you're the guy. But on a floor, with a shitty PA and no monitors, sitting in front of a guy eating the house salad at seven in the evening, that's very hard. Your job is to transcend all of that.' A few months into Buckley's residency, during another set for Nicholas Hill's *The Music Faucet* on WFMU, he echoed Geary's feelings about Sin-E. 'It's threatening. The thing I always wanted to do, before I left LA for the second time, was get in a space that was impossibly intimate, really up close, and Sin-E is like that, you're right in front of the people. Some people come to talk, some come to listen; sometimes there can be a lot of noise. It's a strength I really wanted to get into with my music, my singing, my playing – if I couldn't move people close up there was no point going any further. [But] I've got a lot of learning to do.'[3]

What Shane Doyle lacked in business nous he made up for in observational skills: he could see early on how right Sin-E was for Buckley at this stage of his career. 'I don't know where else he would have had the same freedom,' he figured. 'He was totally experimental, you could see that. He'd be reaching for notes that he didn't even know existed, or that he could reach.' Leah Reid, who would soon get very close to Buckley in her role as Product Manager at Columbia Records, was also convinced this was the best possible place for him to master his craft. And it wasn't just about stretching his voice into myriad shapes and colours. 'Through playing at Sin-E he learned to adapt and not just get completely engrossed in the music. He'd look at the whole room as part of what he was doing. If someone in the crowd said something or did something he'd work it into a song or his between-song patter. As engrossed as he was with what he was doing

103

he was also in tune with what was happening around him.' (Reid was watching a Buckley set at another downtown venue when the power failed. Undeterred, candles were lit at each table and Buckley continued, absolutely unplugged. She says that the half a dozen people in the room agreed it was one of the greatest gigs they'd ever witnessed.)

Mark Geary was one of many who noticed how easy it seemed for Buckley to slip between the sublime and the ridiculous during those early Monday night slots at Sin-E. 'When I watched Jeff... a lot of the songs would go on for 15 or 20 minutes and you could hear a pin drop. But he was also really good at telling stories; he was incredibly witty, a great mimic. He'd do a 15-minute bit on Robert De Niro, quoting him, the whole act. He'd do this thing where he played and he'd be killing the room and then almost in a self-deprecating, bring it back to earth way... it was almost self-mocking.

'I think that levity, that between songs stuff, was really what gave people a sense of what a star this was, because he had this amazing personality. With singers sometimes there's this terrible danger of getting into Celine Dion territory – it can be hell on earth, a total wank. But Jeff never fell for that; he could nail a song and still have this great stagecraft. And it wasn't a scripted thing, it wasn't a gimmick; Jeff just wasn't about that. There was a real bravery to have an audience hanging on your every word and then to throw out a gag. It was compelling.' Geary, who's released several high-quality albums himself, admits that Buckley remains a heavy influence on his own work, especially when playing live. 'I've always gone on stage as me and by the end of the show hope that I've revealed something about myself, where I'm coming from. It took me a long time to build up the stagecraft that Jeff had in spades. And it didn't look like he was trying.'

Photographer Merri Cyr, who'd first shoot Buckley in 1992, witnessed a darker, more belligerent side to Buckley's on-stage demeanour. 'He could be very challenging to an audience, too, he picked fights all the time,' she told me. 'But he could have been a comedian if he wanted to, some mix between Lenny Bruce and George Carlin: he could taunt people. I saw a couple of performances where guys were ready to thump him. It could be very stressful to watch. If he was singing and someone was being a loud-mouth, he'd pick a fight with them.'

Buckley was also an enthusiastic punter at Sin-E. Musician and record producer Jack McKeever, another close New York pal of Buckley's, spotted him standing 'three feet from me and my band' while McKeever played at Sin-E one night. (Keep in mind that no-one really stood at Sin-E. This was a sit-down, sometimes even a fall-down, type of joint.) 'He just went into a

trance while we played,' said McKeever. 'There was a lot of love and cama-
raderie between us [from then on].' McKeever recalled another time when
there was some kind of technical hitch and Buckley started 'moving gear and
amps, even though he was a shit engineer. That was him being a friend, he
was such a solid guy. When he spoke to you he looked right in your eyes. He
was so real, so great.' Buckley told McKeever that his mother had once come
to watch him play at Sin-E and confided in him that they'd shared a joint
afterwards. 'Who smokes dope with their mother?', McKeever wondered.

On another night at Sin-E, when Buckley was performing, something
almost unbelievable occurred: he played a song of his father's (although no-
one present can recall which one it was). Buckley recognised the significance of the moment, too, because he stopped for a moment and pleaded
with the crowd not to record it, if anyone was considering it. Mark Geary,
who was looking on at the time, thought it was odd, because 'Jeff was one
of the hundred who might play Sin-E in any one week, and he's asking people not to bootleg. But cut to now,' he continued, 'and I wonder. But I
remember it more because of what he begged people not to do, rather than
the song itself.' Buckley hadn't gone anywhere near his father's music since
the St Ann's *Greetings* show, so clearly this was an indication of his growing
respect for Tim Buckley's music, if not his parenting skills. Geary, like so
many others who were aware of the troubled Buckley family history, didn't
push his friend for an explanation. 'It's like the guy who just got out of jail,'
he said. 'You don't have that conversation. And there's a reason for that:
Daddy happened to leave his voice and music with Jeff, but Daddy left. He
was in a lot of pain, [he was] a suffering, struggling junkie. That was pretty
heavy.'

Despite Buckley's diligent attempts to keep things at a grassroots level – he
operated a mailing list out of the apartment he shared with Moore, advising
fans of his movement, in his own handwriting – it was inevitable that the
business-card-waving sharks who'd started circling at St Ann's would sniff
him out at Sin-E. But neither George Stein, who now represented Buckley
on an informal basis, nor Buckley himself, were completely resistant to the
interest that was starting to build in this rising star. Shane Doyle witnessed
this first hand, and he felt that Buckley understood what could be achieved
by hitching his star to the right person at the right label. 'I think he knew
he had to have these people in his place,' Doyle said. At the same time,
Buckley also considered Sin-E his retreat, a place he could simply chill, listen to music, talk and drink. 'He tried to keep it his safe haven,' Doyle
added. 'He'd come down and hang out there, even when he was getting

fairly well known.' Doyle said at the time he didn't notice that Buckley was drawing more women to Sin-E, although he did rethink this, sometime after Buckley's death, when he was shown a photo of a woman at Sin-E with a Jeff Buckley tattoo emblazoned across her belly.

Regardless of Buckley's desire to keep his profile low, there was a sense that something magical was in the air at Sin-E during 1992. Writing in the liner notes for the Legacy edition of Buckley's *Live At Sin-E*, Mitchell Cohen likened it to similar scenes that had emerged in the city over the past 30 years: 'Dylan at Folk City, The Spoonful at the Night Owl, maybe The Rascals at Harlow's or the Phone Booth, Hendrix at the Scene, Springsteen at the Bottom Line, The Ramones at CBGBs... we all knew that Buckley at Sin-E was going to be one of those. "You were there? What was it like?"' [4] One night, during a break in compiling a Charles Mingus tribute record, Hal Willner suggested to Steve Berkowitz that they stop in at Sin-E. 'Buckley's kid is playing there,' Willner mentioned in his typically measured manner. Berkowitz, like so many who stopped in at Sin-E purely on a whim, was amazed by what he witnessed, and swiftly became a Monday night regular, as word spread about Buckley's residency.

'We'd go in for coffee,' Berkowitz said when interviewed for the BBC documentary *Everybody Here Wants You*, 'and this little scrawny guy was making coffee and running around and then he'd get up to play: it was very clear, instantly. I grabbed Hal's arm and said, "Am I hearing what I'm hearing?" It went from Jeff making coffee to a sea of limousines out the front. Sin-E was where it's at, it was the happening.' [5]

Of all the players actively involved with what Rebecca Moore described as 'the intense and truly emotionally brutal world of the major label recording industry', Berkowitz was one of the few who seemed to place the artist before the bottom line. A Boston truckdriver's son, who'd tour managed the Cars and was, as I was told, 'really tied into the Boston music scene', he'd joined Sony in 1987 as a product manager, before moving into A&R four years later. He'd carved out a niche for himself working on what his colleague Leah Reid described as 'cool, off-the-beaten-path projects. One side of A&R was looking for the next big rock band, the next alternative band, whatever, whereas Steve was working on the niche stuff.' She described the thick-set, goateed Berkowitz as a 'proud man', who'd stride the corridors of Sony's New York offices, the 'Black Rock' skyscraper on 6th Avenue at West 52nd Street, with his chest puffed out and a constant smile on his face. 'You could see the music behind his eyes. He loves music, loves it. [And] he related to Jeff; they loved each other to pieces. And he was well respected within Sony.' And like Hal Willner, Berkowitz had undergone a serious 'moment' when he watched Tim Buckley perform, at a Boston coffeehouse in the 1960s. But, as Berkowitz's assistant Mike Webb told me, he knew that was a no-go zone with Jeff Buckley. 'Steve knew Tim's music very well, but when he finally met Jeff he was smart enough to never, ever, talk about it. He played it very cool.'

Folkie Eric Andersen, who'd been cornered by Buckley backstage at the *Greetings* gig, had worked with Berkowitz, and felt that he was a man of rare integrity and taste. 'He's good. Steve was with Legacy for a while, then he grabbed hold of Jeff Buckley, which got him back in the top music room. He's got a good ear, absolutely; he's pretty much jazz, blues, roots trained. He marshalled this whole thing; he gave Columbia their orders with Jeff, and they did a great job, I think.' Berkowitz also rated highly with musos Mick Grondahl, who'd soon become Buckley's bassist, and Chris Dowd, who freely admitted to treating Berkowitz with something less than respect when they worked together at Columbia. 'In this business, to find an A&R person with that much information, you know, that much integrity, it's a hard thing to find,' Dowd admitted. 'He was a really strong character,' added Grondahl. 'I think he gave Jeff really good advice and Jeff had faith in him. He was a strong figure in the whole scenario; Jeff could rely on him for advice and was really supportive. He also knew that sometimes the best advice to give Jeff was no advice, to just let him be and do the things he needed to do. Jeff knew what he wanted, you know.'

Berkowitz, however, wasn't a 'typical' A&R guy, according to Mike Webb, who spent almost seven years at Columbia, most of it as his right-hand man. 'I loved Steve, but didn't necessarily love the way he did A&R. He wasn't one of those guys on the street, pounding the pavement, doing the clubs all the time. He'd be waiting for a lawyer to call [about a new act], or be tipped off by someone he knew. I'm sure he was watching every move Jeff made.'

From his first sighting of Buckley at Sin-E, Berkowitz was intent on signing him, but he also knew it would, in some ways, be a tough sell 'upstairs'. 'This was very different to most signing stories,' he told the BBC. 'He didn't have that many songs, he didn't have a demo tape [clearly Berkowitz hadn't heard the *Babylon Dungeon* tape], he didn't have a band. I had no idea what he was going to do: was he going to play solo, was he going to play with a symphony orchestra or the Jeff Buckley Big Band?'[6] Yet the flipside was this: Buckley was easily marketable. He looked like a skate-punk version of James Dean, women either wanted to hug him or shag him (or both), he could sing and play like a fallen angel, while his musical bloodline provided a ready-made angle for the music press. And the buzz from his Sin-E shows was undeniable. As a close friend of Buckley's, who preferred not to be named, told me: 'You're 23, you're beautiful, you're an incredible singer – it's not a hard sell for them.'

Berkowitz wasn't the only industry player drawn to Buckley. Imago's Kate Hyman was still interested in signing him, while reps from Sire and RCA had also drifted into Sin-E to check out his Monday nightspot. Clive Davis, the head of Arista Records, also recognised Buckley's nascent talent and marketability, initially on the advice of his A&R scout Mitchell Cohen. Davis, unlike Berkowitz, was a real heavy-hitter: in a career that already spanned 30-plus years, he'd signed such superstars as Bruce Springsteen, Janis Joplin and Billy Joel, while Arista was home to mega-sellers Barry Manilow, Air Supply, The Grateful Dead, Dionne Warwick and Whitney Houston. In a gesture that would bring an ironic smirk to the face of Shane Doyle, Davis' 'people' called Sin-E and attempted to secure a table. 'The record companies had no idea what kind of place this was,' Doyle said, still laughing at the scenario some 15 years on. When Davis did arrive to watch Buckley perform, he rolled up in a limousine, unlike Berkowitz, who simply walked in off the street.

As the sharks started to circle, two separate Jeff Buckleys began to appear at Sin-E. The first was fully aware of who was in the crowd and what they wanted from him, but when they left the second would emerge to put in a completely different performance. Doyle was one of many who witnessed his metamorphosis. 'He'd do his thing and then when they were gone, he'd still be hanging around, drinking a little wine, and then he'd play later, maybe for two hours, and that would be even more brilliant. It was nice to watch him when he was playing around, experimenting with notes, do a Tom Waits impersonation that would fall into Van Morrison or something. He'd be laughing at himself, it was a lot of fun.'

Yet despite the obvious clout that someone like Clive Davis wielded, it was apparent to such Columbia insiders as Leah Reid that Buckley knew exactly where he belonged. After all, Columbia was the label of choice for such 'serious' artists as Miles Davis, Bob Dylan and Bruce Springsteen, whom he respected not just for their music but for their ability to deal with the music 'biz' and build lengthy, massively influential careers, something of an anachronism in an era of hefty budgets, glossy videos and a 'throw it at the wall and see what sticks' attitude. 'Everybody [at the label] knew that what he was doing and was going to do was important and if you looked at the legacy of the labels that were courting him the only one that made sense was Columbia Records,' Reid said. 'When you think about the legacy of Arista, it's not so much about songwriters as people like Whitney Houston. They probably would have done a great job but Columbia was so right for him.' Buckley's manager George Stein agreed. Speaking in Merri Cyr's book *A Wished-For Song*, he said that the history of the label played a key part in their decision. 'That was the label of Bob Dylan.'[7]

There's no doubt that Buckley wanted to become a 'significant' artist, despite his uncertainty about whether he was ready to take such a large step. 'Why sign with Columbia [if he didn't]?' said Mike Webb. 'He wanted to be big. Maybe he wanted to believe there was a connection between [Columbia legend] John Hammond and Miles Davis, Bob Dylan – he wanted to believe it was still that Columbia, but I don't think it was.' At the same time, Buckley's connection with Berkowitz was strong and that was a big factor in his decision. 'Jeff was close to Steve and trusted him,' said Webb, who witnessed their relationship from close quarters until leaving the label in late 1996. 'And while I wouldn't say that Jeff was [Berkowitz's] only shot, when a Led Zeppelin walks in the door, you know what's in front of you. Steve was definitely aware of that.'

In the early 1990s, Columbia's roster was a mixed bag: they'd signed wayward but brilliant singer/songwriter Chris Whitley, a talent almost as singular as Buckley, while their pop/rock money-makers included Mariah Carey, Michael Bolton and the C&C Music Factory. 'Heritage' acts such as Leonard Cohen, Bruce Springsteen and Dylan had remained faithful to the label over long careers, while fellow icons Ray Charles and Johnny Cash had only recently ended their recording careers with Columbia.

There was also something in Berkowitz's streetwise approach that appealed to the industry-wary Buckley, although he was still quite ready to check out what other labels had to offer. And on June 10, 1992, he did just that, walking into the offices of Arista to hear Clive Davis's pitch, although he first had to endure a five-minute video outlining the many peaks of Davis' own career. Buckley, at the time, was dressed in a ripped T-shirt and carried a see-through plastic bag containing Ajax and bathroom cleaner. Apparently he came straight from some essential household shopping.

By this time, George Stein had, with Buckley's input, sketched out a package deal that would have to be accepted, at least in theory, by any label that was planning to sign Buckley. He'd receive $100,000 on signing, would be guaranteed a three-album deal, a hefty royalty rate of 28% and total creative control. It was a brassy move on their part, especially for an unproven act like Buckley and a relative newcomer to management such as Stein.

They were naysayers whispering in Buckley's ear, including Penny Arcade and Rebecca Moore, who were both convinced that he should sign to an indie label; Gary Lucas felt the same way. But, as one friend of Buckley's told me, he was certain that recording for a major was 'his destiny'. After a few months of to-ing and fro-ing, he and Stein agreed to sign with Columbia, and the first draft of his contract was ready on August 6. In a gesture designed either to prolong the suspense, or leave the label with no doubt that he wasn't to be fucked with – or perhaps it was an indication of his uncertainty – it was another two months before Buckley actually signed the deal. Even then it wasn't quite what he and Stein had demanded: the words 'creative control' were conspicuous by their absence. After the formal signing on October 29, Buckley bought Moore some donuts, and then dropped by his neighbourhood ATM where he slipped a cheque for $100,000 into the deposit slot. Ready or not, he was now a major label contender.

During the bitterly cold New York winter of 1992 and 1993, Buckley continued his Sin-E residency, as well as putting in sets at Fez, where he'd struck up a deal with the management: they'd feed and water him and he'd play for free. Clearly influenced by the 'arty' Moore, he also dipped his toes in more avant-garde waters, performing a musical piece (of sorts) entitled 'Comb Music' at the Anthology Film Archives and then playing at a Hoboken benefit for Projected Images, a Hudson County film archive, a curious one-off that rated Buckley a mention in the *New York Times*. On January 17, he dropped by the WFMU studio to play another set for Nicholas Hill's *Music Faucet*. An earlier set for Hill, recorded on October 11, 1992 and widely bootlegged, included covers of Percy Mayfield's 'Please Send Me Someone To Love', a pair of Elton John ballads, 'Curtains' and 'We All Fall In Love Sometimes', plus the usual Morrison and Dylan tracks and a couple of originals. This was punctuated by lengthy rambles about Sin-E and the joys of coffee, along with generous compliments for the 'good people of WFMU'. He was obviously as comfortable – and charming – in the sterile surrounds of a college radio station studio as he was on the poky stage of Sin-E.

Although overlooked by most historians, the January 17 set with Hill was an especially significant event for Buckley bootleggers. He strummed and crooned his way through nine songs, all covers, including takes of Dylan's 'If You See Her, Say Hello', Morrison's 'Madame George' and 'The Way Young Lovers Do', the old standards 'Parchman Farm' and 'Dink's Song', as well as his rearrangements of The Creatures' 'Killing Time' and The Smiths' 'I Know It's Over', useful reminders that he wasn't restricting himself to 'traditional' songs and classic singer/songwriter fare. But what's most interesting and significant about the set was the disappearance and subsequent chance rediscovery of a recording of the show. More than three years after the performance, during the autumn of 1996, East Village local Barry

Paddock was walking down 2nd Avenue, and at the intersection of 12th Street he noticed a pile of cassettes that had been left on top of a garbage dumpster, like some kind of unwanted foundling. Curious, Paddock stopped and sifted through the cassettes, most of which were pre-recorded albums by acts he didn't rate especially highly, like The Beastie Boys. But one tape was completely blank, except for a hand-written note that read: 'J Buckley Stuff'. Paddock took it home, played it and discovered that it was a rare recording of that WFMU set. It's now known universally as the *New York Garbage Can Tape* and is highly prized by Buckley bootleggers, of whom they are many.

Buckley, meanwhile, decided to acclimatise himself to the workings of a major label during the early months of 1993. On an almost daily basis he'd swing by Sony's HQ, and catch up with Berkowitz. Columbia staff knew that Buckley was in the building when they heard the jangle of his keys in the hallway, but most ignored him. He didn't rate that highly there, at least not yet. 'Here comes Jeff again,' they'd say to each other, and keep working. But he was about to meet another 'booster' at the label, Leah Reid, who was a Product Manager, the position that Berkowitz had held before moving into A&R. Reid, who described her role as 'the guardian of the vibe', responsible for whipping up the necessary enthusiasm amongst all Columbia departments for their new signing, turned out to be almost as useful an ally for Buckley as his man in A&R. Reid was a diehard music lover who'd booked bands at college, worked in record stores and under-took a CBS training program before joining the company in 1991. She'd barely been in the job for a year, but had worked with such reputable acts as singer/strummers Shawn Colvin and Mary Chapin Carpenter and high grade pop band Shellyann Orphan. When Buckley was signed, she immediately put up her hand to work with him. Reid sensed something unique and just a little strange about Buckley as soon as they met, an incident she still vividly recalls.

'One of the things they do at labels is bring the artist in to meet the people they'll be working with,' she said. (In Buckley's case this happened just a few days after many of the staff, Reid included, caught his Sin-E act for the first time.) 'Steve brought Jeff in and I got the call to come and meet him. I sat there and explained what I did and how I felt about his show. He was eating a sandwich, and as I was talking I remembered he stopped eating, put the sandwich down, and just stared intensely as I was talking. He was really listening to what I was saying,' she said. This interest was unusual for most new signings, who either found the inner workings of a major label more challenging than a Rubik's Cube, or simply didn't care about anything but getting on stage or into a studio. Reid's relationship with Buckley strengthened considerably during these early months. According to Reid, 'He'd come into the office every day during that first summer, just to sit, read magazines, watch TV and get a feel for what it was like to be in a record company.' But on one occasion, he walked into her office and made a point of turning and shutting the door behind him. 'He talked to me for about four hours,' said Reid, 'about where he came from, what his issues were [with the label], his hopes, dreams and fears about the record industry. It was like I was OK, he trusted me and now he can confide in me. I just listened. I guess he felt that if he provided me with the same information and ammunition, we were fighting the same fight. It would also help me do my job.' As Buckley and Reid finally walked out into the Manhattan night, he knew that he now had two true believers amongst the Columbia staff. 'He needed to get a comfort level with you,' she felt.

As Reid soon discovered, Howard Wuelfing, the head of Columbia publicity, also had a similar 'sit down' with Buckley. Yet Wuelfing's first encounter with Buckley, as he recalled in Merri Cyr's *A Wished-For Song*, said plenty about how Buckley prized the making of music far more than the selling of it. Wuelfing had been directed to set up a 'trade shot' of Buckley with the head of the label Don Ienner and Berkowitz, to run with a *Billboard* story talking up Columbia's new signing. They were gathered in the Sony foyer, but Buckley had gone missing. 'I combed the A&R offices and everyone's seen this Buckley kid but no-one seems to know where he's gone off to,' Wuelfing recalled. He nervously checked back in on the 'execs' and sensed that they were 'getting restless'.

'I start checking the rest of the floor, room by room. I reach the Special Products division and there's Jeff. He ferreted out one exec who still played in local bands and here they are happily chatting about mutual musician friends, recent gigs, incredibly obscure old records. Jeff's totally oblivious to this little matter of his first official record company trade shot.'[8] On another occasion, while waiting for Berkowitz to finish a meeting, Buckley and Mike Webb – who played bass in a band called Spitball, a favourite of Penny Arcade's – fell into a discussion about alternate tunings. 'Steve had guitars in his office,' Webb recalled, 'and I asked Jeff to play "Here Comes The Sun", and he did it, right there in the office. He was always very kind.'

Howard Wuelfing warmed to Buckley when he sat down and asked him about his early musical influences. Buckley replied that his two most important records while he was growing up were Led Zeppelin's *Physical Graffiti* and comic George Carlin's *AM/FM*. 'I learned George Carlin's routines by heart,' Buckley said. 'When my mom threw parties, I'd do them for the guests.' Wuelfing raised his eyebrows and admitted: 'This is not what I expected.'[9]

By now, several months had passed since Buckley's signing, yet not only had he failed to commit anything to tape, but no-one had a clear indication of what kind of record his debut would be. Even David Kahne, erstwhile Fishbone producer and now the head of Columbia A&R, wasn't sure where Buckley was headed, something he confessed to the assembled masses at a Sony convention, just before he brought 'the kid' out to sing. As Leah Reid recalled, 'I remember [Kahne] saying that he had no idea what he was going to with him, but he knew it would be great. That's how David was, but it was true, you didn't know what was going to happen *but you knew it was going to be great.*'

In February 1993, Berkowitz put in a call to producer Steve Addabbo, who the A&R man knew through their small-scale success with Shawn Colvin, a singer/songwriter that Addabbo had brought to the label. Addabbo had also produced a couple of albums for folkie Eric Andersen, which were released by Columbia, with the help of Berkowitz. The genial Addabbo was best known for his work with Suzanne Vega, co-producing her first two LPs.* Addabbo had set up his own studio, Shelter Island Sound, which was situated at 30 W21st, and Berkowitz felt that this intimate room was the perfect place for Buckley to get something – anything – down on tape. It was time to get moving.

But, as Addabbo told me in 2007, Berkowitz still had no firm idea of what type of record Buckley would make when he called to book three days of studio time. 'Berkowitz said that he'd signed Jeff but didn't really know what he had. He said, "Can he spend a few days with you and play whatever he's got?" He wanted a place where Jeff could feel comfortable with someone he trusted.' Despite a working knowledge of Tim Buckley's music, Addabbo knew nothing of his son, who strolled into the studio with an acoustic guitar, an electric guitar and a harmonium. Addabbo's role was simply to get this stuff down on tape; Buckley's job was to play everything he knew (and attempt some things that he didn't). 'We let him go and kept the tapes running.' Addabbo used two machines, just in case any multi-tracking was required. 'I think he was a little nervous at the beginning,' said

* In 1990 Vega struck paydirt with her unlikely hip-hop-pop crossover hit 'Tom's Diner', which was recorded at Woodstock's Bearsville Studio, a music-making hideaway that would soon play its role in Buckley's life. And just before his sessions with Buckley, Addabbo had been approached by Gary Lucas about some possible recordings, with a new singer, although that never came to fruition.

Addabbo, 'but once he got started he was pretty easy and free about it. You could see his mind working behind his eyes, he was thinking intensely about what was going on and what he could do next. At one point it got really spontaneous, which was really nice.'

Over three cold days in February, Buckley cut enough songs to fill five 90-minute DAT tapes. It was a mammoth outpouring of music, like several Sin-E sets played back to back. On the first tape were his versions of 'Just Like A Woman', The Smiths' 'Boy With the Thorn In His Side', plus 'Lost Highway', 'Satisfied Mind' and a bell-ringer of a take of 'Hallelujah'. ('That version is just ridiculous, it's so good,' said Addabbo.) Dylan's 'Woman' was equally powerful. 'He did it twice in a row,' said the producer, 'and while the first take is good, the second is unbelievably different, just fantastic.' 'Eternal Life', one of the few originals Buckley was ready to attempt, was a feature of the second tape, along with an early version of 'Corpus Christi Carol', plus 'The Way Young Lovers Do' and 'Killing Time'. By this stage in the sessions, Addabbo understood what Berkowitz had spotted in Buckley: he'd never witnessed an outpouring of music like this or such a far-reaching musical talent. And nothing was static; it was clear that every song was a work in progress. 'He'd do two or three takes and every one he did was different,' recalled Addabbo. 'And his guitar playing was fantastic, too. There were also moments when he's cracking himself up and then he'll kick into something and you just go, "What planet am I on?" The skies opened up for three or four minutes and then he'd come back and go, "Oh, that was crap". He wasn't quite aware of the effect his music had on people.'

Buckley still had plenty more songs in the tank. On the third disc he turned to originals – 'Strawberry Street', 'Unforgiven', 'Grace', 'Mojo Pin' – plus covers of 'Dink's Song', Van Morrison's 'Sweet Thing', even an aborted take on Sly & The Family Stone's 'Everyday People'. And just to prove that he really was the human jukebox, he pulled off a parody of The Doors' 'The End' that would have had Jim Morrison turning in his grave. (Buckley broke up with laughter at the end of some of his improvs, proof that he clearly enjoyed the ambience of the small studio.) Another take of 'Sweet Thing' appeared on Disc Four, plus 'The Way Young Lovers Do' and a 'great version' of 'Calling You'. This version was so powerful, in fact, that Addabbo still has plans to send a copy to Bob Telson, a friend who was also the composer of the haunting ballad, a true vocal showcase. A harmonium-and-voice run through Morrison's 'Madame George' was the pick of the fifth and final tape.

If the sessions with Addabbo were merely to help get Buckley comfortable in a studio, they were an unqualified success. But, as Addabbo recalled, if the plan was to help Buckley focus on a specific style, then they fell short. 'It was like watching a wild horse,' he said. 'There were moments when the horse would be really beautiful and others where you'd go, "Whoa, stand back, it's a little out of control." But what was quite evident,' Addabbo continued, 'was that he really knew that he was good and bad sometimes and that he wasn't quite ready for the big producer and all that. But that's why, to me, these sessions are precious: it was relaxed, we weren't "producing" anything, let's just see what you've got. It's so unguarded.' Addabbo was also impressed by Buckley's sharp wit and his ready sense of humour. If he was nervous at the start of the sessions he was more mellow than David Crosby by the time they were finished.

'You could tell he was a bright kid,' he said. 'He knew what was going on: he was witty, he was smart, he was quick. And there's a lot of laughter on those tapes.' There's also a fair wallop of distortion: Buckley's thing for soft-loud dynamics often led to unexpected, crystal-shattering screams that would almost blow Addabbo backwards.*

But as they wound up their mini-marathon, Addabbo, who immediately called Berkowitz and volunteered his services for Buckley's studio debut, remained uncertain about how the kid's career would play out with Columbia. He'd seen first-hand how the label worked and found it 'pretty distasteful. Columbia was pretty promotion-driven. It was all about break-the-single; it was more cut-throat.' Despite the label's impressive back catalogue, Gary Lucas was frustrated by Columbia's corporate-minded attitude towards what he considered to be an art form. Addabbo saw his friend Berkowitz as a 'soft guy in a hard place', which he figured was what drew Buckley to him. 'But Berkowitz still had to feed that machine and to fit Buckley into that machine was a tough ask. They weren't into developing him properly, they just wanted to throw the big bucks at him. You know, "Let's break this thing".'

Though progress seemed to be stalled, there was no question that Buckley's stock was rising all the same. In early 1993 he was invited to sing at Day-O, the country estate of Sony boss Don Ienner, the former home of calypso king Harry Belafonte. It was an indication of just what Buckley meant to the label. Mariah Carey looked on as Buckley, hidden beneath a

---

* Amazingly, despite the posthumous cottage industry that has developed around Jeff Buckley, these five DATs – of which only two copies exist, one with Addabbo and the other safely stashed away in the Columbia vaults – have never been released. True believer Addabbo phones Berkowitz every couple of years to try and convince him that they should be.

blue hooded sweat jacket, improvised a version of Led Zep's 'The Rain Song', a choice no doubt motivated by the day's miserable weather. In the words of Mike Webb, Steve Berkowitz's assistant, Buckley's rendition was 'perfect'. 'I was so blown away that I really don't remember anything else about what he played or the rest of that day,' he wrote in a 2006 blog. 'But for me – who's seen a LOT of live shows – it was one of the most incredible musical moments I've ever witnessed.'[10] Buckley quickly proceeded, in the words of his buddy Chris Dowd, to 'wrap Donny around his little finger'.

Buckley made another A-list connection around the time of his sessions with Addabbo, when his friend Danny Fields got a phone call. Mr Buckley's presence was requested by the McCartneys, who were appearing on *Saturday Night Live*: could Fields please set something up? 'I took Jeffy backstage to meet Paul and Linda at Rockefeller Centre,' recalled Fields. 'She was gushing all over him, as was Paul. I didn't enjoy being in his company terribly much; Linda was my friend, not him. They started talking about music, which I hate anything more in the world, and I figured it was done, I'd brought him to meet them and he was now safe in the arms of Linda and Paul McCartney. I'd known them long enough to know who they were going to embrace and who was not going to get through the stage door much less into the dressing room – and much less into their arms and affection. Now his career was really off and running.'

As for Buckley, he'd just gotten a lot of music out of his system, both during his so-called 'café days' and through his sessions with Addabbo. When the producer checked in with him soon after their few days together, during another Sin-E set, Buckley pulled him aside and said that the novelty of working solo was rapidly fading. 'I want to play with a band,' he admitted. Fortunately for Buckley, one of the musicians he needed was also a Sin-E regular, bassist Andrew Goodsight. And, just as he had with Gods And Monsters' Tony Maimone, they bonded over a mutual love of Led Zeppelin (plus a running gag about Robert Plant's wonky teeth).

Goodsight had been playing bass at Sin-E as part of the band of another regular, Adam Roth. Buckley was in the crowd one night, looking on. Afterwards, he approached Goodsight and they jammed virtually every Zeppelin tune they knew. 'Hey man, give me your number,' he asked Goodsight as they finally packed away their gear, which he duly did. But Goodsight had a confession to make: he had no idea who this thin white Zep-lover actually was. 'I was off the radar, focused on my own writing and playing in a dozen bands,' said Goodsight, who's best known for his role with high-octane punks Black 47. But what did impress Goodsight was

Buckley's ability to channel the mighty Zep. 'I didn't know any of his tunes,' he recalled. 'Instead, I was like, "Wow, this guy can play Jimmy Page better than Page and can sing better than Plant live." And not only that but he knew all the detail, all those changes and parts that people don't learn. And I don't just mean a few songs, I mean the entire catalogue.' (When an awestruck Goodsight pumped Buckley for details, asking him how he got to know their music so intimately, he simply replied: 'I used to sit in my room a lot, listening and learning.')

Goodsight was also impressed by Buckley's apparent total lack of pretension. He walked into Sin-E, not long after they first jammed, and was shocked to see Buckley wiping dishes. 'He didn't need to do that – and I don't think they were paying him. And that was after he got his first major label cheque. He wasn't pretentious, or a jerk, or [someone who'd] burn bridges like so many people I know who've gotten signed.' Buckley and Goodsight convened soon after, along with drummer John McNally, at a rehearsal space called Context, on Avenue A. They started by jamming every Rush song that they could recall, 'mainly for a goof,' according to Goodsight. They also played AC/DC tunes, even some Judas Priest screamers. 'We also did some Beatles, but mainly rock stuff,' Goodsight said. 'We had this saying, "Fuck the Beatles". I loved them, but I didn't need to hear "Yesterday" again.'

But it was also the 'idea' of a band like Led Zeppelin that drew Buckley to these two solid players, and steered him away from the idea of becoming a genuine 'troubadour' (much to the concern of Columbia, who were leaning in that direction on the strength of some of the Addabbo recordings). During rehearsals, Buckley recalled how Zeppelin felt a spark when they first played, and he was trying to bottle some of that for himself. 'Jeff was definitely looking for a vibe,' Goodsight said. When they'd finished playing, he and Goodsight would talk Led Zeppelin until they ran out of breath.

Duly 'vibed', Buckley approached Berkowitz with the idea of the nameless trio putting in a couple of days at the Knitting Factory, to see where it might lead. Buckley planned to record all the sessions. In fact, as Goodsight and McNally quickly learned, Buckley recorded everything, 'every note, even in rehearsals,' Goodsight said. The day after every rehearsal or session he would reconvene with the pair and hand over cassettes, labelled: 'Fun With Andrew and John.'

They played together for something like five days, recording, to Goodsight's recollection, 'a load of covers and maybe 10 or 12 originals'. One of these, the metallic 'Strawberry Street', ended up on the expanded version of *Grace*, much to the bewilderment of Goodsight. 'He would never have wanted that song released,' he said. 'It was the first song he wrote and probably the worst. It's such a crappy song.' Buckley was constantly working on it during those Knitting Factory sessions, but couldn't find a way to make it fly. He also put in several hours tweaking 'Last Goodbye'.

'He'd just keep working on that bassline,' said Goodsight. 'It was a little scary at times how focused he could be, almost to the point of obsessiveness. But he seemed to be struggling with writing, a bit. He was always trying to write the next "Stairway to Heaven", rather than just writing a bunch of tunes.' 'Hallelujah' was another song that Buckley recorded at the Knitting Factory, along with a batch of Dylan tunes. But just like his sessions with Addabbo, it seemed as though Buckley was getting music out of his system in order to begin making something truly original. 'He played old blues songs, hillbilly songs – we did a lot of old jazz songs,' said Goodsight, who felt as though Buckley was 'getting ready to write. That's what people do, they study and study and then they're ready.' (Tapes of these sessions, just like Addabbo sessions, remain virtually untouched by Columbia, apart from the 'crappy' 'Strawberry Street'.)

As grounded as Buckley appeared to be to Goodsight and McNally, there was the occasional reminder that he was a major label signing. On one morning – most of their sessions began in the late morning and stretched to mid afternoon – several hefty crates appeared in the Knitting Factory foyer. Goodsight and McNally were amazed by the contents: vintage gear, including Hammond B3 organs, 1970s Strats and Gibson guitars, plus amps. The bassist, who was used to punk bands that struggled to even *afford* an oily rag, couldn't resist asking Buckley what was going on. 'Jesus, Jeff, what kind of advance did you get?' he asked. Buckley flashed him a Cheshire cat grin and replied: 'I could buy a small island,' and then announced it was time to get back to work.

Once or twice, Columbia staff would swing by and check on their new star's progress. Buckley would nod at Goodsight and McNally and they'd immediately cease playing. 'He had no time for that bullshit,' said Goodsight. 'He'd stop and hope they would leave. He just stayed out of that whole bullshit world.' It was clear, though, that Buckley had faith in Berkowitz; they'd often conduct quiet conversations, out of earshot of the band and Columbia staffers. 'Jeff trusted him and I respect that,' said Goodsight, 'but that was the only [Columbia] guy he'd deal with.'

At the end of several days of rehearsing and recording, Buckley knew that he was moving in the right direction: he definitely wanted to front the next Led Zeppelin. But Goodsight and McNally, sadly, weren't going to become Buckley's John Paul Jones and 'Bonzo' Bonham. And even if he did plan to hire them for some upcoming shows, Buckley's lousy communication skills put paid to that. 'He was always kind of a mystery,' Goodsight said, 'and that was the frustrating part of playing with him. I didn't know what his intentions were.' Buckley made that abundantly clear when he called Goodsight on a Thursday night and asked if he was free for a gig – on the following Friday. 'It was typical Jeff style, on a whim, fast and loose,' Goodsight recalled. There was a problem, though: Goodsight already had a paying gig, and needed assurance from Buckley that 'this was something he really wanted to start doing'. If that was the case, he said, 'I'd hang this band and tell them I can't play any more.' Buckley, however, merely replied: 'Oh, don't worry about it. It's not a problem.' It didn't take Goodsight long to realise that he'd made a huge mistake. 'I felt funny hanging up the phone – and that was the last time he offered me a gig,' he recalled, still uncomfortable with the memory.

To his credit, Buckley didn't alienate Goodsight, even though he'd passed on a chance to make some musical history. He steered him in the direction of numerous choice gigs, including sessions and/or road work with The Rollins Band, Brenda Kahn (where he got to play alongside several Psychedelic Furs, who were backing Kahn at the time) and Mercury Rev. Buckley even tipped him off to a Porno For Pyros audition, although Goodsight was turned away at the door, without plugging in, because he was 'too tall', as he told me. 'Jeff threw a lot of work my way,' he said. 'He was thoughtful.' And Goodsight remains convinced that those Knitting Factory sessions, as exploratory as they were, definitely pointed the way forward for Buckley: he now wanted to make a rock record. 'He was looking for a band,' Goodsight said. 'Everyone at Sony said they wanted to keep him crooning, but he insisted. And he auditioned virtually everybody in the city.'

But while Buckley may have been taking a few steps forward musically, his relationship with Rebecca Moore was suffering. Buckley's rising star meant that the offers were many and varied, and he rarely refused. Writing via email, Moore accepted that his signing to a major, and the due 'fame' that brought, put intense pressure on their romance. By this time, he'd moved out of their shared flat, into what he described as a 'real apartment', for $900 a month, at 233 E12th Street in the East Village. It probably didn't help, as Goodsight admitted, that Buckley 'had sex with every woman on the Lower East Side'. Glen Hansard backed this up, when I asked him about Buckley's love life. 'Who wasn't one of Jeff's lovers?', he laughed. 'Every woman I met in New York had a Jeff Buckley story and it usually involved them kissing him. A female friend of mine who dated him said that whenever you were in Jeff's company, you felt like you were the only person in the world. And that was true.'

119

'I did the best I could, the absolute best – and I know he did too – to weather the intense and truly emotionally brutal world of the major label recording industry,' Rebecca Moore wrote to me. 'I don't think people can possibly understand, unless they go through it, how dark that world can be; how much and how quickly it takes over and causes everything to change if you don't have an impossibly calloused armadillo skin. Part of it is cliché, but part of it is so much more dark than anyone can imagine. Both of us were way too incredibly naive, innocent, green and ultra-sensitive to withstand it or navigate it, despite our best efforts, because the industry thrives on manipulation and control; it is truly about exploiting the artist's vulnerability.' There was, however, no mention of Buckley's rampant libido.

His first 'real' relationship rapidly coming to an end, Buckley had one more move to make, musically-speaking, before he could also bid farewell to his café days. He needed to document the time for history. And that would prove to be a tad more challenging than just another Monday night set at Sin-E.

Notes

1. Diehl, Matt: The Son Also Rises... *Rolling Stone*, October 20, 1994
2. www.jeffbuckley.com
3. Hill, Nicholas: *The Music Faucet*, WFMU, 10 November 1992
4. Cohen, Mitchell: Liner notes, *Live At Sin-E*, Legacy edition, Columbia Records 2003
5. BBC2: *Everybody Here Wants You* documentary
6. See note 5
7. Cyr, Merri: *A Wished-For Song*; Hal Leonard, 2002
8. See note 7
9. See note 7
10. Webb, Mike: www.2walls.com

Chapter Six

Amazing Grace

Jeff Buckley wasn't a prolific songwriter. In fact, throughout his all-too-brief career he suffered from a sort of creative inertia, writing only a handful of great tunes – co-writing, in some cases – and even they were a long time coming. Many of his Sin-E peers doubted his ability to create anything truly original, even though they had total and utter respect for his heaven-sent musicality, on-stage charisma and humble personality. Even Columbia staffers weren't so sure how many tunes Buckley actually had up his plaid-shirted sleeve: Leah Reid spent one night at Fez, sitting alongside Rebecca Moore, asking her after each song, 'Was that a cover? Or was that an original?' Others suspected that the younger Buckley was always comparing his few originals with those of his father, a prolific, freewheeling artiste who pumped out nine studio albums in roughly the same time it takes Axl Rose to hire a drummer. Lee Underwood, Tim's guitarist, who'd had two tumultuous 'sitdowns' with Buckley back in 1989, clearly felt that was the case, but sensed there was also a deeper dilemma within Buckley.

'Jeff felt uncertain of his musical direction, not only after signing with Columbia, but before signing, and all the way to the end,' Underwood wrote in an email in 2007. 'He did not know himself – which musical direction he might want to commit himself to, because taking a stand, making a commitment to a direction, or even to composing and then successfully completing the recording of a single song, was extremely difficult for him. On the one hand, creativity was his calling. On the other hand, any creative gesture that offered the possibility of success terrified him. Hence, his creative inertia, his inability to write very much or very often, his inability to make a commitment to any given take in the studio; his inability to keep appointments, show up on time, respect corporate officials, or even to complete a second recording successfully.'

Columbia's Mike Webb had a different, though equally valid, opinion. 'He was a great mimic, and maybe that came more naturally to him,' he figured. 'He could perform someone else's songs and you felt like he wrote it himself – he could get all the emotions out. But if he's doing it himself, maybe he was touching places that were too painful.' Buckley cast some of those chronic doubts aside, and possibly said his goodbyes to Rebecca Moore, when he casually strode into Sin-E on a spring afternoon in June 1993. It was the occasion of yet another recording for Nicholas Hill's 'The Music Faucet' program, broadcast live. Hill had invited Glen Hansard, who was on one of his many trips to New York, and iconic, wheelchair-bound singer/songwriter Vic Chesnutt. He also asked Buckley to turn up and play, although, as he told me, 'It was not a sure thing he would show', which was hardly out of character. 'It was afternoon,' Hill recalled, 'and there were more folks on the street than in the room.' This was also the first time that WFMU had broadcast from Sin-E, so it turned out to be an afternoon of firsts.

Hansard opened the show, followed by Chesnutt. Then Buckley started to play, singing 'Sweet Thing' with Hansard, just as they'd done during their one-night stand while moonlighting from The Commitments. 'Glen's harmonising was not a real solid thing,' said Hill, 'but the idea was nice.' Buckley then sang 'Lilac Wine' before springing a huge surprise on the few people in the room and gathered outside: he started strumming a completely new song, entitled 'Lover, You Should Have Come Over'. Hansard, for one, was completely gobsmacked. 'Back then Jeff was slightly weakened in my eyes,' he admitted, 'because he didn't write his songs fully.' (Hansard told me that his 'holy trinity' of songwriters is Leonard Cohen, Bob Dylan and Van Morrison, all hard acts to follow.) 'I couldn't understand why this guy couldn't go off with a guitar and write his own tunes. But when he sang "Lover, You Should Have Come Over", it was fucking incredible. That was the first time I went, "OK, dude, you can write songs". Maybe subconsciously I was measuring him against Tim, who was amazing.'

Mark Geary, Buckley's Irish buddy and fellow Sin-E regular, had similar misgivings. 'I always wondered about the quality of his actual songs,' he said. 'But he was so good at what he did at Sin-E that it took a long time to separate myself from that and recognise his songwriting talent. One is being incredibly picky, though, to say, "unbelievable guitar player and singer, but are the songs up to it?"' 'Lover', at least for the time being, dispelled any misgivings Buckley's peers had.

Nicholas Hill knew that he was witnessing a moment of history, because Buckley had been extremely reluctant to play any new tunes since the derailment of Gods And Monsters. (It was also further proof, as Hill says elsewhere, that Buckley 'very much used the airwaves' to his advantage: what better way to debut a song than to a radio audience?) 'The whole time he was woodshedding at Sin-E, and throughout the whole courtship thing with the record labels, he didn't perform any of his own material, at least for a year,' said Hill, who believed Buckley was using the music of others to find his own voice. Hill was ecstatic about getting all this down on tape – he'd already recorded the brief sets of Hansard and Chesnutt – but just as Buckley began to sing 'Lover', he struck some technical difficulties. 'Oddly, out of hundreds of shows, this is the one that got away,' he shrugged. When he saw that his recorder wasn't picking up a signal, he tried to record the song off a radio in the café's kitchen, but the reception was poor, with another station's signal bleeding through. Hill was ready to slash his wrists when Waterboy Mike Scott then strolled into Sin-E, also with a tune to debut, a 'really great topical song', according to Hill, called 'Going Down To Waco'. 'Mike wasn't booked,' Hill added, 'he just happened to be walking by. These were very casual affairs.'

As potent as Scott's protest song undoubtedly was, the debut of Buckley's 'Lover', historically speaking, overshadowed everything else heard that afternoon in Sin-E. Even in its bare-boned acoustic form, devoid of the heavenly gospel choir and lush arrangement that can be heard on *Grace*, this was clearly a great song, a bittersweet valentine, an outpouring of emotion, beautifully expressed and sung in a voice rarely heard this side of, well, his father. Buckley, as always, would be cagey when pushed for an explanation of the lyric. 'I wrote this song while lying [and] listening to the telephone in my apartment,' he said on-stage in Italy during 1995, revealing very little. 'But she never called.'

If the woman in question was Moore, which certainly could be the case, maybe she'd caught wind of Buckley's nocturnal adventures in the East Village. There was definitely a heavy serving of guilt in Buckley's lyrics, especially when he sang: 'Sometimes a man gets carried away/When he feels like he should be having his fun/And much too blind to see the damage he's done/Sometimes a man must awake to find that, really/He has no-one.' There's enough pathos present in the lyrics of 'Lover' to fill several Morrissey purges.

Yet when Buckley finally agreed to record something for his debut Columbia release, it was a flashback to his Sin-E woodshedding. July 19, 1993 was locked in as the day that Buckley would return to the venue and try to recapture some of the magic of his Monday night sets, for release as a live EP. The theory was sound: as Berkowitz stated, it would 'diffuse' the expectations surrounding his major label debut, and it would also (hopefully) document a key moment for someone Columbia believed would become the next Dylan and/or Springsteen. A live EP was also a throwback to an era when 'artist development' meant more than a big budget, an MTV-ready video and a hefty promo push; there was something authentic and rootsy about the concept. According to Leah Reid, 'It allowed us to tell his story, you know, this is who he is, this is where he came from, this is how it worked in New York. There was no commercial expectation, it was just a great set-up and in hindsight the only way it could have worked.'

Photographer Merri Cyr was one of the few Buckley confidantes to know about the planned Sin-E recording. But Cyr was doing her best to avoid getting involved with the project, despite repeated requests from Columbia's new star. For several days, she'd come home to her apartment and find yet another message from Buckley on her answering machine: 'Merri, Merri,' he'd implore in a sing-songy voice, 'you have to call me right away about this Sony thing on Monday.' She was pissed off at Buckley at the time, but finally caved after he'd left something like 10 messages in a row, all with the same request: 'Please come to Sin-E', followed by what Cyr described as 'all this gooey shit'.

They'd known each other for less than a year, but already their relationship was taking some weird turns. She'd photographed him for *Paper* magazine the year before; Rebecca Moore, who had some connections at the mag, helped set up this very early coverage of her then boyfriend. Straight away, Cyr was taken by Buckley, not because he was a serious music talent – she hadn't seen him play yet – but because 'he was a big ham,' she laughed. '[At that first shoot] we had a lot of fun, he was very energetic and was really engaged with me. He was sort of challenging me in a way sometimes.' This was unlike so many other musicians that Cyr had shot. Typically, they rated being photographed with having a tooth pulled or lugging their own gear. Cyr's curiosity was piqued enough to go and see Buckley play at Sin-E. She was totally overwhelmed by the intimacy of the experience, especially when he crooned 'Hallelujah'. 'I'd never seen any performance like that before,' she said. 'I had to stop myself from sobbing.'

But it wasn't just this career-maker of a cover version that impressed Cyr. Buckley was truly unique; he could move seamlessly between musical styles and could also alter the mood in a room quicker than you could say 'Hello, Sin-E'. 'In the course of one performance he could be soft, accessible, angry – and sometimes his anger, which he had plenty of, would pop up,' she said. 'I [also] saw a lot of performances where he wouldn't try and overpower rowdy crowds. Instead, he'd start with a just barely audible, really light tone, and it would increase very slowly. I've never seen an audience shut up so fast. They could hear this weird sound and they'd shut up trying to work out what it is. Sometimes, within 20 seconds, a rowdy crowd would be turned into this gathering where you could hear a pin drop.' Buckley wouldn't walk on stage and start singing immediately; instead he'd scan the audience 'and sort of sniff them out, like a dog smelling the wind,' Cyr said. 'He'd pull you into his space,' she said. 'That's how he'd rein an audience in and take them where he wanted to go.'

By the time of the Sin-E recording (and requisite photo shoot), Buckley had alienated Cyr, for reasons that she's long since forgotten. By now she'd learned that he was volatile and provocative. 'You'd have conflicts [with him]; he'd have those in his personal relationships with people. He'd piss you off and you'd be like, "Fuck off, I'm not going to talk to you anymore, you dick". That was how I felt about him at the time it came to shoot the Sin-E cover: "Ah, fuck that guy, he's an arsehole".'

It's not surprising that Buckley displayed the many sides of his temperament to Cyr early on; the relationship between a 'star' and a photographer can be both intimate and highly volatile. And, as Cyr admitted to me, her friendship with Buckley was a little unclear, intimacy-wise. 'I wasn't his girlfriend or anything, but that line was a little fuzzy sometimes. And I didn't want to be seen like a groupie.' Buckley liked to challenge people, pushing them until they either told him to go fuck himself (as Cyr had done) or bend over and let him have his way. 'You were being tested,' Cyr said. 'Then it was a challenge for him to win you back. This was a process I went through with him a lot.' But Cyr admits that Buckley's ample supply of charm and charisma made him almost impossible to hate forever. 'He respected you only if he thought you'd stand up to him. If you rolled over he wouldn't give you the time of day.'

There was an additional complication with the Sin-E shoot: Columbia had already hired a photographer. When Cyr did return Buckley's call, he told her to get to the label's office straight away. First up, Columbia staffers wanted to see her portfolio, and if they were happy with her work, Buckley needed to get someone at the label to 'un-hire' the other photographer. And quick. 'I had to watch this guy fire her over the phone,' Cyr recalled. 'That was on Friday and Monday was the day of the shoot.'*

---

* Cyr was puzzled by her brief trip to Black Rock, Sony's imposing HQ: she spotted one of her images, framed and hanging on the art director's wall, yet he'd never bothered returning her calls until she started working with Buckley. Like her subject, she was learning a lot about the machinations of the corporate world.

It was a day of firsts: it was Buckley's initial foray into the world of a major label and it was Cyr's debut shoot for a multi-national. Sin-E owner Shane Doyle was bemused, to say the least, as various Sony staff arrived in the morning, and a mobile recording unit was set up in the bar a few doors down. There were cords and cable running in all directions, as a few locals started to drift in, wondering what the hell was going on. 'The recording was never acknowledged,' insisted Leah Reid. 'It was more a case of we press the buttons and you do what you do.'

At one point, Shane Doyle grabbed Buckley and asked: 'How does this work? I'm supposed to get paid for this, right?' Quick as a flash, Buckley replied: 'Charge whatever you like, Shane, it's Sony Records.' When it was decided that a second day of recording was required, Doyle put in a call to Berkowitz. He said: 'What's the story with this? I guess I'll have to charge you the same amount.' When Berkowitz challenged him, saying that the exposure was surely worth far more, Doyle replied: 'I don't need it. You'll have to pay me for another gig.'*

Interestingly, Doyle had never considered recording any of the Sin-E action before. The way he saw it, that ran contrary to the spirit of the venue. 'There was no playing for the camera or a recording device,' he said. 'No one had any inhibitions; you could act the clown, you could be any way you wanted, you didn't have to think about it.' In some ways, *Live At Sin-E* marked the end of an era for Buckley and the venue. Both were now public property.

Even though Buckley had played enough shows at Sin-E to sing the setlist in his sleep, something didn't gel on the first day of recording, which comprised an afternoon and an evening set. It may well have been a simple case of jitters: after all, as Cyr recalled, at the start of the day she was the only person in the room not employed by Sony. 'He was scared of the company, he was scared of doing this first project, there were a bunch of business people there breathing down his neck,' she said. 'It was one of the biggest days of his life. And he was really afraid of failing. It was a very intense experience.' (Leah Reid disagrees with this. 'He wasn't being pressured to do anything,' she told me. 'At that point he realised it wasn't so much about a label as the people inside a label, people he could trust. It wasn't until later on that the

* Today Doyle admits that he had no idea how significant an artist Buckley would become, or how his name would be forever linked to Sin-E. 'In any event I never capitalised upon it, you know?'

pressure of Columbia Records became more of his day-to-day. Back then they gave him the time to be nurtured.')

During the first set the room was virtually empty, but by the evening Sin-E was packed with Buckley friends and fans. 'There were people spilling out the doors,' recalled Cyr. 'At that point he'd developed quite a following,' added Leah Reid. 'The afternoon shows were really just warm-ups, so it wasn't full by any means, just random people, but each night the shows were packed. There were more Columbia people than ever before, but there were also punters there, too.' Between the two sets, Buckley retired to Anseo, the bar two doors down from Sin-E, spread himself across a couple of stools and duly fell asleep, with his head resting in Cyr's lap. 'I remember feeling very protective of him,' said Cyr. 'I'm only a year and a half older than him but he just seemed so young and vulnerable.'

All the time, Cyr kept snapping away, documenting everything. During a break, the two walked to nearby Tompkins Square Park, where Cyr shot some images of Buckley that are now rated amongst the most candid portraits ever taken of the man. (And around which Cyr has built a formidable photographic career.) The one shot that summed up Buckley's first attempt to document his 'café days' was the image eventually used for the EP cover, another clear statement from Buckley that he was doing his best to stay in control of his career: the shot was incredibly revealing and laugh-out-loud funny. Early in the day, Cyr somehow found herself inside the venue, perched on a ladder – to this day she has no idea where it came from – while cradling a panoramic camera and a very wide lens. A soulful Buckley, strumming Janine Nichols' Fender (still on loan), appeared to be looking to the heavens for divine inspiration. A huge Sin-E banner was positioned behind him. So far, so obvious. But on closer examination, you can spot a Sin-E regular, within arm's reach of Buckley, flicking through his morning newspaper, totally oblivious to whatever, or whoever, this skinny white guy was channelling.

'It's hysterical,' Cyr said, 'he didn't give a shit. That was very brave of Jeff to pick that shot, but it also reflected how he felt. He saw himself as this dweeby guy. I think that changed later when he realised he could manipulate people, and get what he wanted, sex and stuff like that, but at that moment he was wide-eyed, a real goober, you know? He didn't want to be a Chris Isaak lookalike. He was this fucking goofball.' (To Cyr, Buckley was a mass of contradictions: he was a control freak, musical marvel, friend, employer, and a constant source of frustration. 'Musically, he was very mature, but emotionally he wasn't. That was confusing in relating to him because you would assume a certain maturity that he didn't possess.')

Amongst the cuts Buckley attempted during those two sets was a pair of originals – 'Eternal Life' and 'Unforgiven' – plus the usual slew of covers, including 'Strange Fruit', Morrison's 'The Way Young Lovers Do' and Dylan's 'Just Like A Woman' and 'If You See Her, Say Hello'. The latter pair were revealing choices for a guy at the end of his first 'real' relationship; one a savage putdown, the other a heartbreaking post mortem of a dead romance.

In the liner notes for the expanded Legacy edition of *Live At Sin-E*, Berkowitz wrote how Buckley was 'in pursuit of a lot of things... the pursuit of beauty, communication, sex, coffee, laughs, music, the pursuit of self.'[1] But Berkowitz didn't necessarily feel that much of this wild beauty was caught on the tapes from the original sessions. He convinced Buckley to return to Sin-E and try again, on a Tuesday, August 17, just to see what happened, even though the label – and Buckley, of course – was already many thousand production dollars down the drain. But Buckley also knew something was amiss; he told Hal Willner that he thought the Sin-E tapes stank. He said something similar to Kathryn Grimm, his old Group Therapy bandmate. 'Sin-E, well, he wasn't really thrilled about it,' she said. 'He was so critical of himself that he could hear every note that was out of tune.'

It was a vastly more confident and assured Buckley that was caught on tape the second time around. Barely taking the time to 'smell the room', he launched into a driving, sexy version of Nina Simone's 'Be Your Husband', powered by nothing more than his mad-dog howl and stomping Doc Martens. There was no chirpy hello, no nervous patter, no jokes – he truly let his voice (and boots) do the talking.

Buckley proceeded to work through what could best be called a Sin-E's 'greatest hits' set, including almost all of the songs he'd attempted three weeks back, as well as Dylan's 'I Shall Be Released', and 'Dink's Song', a hangover from his Gods And Monsters days, plus a much-improved run-through of 'Lover, You Should Have Come Over', a lean, stunning 'Mojo Pin' and his reading of 'The Man That Got Away', 'borrowed' from Judy Garland's version first heard on the film *A Star Is Born*. He also produced a stark rendition of 'Strange Fruit' and dazzling versions of Van Morrison's 'Sweet Thing' and 'The Way Young Lovers Do'. Led Zeppelin's 'Night Flight', a hidden gem from their *Physical Graffiti* album that Buckley had actually shelved a few months back, was another standout, ditto 'Calling You', which now actually sounded more like a valentine to Sin-E – 'coffee machine that needs some fixing/at a little café just 'round the bend' – than a lift from a popular 'fish out of water' indie flick.

Once he'd set the mood, Buckley quite visibly relaxed, and the 'human jukebox' switched on. He searched for a missing chord to a Duane Eddy tune (helped out by an audience member), and experimented with reverb, which led to a quick strum through The Doors' 'The End', delivered Nico-style, where he playfully swapped the 'mother' of the lyric with 'Sony' (as in 'Jeff?' 'Yes, Sony?' 'I want to *aaaahhhhhhh* you'). This could have turned very ugly, but Buckley managed to avoid turning a cheeky piss-take into a very public slap in the face. Possibly there was some antipathy simmering under the surface, or maybe it was just another of Buckley's tests: how far could he push his new bosses until someone told him to back off? This he'd find out soon enough.

Buckley also toyed with the faithful when he went into his usual 'Nusrat is my Elvis' spiel. Initially, the crowd thought it was another example of Buckley's playfulness, but then he dropped into a near-flawless impression of the almost-impossible-to-impersonate Pakistani. (The piece was called 'Yeh Jo Halka Halka Saroor Hai', in case you needed to know, Buckley's first introduction to Nusrat.) When he finally stopped wailing, several bewildering minutes later, you could almost hear the sound of numerous jaws dropping to the floor. It was that powerful.

Columbia's Leah Reid, who was looking on, knew that the Sin-E recording, when it finally reached the stores, was the ideal introduction to the label's new signing – and it would also provide the breathing space Buckley needed to write and find the band that he was so desperately seeking. 'We did get to capture the moment, but we also took the pressure off [his first studio recording],' said Reid. 'We were able to work more organically, more grassroots. It's not like the radio promo department [was going] to get a song from the *Sin-E* record on the radio.' Sony's president Don Ienner, however, nixed Buckley's plan to name the Sin-E EP *Café Days*, as a nod to a line from his beloved Joni Mitchell's 'The Last Time I Saw Richard'. When a mock-up crossed Ienner's desk, he put a large slash through the proposed title, and declared that it should henceforth be known as *Live At Sin-E*. Clearly Buckley's creative control didn't extend into marketing. (Incidentally, the round coffee mug stain on the *Sin-E* cover is real; it was scanned from a coaster saved by a Sony staffer who was at the show.)

Buckley held back 'Hallelujah', now the centrepiece of his set, until the very end of that second recording. The version that would be heard on 2003's complete *Sin-E*, while lacking the sonic bells and whistles of the 'definitive' *Grace* take, was near-flawless, Buckley wringing every last drop of emotion from both his almost-spent voice (and a guitar that drifted in and out of tune) and Cohen's wise, witty, occasionally baffling lyric. It was the perfect song with which to sign off his café days. 'That's all, man,' he managed to utter at the end. 'Let's go drink and sleep.'

Buckley may have struggled with songwriting and fidelity, but he was always moving forward, seeking out new sensations and directions. Cyr was amongst those who felt it confirmed Buckley's suspicion that, just like his father, he wasn't destined for a life of 'three-score-years-and-ten'. 'I believed that he felt he had a limited time. I think he was trying to shove a lot of stuff into his short life, to get as much experience as he could,' she said. 'He wanted to have all these relationships in a full intense way, but in a short time, so I think when he was with somebody he was totally with them.'

With that in mind, and the Sin-E recording finally in the bag, he started to seek out a band in earnest. After several months of scratching around, Buckley was now operating in fast-forward. As Buckley himself admitted in the EPK that helped promote *Grace*, 'I was dying to be with the band, dying for the relationship. You know, the chemistry, people, warm bodies, male, female, you know, bass, drums, dulcimer, tuba, anything, anyway that the band would work out – marching bass drum, whatever.'[2]

In June, he and Berkowitz had met with producer Andy Wallace, who'd first broken through with his work on the 1986 Aerosmith/Run DMC rap/rock crossover smash 'Walk This Way'. He was best known for his mix of Nirvana's *Nevermind*, an album that had transformed three straggly-looking punks into unlikely solid-gold superstars (at Sin-E, Buckley had somehow managed to turn their 'Smells Like Teen Spirit' into a qawwali chant – Nusrat Nirvana). But the bearded, avuncular, 46-year-old Wallace was anticipating a Buckley record along the lines of Sin-E; a vocal showcase, in short. As a solo act, he found Buckley 'magnetic and magical'. But this wasn't what Buckley had in mind, because he'd just kissed his one-man-band days goodbye. Wallace confessed his uncertainty. 'It was very tempting to say, "Yeah, it's got to be all about that", but Jeff, thankfully, was very convinced about doing the band and moving to the next place he had to move to.'[3]

Buckley's first move was to recruit bassist Mick Grondahl, whom he'd met briefly in March, after a show at Columbia University's Post Crypt Café. Though born in Denmark, the 25-year-old Grondahl had grown up in New York, where he was raised by his divorced mother, who owned a cosmetics business. Although Grondahl was never so crass as to talk about wealth, there were suggestions that he came from a 'monied' family. And he wasn't the most upbeat of characters; he was described to me as 'gripey and complain-ey' and 'snobbish'. 'Mick... was a little bit of a shit. He was a little too cool for everyone, he was more of a snob than the rest of them,' said

Mark Naficy, Buckley's long-time soundman. (During our lengthy inter-view, it would be fair to describe Grondahl as polite yet detached.) Just like Mary Guibert, Grondahl's mother was an avid music fan, and introduced her cherubic-faced son to what would now be called 'world music', which Grondahl described as 'bazuki, flamenco, Middle Eastern music'. At the same time she would also play him Talking Heads' groundbreaking LP *Fear Of Music*. 'She had a very open ear to new stuff,' he said.[4]

Grondahl started playing the drums at 12, and shifted to bass when he was 16. He'd met a lot of wannabe guitarists, so he figured that there had to be vacancies for reasonably skilled bassists. Influenced by such classy players as jazzman Stanley Clarke, it also didn't take him long to figure out that 'there is a whole range of things you can do with the instrument'. Almost immedi-ately he was playing in high school bands, but most of them stayed in the garage. 'We couldn't get into bars, not even in New York,' he said. While studying fine arts at college in Saratoga Springs, majoring in art history but also dabbling in sculpture (especially stone carving) and photography, Grondahl continued playing, mainly in a band that mixed funk and reggae standards with covers. Already he was showing the type of anything-goes musical spirit that would prove useful when backing Buckley. His attitude, even then, was: 'Have fun with it, improvise, let's see what happens.' But music was still a hobby for Grondahl; it wasn't until he returned to New York, after graduating, that he considered it as a possible career, answering some 'bass player wanted' ads in the *Village Voice*. But nothing gelled for him. 'I would be in the band for a while,' said the softly spoken Grondahl, 'and if I wasn't happy with it, I would immediately quit. I was kind of disenchanted.'

At the time he met Buckley, Grondahl was in another dead-end band named Glories, who shared rehearsal space with Daniel Harnett's group Glim, who were also on the Columbia University bill with Buckley. Grondahl tagged along, primarily to see his friend's band play. He watched Buckley's set for around an hour, more out of curiosity than anything else. 'I knew nothing about him,' Grondahl told me in 2007. He didn't link Buckley to his famous father until they met again, soon after, at a party. But even Tim Buckley didn't register that strongly with Grondahl. 'I knew him a little bit from sightings in the record bins and stuff,' he said off-handedly. And Tim Buckley certainly wasn't a point of discussion between him and Jeff at the party. Grondahl recalled how they chatted about 'Howling Wolf or something'.

In July, Grondahl spotted Buckley's name in the *Village Voice*; he was play-ing a solo set at Fez as part of the New Music Seminar. Although he didn't have any cash, Grondahl dropped by the venue, with his friend Cynthia in tow. His luck was in: Buckley saw Grondahl and snuck him into the gig. 'Jeff just popped out of nowhere,' he recalled, 'recognised me and we exchanged numbers.' This time around, Grondahl was far more impressed by Buckley's one-man-and-a-Fender approach. 'He'd improved enormously in that time; he'd made huge advances. It was better than the first show; I was knocked out.' In 2007, when asked what was his most vivid memory of Buckley, Grondahl cited this Fez set. 'He walked out with such determination,' said Grondahl, 'and got to the mic and started pounding his feet and doing this rhythm, while singing "Johnny Lee". And he kept pounding his feet and singing. There was nobody talking; nothing. It was just so powerful.'

Grondahl made the next move, calling Buckley a few weeks later and suggesting a jam. (In 1995, Buckley admitted that Grondahl was 'so honest, frank and sincere that I knew I'd have to call him back'.[5] They got together very late in Buckley's apartment for what turned out to be the most inspired jamming of Grondahl's career. 'It was magical,' he told me. 'I really felt, without sounding too airy-fairy, that there were angels present in the apartment while we were playing.' What amazed Grondahl was the fact that they barely knew each other yet 'there was this strong connection that I'd never felt with anyone else. It just seemed like a dream, mythic.' The pair recorded their noodling, on a new Mini Disc recorder that Buckley had scammed from Sony. Known in Buckley folklore as 'The Angel Tape', Grondahl still has a copy, even thought it's barely audible. (Buckley was wary of the neighbours, it being the middle of the night and all.) 'It ended up on really low volume on the tape,' recalled Grondahl, 'and I still wonder whether it did really happen at all, without sounding too strange or obscure. It just had this huge impression on me.'

Speaking in June 1994, Buckley was just as enthused, describing their jam as 'two-o'clock-in-the-morning-type-music'. 'He had all the qualities I dug,' said Buckley. 'There are bass players all over the city that can play rings around him in terms of technique, but nobody else could ever make the music he makes. And that's more powerful.'[6] According to Grondahl, Buckley admired his ability to keep things 'low key'. 'He said he'd experienced a lot of busy bass players and he liked the fact that I was more simple, more methodical in constructing bass figures. When I started out with Jeff I felt that he needed to stay "in front", there was already so much in his voice and guitar. I tried to stay out as much as possible, but when I did come in, I felt that it was mostly to support him. Once that was established I could meander a bit and explore the tonal range.'

The hiring of Grondahl typified Buckley's attitude towards his band. While he could have easily hired road-hardened 'cats', who could match him note-for-note, he seemed intent on finding players that he could connect with personally and musically – and, although he didn't say it out loud, he was probably also looking for musos that would give him the necessary room on-stage to let him work his magic. These guys weren't likely to compete with Buckley; they were there to support him, not challenge him. Gary Lucas considered them to be some 'hand-picked band of young acolytes'. Leah Reid, for one, could see that these guys weren't quite on Buckley's level as players. 'Mick wasn't the greatest songwriter or musician and he felt that maybe he would never get this chance again. Michael [Tighe] would never become a road-weary session guy, and Matt [Johnson] wasn't the best drummer. But it worked.' And it must have pleased his label enormously that the group of 20-somethings he hired all possessed brooding good looks, making them an easier, if not necessarily easy, sell.

Grondahl may have been turned on by the chance to play alongside Buckley, but when he was hired, and then told that he had all of six weeks to get in shape for the *Grace* recording sessions at Woodstock, he started to doubt himself. On two separate occasions he said to Buckley, 'I don't know if I can do this, you may need to get someone better.' Buckley paused, and in a gesture that dispelled all of Grondahl's fears, looked him straight in the eyes and stated: 'No, you're the man.' 'He could tell I was down for the ride,' said Grondahl, 'and that's what he was looking for in musicians.'

Grondahl, however, remains unsure whether Buckley's choice as drummer, Matt Johnson – the first tub-thumper to audition, incidentally – was totally 'down for the ride'. Described by Leah Reid as ' warm and kind and generous, [with] this great smile,' Johnson was a Hollywood-handsome 22-year-old Texan, who'd been living in New York for only four years, playing in a band called the Choosy Mothers and also drumming for singer Dorothy Scott, who'd helped Buckley score his Sin-E residency. A friend of Rebecca Moore had recommended him to Buckley. After finding a message on his answering machine from 'a raspy-voiced Jeff Buckley', as he recalled in *The Making Of Grace* EPK, Johnson first met with Grondahl and Buckley in Context, a New York rehearsal space.

Though not as 'magical' as the 'angel jam' between Buckley and Grondahl, there were sparks, nonetheless: the framework of the track 'Dream Brother' came to them within the first couple of hours of playing. (Buckley had a knack for writing songs during first meetings: he'd also done this with Gary Lucas and later on with Michael Tighe.) It began when Buckley turned to Grondahl and asked: 'Do you have any grooves?' The bassist started to play something he'd actually discarded from a previous jam, and Johnson settled into what Grondahl described as 'this really nice cymbal and snare and bass drum kind of figure'[7] Buckley then began to play a 'snakelike pattern'. Grondahl, for one, wasn't sure that the song was flying – his initial reaction was 'Oh God, this form sounds really bad', partly because he was using a 'crappy' amp and was also having trouble muting his strings – but they continued, and the jam, in Grondahl's words, 'started to take off more and more'. Straight away, Buckley knew he'd found his guy; as the instrumental wound down he told Johnson he should join the band. 'I asked Matt what he was doing the next few months,' Buckley said in *The Making Of Grace*, 'and he said nothing was going on, which wasn't quite true. Maybe nothing special, but he had this whole life that I was upsetting. So was Mick. Things were happening fast and I kind of ruined their lives and made a new one.'[8]

The Grifters' Dave Shouse, soon to become a Buckley insider, recalled hearing a story from Johnson about that jam. '[Johnson] said that the first time all three of them played, Jeff didn't play any songs or sing, he just did these weird guitar pattern things, because he wanted to make sure that he took a person's safety net out of play,' he said. 'Sometimes being a really good musician doesn't always cut it. Jeff wasn't sure who he was playing with and kind of said, "Let's all be green at once." Intuition, that's what he was looking for.'

A few days after that night at Context, Leah Reid collected Buckley to drive him to a gig in Philadelphia. 'He had a mini disc,' she said, 'and he told me, "I jammed with Matt Johnson." And in my head I was thinking, "*The guy from The The?*" I didn't want to not be cool, but I just couldn't understand why he'd be playing the drums with Jeff.' This just went to show that while Johnson may have been a drummer of repute in certain dark corners of New York, he was no Keith Moon.

Yet almost immediately, Grondahl, at least, sensed that Johnson's attitude towards the band differed to his. 'Part of the situation with Matt Johnson,' he said to me, 'was that he wasn't necessarily down for the ride in the long term. He was more focused on doing this for a while and then moving onto another thing.' (In hindsight, Grondahl was spot on: Johnson has since played with Rufus Wainwright, Joan Wasser, Beth Orton and many others and is now one of the most in-demand timekeepers in modern rock.) Grondahl's attitude towards Buckley was different. 'We wanted to be like The Beatles and continue on and on,' he said. 'So that was an issue.'

Grondahl, however, stressed that Johnson was 'super talented' and 'easy to work with musically'. And even though they came from very different places on the map – Europe and New York in Grondahl's case, 'trailer trash' California with Buckley, and Texas and Ohio, in the case of Johnson – they 'shared the same sense of humour,' according to Grondahl. 'There were some differences, but we related really well, laughed a lot and felt good about each other's playing.' He emphasised that the 'deeper part' of their connection happened through music, not some craving for chicks and dope, like so many bands (although Grondahl would have trouble with the latter in the near future). '[Music] was the thing that stitched us together,' he said.

One thing that Johnson did share with Grondahl, at least at the start of their Grace odyssey, was a sense of panic: the trio was now only weeks away from heading to Bearsville studio in Woodstock and starting work on Buckley's 'proper' debut. 'It was very, very quick, very shocking,' he said in *The Making Of Grace*, 'to go from meeting someone to playing with them and then recording a few weeks later. It was really scary.' If anything, Columbia's Berkowitz was relieved when Johnson was hired. '[Until then] I was concerned a lot as to where he would find a drummer that could hang with him,' he confessed.[9] Mike Webb, Berkowitz's assistant, gives due credit to his boss for allowing Buckley to hire such a bunch of greenhorns. 'Within himself he knew Jeff could choose better guys but within his heart he wanted Jeff to make the album he wanted to make.'

Grondahl once described their six weeks shut away in New York's Context Studio as a 'kamikaze mission', but he tones that down today. 'I think what I meant by that was that it was too strong; we were just very full-on, we lived and breathed that music for six weeks. [But] it was exciting to work with him. We were all constantly discovering new things and new approaches, new ways to attack the songs, and that kept us going.' Producer Andy Wallace dropped by Context two or three times a week. 'We'd be blasting away, jamming, and he'd be taking notes,' Grondahl recalled. At one stage, Wallace turned to Buckley and asked: 'Is this song meant to be 15 minutes long?' Buckley smiled and replied: 'Well, could be, right?' Wallace admitted that it very well could be the case, but he didn't hear the structure. Not yet, anyway. 'It was clear after talking with Jeff about it that they were just jamming. He was, at the same time, I think, really trying to grab things that worked arrangement-wise.'[10] Wallace was too polite – or possibly too scared of the possible response – to ask the key question: 'Where are the songs?'

Within a few months, Jeff Buckley's career had shifted from cruise control to hyper-speed: he'd gone from a Monday night residency at Sin-E hanging with Tree Man to near boiling point. He barely had times to shake hands with Grondahl and Johnson before they were to be shut away in one of the most renowned (and expensive) studios in the USA. And it's worth bearing in mind that Johnson and Grondahl were as 'green' as Buckley when it came to working in a major studio like Bearsville. 'We weren't sea-soned professionals,' said Grondahl. 'I'd had some experience, but more home-made studios and what not, not 24-track studios.' Established in 1969 by the imposing figure of Albert Grossman, Bob Dylan's first manager, Bearsville studio had been instrumental (pun intended) in the creation of such albums as R.E.M.'s *Automatic For The People* and *Green*, The Band's *Cahoots* and *Get Close* from The Pretenders. It wasn't the kind of space that was used by novices. It was a massive risk on the part of Columbia: there was every chance they'd be kissing several hundred thousand dollars goodbye, and if it fell apart it could have spelled the end of very brief musical careers for Buckley, Grondahl and Johnson. And Buckley certainly didn't have an album's worth of new material ready for recording; he was incredibly fortu-nate that the nucleus for 'Dream Brother' emerged from his first jam with Johnson.

Nonetheless, Buckley's stock was very much on the rise within the cor-ridors of 'Black Rock'. Leah Reid witnessed that first hand during one of Buckley's regular visits to her office. It was her birthday, and a cake had been organised. 'He came and got me from my office – and everyone swarmed all over him. It was like, "ooh, that's weird".' The key-jangling guy who until recently had been studiously ignored by staffers was suddenly a very hot property. According to Mike Webb, 'The women at Columbia were all giddy about the guy.' It was like Sin-E all over again.

Late September 1993 wasn't too bad a time to be alive. Execs at Columbia, for one, were chuffed; no less than three of their hit-makers – Billy Joel, Mariah Carey and scruffy rockers Soul Asylum – were riding high in the US Top 20 with 'Dreamlover', 'The River Of Dreams' and 'Runaway Train', respectively. And the scrawny 26-year-old who could well be their next superstar was unpacking his bags and taking the country air in Woodstock, a rural retreat with a weighty musical history. Bob Dylan, who had broken his neck there, had made some of his finest music with The Band at Big Pink, their Woodstock HQ (as heard on the legendary *Basement Tapes*). There was also the music festival at nearby Bethel in 1969, 'three days of peace and love and joy', as the heady, epic *Woodstock* rockumentary informed those who weren't amongst the half-million or so mud-caked hippies who witnessed career-defining sets by Joe Cocker, Santana, Country Joe McDonald, The Who and many others.

But the area's musical past wasn't necessarily the reason that Bearsville Studio was chosen for the *Grace* sessions, at least not in the case of Buckley. 'Somebody Jeff's age and temperament,' producer Andy Wallace told me with a very significant pause, when we spoke in 2002, 'well, there was bound to be plenty of distractions in the city.' (Buckley backed this up in *The Making Of Grace*. 'I'm an easily distracted person,' he admitted, as Ernie Fritz's camera tried to keep up as he wandered along some rustic Woodstock back road. 'So this is great.') Wallace, who'd worked at Bearsville with R.E.M., also had more traditional reasons for choosing Bearsville. 'There's a real music history there,' Wallace said. 'And the main building is huge; it has two studios and a residential apartment. Studio A has a huge live room – airplane-hangar huge. It's a beautiful sounding room.' Buckley summed it up neatly when he sat down, looked around him, uttered a few words to test Studio A's acoustics and said, simply: 'This room is awesome.'

Producer Steve Addabbo, who'd recorded a solo Buckley in New York, wasn't entirely sure that Bearsville was the right choice. 'It's a very big studio and it can be very impersonal, the room is about 40 by 80 with this huge ceiling. Very cavernous. It's on a grand scale and to go up there for your first record... The thing that is great is that you're living there all together. I love that atmosphere, that woodshedding, an isolated, concentrated environment.'

For the band, Bearsville and Woodstock, despite its distance from New York, was actually a relief after the intense sessions at Context. This type of cabin fever was far preferable. 'It was late September,' said Grondahl, 'and the leaves were changing, we were living together, getting to know each other, listening to The Cocteau Twins and whatever music we liked. And we were sharing time together, which we hadn't the time to before, when we were really thrown together. It was good to have a change of scene,' he added. 'Going to Bearsville was fantastic.'

Buckley, Johnson and Grondahl would record with Wallace on weekdays, while at the weekends, the producer left Bearsville to see his family, so they'd either check out their surroundings or return to New York. 'It was a really fun time,' said Grondahl. 'We were trekking around, seeing the deer walking along the creek. It was quite cosy, a welcome change. It was perfect for where we were at then: we could focus on the music but we were close enough to New York to resume our social life.'

The ever-savvy Wallace worked hard to create the right mood in the studio, so he arranged to have several distinctly different 'set-ups' available to Buckley at all times. 'There was a loud, electric set-up,' said Steve Berkowitz in *The Making Of Grace*, 'an acoustic set-up and like a one-person folk club set-up. And everything was miked.'[11] The concept was ideal: Buckley could either work out songs with the band and Wallace – most of the writing and arranging took place in Woodstock – or cool off by playing covers and

137

curios, just as he had at Sin-E. And Buckley's attitude was definitely any-thing goes: one morning Wallace clocked on for duty and Buckley was tear-ing a hole through 'Hocus Pocus', a chaotic collision of yodelling and soloing from Dutch prog-rockers Focus.

All up, Buckley recorded at least an album's worth of covers while in Bearsville, including numerous stabs at Dylan's 'Mama, You've Been On My Mind', 'Just Like A Woman' and 'If You See Her, Say Hello', along with takes on Cohen's 'Hallelujah' (also in several different flavours), Led Zep's 'Night Flight', the blues chestnuts 'Parchman Farm Blues' and 'Dink's Song', plus his gravel-and-sand assault on Screamin' Jay Hawkins' 'Alligator Wine', a rave-up that clearly gave Buckley the chance to blow off any built-up steam. Most of the covers were done in the morning, before Buckley attempted to nail vocal takes on the album's 'proper' songs. 'He'd do that more or less to warm up and get his voice started,' said Grondahl. (Or, in the case of 'Alligator Wine', discover if it really was possible to cough up a lung while singing.) 'He did a lot of covers,' said Wallace, 'and a couple of very funny things, [including] a take of an old Delta blues that had us cracking up.'[12] (It wasn't all laughs in the studio, though; Wallace was nicknamed 'The Fist' for his habit of illustrating a point by thumping the console.)

A few weeks in, Leah Reid swung by Bearsville, with director Ernie Fritz and his film crew in tow. As she recalled, her luck was in: Buckley was attempting to cut definitive vocals for 'Grace' and 'Hallelujah'. 'It was a good day,' she laughed. Buckley's perfectionist streak was on full display; after swooning and crooning his way through a remarkable 'Hallelujah', he turned to the awestruck production crew, who were filming everything for the Sony EPK, shrugged and said: 'It was OK.' Reid laughed it off as typical Buckley. 'These guys are blown away and he thought it was OK,' she said. 'It was an incredible opportunity to experience him doing that in the studio but at the same time, with the camera crew there, he felt the presence of "the machine". He was very aware. There were uncomfortable moments for him, where he thought, "Oh, oh, it's starting." So it was a day of mixed bless-ings. He performed this magical song but then we'd be strapping a micro-phone on him so we could walk up this gravel road in Woodstock and do an interview.'

Another Bearsville drop-in was guitarist Gary Lucas. Buckley, in another demonstration of his almost over-powering sense of loyalty, invited his for-mer bandmate to place his avant-garde stamp on 'Grace' and 'Mojo Pin', despite the messy falling out they'd had at the end of Gods And Monsters. (Admittedly, Lucas co-wrote both songs, so there was also some payback involved.) While Lucas was in the studio, Buckley began working on the vocals for the album's title track. 'He came out of the booth with this sheep-ish, little boy look, like "Did I do good?"' Lucas recalled. 'He knew it was fucking great.'[13]*

Karl Berger, an acclaimed Woodstock-based jazz composer, arranger, pianist and vibraphonist, also dropped by, adding sweeping string arrange-ments to several *Grace* tracks. Buckley was in awe of the 58–year-old peer and pal of jazzman Ornette Coleman, whose greying temples and glasses suggested a college professor rather than a jazz great. As Buckley declared, 'It's like having a regal visitation, having someone arrange for strings. He can do, you know, a chord progression with strings that makes [a song] com-pletely different. It was a really great treat.'[14]

The recording of 'Mojo Pin', which came about three weeks into the ses-sions, was a key moment for Buckley and the band: it finally seemed that, after a few hit-and-miss weeks, some sonic sparks had started to fly. But this discovery didn't come to them in the studio; instead, it sunk in as they motored around Woodstock in a rented van, listening closely to a cassette (their preferred method of reviewing works-in-progress). 'It was such a privilege,' Grondahl said, 'because you could drive around listening to it in such a precise, acute way. You could just hear it so much better – it was a really good gauge of what the song was doing, whether it needed anything more.' Grondahl recalled how they felt that 'Mojo Pin' – which was cut in one take – 'was the point when all of a sudden things turned into something more. Before that it was coming along, but now you could hear a certain potential for how other songs could be defined.' Steve Berkowitz agreed. He was amazed how this song that stretched to almost five minutes felt any-thing but drawn out. It was almost Dylan-esque.

Speaking in *Everybody Here Wants You*, Berkowitz felt that this was really the leaping-off point for the making of *Grace* (although Grondahl felt that Berkowitz was exaggerating when I repeated the following statement to him). 'This volcanic eruption of artistry came booming out of him, that was just wild,' said Berkowitz, with the type of fervour usually reserved for polit-ical rallies. 'It was hundreds of ideas, guitar parts, vocal parts, backwards parts, extra drum parts and tablas – baboom!'[15]

Drummer Johnson didn't share Berkowitz's unbridled enthusiasm, as he admitted in the same documentary. 'As I was playing I was thinking, this is so over-the-top, this has got to be sucking. Then I'd listen back and think,

---

* King Buzzo, of psychedelic grunge band the Melvins, became an unlikely friend of Buckley's when he dropped by the studio.

this is kind of garish, that voice going up really high like that at the end, dragging along with this outro, with these descending chords and this high vibrato on the voice. Then I went, no, *this is really great*.'[16] 'Mojo Pin' may have been a major moment for Grondahl, but Johnson felt that 'Dream Brother', even in its vocal-less, lyric-less form, was his personal turning point. 'I thought it'd never make the record,' he confessed. 'It was this droney, Eastern thing, like a backing music for a mantra or some big Led Zeppelin thing. When he came up with that melody, I heard it over the headphones and I thought it was amazing, so beautiful. I never would have thought of that melody in a million years.'[17]

Five weeks in, though, as the *Grace* sessions drew to a close, something unspoken lingered in the air at Woodstock: Buckley simply didn't have sufficient material to fill an album; certainly not enough originals, anyway. (By this stage they'd recorded 'Mojo Pin', 'Grace', 'Last Goodbye', 'Lover, You Should Have Come Over', 'Eternal Life' and 'Forget Her', which failed to make the final cut.) As Johnson reflected, 'We didn't have enough songs to make a, you know, "Jeff Buckley wrote every song kind of record". At least he didn't have enough songs that he liked. He might have had them but he didn't pull them out.'[18]

Buckley's stump-speech, when the album was finally done, was that he decided to include the numerous covers – 'Hallelujah', 'Corpus Christi Carol' and 'Lilac Wine' – in a concerted attempt to 'link this album to my past'. While there's little doubt that Columbia always intended for some Sin-E era songs to make the record, the reality was more likely that Buckley was either reluctant to unveil any new songs he had – or possibly he had nothing left, just as Johnson suggested. The mixture of his stifling creative inertia, and relentless perfectionism, which would really come into full view a couple of years later when attempting a follow-up to *Grace*, was obviously a problem for Buckley as early as 1993. Lee Underwood believed that Jeff suffered a sort of 'neurotic inner division' when he wrote; in short, he feared being compared to his father. Underwood wrote about this in private notes for his book *Blue Melody: Tim Buckley Remembered*. 'It seems to me that if Jeff paid his respects to Tim and did it honestly, opened his arms to Tim, embraced Tim with love and acceptance and appreciation, that he would heal this terrible wound that is dividing him and setting him at war – not against Tim – but against himself. If he does acknowledge his biological and musical influences, he reunites himself with his father, stops alienating everyone who liked Tim, and, most importantly, frees himself from this rather sad, self-destructive, neurotic inner division.'[19] (Underwood, nonetheless, remains a huge admirer of Buckley's work, praising his voice, 'his intensity' and his 'improvisational courage'. 'He's not getting all this recognition for nothing,' he wrote while Buckley was still alive. 'He's a first-rate contemporary artist and deserves every ounce of respect and appreciation he receives from audiences and the press.')

The closest that Buckley ever came to addressing this turmoil was when he referred to the overall album as 'an elegy, sort of a child's coffin... full of past ghosts, exorcised in song'.[20-22] Certainly none of his bandmates were bold – or tacky – enough to ask about the impact, positive or otherwise, his father had on his work. 'I had the suspicion that to talk about that would have been bad taste,' Grondahl figured. 'I wouldn't feel inclined to go up to Ziggy Marley and go, "*Rastaman Vibration* is the greatest album".' A few years later, though, Buckley did sit down with Grondahl and talk through his 'father issues'. 'He forgave his father and didn't want to hold this anger, this weight, against him,' Grondahl told me. 'He was very sincere about that.' Grondahl wasn't so sure that Buckley had resolved his concerns with his mother, however. 'I feel like he still had some difficulty with her, right up until he passed away.'

Though still a song or two shy of a completed album, the Bearsville sessions had been rewarding enough for Buckley and his new band, as they packed away their gear in late October and returned to the city. Wallace had added the necessary brawn and brain to Buckley's originals, especially the emphatic 'Eternal Life', at the same time keeping most of his covers in a relatively pristine state. Meanwhile, back at Black Rock, Sony boss Don Ienner was impressed by the rough mixes being sent down from Woodstock. 'He was always supportive of Jeff,' said Leah Reid, 'but that's when he sensed there was a commercial potential. It was a genius move to get Andy Wallace for that record. So it was at that point that Donny got vocal. It was one of those things that people sensed; he'd mention Jeff's name in a meeting and you'd go, "That's who he likes." Once Donny was in, everyone wanted a piece of it.'

Not everyone at Columbia HQ shared this opinion, though. Mike Webb, who'd listen to the rough mixes with Berkowitz, could see what Wallace was doing with Buckley's songs: he was giving them a radio-friendly sheen. The first thing he and Berkowitz heard were rough tapes of Buckley playing solo, followed by basic band recordings, 'and that was great stuff. Then we heard the Andy Wallace mixes and we went... *hmmm*. He clogged the sound right into the middle [of the mix], for radio. What I heard before was much bigger and better than what Andy did.' He cited the removal of a guitar part from 'Eternal Life' as one example of Wallace's sonic intervention.

141

'Andy should not have done what he did,' Webb said. (He nominated Daniel Lanois or Hal Willner as producers who might have done a better job. 'Jeff needed someone very creative, someone who could make sure the tape was rolling and then encourage him: "Go for it! Go for it!" ')

Buckley, Grondahl and Johnson had clearly formed a bond during the past few months; while they weren't necessarily ready for group hugs, there was a chemistry building between them that would truly come to fruition once they took this album on the road (with the addition of guitarist Michael Tighe, who'd soon get on board). But all this was still some way in the future: right now, Buckley had to journey back to his past and start talking up *Live At Sin-E*. He was also about to have an uncomfortable encounter with his biggest idol of all, Bob Dylan, in a poorly handled reminder that he may not have been Sony's golden-haired boy after all.

Notes

1. Berkowitz, Steve: Liner notes, *Live At Sin-E*, Legacy Edition, 2003 Columbia Records
2. Fritz, Ernie: Columbia Records: Grace EPK
3. See note 2
4. Keleman, Gayle: Mick Grondahl interview, www.jeffbuckley.com, November 2, 1995
5. Perret, Philippe: Get Your Soul Out, *Les Inrockuptibles*
6. Diehl, Matt: The Son Also Rises... *Rolling Stone*, October 20, 1994
7. See note 2
8. See note 4
9. See note 2
10. See note 2
11. See note 2
12. Irvin, Jim: It's Never Over, *Mojo*, August 1997
13. See note 12
14. See note 2
15. BBC2 *Everybody Here Wants You* documentary
16. See note 15
17. See note 15
18. See note 2
19. Underwood, Lee: *Blue Melody: Tim Buckley Remembered*, Backbeat Books, 2002
20. Smith, Andrew: His Father's Son, *The Sunday Times*, June 8, 1997
21. Creswell, Toby: Grace Under Fire, *Juice*, February 1996
22. www.jeffbuckley.com

Chapter Seven

On The Road

In November 1993, with little in the way of corporate fanfare, the EP briefly known as *Café Days* was finally released. Columbia's expectations were realistic, although they couldn't have predicted that the four-track EP and its subsequent double disc Legacy companion would become such steady sellers over the years. Leah Reid and others at Columbia understood completely that the EP was never going to be a mainstream hit. As she admitted, 'At this point it was more about the alternative marketing people, college marketing, it was their baby. It allowed us the perfect set-up for the album.'

Reid and other true believers at Columbia figured that the best thing they could do with Buckley was to simply spread the word, by whatever means possible. 'It was more like, "Let's turn people on",' she recalled. 'You'd spend a day going into record shops and letting people in on your secret. At the same time it wasn't something that everyone understood, some would simply not get it. And I was like, "That's OK, that's fine, I'll move on and find someone who does".' The term 'hype-free' was kicked around like a football; the goal was to establish Buckley as a credible, 'serious' artist, even though they knew he'd be a tough fit with the rigid American radio formats (which goes a long way toward explaining his subsequent Australian success, where both commercial and non-mainstream radio are more tolerant and less format-driven than their US counterparts).

The selection of songs for *Live At Sin-E* was another astute move on the part of Columbia, combining two Buckley originals – 'Mojo Pin' and 'Eternal Life' – with a pair of covers: Morrison's 'The Way Young Lovers Do', an outstanding showcase for Buckley's voice and guitar, and 'Je N'en

Connais Pas La Fin' (or 'I Don't Know The End Of It' in English), a nod to his broad range of influences, in this case, French songbird Edith Piaf. The EP showed that he was more than the human jukebox; he could also write his own material (as strained as that process proved to be for Buckley). Reviews came in a trickle rather than a flood. *Guitar Player* drew valid comparisons with Robert Plant, Nusrat Fateh Ali Khan and, surprisingly, the Metal Guru himself, T Rex's Marc Bolan, while paying due respect to Buckley's stringwork and its shades of 'funk, Gypsy jazz and early punk'.[1] Australian daily, *The Age*, was underwhelmed. 'One guitar, one amp, one trendy New York café, one sensitive New Age *tres* serious muso,' they sniped. 'One big yawn.'[2] Buckley's acclaim south of the equator would come soon enough, but this was a less-than-brilliant beginning.

The *Denver Post*, in what would become pretty much the norm for every Jeff Buckley-related profile, review and feature, mentioned his father – whose name was noticeably absent in the bio material that accompanied *Live At Sin-E* – noting that it was curious how Buckley had chosen to cover a song from Morrison's *Astral Weeks*. 'That album and Tim Buckley's *Happy/Sad*, from the same year, were as close as anyone got to mixing pop music's finest elements into an elixir of sound that floated dream-like in and out of a listener's consciousness,' their breathless reviewer gasped, before admitting: 'I don't like *Live At Sin-E* that much.' There was one concession, though; they considered Buckley's spin on 'The Way Young Lovers Do' 'a smashing success'.[3] The *Austin American-Statesman* observed that the Buckley bloodline was 'impossible to deny', comparing him to a younger Robert Plant and declaring that he displayed 'a profound Van Morrison influence'.[4] *In Fashion*, meanwhile, poured on the praise. 'Jeff Buckley is quite possibly the most uniquely talented artist making music today,' their reviewer stated. Highly-regarded scribe JD Considine, writing in the *Baltimore Sun*, was another convert, spotting the mark that both Led Zep and Jane's Addiction had left on him. 'Buckley's choirboy voice and razor-edged guitar make for a stunning combination,' he wrote, 'one most listeners won't soon forget.'

In short, most *Sin-E* reviews were neither wildly effusive nor overly damning. Most outlined the obvious touchstones – Van Morrison, Robert Plant, Nusrat Fateh Ali Khan – and talked up the Buckley bloodline, much to the dismay of both Jeff and his label.*

---

* When *Grace* was finally released, Columbia's head of publicity Howard Wuelfing requested that reporters refrain from mentioning his father during interviews. This, of course, simply meant the question was moved to the top of the list.

There was one notable exception, a review from *Newsday*, a New York daily, which ran in December. In a move that horrified Buckley, *Live At Sin-E* was not only reviewed alongside Michael Bolton's latest release, but was actually likened to his bombastic balladeering. The word 'oversinging' all but leapt off the page, striking a startled Buckley where it hurt the most: his ego. (By bizarre co-incidence, Buckley's Group Therapy bandmate, Kathryn Grimm, can be spotted cavorting as an extra in the glossy, M-rated video for Bolton's 'Dance With Me'.)

When the review ran, Buckley was back in New York, working on *Grace*, going overdub-crazy in various studios, while still trying to cut definitive vocals for 'Corpus Christi Carol' and 'Hallelujah' (eventually producer Wallace stitched together a composite version of each, culled from the dozens of different takes). Apparently, all work ceased for a couple of days when the *Newsday* piece surfaced, as Buckley mulled over the review, wondering how the hell he could be compared to his big-haired labelmate Bolton. Eventually, in a one-on-one with *Interview*'s Ray Rogers in February 1994, Buckley had regained enough composure to vent. He described the comparison as 'really disgusting', then added a knockout blow: 'Michael Bolton wants to be black, black, black. He also sucks.' He also let loose during an on-air chat on Santa Monica station KCRW, on January 4. 'Critics hate this fucking CD,' he said of *Sin-E*. 'They don't like it. Somebody in New York called me a cipher, called me a zero, because they really couldn't figure out anything. They usually like to know where to put the thing in the hole and they have this problem with me.'[5] *Grace's* release date, meanwhile, virtually slid off the Columbia schedule, moving from January to March 1994 and then, finally, to August.

Another distraction was about to steal Buckley's attention away from his seemingly endless album sessions and the occasional discouraging review. On November 16, 1993, Bob Dylan, another labelmate of Buckley's – and one to whom he accorded a great deal more respect than Michael Bolton – plugged in at New York's Supper Club (concert number 535 of his Never Ending Tour, for those who need to know such things). Buckley, taking advantage of his elevated status within Sony, accompanied Berkowitz to the show, and looked on, transfixed, as Dylan mixed such traditional folk tunes as 'Ragged And Dirty' with his own masterworks, including a rare 'One More Cup Of Coffee', from *Desire*, plus 'My Back Pages', 'Ring Them Bells' and, crucially, 'I Want You', from 1966's peerless *Blonde On Blonde*. Afterwards, Buckley headed backstage for a meeting, during which Dylan mumbled something about Jeff's good looks and his eerie resemblance to his father. Clearly in awe of the great man, and a little confused by his unsettling aside,

Buckley didn't say a word. 'I was petrified,' he admitted some time later. '[But] he told me something I will never forget: "Make a good album, man. *Just make a good album*".'[6]

The next night Buckley played a solo set at Sin-E. In the past, while on-stage, he'd quite readily and good-naturedly impersonated everyone from Robert Plant to Nusrat Fateh Ali Khan, Jim Morrison to The Cranberries' Dolores O'Riordan, and no-one had considered it in bad taste. So it seemed perfectly reasonable to 'do' Dylan, whose nasally, mid-western whine and clipped diction was absolutely ripe for satire. Buckley launched into 'I Want You' – 'the guilty undertaker sighs/the lonesome organ grinder cries' – complete with a Dylan-esque twang, then played 'Grace', all the while maintaining his Dylan inflection. In between songs, Buckley mentioned how he was torn about the show he'd just seen: he felt that Dylan had 'sailed through some songs and was brilliant on others'. 'But he's still got it, right?' asked someone in the crowd, to which Buckley replied: 'No. This is not *Blonde On Blonde*. This is him now. You guys are living in the past.' Then Buckley returned to his regular set, and thought little more of the exchange. It wasn't the first time he'd referred to Dylan on stage, or gently mocked his singing style: he'd been doing that back in the time of Gods And Monsters.

What Buckley didn't know was that a collection of Dylan's people, including members of his management team and some friends, were at Sin-E, looking on. They reported the events of the night to Dylan, who placed a call to Columbia brass. Right away, Berkowitz phoned Buckley. 'Well,' he said firmly, 'Bob feels dissed.'

Buckley was gutted. Just as with all of his impressions, it was done out of admiration; 'dissing' Dylan was the last thing on his mind. His comment about Dylan's show was simple, straight-up honesty; he'd have said the same to anyone who asked him in the street. The next day Buckley sat in Tompkins Square Park, head in his hands, oblivious to the falling snow, 'wishing I was never born,' as he admitted. 'I just loved him so much I sent him up.'[7] Later on, he called Rebecca Moore – despite their split they remained close – in tears. He also spoke at some length with Merri Cyr. 'I remember him telling me about that and going through this big rigmarole,' she said. 'I thought it was really funny, like, "What did you do?" I think he was imitating Bob in a Lenny Bruce kind of way, a bit mean. He was going on and on about how he had to write a letter to Bob Dylan.' It was agreed that Buckley would write an apology to his idol, explaining his side of the story. For reasons that still remain unclear, the letter was reproduced in the liner notes to some versions of his posthumous LP *Sketches For My Sweetheart the Drunk*. In part, it read:

'You were really gracious to me, to even allow me backstage to meet you. I'll never forget what you told me as long as I live. [Buckley was referring to Dylan's 'just make a good album' comment.] I'm very, very honoured to have met you at all.' The first draft of the next sentence was scrawled out, although the final three words, 'regret this incident', made it very clear that Buckley was doing his best to swallow his pride. Then he continued: 'I'm only sad that I didn't get a chance to tell you before all this intrigue. This intrigue is not the truth. Lots of eyes will read this letter before it gets to you, Bob, which I accept. Someday you'll know exactly what I mean man to man. Always be well.' *Jeff Buckley*.[8] Soon after composing the apology, Buckley decided to read it from the stage at Poet's House, a New York library centre and poetry archive; this was recorded and turned up on the 2007 LP, *The Spoken Word Revolution Redux*.

Clearly, the liberty that Buckley had enjoyed until signing with Columbia was now long gone. He'd just learned an object lesson in corporate politics: never send up a star, no matter how well intentioned and light-hearted it may be, and certainly don't do it when their 'people' are looking on. This was a reminder, just in case Buckley needed one, that he was now in music's major league, where the rules – and the stakes – were vastly different from what he was used to. Black Rock was now no longer a safe haven for Buckley, as Leah Reid recalled. 'People bothered him more,' she said. 'So we'd go out and drink or have dinner, that kind of thing. His anonymity was gone by that point.'

Nonetheless, Buckley's relationship with Berkowitz, his Columbia patron and protector, remained strong. A few days after a set with Johnson and Grondahl at legendary downtown punk club CBGBs on December 18 – where he combined Sin-E era standouts with bruising anthems-in-waiting 'Grace' and 'Eternal Life' and ended his nine-song set with a breezy, 'This is Matt Johnson, this is Mick Grondahl, and this is your brain on drugs, good-night people' – Buckley turned up at the Berkowitzes for Christmas lunch. (Berkowitz was married, and had two very young sons, Nick and Ben.) As always, Buckley was ridiculously late – several hours had passed since his expected arrival time – but seemed oblivious to his tardiness. He appeared at the front door, decked out in his latest thrift store acquisitions, a top hat and fur coat (one sleeve of which was held together by safety pins). Tucked under his arm was his contribution to the Berkowitz festivities: a re-gifted, half-demolished Christmas basket, which Buckley had received from Columbia a few days earlier. Buckley, who was leaving to visit friends in the UK soon after – Chris Dowd had been spending some time in London – walked in, smiled at the startled Berkowitzes, and placed what was left of the hamper under the Christmas tree. But Buckley redeemed himself later in the day. Nick Berkowitz was idly watching some cartoons on TV, with Buckley, a man who loved kids almost as much as he loved women, seated alongside him. At one point Buckley leapt off the couch, stood alongside the TV set and mimed each cartoon, pulling off perfect renditions of the characters' voices and the deceptively complex soundtracks. The human jukebox was in the house. For several minutes, Nick's eyes darted between Buckley, the TV and his father. Then he asked: 'Dad, how is he doing that?' 'I don't know, Nick,' Berkowitz replied, shaking his head. 'Just sit down and watch him.'[9]

With *Grace* still nowhere near completed, Buckley's immediate plans were quickly altered. As part of the low-key promotion for *Live At Sin-E* it was decided that he'd hit the road, beginning with some New York shows with his band, before leaving them behind and heading west, then continuing through Seattle, Canada, Dallas, Austin, Chicago and onwards, ending his first 'proper' US solo tour with a date at Lulu's Restaurant in R.E.M.'s hometown, Athens, Georgia, on March 5, 1994. Critical word was positive from the get-go. *Rolling Stone's* coverage of his January 12 set at Wetlands in Manhattan saw beyond the technical hitches and Buckley's reluctance to acknowledge the gathering, apart from a cheeky, 'I just wanna thank everybody for being on the ticket-buy list,' a less than subtle dig at the industry-heavy crowd. There was fulsome praise for his voice, 'a big, soaring, passionate critter that swooshes and trembles... that's a brilliant and disquieting cross between Bob Dylan's and Diamanda Galas', with a little Siouxsie Sioux thrown in for good measure'. Buckley was described as 'the coffee-house circuit's great hope' – a comment he would have bridled at, given that he was moving into his Zeppelin phase – while 'Lover, You Should Have Come Over' was singled out for its inability to 'decide whether to be Zep-like or country tinged, so it decides to be both. The punch line is,' the review declared, 'Jeff Buckley can get away with anything.'[10] Columbia's Mike Webb, who was in the moshpit at Wetlands, still revels in the memory of Buckley silencing what was, at first, a noisy, disinterested gathering. 'The crowd was talking, almost ignoring Jeff,' he said. 'Then he started in on what sounded like a Buddhist chant' – this seductive hum was christened 'Chocolate' and usually preceded 'Mojo Pin' – 'and bit by bit, it was like he was turning down the volume in the crowd. You could hear them mellow out. Then it was silence, except for Jeff – and *then* he launched into "Mojo Pin". He knew how to take the temperature of a room.'

Buckley would also use this 'chant' as a form of musical cue for his soundman Mark Naficy. 'I could tell what song he would play when he was doing

that,' the Seattle-based Naficy told me. 'Those chants revealed what was coming next, from the very first strum of the guitar, or the first noise he made. In
a lot of ways they were the first part of those songs. He was building into starting the song, maybe warming up his voice a bit. It was easier than "1, 2, 3, 4,
go!" It was a way of feeling out the room, getting everything right; it allowed
him to make changes and not have to stop in the middle of a song.'

Good press and monk-like chants aside, plenty happened off-stage as well
during this tour: Buckley moved one step closer to completing *Grace* while
in LA; he met a future lover in Atlanta; and bonded with tour manager Dave
Lory, George Stein's business partner, who was now in control of the day-
to-day routine of Buckley's life – playing, resting, meeting-and-greeting,
smiling on demand. Unlike manager Stein, the 36-year-old Lory was a
music biz veteran, who'd tour-managed bluesy southern rocker Greg
Allman, no small challenge since Allman was known to be 'difficult'. He also
worked with the reunited Allman Brothers Band (it's been said that Lory
actually resembled a Confederate soldier, a look that would have impressed
Allman and co). He also knew Steve Berkowitz. Lory recalled his first trip
with Buckley as 'just him and me puffing into bad truck stops and buying
bad cassettes and talking about music.' Almost immediately, Lory admired
Buckley's on-stage instincts. 'The joke was,' as Lory recalled, '"We're gonna
jump off the cliff and the parachute always opens". That was the fun of
managing Jeff Buckley, jumping off that cliff.'[11] 'Dave knew touring inside
out and had a manager-type background,' said Leah Reid. '[Stein and Lory]
were on the surface a 50/50 partnership, but those of us who worked with
them knew who did what. I was on the phone with Dave constantly. He got
it and understood how things worked.' By February 1994, Lory and Stein
had officially taken on the role of managing Buckley, for a shared 15% commission. Buckley now had 'people'.

While in LA, Lory delivered Buckley to a studio, where he met with pro-
ducer/engineer Clif Norrell (misspelled as 'Cliff' on the *Grace* liner notes,
incidentally), to continue work on *Grace*. Norrell, who came recommended
by Andy Wallace, and whose wife Michelle was a Sony staffer, had worked
on Fishbone's *Reality Of My Surroundings*, and knew that Buckley and
Dowd were close. He checked out one of Buckley's LA shows a couple of
days prior to their session, and, like so many others, 'was completely blown
away by his performance'. Up until then, apart from the Dowd connection,
he knew nothing of Jeff Buckley and was merely 'familiar', at best, with the
work of his father.

The key song that they worked on was 'Dream Brother', which, apart
from Buckley's vocal, as Norrell told me during our interview in 2007, was

'pretty much finished' otherwise. Buckley, as usual, waited until the last possible moment to complete the track. 'We didn't actually start working on the vocals until about 11pm on the last night we could do it,' Norrell recalled. Buckley began by recording a few vocal takes of the chorus, then looked at the clock, and then at Norrell and said: 'OK, it's 11.30 now. How about I meet you back here in two hours?' 'I was pretty sure that we would be there all night getting it right at that point,' admitted Norrell. But Buckley did return, sometime around 1.30am, ready to sing. 'And we got right into it,' said Norrell. 'He sang the verses and completely nailed it in a few takes and we were out of there within a half hour or so.' For a song with such a lengthy genesis, from LA to New York and back to LA again, and spanning a few years, the completion of 'Dream Brother' was, by Buckley's standards, done in record time.

Maybe, as Buckley's friend John Humphrey told me, he needed a good chunk of time to create something truly original. 'I think Jeff was weighed down by his own sense of responsibility – to the world – to create something so powerful and beautiful that it could serve as an antidote,' Humphrey wrote via email. 'Ultimately I think he found himself in the same paradox that many young, inspired artists find themselves in: How can you deliver a message of liberation from within the very structures [i.e. Columbia] that confine, and commodify? I think that was fucking with him.'

While with Norrell, Buckley also cut the album version of 'Corpus Christi Carol', an entirely different version, in trademark Buckley style, to the take he recorded at Bearsville with Andy Wallace. Norrell's plan was to keep it really simple. 'Since this version, and probably the earlier versions as well, was only a single vocal and electric guitar,' said Norrell, 'I kept it to a very simple set-up to capture the moment.' Once again, several different versions were recorded with Norrell; surely, the seemingly endless number of takes for each *Grace* track deserved a mention in the Guinness Book of Records. But Buckley gave Norrell the impression that he was in control. 'Jeff was very focused,' he said. 'Although we had plenty of fun and laughs, not much time was wasted. It was very much like, "This is what I want to do" and we would do it and then pretty quickly move onto the next thing.'

By the time he got into the studio with Norrell, Buckley was showing signs of the strain of finishing the album. 'I kept everything we did purely on a musical and creative level,' Norrell said. '[But] I do not think that Jeff responded well to pressure, and it's natural to assume that he was feeling some pressure towards the end of the recording of the album.'

This wouldn't be the last time that Buckley worked with Norrell during the days of *Grace* (he was actually shortlisted for Buckley's uncompleted second album). Norrell recorded Buckley and band on-stage at Wetlands in New York and oversaw the recording of a live session for a program called the *Columbia Radio Hour.* They also collaborated on what became known as the 'road version' of 'Eternal Life'. One of Norrell's most vivid memories of Buckley's anything-goes approach was during another session, a few months after they recorded 'Dream Brother'. Ostensibly they got together to nail the definitive version of 'So Real'. ('So Real' was originally planned as a B-side, but, according to Norrell, 'Everyone loved [it]; pretty much everyone agreed that it needed to go on the album.') But Buckley was also keen to capture a version of 'Kanga-Roo', a frenzied Big Star pop-rock purge that the group had recently incorporated into their set. In much the same way that 'The Way That Young Lovers Do' gave solo Buckley the chance to stretch out, 'Kanga-Roo' enabled the band to truly kick out the fucking jams, sometimes for 20 minutes or more, often to the concern of Sony staffers, who thought it might be better to squeeze in a few more originals and 'push the product' harder. Mike Webb, who was responsible for dubbing DATs onto cassettes, recalled that when he played 'Kanga-Roo' at full volume in Sony's tape dub-bing room, 'it'd drive people insane. In the end... they wouldn't let me play it that loud. And I know it created tension higher up; I think they thought it was a big "fuck you" to the label. I totally sided with Jeff on that one.'

Just before Buckley and the band began to play, he turned to Norrell and asked: 'How much time can we fit on a reel of tape?' Up until then, the pro-ducer figured that 'Kanga-Roo' was essentially 'a normal three minute song with an 11-minute drum solo'. 'At that point,' Norrell admitted, 'I had a feeling what he was up to, and knew that he wanted to make it as long as he possibly could.' So Norrell lied; he knew that there were ways to capture as much as an hour's worth of music on a reel, but told Buckley that 15 minutes was the limit. 'OK,' Buckley replied, 'signal me when we get to 13 minutes.' There was one hitch: the studio's control room and the 'live' room weren't directly attached (most are separated by a glass window), so Norrell was forced to run down the hall at the 12-minute mark and give Buckley the signal, 'trying to shave off a little more time', as their firestorm of a cover version continued. On playback, at least at first, Norrell thought it was 'fairly indulgent', but then gradually revised his thinking. 'Upon further listenings I really got into it,' he said. '[I found it] hypnotic and intense, and I was just in awe of Matty Johnson's unbelievable drumming.' To this day, Johnson's brawny, brainy playing on the song remains one of Norrell's all-time favourite performances.

Norrell did get the chance to witness Buckley's wild side away from the studio, too, one night in New York, soon after *Grace*'s completion. Chris

Dowd was also along for what Norrell described as a 'long and late night' of club hopping. Somewhere during the evening they drifted into a club, where Soundgarden's dark grunge valentine, 'Black Hole Sun', was blaring over the PA. (Soundgarden's Chris Cornell would become a key player in Buckley's posthumous legacy.) Buckley loved the band and the song – he was also a dedicated Nirvana fan, too – and raced through the crowd, not stopping until he reached the middle of the dance floor. Then he began to wail. 'He sang the song in a full screaming loud voice while doing the full rock star pose and moves along with the song,' Norrell laughed. 'A lot of the club-goers were looking at him strangely.' Norrell was amused, but he just couldn't stop himself from listening closely. Despite being in the thick of a wild Manhattan night, Buckley still nailed the song. 'Even when he was screwing around musically, it always sounded amazing,' Norrell said.

In early March 1994, Buckley's solo roadshow paused in Atlanta, Georgia, for a three-night stand. Looking on at one of the gigs was a pair of Cocteau Twins, bassist Simon Raymonde and vocalist Elizabeth Fraser. Eight years older than Buckley, the Scottish-born, dark-haired, vaguely androgynous Fraser had also been the recipient of high praise for her unique, albeit unintelligible vocal style: one English scribe said she had 'the voice of God'. The Cocteau Twins, by this time, had peaked; the title track of their 1990 LP, *Heaven Or Las Vegas*, even contained lyrics that made some kind of sense, backed by a million-dollar hook. Their dense, gloomy earlier work, including 1983's *Sunburst and Snowblind* EP, and 1986's *The Pink Opaque*, was characterised by Robin Guthrie's orchestral guitar work and Fraser's ethereal voice and obscure lyrics – it seemed as if she was singing in tongues. Though they never had an actual hit, per se, *Heaven Or Las Vegas* was this black-clad band's commercial high-water mark. By the time she met Buckley, Fraser had a daughter, named Lucy Belle, who was born in 1989. The child's father was the Cocteau's other main-stay, guitarist Guthrie, whose relationship with Fraser ended in 1992.

Buckley astounded Fraser. 'He knocked me sideways,' she said afterwards. She and Buckley already had a strong karmic connection: while moon-lighting with the band This Mortal Coil in 1984, she recorded an other-worldly version of Tim Buckley's haunting, stately 'Song To The Siren'. She was equally thrilled by Tim's vocal gymnastics, as she admitted on the BBC's *Everybody Here Wants You*. 'I could hear his soul [in "Siren"],' she said. I found it very powerful, very human music.'[12] Oddly enough, This Mortal Coil also covered Big Star's 'Kanga-Roo' on the album, which was entitled *It'll End In Tears*. If sonic signposts were anything to go by, she and Jeff Buckley were destined to connect. Eventually, the pair became lovers.

By the time he returned to New York, in late winter 1994, after more than 30 solo dates, he invited a friend, 21-year-old guitarist Michael Tighe, to audition at Montana, a rehearsal space. Tighe was hardly a seasoned musician; if anything, he made the inexperienced Grondahl and Johnson seem like studio veterans. An aspiring actor, he hadn't actually been in a 'proper' band before Buckley asked him to sign on, but had been playing guitar since his teens, when a degree of proficiency was required for a part in a play. Again, Rebecca Moore was the connection: she knew Tighe and introduced him to Buckley in 1991, soon after he moved to Manhattan. He and Buckley were friends; during those early days together they'd take walks, find cheap places to eat, or simply hang out, playing pool and pumping quarters into a jukebox, rapping about their shared love of bluesmen Son House, Muddy Waters, Howlin' Wolf and Robert Johnson (all key influences on Tighe's spare playing style). On several occasions, even then, Buckley told Tighe: 'If I ever get a band together, you're in.' As bassist Grondahl recalled, 'Michael had very little band experience, let alone studio experience.' He also had very little gear: he arrived at the rehearsal space with a malfunctioning plug for his guitar, a broken strap and a churning stomach. He opted to play sitting down.

Many people in Buckley's circle, including his management and Columbia staff, were confused by his decision to hire Tighe; not only was he impossibly green and relatively unskilled, but Buckley was such a deft guitarist – 'the Hendrix of my generation,' to Grondahl – that it seemed unnecessary to have a second axeman in the band. 'I remember the debate,' said Mike Webb. 'Is this a real band or are they Jeff's backing guys? Publicly, Jeff was saying they were a real band, but he would have known he was the star attraction; he was the Jimi Hendrix of the thing. I also wondered what Michael added, but if you can take your buddy on the road with you, what the hell.'

Nonetheless, Grondahl, for one, saw a certain logic in Buckley's move. 'In a way I wasn't surprised,' he said during our 2007 interview. 'I'd seen guys who could really rip it up' – Tighe was the ninth player to audition for the band – 'and play fast and stuff, but we were looking for someone who had character and a certain style: enthusiasm and originality over technique, that attitude was more important. I felt safe about it,' he added, 'because if worse came to worse, Michael could lay out and we could do something interesting as a trio.' Buckley, as cryptic as ever, said he was drawn to Tighe's 'rhythmic sense', although, as he stated in the EPK for *Grace*, maybe he just enjoyed the company of his bandmates. 'I really can't stand being alone all the time,' he shrugged. Regardless, Tighe would bring some added muscle to Buckley's on-stage sound, especially, much later on, when volume began to overpower nuance, as the quartet's exhaustion and frustration with their seemingly never-ending touring took over.

Not everyone within Columbia, however, was enthralled by the idea of Buckley hiring a group in the first place. One former staffer saw them as a handicap for Buckley when he played live. 'They played the same set list every night; that was anti-Jeff; [he was] a guy who lived in the moment. I felt that he could go so much further than the band.'

It did help that a new song began to emerge from that first jam with Tighe at Montana, built around a guitar line that the new recruit threw into the mix (played on Buckley's guitar, incidentally; he was playing drums at the time). Buckley had a lyric that fitted perfectly and the song quickly became known as 'So Real'. At first, Buckley recalled, 'it was disjointed and it wasn't together; it wasn't anything. [But] everything about his style is right there. I made it into a song. If I didn't come along, it would have just been a blob.'[13] However, Buckley was soon so excited about 'So Real' – later described by a writer as 'one of the most intensely sexual songs I've ever heard'[14] – that he decided it needed to be recorded, straight away. And he made another quick decision: 'Forget Her', a mid-tempo moodpiece cut with Wallace, who thought it was 'a wonderful song',[15] had to go. ('For personal reasons', said Grondahl in the liner notes to the Legacy edition of *Grace*.[16]) 'So Real' was cut at the same Clif Norrell-engineered session as 'Kanga-Roo'; Buckley nailed the vocal at three in the morning, first take. 'I love it,' Buckley said, 'because it's the actual quartet that you see in that picture right there that you have on the wall, on the album. And that one I produced live.'[17]

Leah Reid swung by the Tighe audition just in time to witness the sight of Buckley drumming and the riff for 'So Real' developing into something that resembled a song. 'We were going to dinner afterwards and Jeff turned to me and said, "I found my guy",' she recalled. Buckley's 'dream' band was now in place.

Due to depart for his first solo UK date on March 11, Buckley believed that with the recording of 'So Real', *Grace* was finally completed. He felt an overpowering sense of pride towards the songs, especially those – 'Last Goodbye', 'Eternal Life', etc – that he'd been sticking by for so long. 'At the time I wrote them,' he said, 'a long time ago, I was around an environment that thought that they were completely loser songs. I put them on the album to prove... to the songs that they weren't losers. Sort of like finding kids have been told all their lives that they're pieces of shit and finally you have to go around proving to them that no, they are worth knowing and loving.'[18] Of course, it wasn't as though Buckley had a spare bunch of sub-stitute 'loser songs' ready to roll; he'd recorded pretty much all he had. As for late addition 'So Real', the closest Buckley ever came to a definitive expla-nation of this knotty, deeply-felt slowburner was from a London stage later in the year, when he announced: 'Of course, when you say fuck off, it means I love you. Speaking of which, fuck you *and* I love you, here's a song that combines both.'[19]

The response from Columbia was not good when Buckley announced that 'Forget Her' was to be dropped. At this point, the song had actually been included in advance cassette copies of *Grace*, which had been sent to writers for 'long-lead' magazines in the hope of creating some sort of criti-cal 'vibe'. (Now another hugely collectible Buckley item, of course.) It was also slated as a contender for the album's lead single. Just like the 'Bob Dylan incident', it was another part of Buckley's crash course in major label poli-tics. He thought he was untouchable and that every decision he made was final and non-negotiable. Of course that wasn't so.

Mike Webb recalled how Buckley 'just walked in thinking, "OK, I don't want this song on the record", and that it was done. But no, it turned into a debate and a very long discussion. I think Donny [Ienner] put intense pres-sure on Jeff to include the song, and I don't think Jeff wanted to piss the label off. I think Jeff struggled with that. And I have no idea, to this day, what his motivation was: it would have been a hit song. *Jeff took the hit song off the album.*' According to Webb, Steve Berkowitz had 'very grand visions' for the song. One of these, you'd think, was to make it a number one single.

To Leah Reid, Buckley's decision was another indication of his ruthless perfectionism. 'Jeff said that he really liked it but said the song, as it sits right now, was only 10 carat and he wanted it to be 24 carats,' she admitted. 'And he said it was too personal. In his mind it wasn't what he wanted it to be, it was falling short. He said, "One day I'll get it to 24 carats".' (Of course, that never happened; the Wallace-produced original was included in the Legacy edition of *Grace*, released in 2004.) It's never been clarified what exactly was so personal about the song, although Reid suspected that 'Forget Her' was another valentine to Rebecca Moore, Buckley's ex girlfriend. 'I pictured them [all] being about her, but have no clear evidence,' she said. 'I felt that his songs were so personal that I couldn't ask about them. His heart was so far out on his sleeve.'

There's also another, more radical theory behind Buckley's decision. As much as he had grand plans – after all, one of his touchstones was Led Zeppelin, who never understood the term small scale, both with their music and career path – Buckley feared success. He was possibly flashing back to other Columbia 'heritage' artists, such as Dylan and Bruce Springsteen, who'd taken a few albums and several years to really blossom as songwriters and stars. Maybe, if 'Forget Her' really hit hard and fast, it would simply be too much for a guy still on his first album. 'I think he had some fear, some understanding of what fame can do to you,' said Mike Webb. 'Maybe that's one of the reasons he took that song off; maybe he didn't want that fame so quickly.' As *Grace* started to break in different corners of the planet, especially the UK, France and Australia, Buckley had many long conversations with friends about what success meant to him, and how it wasn't filling any holes in his soul, so maybe Webb was right.

Buckley's contrariness regarding 'Forget Her' was only one of several moves he made at the time that seemed, at least on the surface, to distance himself from Columbia's commercial instincts. As early as February 1994, even before the 'Forget Her' debate (which Buckley won, in the end), he was talking up a 'no video' policy like a mantra, during an on-air interview for WXPN's *World Café* radio show, broadcast out of Philadelphia. 'I love visuals,' he said, 'but they're commercials for the album and I wouldn't want that to be the object. That's why I'm not making a video for this album.'[20] That, of course, didn't quite prove to be the case, although Buckley kicked long and hard against this particular prick. 'It's always a dilemma for everyone who gets signed, the way the rules are set up, the way that it's structured for some artists to really succeed and others to really not do anything,' he said during the same interview. 'And sometimes I have a pretty black soul; the music business will bring out the cynic in me.'[21]

Leah Reid, to her credit, understood where Buckley was coming from. 'He was concerned about being portrayed as a poster boy, a pretty boy. He didn't want to be part of the MTV generation,' she figured. 'The reason that the *Grace* EPK existed was that part of it was shot at Sin-E; it already existed. It was more about questioning why he needed to make a video.' 'Last Goodbye', the first video that was eventually shot for *Grace*, and covered in more detail later on, was one of the biggest financial gaffes of Buckley's brief career. In Reid's summation, 'It was a giant cluster fuck.'

Bassist Grondahl was another Buckley insider who caught a glimpse of his boss's reluctance to buy into the star-making machine. 'There was some talk about how to market him; I remember some talk about him having a non-image,' he said. 'You see some of those videos and he has the messy hair and the wrinkled plaid shirt, the grunge kind of thing, but it was such a moot point, that whole world, to us, the MTV world. We wanted to do whatever we could to deflect the attention away from that and towards the music and the songs.'

Tony Maimone, who played alongside Buckley in Gods And Monsters, and got to know him well, also sensed Buckley's struggle with the idea of becoming a product. 'They did put the rock star mantle on him, you know, and it wasn't that he didn't want it, but when you're young and you want to be famous and do these things, you don't realise the can of worms you're opening.'

All of Buckley's concerns, fears and contradictions were outlined in an exhaustive marketing document prepared by his managers Stein and Lory – with Buckley's input, according to some – that spelled out many things: their client's wariness of music videos; his thoughts about publicity, insisting that Buckley be interviewed only by 'alternative fanzines' (a big call when *Rolling Stone* came knocking, incidentally); his reluctance to discuss certain personal matters (number one being his father); even his insistence on being a headliner, wherever he played. It was a particularly brassy, even arrogant move on the part of Team Buckley and proof positive that Stein and Lory were working hard for their 15%. While this hefty report was crossing numerous desks at Black Rock, Buckley got back to the business of making music. London was calling.

Almost 26 years earlier, Tim Buckley made an astonishing UK debut at London's Queen Elizabeth Hall. The shows, documented on the *Dream Letter Live In London 1968* CD, were described in the liner notes by his guitarist Lee Underwood as 'the real thing, with real fire and real tenderness. It's alive in the moment, right here, right now.' It wouldn't be too far from the truth to describe Jeff Buckley's first UK shows the same way. He began with a set at Ratners in Sheffield, on March 11; four nights later, the solo Buckley played the Borderline in London, where he silenced the normally rowdy industry crowd with a deadly run through 'Hallelujah'. After subsequent must-see shows at Bunjies, the long running folk venue, and an in-store at Rough Trade Records, Buckley was, in the words of writer Jim Irvin, 'the talk of the town'. Looking back on this handful of dates for *Mojo* magazine, Mick Houghton was just as fulsome in his praise, stating how Buckley's 'mesmeric solo performances' were greeted with 'ecstatic drooling'.[22] Given that the airwaves at the time were clogged with the likes of Celine Dion, Ace Of Base and M People, human jukebox Buckley might well have descended on England from some alien planet of sound.

Buckley continued to draw A-listers to him like a magnet. Former tennis champion John McEnroe, a long-term rock fan who often mingled with the stars, helped lug Buckley's gear after a set in London. Pretender Chrissie Hynde, who'd interviewed Tim Buckley, and became a huge fan, was also at that show, genuinely enthralled. 'Tim Buckley seemed to be just about everything that was right about the hippy '60s. He was certainly one of my all-time top five favourite artists,' Hynde said during the *Everybody Here Wants You* documentary. 'People my age all flocked to see Jeff, just to hear that voice again. He would be so pissed off with it by now; all these toothless hags hanging around the stage door, [saying] I knew your Dad. Well, I didn't!' Manic Street Preacher James Dean Bradfield was another convert after witnessing a thrilling Buckley set later that year in Dublin. 'It was as close to spiritual as I'd ever like to get,' he gushed.[23]

During that first UK visit, Buckley put in an unadvertised appearance at Bob's Blues Bar on Denmark Street, while also playing shows in such unfashionable spots as Wolverhampton, Stevenage and Hitchin, prompting an *Evening Standard* reporter to declare it 'one of the oddest promotional visits in recent memory'.[21] 'A vocal chameleon with an ambitious range,' noted the same writer, 'he has inherited more than his dad's unkempt curls and arched eyebrows. A wider stage is calling.'[22a] While in London, Buckley took the opportunity to check out grunge stars Soundgarden, and after their set went backstage to meet heartthrob Chris Cornell, a guy who shared some of Buckley's moody musical inclinations. A bond was formed.

According to Mark Naficy, soundman for both Soundgarden and Buckley, the Seattle band were big fans of Buckley. 'They were always talking about him,' Naficy said. The admiration was mutual, if Buckley's impromptu New York karaoke version of 'Black Hole Sun' was anything to go by. When Buckley hired Naficy, not long after this London meeting, he requested the same set of monitors that Naficy had hand-made for Soundgarden. 'I think Jeff just wanted them because Chris Cornell had some built,' Naficy laughed. 'They're really big and powerful monitors. I literally cut and routed the wood, glued and screwed them.'

Another Seattle band was soon dominating Buckley's thoughts. Back home in early April, he awoke to some devastating news, and put in an emergency call to Steve Berkowitz. Nirvana singer, songwriter, guitarist and tortured soul, Kurt Cobain, had been found in the garage of his Seattle home, dead from a self-inflicted bullet wound. Cobain, like Jim Morrison, Janis Joplin, Jimi Hendrix and many other dead stars before him, was aged 27 – as was Buckley at the time. Buckley understood his rock and roll mythology; he knew that 27 could be a dangerous age. He was a huge admirer of Cobain, who'd changed the entire complexion of the rock music biz with his explosive anthem 'Smells Like Teen Spirit' and its parent album *Nevermind* (which was mixed by Andy Wallace, not coincidentally). 'Smells Like Teen Spirit' was one of the many 'popular' songs that Buckley often dropped into his solo sets; he even played snatches of it while in Gods And Monsters. 'Jeff was a total fucking Nirvana freak,' according to his friend Glen Hansard. He was certainly remembered fondly by Buckley. In a letter to a fan, dated April 10, 1994, he signed off: 'Kurt Cobain, rest forever in peace.'

He also related very closely to the major label conflicts that Cobain had endured with Geffen. Just like Buckley, Cobain wanted a lot of people to hear his music, but he was also deeply uncomfortable with the idea of being 'marketed'. The frequent mention of the term 'spokesman of his generation' turned Cobain's constantly queasy stomach just that little bit more. 'I remember when Kurt Cobain died, Jeff got really, really upset and really needed to talk with Steve,' said Mike Webb, who intercepted the call. 'He took that hard, which kind of surprised me. I definitely think Jeff was a different kind of human being; he probably was more in touch with that side of his brain, or that side of life, whatever you wanted to call it.' Maybe, as many of Buckley's friends and peers told me, he had a sense that his time on the planet was in short supply, and Cobain's death – even though it was a cowardly act of suicide – reminded him of that.

When asked to formally comment on Cobain's death, Buckley unleashed what sounded like an anti-corporate manifesto. 'You gotta make your own life,' he said. 'You can't leave it up to the leaders. Jesus, JFK, Kurt Cobain, they all got fucked up. Kurt didn't feel loved, or maybe he didn't know how to recognise it. But it won't ever happen with a leader; independence has to come or you'll die. You'll end up like someone's puppet and you'll be gone like a chump before you're 30.'[23] Given what lay a few years ahead in Buckley's future, his comment couldn't have been any more ominous.

June 2, 1994, marked another key moment in Jeff Buckley's musical rise: it was the official debut of his new, if not particularly road-hardened, four-piece band, at a low-key private show at the legendary Stone Pony in Asbury Park, New Jersey, the former haunt of Bruce Springsteen and his E Street Band. Throughout April and May, the band had rehearsed hard, preparing themselves for the Peyote Radio Theatre tour, which would keep them on the road until the August release of *Grace*. (It may have been barely 13 years ago, but the idea of a band doing major dates *before an album drops* is now almost unheard of.) Immediately, Buckley made a statement: rather than stand centre stage, as most 'frontmen' preferred to do, he stood stage right, which gave him a far better view of his more timid bandmates, allowing him to 'direct' the group. The many women now coming to see and hear him were confused; they'd push their way to the front of stage, only to come eye to eye with Mick Grondahl.

The bassist's explanation of Buckley's decision to stand stage right was relatively straightforward. 'It was mainly a result of sound dynamics,' he said. 'Jeff liked his voice, and in particular his guitar, to be loud, and so we chose to put him on one side of the drum kit. Also, by putting him to one side, we, the backing band, were able to observe visual clues, like raising his guitar neck.' Gary Lucas felt it was Buckley's way of getting the full attention of his 'adoring fans'.

Buckley's unusual placement would also reap benefits for some of his support bands, according to Dave Shouse of The Grifters. 'We did our stage set-up a little bit differently [from Buckley and band], with three mics across the stage and mine in the centre,' he recalled. 'Well, they would open the doors and all the girls would go straight for the centre mic. But Jeff would always play stage right. So by the time he came on all these girls would be trapped at the centre of the stage. So I had eye candy for rows and rows; I'd play shows just looking out over all these gorgeous women, going "This is not what it's really like, but I'll take it for right now." I'd announce that we had one more song and that all the women should take a few steps to their left straight away.'

Mark Naficy had yet another take on his on-stage set-up. 'I think he wanted it to come across as a band. By not standing in the middle he was just one of the four members,' he said. 'Maybe by standing where he was they could all see, he could face them all at once. But my impression was that he was not trying to take centre stage, not trying to take the attention away from the band.'

The Peyote Radio Theatre Tour was named in honour of a three-track *Grace* sampler released in June 1994. (The EP's tracks were 'Mojo Pin', an instrumental version of 'Dream Brother' and the marathon 'Kanga-Roo'.) Its name, in turn, was taken from a band in-joke; after seeing a drug-fucked tragedy stumbling along a New York street, they agreed it was an example of 'chemical theatre'. As Grondahl recalled, the sense of expectation within the band was tangible – there was a touch of Jack Kerouac about the whole adventure. 'It was exciting,' he said, 'we were all together, it was our first time going out like this and we really felt like we were on the road, in that sense.' The band, plus Lory, travelled in a 10-seater van; Grondahl came up with the savvy idea of slinging hammocks out the window of the van and over the roof so that they could get some rest on their lengthy between-gig trips. 'Even though it was cramped, we felt good about it,' said Grondahl. 'Later on, when we got the bus, we kind of missed those days in the van, even though they were incredibly inconvenient.'

Within the first couple of weeks of the tour, and well before *Grace's* official release, the good word started to spread on the album, based on the cassette copies passed around by Columbia. On June 17, as the band set up for the first of two nights at New York venue Fez (where Buckley had played many solo sets), the *Boston Herald* laid on the praise. *Grace* was described as 'a diverse, forceful record that showcases knife-through-the-heart vocals... it could be the album of the summer. Except that it won't be released until late August.'[24]

Not all Buckley-related press was so upbeat, however. On June 28, the band played a sold-out gig at Toronto's Albert Hall, but unlike most of these early shows, Buckley didn't seem to be in the moment. 'Jeff Buckley gives brave and enigmatic shows,' stated a reporter for the *Toronto Star*, 'but [he] didn't seem comfortable... mumbling between songs, offering little acknowledgement of the full house and exhibiting a throwaway attitude that underlined and ultimately undermined his songs of dislocation.'[25] But this was the exception; a Chicago show was described as 'magical', while Buckley's voice was singled out as a 'pretty phenomenal object'.[26]

Yet the name of his father appeared alongside virtually every mention of the name Jeff Buckley. 'Buckley,' wrote one critic, 'is a vocalist whose melding of folk, jazz and rock styles recalls the music of his late father.'[27] 'Jeff Buckley was the subject of a record company bidding war,' pronounced another. 'He's [also] the son of the late Tim Buckley.'[28] It appeared that Columbia's plan to separate the two wasn't working quite as they'd hoped. It was also understandable, to some extent, when Buckley began to publicly denounce Tim; having the name of your long-gone father thrown at you in almost every media conversation must have been incredibly dispiriting. Even before *Grace's* release, Buckley was cutting short questions about his bloodline. 'I can't tell you how little he had to do with my music,' Buckley told *Interview* magazine. But the truth, however, was quite different: if any one artist had a direct influence on Buckley's genre-jumping style and wildly expressive voice, it was his father – with all due respect to Led Zeppelin. And he clearly knew Tim Buckley's work inside out, as he'd confirmed in correspondence with numerous people, including Lee Underwood. It was a complicated situation; he genuinely admired the work of the man who'd walked out of his life and then died before they got the chance to connect. It would have been much easier if the guy hadn't been his father, because then he could have respected him as a fellow musician.

But despite the unwanted and frequent diversion, even this first tour was heavy with on-stage chemistry. 'There was just this magic; they were spot-on from the start,' said Mark Naficy, who was in the perfect position to size up the band. He acknowledged that Tighe was probably in the band more for his personal relationship with Buckley than his playing (Buckley had to teach him his parts as they went along). 'But you wouldn't have known it from the very start. They were a very pro band. They really were the four right guys: Matt was amazing, Mick was a great bass player. Of all the bass players I've worked with, he was the one: so tasteful when he played. And of course Jeff was the mainstay. The whole thing worked so well.'

Interestingly, Naficy's role with Buckley and his band was relatively simple, in contrast with some of his other high-profile jobs. This wasn't a band with any delay settings or audio cues – or pyrotechnics, for that matter. 'It was just me amplifying and balancing what they were doing,' he recalled. 'With other bands there's all this effects mix, but not with these guys. I'd walk in, make sure the speakers were placed right, all that kind of stuff, get the different levels balanced, get some equalisation for what the room needed, and that was it.'

On July 9, the bandwagon, hammocks and all, rolled into Iowa City, to play a venue called Gabe's, where Buckley headlined a bill that also featured Dave Shouse's band The Grifters, and The Dambuilders, whose numbers included a violin-wielding firebrand by the name of Joan Wasser. It was the beginning of a deep, if occasionally tormented series of relationships for Buckley. Shouse and his wife Tammy would become his Memphis-based hosts and confidantes (and the bluesy, psychedelic rock of The Grifters would be a massive influence on Buckley's post-*Grace* sound), while Wasser, in the words of Chris Dowd – who also knew her very well – would become the 'man sized love' of Buckley's life. A few weeks shy of her 24th birthday when they met, Wasser was raised in middle-class Norwalk, Connecticut, and had been playing violin since the age of eight. She enrolled at Boston University, studying under the renowned Yuri Mazurkevich, and played with the Boston University Symphony Orchestra. But then she discovered indie rock, playing in such acts as The Lotus Eaters and Hot Trix, before joining The Dambuilders.

Wasser was no natural beauty – she was described to me as 'plain Joan' – but her physical, passionate violin assaults on-stage were matched by an equally frenetic off-stage manner. 'She wasn't Kylie Minogue, she was rough as tacks back then, but he was in awe of her, I think,' said Jon Pope, who met Wasser while tour-managing Buckley's 1996 Australian visit. But Wasser's influence on Buckley had its limits, Pope figured. 'I got the feeling that if she tried and influenced the band, he'd tell her to get fucked.' Dave Shouse described Wasser as 'very impulsive', a trait that had obvious appeal to the anything-goes side of Buckley.

Their first night in Iowa didn't start so promisingly, though, as Shouse told me. 'We had no idea who the dude was. Someone said that Tim

Buckley's son was going to headline, and we were like, "What the fuck?" I didn't know about the Sin-E stuff or him singing at his dad's thing at Brooklyn. Nothing. The grapevine wasn't working.'*

At the after-party that followed the Iowa City gig, Buckley made it very clear that he was interested in more than violin lessons from Wasser. It was the talk of The Grifters' tour van the next day, as Shouse recalled. (Shouse, being the designated driver, missed out on the party.) 'Everyone came back talking about how they'd all gone out and that Jeff was super hyper, entertaining, working hard to catch Joan's eye,' he said. 'It was infatuation at first sight and it snowballed from there. I think they had a very spirited relationship. They seemed happy, so we didn't talk about that. You're happy? Cool.'

A smitten Buckley and band then headed west, for shows in St Louis, Denver, Seattle, Portland, San Francisco and LA. Meanwhile, press coverage, and the hype that comes with that, started to build, and the expectation surrounding *Grace* reached boiling point. But Buckley had just met the love of his life, and for a day or two, at least, the imminent release of his 'proper' recording debut didn't weigh so heavily on him.

Notes

1. Bell, Max: Contemporary Drift On New York's 60s Club Scene, *The Evening Standard*, March 22, 1994
2. Saunders, David: Cornflake Girl, *The Age*, February 18, 1994
3. See note 1
4. See note 2
5. Anon: Man In The Moon, *KCRW*, January 4, 1994
6. Perret, Philippe: Get Your Soul Out, *Les Inrockuptibles*
7. Simpson, Dave: Grace Under Fire, *The Guardian*, May 1, 1998
8. Buckley, Jeff: Liner notes, *Sketches For My Sweetheart The Drunk*, Columbia Records, 1997
9. Cyr, Merri: *A Wished-For Song*; Hal Leonard, 2002
10. Darzin, Daina: Live review, *Rolling Stone*, January 1994
11. Irvin, Jim: It's Never Over, *Mojo*, August 1997

---

* Later on, Shouse did get a feel for the kind of adulation that was directed towards Buckley. When he moved to Memphis in 1997, on the suggestion of the Shouses, Buckley tried to re-create his 'café days' at a tiny hole-in-the-wall called Barristers. 'The word got out and the freaks would start to come into town,' Shouse told me. 'They'd drop by his house, things like that.' So much for Memphis as Buckley's escape.

12. BBC2, *Everybody Here Wants You* documentary
13. Creswell, Toby: Grace Under Fire, *Juice*, February 1996
14. Danielsen, Shane: You Read It Here – Album Of The Year, *Sydney Morning Herald*, October 17, 1994
15. See note 11
16. Anon: *Grace* Legacy Edition liner notes, Columbia Records 2004
17. See note 13
18. See note 13
19. www.jeffbuckley.com
20. Anon: *WXPN World Café*, February 1994
21. See note 20
22. Houghton, Mick: Jeff Buckley, Grace, *Mojo*, September 1994
22a. Reese, Joel: Genius Unleashed?, *Chicago Daily Herald*, July 17, 1998
23. Taylor, Sam: Inherited Torment, Just Like His Dad, *The Observer*, June 8, 1997
24. Lozaw, Tristram: Boston Beat, *Boston Herald*, June 17, 1994
25. Stoute, Lenny: Project 9 Parties For Unity Through Diversity, *Toronto Star*, July 7, 1994
26. Rosen, Steven: Critics' Choice, *Denver Post*, July 10, 1994
27. Blackstock, Peter: There's Nothing Slow About Summer At Moe's, *Seattle Post-Intelligencer*, July 15, 1994
28. See note 26

Chapter Eight

Inside The Star Making Machinery

Steve Berkowitz may have been Jeff Buckley's number one cheerleader within the corridors of Black Rock, but it wasn't until a few weeks before *Grace's* release that he went 'public' and began to talk up his new(ish) signing to the media. In July, he went on the record with *Billboard*, the music industry bible. The underlying 'mantra' of the feature, written by Jim Bessman, was that Buckley defied categorisation. 'We didn't have a preconceived notion of what album we should make,' said Berkowitz, a surprisingly frank admission for a story that was essentially advance spin for the record. 'He's not the next X or Y or superstar or folkie or jazz musician – just Jeff Buckley, who does exactly what he does.'

Berkowitz continued to cut through the crap, too, understating massively when he told Bessman that the lack of planning behind *Grace's* creation was not the way things are typically done at a major label. 'It's very unusual to start a record with an artist and not know pretty much what would happen,' he said. Berkowitz revealed how the band had only just met when *Grace* rehearsals began, but added that they 'were fresh and great improvisers and the music kept growing.' When pressed on Columbia's marketing plan for the album, Berkowitz stressed that, just like the music, 'the [plans] will evolve naturally,' adding that college radio, alternative rock press and retail were the label's target areas.[1]

Leah Reid insisted that *Grace* was a 'worldwide priority' for Columbia, in part because of Donny Ienner's very vocal support of the record. Mike Webb, Berkowitz's assistant, agreed. 'I always sensed, and this came from

Steve, was that Jeff was a high priority artist, period. But the problem for the label was "How do we make him a hit-making machine?" I feel that Steve's vision was – and I hate to compare him with Springsteen – but it took a few albums for Bruce to blow up. That was the path that Steve wanted to follow, and making Donny understand that it's not going to pay off on album one, that was the battle. But I always felt that the label was committed to Jeff.'

In the same *Billboard* piece, Berkowitz pointed out how important touring would be in 'breaking' Buckley. And that's essentially what Buckley and band continued to do, initially in the US, until mid August 1994. On a rare day of downtime, Buckley and Merri Cyr reunited to shoot the cover image for *Grace*, at the Brooklyn loft of a friend of Cyr's. Once again, the end result would become the subject of much heated discussion within Columbia. Buckley was more playful and engaged at this shoot, unlike the long, stressful day that generated the cover photo for *Live At Sin-E*. With *Grace*, Buckley had an image in his head, 'borrowed' from the cover of the Leonard Cohen LP, *I'm Your Man*, where the worldly composer of 'Hallelujah' was caught mid-thought, eyes closed, his hands clasped around a beautiful vintage microphone. As provocative as ever, Buckley figured that the shot needed some 'glamming' up, so he decided to go shopping. Cyr, for one, loved the slightly ridiculous outfit he unveiled at the shoot.

'I called that his Judy Garland glitter jacket, this junk store jacket, all sparkling [and] his hair was all sort of boofed up,' she recalled. 'There was one point where he was eating this banana and I went, "OK, it's sort of Sid Vicious meets Leonard Cohen meets Elvis, or something like that." Even the one where he's looking so broody is from a comic series of pictures; he was just fucking around, you know?'

Leah Reid was also at the shoot. 'I think there were eight mock ups,' she said, 'and we all had our favourite.' Reid's pick was an oft-seen shot of Buckley in a Hamlet-worthy pose, absorbed in his reflection in a mirror. Buckley probably rejected the photo, not due to its narcissism, but because it portrayed him as a little too broody. The one thing he didn't want to do was to conform to a grunge-rock stereotype, a broken-hearted Eddie Vedder with a far better voice. When Reid told label boss Donny Ienner she thought it was the right photo, he snapped back: 'If you think that's the album cover you don't know who this artist really is.' 'I thought that was ridiculous,' Reid said. 'It was a great picture. [But] the first and only shot [Jeff] wanted was the one that ended up on the cover.' Reid then met with Buckley on the road, in Philadelphia, to show him the various mock-ups. 'He told me, "I love it because I'm listening to music".' (At the time he was tuning into an instrumental version of 'Dream Brother'.) 'I think it captured a moment he was having with himself,' she added.

Typically, other Columbia staff weren't so sure that was the right photo. 'People started to get a bit micro-managey with it,' said Reid. 'There were meetings and discussions. [But] I thought we were making a bigger deal out of it than necessary. It was him, it was what he looked like, what he would wear, deal with it. It was also Jeff putting his foot down, saying, This is what I want.' In a classic case of decision-by-committee, numerous questions were kicked around by Columbia staff: Was it too gay? Was it a little too Judy Garland? 'Some people even thought he looked too much like Adam Ant,' Reid recalled. 'That came up all the time.' Eventually, a decision was reached between Ienner, Reid, Berkowitz, the Sony art department, Stein, Lory and Buckley: for once, the 'star' was going to get his way and the now-iconic image remained. According to Reid, 'It became pretty clear that most people wanted what Jeff wanted.'

To Merri Cyr, this argy-bargy typified Buckley's turbulent relationship with Columbia and his own uncertainty regarding major label life. 'The record company didn't like that shot, especially what he was wearing, that it didn't fit the image they had in mind for him,' she said. '[But] he was in conflict with them all the time, about everything. That was part of his split personality; he wanted to be on this major label and get all this worldwide exposure but he wanted to act like he was on an indie label. I think he envied that freedom he had in the beginning at Sin-E, where he wasn't being judged by this specific point of view. I was party to him talking about all the problems he had with them.' The Grifters' Dave Shouse also became a sounding board for many of Buckley's problems. 'We never talked about music, but we talked about the fucked-up business,' Shouse laughed. 'He was dealing with Sony, and The Grifters were dealing with Sub Pop, so we'd bitch a lot about the business.'

Now, with his latest major label dilemma finally resolved, Buckley and band had one more US date to play, on August 16, a week before *Grace's* official release. Then they'd begin a month of UK and European dates, the first that Buckley would play there with his backing band. In a twist that surely wasn't lost on Buckley, he planned a 'farewell' shot at Sin-E, but the box office response was so enthusiastic that the show was shifted to the far roomier Wetlands. So much for a chance of paying dues to the venue that kickstarted his career.

Forty thousand copies of *Grace* were shipped to stores on the day of its release, which was a reasonably conservative estimate on Columbia's part.

(Yet accurate, as it turned out; *Grace* was the definitive 'sleeper' hit, selling only a few thousand copies in its first week.) As the album found its rightful place in the stores, alongside the many albums of his father, Buckley was in London, reconnecting (in more ways than one) with Cocteau Twin Elizabeth Fraser. The infatuation that began at the show in Atlanta earlier in the year briefly became a full-blown affair.

Speaking in the BBC's *Everybody Here Wants You*, Fraser admitted that Buckley brought some joy back into her life. 'I was having a hard time in the band,' she said. 'To me, Jeffrey had been given this set of paints; I had all this colour in my life again.' Fraser was aware, when they met, that Buckley idolised her, which she found 'creepy'. (The Cocteau Twins had been on high rotation for Buckley and his band while they were recording at Bearsville, while Buckley included Fraser amongst his many vocal impersonations.) But this admiration ran both ways. 'I was like that with him,' she confessed. 'It's so embarrassing, but it's the truth. He was really spontaneous and exciting.' In the little time they actually shared, she and Buckley would exchange diaries, reading each other's most intimate thoughts. 'It was very personal stuff,' she understated neatly. 'I couldn't help falling in love with him; he was so adorable.' It seemed inevitable that they'd record together; the result was a lovely, languid ballad, 'All Flowers In Time Bend Towards the Sun', still officially unreleased, but easily traceable on-line.

Their affair wasn't built to last. Fraser said that although 'there was a great deal of intimacy, other times I'd feel like I just wasn't penetrating this Jeff Buckley boy at all. Sometimes I felt like a groupie.' Like many others who knew Buckley, Fraser got the feeling that he was a man in a hurry. 'His was a life of experimentation... to experience as much as possible.'[2]

That was on full and obvious display during his first visit to Ireland, which began with a gig at a Dublin venue called Whelans. Glen Hansard, Buckley's running buddy from his days in the Commitments touring band, opened for him, with his band The Frames. 'This is my mate Glen and we're going to hang out for the next few hours,' Buckley told the band, as he and Hansard boarded the tour bus. With Columbia staff and management out of earshot, Buckley told Hansard that it cost a 'fucking bomb' to make *Grace*, but that he was proud of the album, slipping Hansard a copy. Hansard, admittedly, was having trouble adjusting to his old friend's career upgrade. 'It was my first time travelling in a tour bus,' he recalled. 'You have to understand that I only knew him as a bloke from LA that was in a hair band, so I was saying to him, "This is fucking amazing; you're huge".'

Hansard also got to witness first-hand the fervent response Buckley was now receiving from the press, especially in the UK. 'In Dublin, all these fucking journalists who wouldn't talk to my band were all over him like flies. It was this weird atmosphere. These guys, cynical old bastards, were starstruck, which made it clear that he was special. [A writer from a French magazine awaited Buckley in Dublin, as did an American journalist, flown in to cover the tour.] In the naivety of my youth I thought the journalists were all idiots. Not that Jeff wasn't brilliant – he was. I always though that Jeff was an amazing singer but I'm not sure that his songs were that great. But as a singer, fucking hell, he could sing his balls off.'

As Hansard discovered the next day in Belfast, Buckley didn't restrict his singing to the stage, either. Bored by the interminable rain and yet another hotel room, Buckley grabbed his acoustic guitar and hit the streets, in the process blowing out various interviews and a sound check. His 'people' had no idea where he'd gone. To Hansard, the incident illustrated Buckley's need to be totally 'in the present'. 'Jeff disappeared in the middle of the afternoon. It was pissing rain, but he went off with his guitar, a Gibson acoustic, literally wandering around town singing, in the rain, for an hour and a half,' Hansard laughed. 'We only knew about it because people at the gig told us, "We saw Jeff Buckley today, walking in the rain singing." He was like the Pied Piper. He wasn't even busking, just walking around, with the rain pissing down, singing. He was one of these guys who was always right in the moment, totally in the present, and I think that's what got him into loads of trouble with women. The present was the only thing that mattered, it was more important than the recent past or his potential future.' Mind you, Buckley and band weren't exactly lady-killers, at least according to Mark Naficy, who spent the best part of two years working with them. 'Yeah, they could have [been] but they didn't really work that angle. Compared to other bands I've worked with they were indifferent. They didn't really search that out, or show as much interest as I've seen in other bands. And I've seen the worse; I came up through the 1970s and '80s.'

While Buckley wiped the Dublin rain from his Gibson, media from one end of the globe to the other ran their eyes over the Sony press release that accompanied *Grace*. It was another telling document, a key part of the Jeff Buckley manifesto, which read as though his father was nothing more than the dead guy in the next record store slot. Somewhat naively, the name Tim Buckley didn't appear anywhere in the album bio. Instead, the younger Buckley talked up his roots ('rootless trailer trash born in southern California'); his love of New York ('more than any place, this is where I felt I belonged; I never fit in in California'); and his desire to make a 'band' album, despite his love of such singular talents as Dylan, Robert Johnson and Thelonious Monk ('there are so many other areas you can go with other instruments going at the same time... it's the difference between the eight year old and the 28 year old'). He also talked up his newfound connection with Tighe, Grondahl and Johnson ('we really became a band during the album; even now, we're still evolving'), plus his willingness to wear his heart further out on his sleeve than any of his musical peers. 'Sensitivity isn't being wimpy,' Buckley said, 'it's about being so painfully aware that a flea landing on a dog is like a sonic boom.'

Within two A4 pages he'd declared himself to be a drifter, a dreamer, a bandleader and a poet. Buckley also portrayed himself as a deep, if somewhat oblique thinker when asked to describe his music. 'It's part quagmire and part structure,' he figured. 'That's my musical aesthetic; just this imperceptible fleeting memory.' And then this ominous coda, while still on the subject of music: 'It's like there's a guard at the gate of your memory and you're not supposed to remember certain things because you can only obtain the full experience by completely going under its power,' said Buckley, in full rhapsodic flow. 'You can be destroyed or scarred [by music] – you don't know. *It's like dying*.'[3]

On release, *Grace* kept some interesting company, alongside new albums from noise addicts Dinosaur Jr (*Without A Sound*), Cali punks Bad Religion (*Stranger Than Fiction*), *Definitely Maybe*, the emphatic debut from Britpop frontrunners Oasis, Body Count's politicised thrash-rap (*Born Dead*), even the watered-down soul-pop of Boyz II Men (*Boyz II Men II*). The US airwaves were no less confusing, given that the suicide of Kurt Cobain had effectively killed off grunge's era-defining surge. Instead, the charts were clogged with the usual uninspired fluff: bespectacled coffee-shop strummer Lisa Loeb, R&B acts such as Coolio and Babyface, and the rootsy pop of Sheryl Crow. With its epic, slowburning grandeur and distinctive timelessness, *Grace* zapped the 1990s back into life, and many critics immediately responded to its high voltage charge.

Billboard was one of Buckley's first champions, describing *Grace* as 'a fully realised debut album plumped with a thick band sound that borders on dreamy and a vocal that crosses over into the amazing.' And then the unavoidable rejoinder that was echoed in so many reviews: 'It's in that voice that the bloodline shows.'[4] The *Austin American-Statesman* picked up on this theme. 'Unabashedly romantic and overwhelmingly passionate, Buckley sounds like Robert Plant without the sexual squealing, or like an edgier version of his late father Tim.' Their critic also took the time to acknowledge the links between *Grace* and other equally idiosyncratic singer/songwriters. 'It's a rare artist who dares to create something as exquisite as Van Morrison's *Astral Weeks*, Nick Drake's *Five Leaves Left* or

170

Tim Buckley's *Happy/Sad*.[5] Buckley must have squirmed at the idea of once again being likened to his late, often great father, but the comparison was valid: few artists since Tim Buckley had dared to mesh such a conflagration of styles and sounds with emotions that appear to have emerged straight from his very soul.

You could hear that throughout *Grace*, from the aching-hearted splendour of 'Last Goodbye' to the haunting, baroque 'Corpus Christi Carol', and, especially, in the dazzling 'Lover, You Should Have Come Over', a song that had morphed from a simple Sin-E strum to an epic embellished with gospel choruses and angelic harmonies. Andy Wallace had earned his keep – *Grace* was an album that reached (sometimes over-reached) for the stars. Then there was 'Hallelujah', which was aptly summed up by *Time* writer Josh Tyrangiel some time after Buckley died. 'Cohen murmured the original like a dirge,' he wrote, 'but except for a single overwrought breath before the music kicks in, Buckley treated the 7-min. song like a tiny capsule of humanity, using his voice to careen between glory and sadness, beauty and pain, mostly just by repeating the word hallelujah. It's not only Buckley's best song – it's one of the great songs.'

The *Boston Herald* was another daily that supported Buckley pretty much from the get-go; they announced that *Grace* was 'nothing short of amazing'. Even the dodgy pun was excusable, at least in this case. Alongside a Zeppelin comparison that Buckley no doubt respected, there was yet another link to Tim: 'Like his late father,' the overwhelmingly positive review stated, 'Jeff's vocals surge and soar in brilliant tugs of war with his songs. *Grace* [is] a perfect late-night listen and one of the year's most beautiful albums.'[6] In an odd harbinger of what lay ahead for Buckley, the *Washington Post* suggested that Buckley's 'shimmery, dynamic style suggests careful study of Tom Verlaine', even though there was, as yet, no evidence that Buckley had Television's *Marquee Moon* on high rotation.[7]

Soon after, Australian critics started to join in this chorus of approval. 'You read it here – album of the year,' announced the *Sydney Morning Herald*. '*Grace* is, like all the best rock music,' the review continued, 'a work of equal parts drama and exhilaration... [it also] presents a compelling argument for the genetic inheritance of genius.' There was something else that Buckley shared with his father; despite being overwhelmed with critical superlatives – 'sublime', said the *Columbus Dispatch*; 'rarely has a tortured soul been so appealing,' insisted *Mojo* – he soon learned that high praise didn't necessarily translate into sales. It wasn't until 1995 that *Grace* entered the *Billboard* Top 200 album chart, clawing its way to the lofty plateau of position 149.

Nevertheless, a creeping antagonism towards the press began to sneak into Buckley's many interviews. Speaking with the *Toronto Star*, he dismissed a positive UK story as 'so by-the-numbers... it wasn't reviewing, it was just saying where I failed and succeeded – meagrely,' he sniped. (Buckley had just been voted #12 in *Mojo's* 100 Great Voices poll, a few spots ahead of his father.) 'It's such a hard relationship you and I have,' Buckley continued, with no small amount of hubris, referring to the interaction between singers and critics. 'It's so alien, because you will never make an album, or write a song that will be recorded or will last. I mean, I will be dead and [*Grace*] may still be in print – that's quite possible. [Songs] are not meant to be broken down into bits, because you can't love a bit.'[8]

Inevitably perhaps, Buckley saved his harshest putdowns for those reprobates who dared to bracket his music with that of his father. He truly unleashed when he sat down with a writer from the *St Louis Post-Despatch*. 'I'm tired of this,' he growled. 'I'm tired of every single journalist seeing fit to keep [bringing it up]. Everybody knows my attitude on it. Nobody wants to observe it. So I'll just have to deal with it, I guess.' Then this bilious, sarcastic salvo: 'Maybe I'm not a good enough artist that people just think of me. Maybe in the future, I'll bloom into something that will just make people look at me for what I am.' Somewhat unwisely, he insisted that he neither sang like his father, or even owned any of his records, which wasn't the absolute truth. 'I have no intention of taking on a legacy that wasn't bestowed on me,' he sneered.[9]

This was just the kind of curt dismissal that alienated people such as Lee Underwood, his father's friend and sidekick, who'd spent two days with Buckley several years earlier, relating everything he could recall about life with Tim. They also exchanged numerous letters on the subject of his father. As Underwood wrote in his book *Blue Melody*, and later confirmed with me via email, 'In his own recordings, it was patently apparent to me that [Jeff] had listened carefully to Tim's every album, had wisely chosen Tim as his foremost mentor, had learned dozens of vocal inflections, phrasings, and "gymnastic" techniques from Tim, and had masterfully incorporated his knowledge and experience of Tim's music into his own unique, powerful, and exceptionally heart-touching creations. More than any other artist before Jeff or since, Jeff was directly influenced by Tim and his music, perhaps particularly *Starsailor* – and there was absolutely nothing wrong in that. He was the only singer I have ever heard who was vocally or temperamentally even *capable* of being influenced to that degree.'

Mick Grondahl witnessed Jeff's conflict almost every night, as Tim Buckley fans continued to appear at show after show, waving their dog-eared copies of *Happy/Sad* in the bewildered, frustrated face of his son. 'He'd have people coming backstage with old Tim Buckley vinyl for him to sign,' he recalled, with noticeable distaste. 'The worse was when he was once advertised as "Jim Buckley", that was pretty bad. He hated that. He met his father for an afternoon or whatever, he really had nothing to do with him.' During the live set filmed for the *Mystery White Boy* DVD, Buckley responded to repeated requests for his father's songs with a blunt and emphatic 'fuck off', before losing himself in an 'everything sucks' rant – 'except The Smiths', he hastened to add. At later shows, at the mention of his father's name, Buckley would strike the pose of a junkie shooting up. During a gig in Ferndale, Michigan, a female Tim fan yelled out a request between songs. Buckley locked eyes with the woman and replied: 'I don't play that hippie shit.' He drove his point home when he rammed his guitar repeatedly into his amp, Pete Townshend style.

Buckley found an outlet from the stress of touring and dealing with Tim Buckley nutters; he started to drink heavily. A story circulated that he was so smashed during a show in California that he fell off the stage. He also got so drunk at a Joni Mitchell gig at New York venue Fez that he fell asleep under a table and snored his way through a rare set from one of his musical heroes. And there was another gig, at a Chicago venue once owned by gangster Al Capone, called the Pepper Mill, where Buckley virtually rolled on stage. 'Jeff was really drunk and started doing one of his father's songs,' said Grondahl. 'He was so bombed on tequila. He just got drunk and started being destructive or whatever you want to call it. Something must have gone really wrong.' What appears to have happened was another case of Buckley speaking without engaging his brain; he had made a disparaging remark towards MTV, and was duly reprimanded by Columbia staff. It felt like the Dylan situation all over again. 'But that was pretty rare,' insisted Grondahl, 'and luckily we had two more nights there to make up for it.'*

A few months after the Chicago incident, Buckley referred to it in his first on-line posting (he was a reluctant, and somewhat wary, Internet user). 'NO MORE CUERVO NIGHTS!!!,' his post screamed. 'DON'T WORRY CHICAGO!!!!' He also took the time to point out that the band

---

* As far as Grondahl was concerned, the mounting number of in-studio sets at radio stations was far more demanding than his boss' boozing. 'Radio was a drag because it was usually early in the morning, after having played a show late the night before,' he said. 'It was tiring. You'd have to bring gear up and down. In the end Matt started to use an Indian hand drum for percussion when we did the record stores and radio stations.'

'mashed the night before into goatshit.'[10] Unfortunately for Buckley and band, a reviewer turned up to his drunken first night and slagged the show, quite justifiably, noting how the gig was 'pathetic one minute, galvanising the next'. 'Of course,' Buckley wrote, 'the stinking journalists didn't turn up for night number two at the Green Mill gig.' He summed up 1994 thusly: 'This has been the most surreal year of joy and utterly satanic bullshit mixed together.' (His warped sense of humour shone through in a letter to his fan club, postmarked Austin, Texas, November 29, 1994, 5:10am, where he praised the fans 'who channel dead spirits from space and also [the] ones who want to murder me. All my hugs and kisses. In hell, baby.')

A little further down the road, when Merri Cyr caught up with the band in Louisiana to document what was beginning to seem like an endless tour, she was stunned to see the change in her old friend and favourite photographic subject. 'I remember the first day I got there... he was pretty fucked up then, in really rough shape, drinking a lot of booze, and the band was on the verge of breaking up. During that first day we walked to this bar and he quaffed down like four Cuervos and I said, "What the fuck are you doing?" ' Cyr felt that Buckley needed someone to put him in line, but there was no-one in his entourage willing to do that. 'I don't blame the other people, exactly, but all the people around him, like Dave [Lory] and Gene [Bowen, Lory's assistant] and the band members, they all worked for him. I don't think any of the band guys confronted him. Jeff might have been small in stature but he could be quite intimidating and quite scary. I didn't have to care that much about being fired because I was only there for a short time, but he was such a mess.'

Yet Jon Pope, Buckley's Australian tour manager, suggested to me that Gene Bowen, who has since admitted to his own 'active drug/alcohol addiction', was hired specifically to 'babysit' Buckley, who he sensed may have had a 'junkie past'. The veteran Pope had a solid radar for this type of thing, too, telling me how during his lengthy career, 'I've had to call police, I've had to take [musicians] to NA and AA meetings, I've had wives lock husbands out of hotel rooms, the works.' (Pope, nonetheless, shared a few backstage joints with Buckley.) 'When he drank it was scary; he was hard to reach,' said one of Buckley's friends. 'It was like he was on an emotional asteroid.' Buckley's New York supporter Danny Fields was a tad more understanding when it came to the subject of alcohol, possibly because he'd seen the dent that Tim Buckley could make in a bottle of booze. '[Jeff] sure could drink,' he said to me. 'You know, *Irish*.'

Yet the respect for Buckley continued to roll in, and not all of it was from a fawning music press. On stage at the annual Reading Festival in late August

1994, Radiohead's alien-like singer, Thom Yorke, broke into an unaccompanied, impromptu version of Tim Buckley's 'Sing A Song For You'. This little-known tune, from the 1969 album *Happy/Sad*, was totally lost on a huge gathering awaiting 'Creep', their anthem for the disaffected. Though Yorke was paying his dues to Tim, he was also tuning into the music of Jeff Buckley. Chris Dowd recalled how Yorke appeared in the moshpit at one of Buckley's New York shows – possibly the CMJ showcase at the Supper Club, on September 24, 1994 – but left the gig well before it ended, much to Buckley's dismay. 'It bothered him a lot, enough to where he mentioned it to me,' said Dowd. 'I told him he probably heard you sing in person and got freaked and left. As far as artistic respect goes, well, Thom Yorke was a contemporary and when he walked out, Jeff was like, "I must have sucked that night". [But] if *OK Computer* doesn't sound like Jeff singing, I don't know what. It's freakish. You listen to *Pablo Honey* and *The Bends* and then listen to *OK Computer* and there's this quantum change in his voice, a really weird inflection.

'When I was living in London,' Dowd continued, 'a friend of mine said: "Did you hear Radiohead on the BBC? They were playing *Grace*." And I was like, aha, there you go. Meanwhile, he went to his grave thinking that Thom Yorke hated his voice.'

The long-lasting relationship between Buckley and French audiences began to blossom as the *Grace* tour reached Paris in late September 1994. It would reach a dizzying peak during their next visit to France, when Buckley and band headlined iconic venue L'Olympia, a hall that had hosted everyone from French songbird Edith Piaf to The Beatles, The Velvet Underground and James Brown. 'Such an honour, [but] just terrifying,' said Buckley, when asked about following in these particularly sizeable artistic footsteps. 'How am I supposed to follow Piaf? I don't understand why I'm so successful in France. Maybe it's because the French love the underlying stories, and that's what I give them. There's a whole novel waiting to unfold. They love the poetry and the lyricism of a certain idea of America.'[11] However, Buckley and German audiences didn't click with the same sort of immediacy. During a show on September 11, 1994, at a Berlin venue called Loft, Buckley asked: 'How many people have the album?', and was met with a deafening silence. 'None?' he replied. 'Awesome.' At least the guy understood humility and hadn't lost his sense of humour. He ended that gig with a pithy: 'Ich bin eine New Yorker; come up and see me some time.' Only Buckley could simultaneously channel JFK and Mae West.

It was during another French stopover, in January 1995, that Buckley finally caved in to Columbia pressure and agreed to shoot a video, for 'Last

Goodbye'. The underwhelming sales of *Grace*, at least during its first few months, meant that Buckley's strident 'no video' policy was now rendered obsolete; if Columbia couldn't break a track on radio, maybe they'd have more success with MTV. It made perfect sense: after all, Buckley and his not-so-merry men weren't bad looking guys, a handy attribute in a visual medium. But the shoot, and the general confusion regarding the video – what Leah Reid delicately described elsewhere as a 'cluster fuck' – was more evidence of a growing malaise between Buckley and Columbia. It also further alienated Merri Cyr, another of Buckley's many boosters, to the point where she virtually turned her back on him. She called the entire production 'a fiasco; just stupid', proof that Buckley had folded to pressure from both the label and his management.

From the very beginning, it was a big budget disaster. For reasons he never explained, Buckley had arranged to have both Cyr and John Jesurin, a theatre friend of guitarist Michael Tighe – someone Cyr described as 'a sort of relatively famous underground play director' – direct the clip. 'This is part of how Jeff was weird,' said Cyr. 'He'd set it up so he had *two directors.*' Cyr's plan, which she'd mapped out in detail with Buckley, was to pay homage to famous French director Jean Cocteau, while at the same time developing a storyline based on Buckley's lyrics. 'I was trying to do this romantic imagery but make it look like an old film,' said Cyr. 'Jeff and I talked for a number of days about the idea; he loved it, but at that time he was convinced people at Sony were spying on him, so he was saying, "Don't tell anyone." I was like, whatever.' But Cyr's idea was never relayed to Jesurin, so a bizarre situation developed where two distinctly different 'visions' of 'Last Goodbye' were being shot at the same time. 'I'd worked on this concept for a long time with Jeff and that wasn't being communicated to this other guy,' said Cyr, still frustrated by the memory. 'I had nothing to do with him.'

Cyr, to her credit, did her best to defend Buckley. When she learned that the catering for the clip was coming in somewhere around $US10,000, for two days worth of food – the rumoured cost of the video was in the vicinity of $300,000 – she snitched to Buckley. 'I kind of fucked myself, I guess,' Cyr said. 'I told him they were going to spend a tremendous amount of money for nothing and I got punished. They [the label] cut back my days of shooting.' Buckley could see that the project was out of control and expressed his concerns to Cyr. 'He gave me an earful about how pissed off he was during the John Jesurin shoot. I think they shot it in France and then transferred it to Kinescope, which cost about another fifty thousand bucks, all kinds of junk, you know? You can see he's pissed off in it, he's looking at

uckley was most at home playing live: 'In the course of one performance he could be soft, accessible, angry – and sometimes his anger, which he had plenty of, would pop up,' said a friend. (KELLY DERVISH/RETNA)

'Touring changed him,' said Columbia's Leah Reid. 'Before he left he was very in touch with his feminine side. When he came back from tour he was a farting, belching guy.' (MERRI CYR/WWW.MERRICYR.COM)

'He was sort of nomadic,' a friend said of Buckley. 'There's also some sense of security that comes from someone saying to you: This is where you're going, here's your money for the day, we need to be at this place at this time.' (MERRI CYR/WWW.MERRICYR.COM)

A live radio show in Dallas, Texas, November 30, 1! 'He wasn't a gracious guest,' said Nicholas Hil of WFMU, a radio station that supported Buckle early on. 'He very much used the airwaves.' (MERRI CYR/WWW.MERRICYR.COM)

Mixing the European release of 'Eternal Life', Miami, Florida, December 1994, with producer Clif Norrell:
Soon after, Buckley would amaze Norrell in a New York club when he stood on the dancefloor and crooned
Soundgarden's 'Black Hole Sun'. **(MERRI CYR/WWW.MERRICYR.COM)**

Life on the bus during the seemingly never-ending tour pushing *Grace*. Drinking became one of
Buckley's indulgences. 'When he drank it was scary; he was hard to reach,' said a friend. 'It was like
he was on an emotional asteroid.' **(MERRI CYR/WWW.MERRICYR.COM)**

Another day, another in-store. Budding singer / songwriter Duncan Sheik looked on at Tower Records in LA and almost quit music on the spot. 'It was very intimidating. I just thought, well, this is tough competition in the guys-with-guitars racket.' (MERRI CYR/WWW.MERRICYR.COM)

Live at the Fleece & Firkin in Bristol, England, January 15, 1995. A-listers were in abundance wherever Buckley played; Chrissie Hynde was at his earliest London shows and tennis player John McEnroe helped lug his gear. (ROB WATKINS/RETNA)

Buckley at Glastonbury, 1995. Buckley connected much more strongly with English, French and Australian audiences than he did at home – at least until he died, when his version of 'Hallelujah' became a staple in the closing credits of films and TV shows

(BRIAN RASIC/REX FEATURES)

Backstage with Paul and Linda McCartney. 'She was gushing all over him, as was Paul,' recalled Danny Fields, who made the introduction. 'Now his career was really off and running.' (MERRI CYR/WWW.MERRICYR.COM)

According to Chris Dowd, Joan Wasser, pictured here backstage with Buckley, was the singer's 'man-sized' love, the one real love of Buckley's life. She later achieved solo success under the name Joan As Police Woman (MERRI CYR/WWW.MERRICYR.COM)

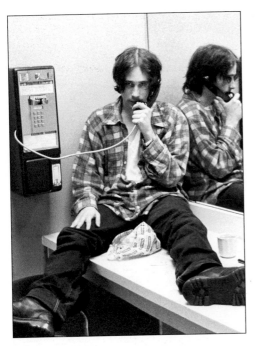

'It's not the real world, touring,' said Buckley bandmate Mick Grondahl, who felt that the *Grace* dates dragged on for too long and tried to shut it down. 'I should have listened to my body, which was saying, "Enough is enough".' (MERRI CYR/WWW.MERRICYR.COM)

Buckley on Broadway with Courtney Love, 1995, an invitation he should have rejected. 'Dude, I want buy every newspaper and burn it,' he told his frien Chris Dowd. 'I'm so embarrassed.' (LFI)

In awe of legendary Pakistani qawaali singer, Nusrat Fateh Ali Khan, a huge influence on Buckley's singing sty When asked about the connection, Buckley simply said: 'Nusrat is my Elvis.' (© 1995 JACK VARTOOGIAN/FRONTROWPHOTOS

The remaining members of Buckley's band play at his memorial service at Brooklyn's St Ann's Church, August 1, 1997. 'The whole thing was horrible,' said one mourner. 'They were putting chairs around in a circle like an AA meeting.' **(BOB BERG/RETNA)**

Buckley's mother Mary Guibert hosts a tribute show at the Garage, Highbury, London in December 2003. Many Buckley insiders have criticised her handling of his legacy. 'He would have given everything with his name on it away,' said one. **(HOWARD DENNER/RETNA)**

Jeff Beckley: A pure drop in an ocean of noise.

the camera like he's really mad, but he set up that situation. I think he wanted to please people all over.'*

That look Buckley gave the camera at the end of 'Last Goodbye' neatly summed up the whole debacle; it wielded the same 'fuck you' as Kurt Cobain's screwed-up mug at the close of the Nirvana video for 'Smells Like Teen Spirit'. If you needed a visual indicator of how Cobain and Buckley reacted to life in the mainstream, it's right there on the small screen. Simply put, neither enjoyed the taste of the so-called good life, even if the Buckley video did score some rotation on MTV's *120 Minutes*, a program he and Tighe reluctantly hosted, and helped *Grace* crawl into the Billboard Top 200 chart. (It was also nominated for Best New Artist clip at the 1995 MTV Music Video Awards.) The budget blowout certainly didn't win Buckley any brownie points at Columbia. 'I'm sure Donnie and co were pissed about it,' said Mike Webb, 'but the fact that they were willing to spend as much as they did tells me Jeff was a priority and that they were willing to work with him. I don't remember where Steve [Berkowitz] stood in all this, but I do seem to remember him shaking his head about the whole thing.'

Leah Reid thought that Buckley's sneer told the story of the making of that video. 'He was so pissed off; he was just hating it. That's what I think of when I see that video; how difficult the process was and how it showed in his face,' she said. 'This was one video that may or may not get played on MTV, and 300 grand meant he'd have to stay out on the road for months [to cover its production costs]. I thought it was an interesting video, but not a 300 grand video.' Reid, however, insisted that Buckley warmed to the 'art' of videos during the making of 'So Real', *Grace's* far more playful second clip, which was directed, several months later, by the highly-regarded Sophie Muller. 'He was way into it, he loved working with Sophie and being in the gorilla suit,' she recalled, referring to various hairy cameos in the clip.

Buckley's drinking, and the physical and mental demands of the road, were clearly taking their toll. A month before the 'Last Goodbye' shoot, he'd appeared at Sony's annual conference in New York, looking more than a little dishevelled. He certainly didn't seem like the same guy who'd worked his magic on Mariah Carey and others with Led Zep's 'The Rain Song' at Donny Ienner's farm, not so long ago.

'Touring changed him,' Reid told me. 'Before he left he was very in touch with his feminine side and gravitated towards women and was very

---

* Cyr eventually edited her own version of the disjointed, relatively meaningless clip, which she now streams on-line at www.merricyr.com.

gentle. When he came back from tour he was a farting, belching guy. That really struck me. He'd spent a lot of time with a lot of guys. But the thing is that he lived to play music and the opportunity to play it every day appealed to him. And he was sort of nomadic, too. There's also some sense of security that comes from someone saying to you: This is where you're going, here's your money for the day, we need to be at this place at this time.'

Yet Buckley hadn't lost his ability to shock. Around the time of the 'Last Goodbye' shoot, he scored a ticket to the ritzy Rock and Roll Hall of Fame induction night, the annual $2,000-and-upwards-a-plate affair held in the Grand Ballroom of New York's Waldorf Astoria Hotel, an event which traditionally attracts the great and the good of the rock industry, everyone from past and present record company presidents to genuine superstars. On this particular night, January 12, 1995, Frank Zappa – whom Buckley had idolised all those years ago in LA – was a posthumous inductee. Moon Unit Zappa, with whom Buckley had become quite close, was there to accept the award on her father's behalf. Danny Fields, meanwhile, had volunteered to help out; his main role was running the backstage press conference, 'telling people to shut up, that kind of thing,' he laughed.

Fields was required to walk between the backstage area and the main hall, via a space between the stage and the main VIP table, where Jann Wenner, the editor and publisher of *Rolling Stone*, and Seymour Stein, the Hall of Fame's then president, held court. 'I was running back and forth and saw a flash of pink,' Fields recalled, 'and it was Jeffy, he was sitting at Seymour's table, wearing a shocking pink Steven Sprouse jacket. I put my hand on Seymour's shoulder and told him how lucky he was to have Jeff Buckley at his table, and I asked what he was doing there. Seymour was the head of Elektra at the time, and he said: "He's my artist." ' Fields was confused: Tim Buckley was on Elektra, not Jeff. When Fields disputed this, Stein replied: 'Oh, he's *like* my artist.' Just as Fields moved away from the table, Buckley spotted him and called out his name. He stopped in his tracks.

'So Jeffy gets up in this pink jacket that you could see across the river, runs between the VIP tables, puts his arms around me and in front of 4000 people plants a smacker on my lips. On the mouth! And he wouldn't let me go. We were standing there, locked in a kiss in front of the whole music business,' Fields said, laughing wildly. 'There were gasps. I mean, that's Danny Fields, and he's kissing Jeff Buckley in front of everybody in the music business. And I thought, "Fuck you all – this is what I do." And I hope you notice that *he kissed me*. I did dine out on it for a while.' Later that night, Fields saw Buckley again, this time in a teary embrace with Moon Unit

Zappa backstage, after her acceptance speech. 'They just sobbed and cried in each other's arms. I thought it was so touching.'

Glen Hansard saw up close the toll that touring and promotion had taken on his friend's mind and his body, when Buckley and band returned to Ireland for more shows in January 1995. This time around, Buckley was no pied piper, serenading startled fans on the streets of Dublin. Buckley called Hansard and offered him the opening slot, which he played solo. When he arrived, Hansard was shocked by the sight of his buddy. 'He just looked fucked,' said Hansard. 'I said to him, "Are you all right man?" I was kind of worried about him. He said, "Glen, I've got all these Sony people hanging around my neck that want a piece of me and I can't talk to you." ' Buckley gave Hansard his mother's phone number in Orange County, which is where he was heading soon after, to hide out for a while. He said to Hansard, 'Call me there, I'm in a really fucking mad place, I'm fucked.'

Having only arrived in Dublin about an hour before he was due on-stage, the set he played that night showed how fatigued Buckley had become. 'They were very, very tired, and he had a really shit gig,' continued Hansard. After a desperate 'Eternal Life', Buckley did something totally out of character: he threw himself into the crowd, Eddie Vedder-style. When Hansard caught up with him backstage and mentioned that he didn't take him for a stagediving type, Buckley replied: 'Dude, I couldn't give them my music, so I gave them myself.' 'Fair enough,' Hansard replied, and reached for another beer.

Hansard had no clear-cut explanation as to the root cause of Buckley's deterioration, apart from the obvious demands of life in constant motion. He's also not sure that drugs were to blame, either, despite frequently hearing rumours that Buckley was using heroin. 'Lots of people were saying that he was on smack, but I don't know. I never did it so I don't know that look,' he said. 'I didn't know where his head was at. When I knew him at the start he was golden, he had this mad energy coming off him. But you spend a few years touring and you do change. He didn't look like he was doing smack or anything, but he was drawn and pale; he just looked tired. I never knew Jeff Buckley the celebrity, I knew the guy I hung out with in Ireland and a few times in America at the very beginning.' Sadly, he'd never see Buckley again.

Mark Geary, another Buckley buddy from the Sin-E days, agreed with Hansard's assessment. 'Touring will [wear you down] quicker than anything. You get to a point where it's just burnout: it's got nothing to do with the booze or the drugs you're taking, it's just fatigue and an expectant audience who have a notion of what you do and what you can do for them. It's really tough.' Mick Grondahl was also starting to feel the pinch, as he told me. 'It's not the real world, touring. To live in that for more than a certain period of time – and this was our first time, so we didn't know what to expect in a lot of ways... but I should have listened to my body, which was saying, enough is enough.' (It's likely that Grondahl, who'd allegedly develop serious drug problems, was already getting wasted on the road. An insider who I spoke with for this book recalled being asked by members of Buckley's band to score cocaine for them.)

Buckley's former Musician's Institute pal, Tom Chang, related how, as *Grace*-mania was unfolding, he ran into Buckley on a scorching New York summer's day, and found his old friend draped in a massive fur coat. The feeling that Buckley was doing serious drugs was impossible to ignore. 'I just said, "What the fuck are you doing?" It was pretty clear something was going on. There was such a change in his persona from the guy I knew, you know? The Jeff I knew was this really reserved, humble guy and suddenly he was this other person. I just think he was evolving, well, maybe *devolving* as a person. But I always got the sense that he knew who he was and what he was doing, regardless of how far he was pushing it. I wasn't worried.'

Not that Buckley and the band had much time to stop and reflect, or even catch their breath. Sure, there was a brief respite with Guibert in Orange County, but the *Grace* bandwagon kept on rolling through the early months of 1995, with heavy promotion and the occasional show in France and England, then to Tokyo for their first dates there, before returning to France, Germany, Holland, Belgium and the UK, for gigs that would consume all his energy right through to early March. Despite their relentless schedule, however, Buckley continued to tinker with his songs; during a soundcheck for their oft-bootlegged show at Paris venue The Bataclan, French writer Philippe Perret looked on while Buckley and Tighe devoted the best part of an hour to perfecting the arrangement of 'So Real'. '[It was] evidence,' Perret wrote, 'that he's not tired of his songs and that he always looks for ways of improving them.'[12]

Mark Naficy, who recorded every show of the tour directly from the sound desk, at Buckley's request, was willing to accept a certain amount of blame for this relentless perfectionism. 'It was because I insisted on it to get it right,' he admitted. 'Unless they were working on a new song they were done when I was done. The demand for the good audio systems and long sound checks was from me. I am the culprit.' Jon Pope, Buckley's Australian tour manager, was amazed by Naficy's attention to sonic detail. 'He'd spend hours setting up for each show, primarily so he could record the gig for the band's playback and analysis afterwards,' he recalled, shaking his head.

By early March 1995, the band finally returned home, but only for more rehearsals, followed by yet another lap of America and Europe, beginning in the middle of April and continuing for another seven weeks. It was at this point that bassist Mick Grondahl pulled aside Dave Lory and suggested that maybe they'd done enough touring for the time being. Grondahl may have been 'down for the ride', but he admitted that the road was losing its magic, not just for him, but for everyone in the band. 'I sensed that things had started to fall apart,' Grondahl said to me. 'Matt [Johnson] was certainly becoming less and less satisfied. I was stressing to the management, Dave Lory especially, that to do the States and Europe twice was more than enough and when they went for the third time, they were pushing it.'

Grondahl, like Buckley, had already started thinking about what came next: as good as *Grace* clearly was, and despite the steady flow of positive press, maybe the record just wasn't going to sell in the numbers Columbia had hoped. 'I think we needed to buckle down and start working on the next album, looking at the ideas we'd created on the road,' Grondahl said, 'but they kept saying, no, you need to do this. Part of it was Jeff trying to pay back the money he owed the record company. That was practical, but in the long run it wasn't good, we started to get irritated with each other and things started to devolve. Touring had a lot to do with that. No-one wanted to leave Jeff high and dry, but this was taking its toll. It was one of the more unfortunate aspects of that whole tour.'

Merri Cyr saw how things were falling part when she caught up with the band in Louisiana, primarily to record some kind of on the road video-verite documentary. According to Cyr, 'Jeff was mental; the first couple of days I was there were very difficult. He was now a bit polluted from being on the road so much; he got no rest, he had things that he couldn't work out while he was on the road, people wanted a lot of stuff from him, he was nervous about producing another album – he was afraid about that. It was just really difficult. I was going to split at one point; it was too much for me.' Although never formally released – at least not yet – Cyr's footage reveals in precise detail just how 'mental' Buckley's life had become; there's a surreal, almost deranged quality to the grainy, rough-as-guts footage that accurately portrays the unreality of touring and the psychological damage it can inflict, no matter how much of a 'gypsy' Buckley clearly was. And his boozing didn't help.

There was a sense of Buckley's 'polluted' mindset in one of his rare on-line postings, dated March 31, 1995, where he made clear his discomfort towards the Internet, amongst other things. 'Unfortunately, in this age of Internet, one can't avoid having one's dreck smeared all over the computer waves by curious Net-surfers,' he wrote. 'I'll guess I'll just have to learn to deal with it. Since any show is going to be culled via bootleg for Internet consumption, I assume,' he continued, 'I will be obsessed with the potential humiliation.'

Buckley was right, too; the amount of bootlegs of his shows that had begun to circulate, and still do today, is astounding. He did, however, have a solution to this problem: 'I'll just have to work all the harder to make [the shows] as good for you as it is for me. Any band will tell you: monitors suck. [So] I'm shelling out some dough for my own monitor system.' (These were the speakers that Mark Naficy hand-crafted for Buckley.) 'What a fucking drag,' Buckley concluded. 'I'm so embarrassed. Oh well, that's the way the cookie bounces. Fuck. I love you, anyway.' *Vive la roque, Jeff.*

As often seemed to be the case with Buckley, such downbeat revelations as this were contrasted by frequent highs. On April 13, *Grace* was awarded the Grand Prix International du Disque – Academie Charles Cros, a prestigious prize granted by the French equivalent of the US Recording Academy. It was a rare achievement for anyone, let alone an artist still on his first album. The roll call of previous recipients read like a who's-who of modern pop: Edith Piaf, Jacques Brel, Yves Montand, Leonard Cohen, Joni Mitchell and Buckley's Columbia label-mates, Bob Dylan and Bruce Springsteen, had all been granted the Grand Prix. Buckley was keeping some remarkably lofty company. It was also ample proof just how strong his French connection truly was: France, along with Australia, were the first countries to grant *Grace* gold status. (It wasn't until 2002 that the LP reached gold sales in the USA.)

With Buckley's next US tour now in full swing, he seemed to finally be revelling in yet another round of interviews and on-stage explanations of his music. Speaking with the *San Francisco Chronicle*, Buckley described *Grace* as 'a low-down dreamy bit of psyche', which the daily's music critic figured was 'as good an explanation as any'. During a Canadian TV show, he was quizzed about 'Last Goodbye' and his explanation seemed to clarify – sort of – Kathryn Grimm's feeling that the song documented his doomed romance with 'an older woman'. 'Some people,' Buckley said, 'they get into affairs that they know in their bodies won't last... but they go for it, anyway. People are very talented at falling out, torture, like truffles in the forest. And they eat them, a lot. But I was 22, she was 37,' he added, finally cutting to the chase, 'it wasn't gonna work out.'[13] A couple of days later, he said that 'Goodbye' was 'fag rock for straight people'. Then, during a show at San Diego's Back Door, he introduced 'Eternal Life' as 'a song about Republicans, religious fanatics and morons who cut school and shit.'[14]

Funnier still was his intro to 'Kick Out The Jams', mid set at the Great American Music Hall in San Francisco: 'And then on the seventh day,' Buckley said, grinning, ready to rock, 'God got into his underwear and got a broom and he invented rocking out!'[15]

On May 3, 1995, the Buckley bandwagon returned to Los Angeles, where, amongst various promo duties, he pulled off a devastating in-store set at Tower Records. Amongst the throng were Buckley's rarely-seen mother, Mary Guibert, and his former bandmate and object of affection, Carla Azar. She, in turn, invited along her friend, singer/songwriter Duncan Sheik, who was about to become the latest Jeff Buckley convert. 'She said he was a friend and that I might really like it,' Sheik said, when we spoke in early 2007. 'He played four songs, among them were "Grace", 'So Real" and "Lover, You Should Have Come Over" and I remember being just amazed by how great the band was and how good Jeff's singing was.' As he and Azar left, however, Sheik was overwhelmed by a sense of gloom. 'Here I am,' he recalled, 'trying to be this troubadour singer/songwriter, doing things in a sort of progressive way, and here's this guy who's got this record out and has done it better than I'll ever be able to do it. It was very intimidating, I have to say. His voice was so singular, so strong and so unique. I just thought, well, this is tough competition in the guys–with–guitars racket.'

Soon after, Sheik watched a Buckley set at LA club Largo, and witnessed the human jukebox in full comic action. 'He seemed a bit nervous,' he said, 'but once the crowd warmed up to him he started doing all these hilarious musical jokes, pretending to be a trumpet player, things that had nothing to do with his record, little skits that created a sweet interaction with the audience. That was charming.'

On reflection, Sheik believes that this LA visit was a turning point in *Grace's* commercial worth. 'When Carla and I saw Jeff at Tower Records, the record had sold about 40,000 copies in America and it looked like it was going to end there,' he said. '[The thinking would have been that] the single was done, nice first try, go back into the studio and make another record. But there was this strange, slow, steady build that happened here, and I guess his star really rose in France and Australia. Things changed.'

Notes

1. Bessman, Jim: Columbia Set For Jeff Buckley's Graceful Bow; *Billboard*, July 16, 1994
2. BBC2: *Everybody Here Wants You* documentary

3. Anon: *Grace* press release; Columbia Records, 1994

4. Anon: Sound Bites; *St Petersburg Times* (from *Billboard* magazine), September16, 1994

5. McLeese, Don: Grace review, *Austin American-Statesman*, September 22, 1994

6. Lozaw, Tristram: Singer's 'Grace' Is Nothing Short Of Amazing; *Boston Herald*, September 23, 1994

7. Jenkins, Mark: New Releases: Pop; *The Washington Post*, October 23, 1994

8. Howell, Peter: Writing Tunes, Doing Dishes: It's All The Same To Buckley; *Toronto Star*, October 27, 1994

9. Sculley, Alan: A Voice Of His Own: Buckley Avoids Dad's Shadow; *St Louis Post-Dispatch*, October 28, 1994

10. www.jeffbuckley.com

11. Beauvallet, JD: *Live At L'Olympia* liner notes; Columbia Records, 2001

12. Perret, Philippe: Get Your Soul Out, *Les Inrockuptibles*

13. See note 10

14. See note 10

15. See note 10

Chapter Nine

The Wizard Of Oz

Buckley had sunk into a brief depression when *Live At Sin-E* was bracketed with bad-haired belter Michael Bolton, but he felt even more uncomfortable when he appeared in a *People* magazine poll of the '50 Most Beautiful People In The World', published in May 1995. (He was ranked number 12 and was declared 'dishy'.) Some of his friends, including Nathan Larson, from indie rock band Shudder To Think, thought it was hilarious, and went to some lengths to rub it in, but for Buckley it represented everything that he didn't want from stardom. He may have sought out success, but he was a musical purist and borderline control freak who didn't fancy the idea of being some 'hot' pin-up on a teenager's bedroom wall. Almost immediately, he dyed his hair jet black, and stopped shampooing. It just sat on his head, in a messy, unkempt pile, as if to say 'who's beautiful now?' According to Mary Guibert, 'He started uglifying [sic] himself.' 'He was embarrassed by that *People* 50 Most Beautiful thing,' said Chris Dowd. 'He was *so* embarrassed by that shit.' A few days later, during the Chicago set that was filmed and released as the *Live In Chicago* DVD, Buckley aired his grievances, dedicating the show to '*People* magazine and Cuervo tequila – both induce failure.'

Buckley also found the time to vent off-stage. When he and the band were in Seattle, he re-connected with Kathryn Grimm, his vibrator-toting friend from Group Therapy. To Grimm he was just Jeff, but, as she witnessed, Buckley was held in serious esteem by his fellow musicians. 'I was hanging out afterwards and there was a lot of people hanging around, when the drummer of Pearl Jam walked up to Jeff, and it was like he was talking to Jesus. He was so in awe and enamoured of Jeff. It was very interesting to watch.' During this catch-up, Buckley told Grimm that the recognition and acclaim that he'd achieved was not necessarily all he dreamed it would be. 'He wanted to be big,' Grimm insisted, '[but] I'm not sure he was feeling the same way once that happened. We had a couple of personal conversations about that. There was a lot of pressure on him, after *Grace* was out for a while. The expectation was that he had to write another *Grace*. It seemed more like commercial pressure. They wanted to squeeze every dime out of him, [but] I think he wanted to be left alone.'

Still the tour van kept on rolling. Back in New York in early June, for a show at Roseland, Buckley stepped out in front of the faithful wearing the glittery jacket he sported on the cover of *Grace*. Tonight, at least, Jeff Buckley the Rock Star was in the house, and the band could barely be heard above the din of screaming women. Looking on was Paul McCartney, in disguise, along with his two daughters. According to Danny Fields, who'd instigated the first meeting between Buckley and the McCartneys, it was further proof that 'his career was really off and running'. McCartney joined Buckley at the after-show party, at a club called the Batcave. Daniel Harnett, Buckley's friend from Sin-E, was also there. Later on, he expressed some uncertainty about what he'd witnessed at that night's gig.

'We, who had known him in the beginning, felt some weird discomfort seeing him on stage at Roseland, in front of a full rock band, singing through a sound system designed for arena shows, emphasising a hollow, contemporary, vocal-and-drums mix style inappropriate to his intimacy and exquisite technique. We saw... another rock star in the making.'[1] His take echoed that of Mike Webb, who felt that Buckley's band was holding him back. It seemed as though the human jukebox had turned into a karaoke machine.

By this stage, Buckley was rejecting as many offers as he accepted, turning down a Gap commercial, appearances on *Saturday Night Live* and *Letterman*, a Prada photo shoot, even a role in the Barbra Streisand film *The Mirror Has Two Faces*. But one offer he probably should have rejected came from rock's black widow, Courtney Love, who invited him to a new Broadway production of *Hamlet*. In some ways, this showed how naïve Buckley could be: Love was a renowned publicity junkie, who, in the wake of Kurt Cobain's death, had tried hitching her star to numerous young-things-on-the-rise, including Lemonhead Evan Dando. Buckley, who was now dating Boston-based Joan Wasser, foolishly thought it was nothing more than a friendly invite to a show, and being a huge fan of her late husband, couldn't help but be intrigued by Love. But as they left the theatre, they were swamped by paparazzi, and tabloid stories revealing their 'affair' started to spring up like poisonous mushrooms.

Many have suggested that Love stage-managed the entire event, purely for the coverage. Penny Arcade said that Buckley was 'shocked' by the scene outside the theatre. Buckley even put in a call to *Rolling Stone* writer Jason Cohen, who was working on a Hole feature for the magazine, in an attempt to water down the so-called story. 'I went out for one night,' he told Cohen, 'and I'm thrust into this weird, rock-star charade heavy thing.'[2] Buckley also talked it through with his friend Dowd, telling him: 'Dude, I want to buy every newspaper and burn it. I'm so embarrassed.' According to Dowd, 'I know there were some things he got off on, but being written up in tabloids, with Courtney Love and shit, that freaked him out. He was kind of like this reluctant rock star.' In an on-line posting, Mary Guibert described the conversation she had with her son. '[He said] "I should have known that she was as shallow as her lyrics".' And Guibert's take? 'The Love-less one turned Jeff off BIG TIME! I think she's scum.'[3]

A more worthy invitation came soon after, this time from Elvis Costello, who was curating the third annual Meltdown Festival, held at the Royal Festival Hall in London. He wanted Buckley on the bill. Along with McCartney and, soon after, David Bowie and Jimmy Page – who'd adorn the cover of *Mojo* magazine holding aloft his prized copy of *Grace*, calling it 'the best thing I've heard all year' – the veteran Costello was the latest member of rock's A-list to join the Jeff Buckley Appreciation Society. According to Janine Nichols, Buckley's early champion from St Ann's, who'd eventually meet Costello in the most unfortunate of circumstances, there were some similarities between the two. 'I think that Elvis and Jeff both had that photographic memory for music, and Jeff was born with the voice that Elvis wished he was born with. Elvis has the heart and soul of a singer but maybe not the pipes,' she said. Buckley's reaction was to joke about becoming the poster boy for 50-year-old rock stars.

This latest overseas jaunt, which also included appearances at the high profile Glastonbury and Roskilde festivals, was a welcome escape from the tawdry 'Love affair'. His Meltdown cameo also provided Buckley with the chance to veer away from what was now becoming a fairly predictable set list. Accompanied by a solitary piano, he headed back to Sin-E for a beautiful, haunting 'Corpus Christi Carol', channelled 17th century composer Henry Purcell during 'Dido's Lament', morphed into a chanteuse for a take on Nina Simone's 'The Other Woman' and paid his dues to Morrissey with a sprightly cover of 'The Boy With The Thorn In His Side'. Only the set-closing 'Grace', with the 'Flying Buckleys' in full cry, hinted at anything that remotely resembled 'pushing the product'. It was a rare chance for Buckley to just let loose and sing, which he did, to the obvious thrill of the crowd.

Mid way through 1995, with *Grace* on the shelves for almost a year, Buckley's thoughts should have begun to turn towards its successor. Yet Buckley had been listening closely to Penny Arcade – amongst other things, they shared therapists, a 70-ish woman known to her clients as Mrs Williams – who'd been telling him about the vibrant music scene in Australia, where she'd performed her *Butch! Dyke! Faghag! Whore!* show more than 100 times, and toured so often that she could have taken out residency. She also had a long-term relationship with an Australian, known simply as 'Henry'. As Arcade recalled, 'Australians are very educated about music. Jeff was mad for the uniqueness of the Australian experience.'

Buckley was intrigued, and asked Columbia about the possibility of touring there. When they rejected his request, on the grounds that it was simply too expensive – and Buckley was now in no small amount of debt to Columbia, especially after the 'Last Goodbye' video fiasco – he used Arcade's Australian success as a case study as to why he and the band should tour there. 'Penny Arcade doesn't even have a record company,' he told the label. There was also a certain commercial sense to a visit to Australia: if *Grace* wasn't going to become a bestseller in the USA, maybe it was time for Columbia to start considering new markets. France and the UK, after all, had proved to be successful forays outside of America, so why not Australia? Buckley insisted, and on August 25, 1995, star, band and entourage – Dave Lory, Gene Bowen, George Stein, plus Mark Naficy and three other crew – touched down in Sydney for what would prove to be one of the most exhilarating and wildly received tours of the entire *Grace* era.

Despite Penny Arcade's upbeat descriptions of Australia, Buckley had no real idea of the response he would receive there, at least not until he strolled onto the stage at Sydney's Metro Theatre, a cosy, 900-odd-seat venue, on Monday, August 28. He proceeded to play a blistering set that briefly galvanised the local music scene: within hours, everyone was talking about Jeff Buckley. The gig was described as 'one of the greatest musical performances ever witnessed in this city'. It also helped that public radio station Triple J, the so-called 'Youth Network', took to Buckley straight away. The network had a nationwide audience, and quickly playlisted *Grace*. One of the station's on-air announcers, Jen Brennan, became a particularly strong Buckley advocate. (She also managed indie rock band Crow, who'd support Buckley on most of his Australian shows. Buckley, in turn, talked them up as 'this awesome Australian band'.)

But even before the tour, the Australian wing of Columbia Records was working the phones. One staffer called local rock magazine *Juice* and placed this succinct pitch: 'The record is fantastic; you and I know that. The band is really great and let's face it, all the women want to get into his pants.'[4] Extra Sydney gigs were swiftly added to the itinerary and, as he headed south to Melbourne for a trio of equally dazzling shows, a proposal was considered to add Buckley to the upcoming 1996 Big Day Out line-up. Guitarist Michael Tighe later referred to the scene at these first Australian shows as 'Beatlemania-like'.*

According to Mick Grondahl, the Australian tour was almost like an escape for the band. 'I remember the weather was lovely, we were on the other side of the world, we were really excited to share our music in this distant land, we were thrilled,' he recalled. 'That first batch of shows we did there I thought went over really, really well.' 'I'll always remember that first show,' said Mark Naficy. 'We blew people away pretty good.'

Jon Pope, who'd tour-manage both of Buckley's Australian visits, became yet another devotee, all on the strength of the one Metro gig. 'I didn't know anything about him; I had friends who were into Tim Buckley, but I wasn't. When Jeff first came, it was hard to find out anything about him. After I saw him play, yes, I knew there was something special about him; I think he had magic. For fuck's sake, you'd never forget it if you saw him. I remember the first show struck me as dynamite.'

Sydney critics agreed, describing Buckley as 'one of the most significant and innovative performers to have emerged in the past five years, [who gave a] performance of great power and integrity'.[5] After that first Sydney show, Buckley kicked on at an after-party at the cheesy Hard Rock Café. Penny Arcade, who was in his entourage, refused to step inside this shrine to rock excess, but did introduce Buckley to the sleazy charms of Sydney nightspots Barons and the Piccolo Bar, both located deep in the heart of Kings Cross, the local red-light district. She also hooked Buckley up with a friend, Kristina Karasulas, who, along with her husband Peter, would 'babysit' the band during their Oz tours.

'I am out of my element,' Buckley whispered to a journalist at the Hard Rock. 'It's really weird to be here.' The writer laughed and then watched in awe as Buckley 'was besieged by women'. 'People wanted to bathe in his presence,' recalled Jon Pope, who was also there. Buckley proceeded to knock back tequilas at an alarming rate, going drink for drink with his Australian promoter, a local legend in both matters of business and partying.

---

* Many Oz recordings, from tours in 1995 and 1996, would end up on various Buckley posthumous live recordings, including the *Mystery White Boy* LP.

Then, without any sleep whatsoever, he rolled into Triple J's Sydney studios for a now legendary live interview, ostensibly for a segment known as 'High 5', where he was asked to talk up five songs that have changed his life.

Buckley, of course, turned a simple 20-odd minutes on air into an event. He did manage to nominate some favourites – Diana Ross' 'Ain't No Mountain High Enough', Patti Smith's 'Ain't It Strange', as well as tracks from The Grifters ('Dave's voice; he hurts real bad, he hurts real good; check it out'), Shudder To Think ('they're beautiful') and Jon Spencer Blues Explosion ('I pretend I'm [guitarist] Judah from the band in my apartment'). But he also rambled, a tad incoherently, on such subjects as his youth, his love of ''70s cheese pop', Nusrat Fateh Ali Khan and The Smiths, also revealing why the band had recently added MC5's sonic firestorm, 'Kick Out The Jams', to their live set.

'We were in Portland and someone said "[MC5 guitarist] Fred Sonic Smith is dead",' he recalled. 'I noticed that people were dying while we were on tour, dropping like flies. It was sad; I didn't expect it. It's great to play.' (After tearing through 'Jams' at their first Sydney show, Buckley actually collapsed in a heap on the stage, totally spent.) Then, after talking up Bad Brains' 'How Low Can A Punk Get?', the sixth song from his High 5, incidentally – it was that kind of interview – Buckley, still on air, smiled at the announcer and cheekily asked: 'Do you have a spliff?' With that, the interview was over.[6]

Equally strange events took place during his shows in Melbourne. During the August 31 gig at a venue called The Lounge, Jon Pope sized up the mood in the room and requested that the bar's cash registers be shut down during his set, something unheard of in a country where drinking (especially during gigs) is almost a national pastime. 'Everywhere we played had to be that quiet,' said Pope. 'He played at the Prince Patrick in Melbourne [on September 2], which was the smallest gig he played, it's this old-fashioned pub with stairs leading up to the top level, and there were people standing on the stairs, stuck there. You could hear that people were so intent; if you coughed in that audience you were obvious. It was this pristine environment.' To Buckley, it must have felt like Monday nights at Sin-E, all over again.

During one of their numerous after-show parties, Pope was again privy to the amazing amount of female attention Buckley – who'd taken to wearing a T-shirt that proclaimed 'Take That, Leave You' – was receiving, even if he was looking a little road-soiled. 'He could have had any woman he wanted,' Pope laughed. 'One night in Melbourne, we went to this nightclub after the show, and the women there were queuing up for him. And yet he

ended up taking home this really ugly girl.' As for other on-the-road indulgences, Pope admitted to sharing a few joints with Buckley and the band.
But, he admitted, it was nothing like previous non-stop-parties he'd tour-
managed for such legendary users and abusers as Red Hot Chili Peppers
and Steve Earle.*

Back in Sydney for the final two sold-out shows, Pope took Buckley and
the band to a nondescript Thai restaurant in inner city Redfern, one of the
city's less salubrious neighbourhoods. When they adjourned for a cigarette
– smoking was another vice Buckley had picked up while on the road – the
scene streetside remains vividly etched in Pope's memory. 'I'm with this
mildly famous person, all hanging out on the bus seat having a cigarette, and
thinking that all of Redfern would have no idea of who's sitting here. He
was totally at ease. It would have been the perfect album cover shot.'

'It was quite beautiful,' Buckley said of this first Australian tour. '[On the]
last night I hung out in this bar, a shithole, but there was this woman
singing, with an acoustic guitar, singing old hippie songs. But then she sang
this Gallic song, to the key of the air conditioner that was in the bar –
[shades of Buckley singing in tune with Sin-E's cappuccino machine] – so
it was this long drone, completely unintentional and natural. But she had a
voice that was divine. I was pleasantly stoned, sitting with some very nice
people, talking about *Perfume* the novel or something, not prepared for what
was going to happen. And she was amazing; she had this really pure voice, a
real pure soul behind it. She didn't know what she was doing, but I hadn't
seen that in a long time.'[7]

The near hysteria of their first Australian tour seemed to briefly revitalise
Buckley and the band – even though at least one insider thought he was
'miserable' throughout the entire trip – but on their return to the USA,
Matt Johnson, increasingly distanced from Tighe, Grondahl and Buckley,
started to think about moving on. 'I think he had a complicated relationship
with Jeff,' said Johnson's close friend and sometimes musical collaborator,
Duncan Sheik. 'Matt was someone who saw the human side of Jeff that
maybe wasn't that pretty. Matt was completely turned off by some of the
excesses of the music industry – the smoking, the drinking, the rock star
behaviour, the girls. Matt, who was trying to be incredibly spiritually pure,
was none of those things. But I don't think Jeff was the main culprit, incidentally.' Or, as Chris Dowd, who'd work with Johnson in the studio, neatly

---

* Jane's Addiction guitarist Dave Navarro apologised 'categorically' to Pope for his
  behaviour on an Australian tour, even though he couldn't actually recall what he did.

surmised: 'He was a different cat to the other guys. And just a fucking amazing drummer.'

Buckley sought respite by throwing himself into one of the many cameos he would make during his life, this time with another of his heroes, New York punk poet Patti Smith. Buckley was once asked what drew him to Smith's sonic outpourings. 'Same thing I like about any artist,' he replied. 'Her voice, her music, her words, all equally special and strange and energising and understanding. They're all integrated: I can't separate her from her voice; I see a picture of her face and can only imagine that sound coming out of her. Such a force of nature.' A few days before leaving for the Australian tour, Buckley had scored tickets to Lollapalooza, which was being held at Randall's Island, on the outskirts of Manhattan. What seemed like another day spent mixing it with alt-rock's A-list changed dramatically for Buckley when he caught Smith's surprise 'comeback' appearance on the festival's second stage.

As he recalled, 'I suddenly saw [guitarist] Lenny Kaye go by on a buggy. I couldn't believe it. "Lenny, what are you doing here?" ' (Buckley and Kaye had become friends when they continued to run into each other in the East Village. They'd often hang out, drinking beers and listening to doo-wop records.) 'It was completely unannounced. I took a chair and set it up next to the stage and watched the Patti Smith Group play. It might have been her first gig in 15 years. She rocked. "Dancing Barefoot", "People Have The Power", a new song she wrote for Kurt Cobain, "About A Boy". It was great. It ripped me apart.'[8] What made it all the more poignant for Buckley was that Smith's husband was the recently departed Fred 'Sonic' Smith, whose death had inspired him to include MC5's 'Kick Out The Jams' in his live sets.

By some strange co-incidence, Buckley was in New York's Electric Lady Studios, just as Smith and Kaye had commenced work on *Gone Again*, her first album in eight years. When they needed a vocal part for the song 'Southern Cross', they turned to Buckley, whose voice was a perfect match. He also contributed an Eastern-influenced instrumental passage to another track, 'Fireflies'. In conversation with a colleague of mine in 2007, Smith, who was a friend of Tim Buckley's, recalled the session with Jeff. 'I remember telling Jeff how happy I was that he was alive and working and so gifted because his dad didn't make it.' As Smith told the BBC, she was struck by 'his passion – he couldn't resist being a part of anything musical around him.'

Also at this session was guitarist Tom Verlaine, who'd played on Smith's debut single from 1974, 'Hey Joe'/'Piss Factory' and co-wrote, with Smith, the searing ballad 'Break It Up', from her first, brilliant album, *Horses*.

Verlaine was a mainstay of seminal New York rock band Television, whose elegiac, epic *Marquee Moon* was one of the quintessential LPs of a time and place that produced such notable bands as Blondie, The Ramones and Talking Heads (all these groups had gotten their start at downtown venue CBGBs, a dump that became punk rock's very own ground zero). Born Thomas Miller – he changed his name in honour of poet Paul Verlaine – Verlaine was 17 years older than Buckley, who respected him almost as much as he did Patti Smith. When they met, Verlaine hadn't released a solo record since 1992's all-instrumental *Warm And Cool*, although he had recently composed the score for a film entitled *Love And A .45*. Verlaine's reputation as a maverick must have impressed Buckley, because as soon as they connected during those sessions for *Gone Again*, Buckley decided that Verlaine should produce his next album.

Buckley had planned some exploratory jams, with a view to working out some songs for his second LP, at a home owned by the Grondahl family, located in Sag Harbour, a village in the smart and leafy Hamptons on Long Island. Grondahl said that the sessions were an attempt to 'make something happen', but it was obvious the band just weren't in good shape. '[Management and Columbia] knew that the second record was a key part in the development but they wanted us to tour more, which jeopardised our way to approach the second record in the way we should have been,' Grondahl said. 'We didn't want to feel like we were burned out, that we didn't want to look at our guitars for a few weeks.' Soon after the sessions began, Johnson told Buckley and the others that he'd had enough; he was leaving. According to Grondahl, 'He just felt he was going in a different direction and didn't so much care for the more metallic, hard rock stuff and was interested in pursuing all different kinds of music: a horn section, violins, studio work.'

Eric Eidel, a friend of Grondahl and Daniel Harnett, who'd helped Buckley secure his Sin-E residency, sat in on drums for the remaining sessions. The Sag Harbour jams began in November 1995, and as Eidel told writer Antony Fine, there was a looseness to the entire affair, as if Buckley was searching out his next musical direction. 'He'd bring in songs and we'd work out arrangements. Sometimes the songs had words, sometimes they didn't. It didn't fall neatly into a style. But there was a conscious decision not to do any more covers. I think he was growing as a writer, deliberately focusing more on his own compositions.'[9]

A growing influence on Buckley was Woodstock-based space rockers Mercury Rev and, especially, indie rockers The Grifters, who he'd befriended at that fateful Iowa City gig more than a year earlier when he'd met Joan Wasser. Grondahl was also a fan of The Grifters, having seen them play New York's Knitting Factory back in 1992. He readily acknowledged that they left their mark on songs that Buckley and band were developing around the time of Sag Harbour. 'I always loved their sound, that hard-hitting, bluesy, psychedelic sound, and we thought that was something we were interested in reflecting in our own way,' he said. 'And I think something like "Sky Is A Landfill" is kind of our tipping the hat to The Grifters, and some other things in the works that never came to fruition. I'd say "I Woke Up In A Strange Place" is another; it has that Grifters-esque feel.'

The Grifters' Dave Shouse felt a strong personal bond with Buckley – they became good friends – but he could never quite work out what Buckley admired about his band. 'It was always like, "What is this dude hanging out with us?",' he laughed. 'Like so many people we were in awe of Jeff; we were dumbfounded by him. Being the nice southern boys that we were, we didn't make a fuss. And he was being really cool, treating us well, and we didn't want to throw the Spanish Inquisition on him, like, "OK, dude, you're really good and it's effortless for you, and we're kind of fucked up, so what's going on?" ' Shouse learned that Buckley was 'like our number one promo guy, hauling our records around to radio stations who may not necessarily want to play Grifters records'. (Buckley did likewise for Sydney band Crow, who pursued a similarly gritty, raw aesthetic as The Grifters.) Speaking with *Rolling Stone* for their September 1995 issue, Buckley listed The Grifters amongst his favourite bands, yet again.

Quite possibly, it was a situation very similar to Buckley's making *People's* Most Beautiful list. Whereas then he set out to 'uglify' himself, now he seemed intent on 'dirtying up' his music, pushing it somewhere new, with an emphasis on energy, volume and danger rather than his glorious, soaring voice and heavy heart. He now seemed more interested in brawn than brain.

Late in November 1995, Buckley sought escape from Sag Harbour at Sin-E, when he played two unannounced solo shows (he played there again on New Year's Eve, along with a gig at the Mercury Lounge). Then, in December, Buckley got back on-line, writing from a 'bloody freezing' New York, updating true believers on his latest movements and his plans for 1996. Firstly, he thanked his fans for their positive letters, writing how 'sometimes things get my brain in a twist and reading your words of support does my heart good'. He then revealed that he and the band 'are in writing mode now, doing well together. They send their love.' (No mention of Johnson's departure plans, interestingly.) He hinted at possible recording sessions in the spring, although he stressed: 'Don't know yet.' Then followed a trademark Buckley coda, loaded with many possible meanings: 'Don't feel down!' he stressed. "'96 must rule! New positive mental attitude slogan: "Dude, future . . . it rocks." You have our best. We love you, too.' *Sincerely, Jeff Buckley*.[10] A few weeks later, speaking on Australian radio, Buckley elaborated on the next album: 'It's a really radical evolution from *Grace*,' he said. '*It'll be better*.'

Yet before Buckley and the band could turn their full attention to *Grace's* successor, they had one more road trip to take, a return visit to Australia, plus New Zealand, for what was christened 'The Hard Luck' tour. But it could easily have been called 'Matt Johnson's Last Hurrah'. It was also another respite for Buckley, because the Sag Harbour sessions had fallen apart a few weeks earlier, with Buckley sinking a further $25,000 or so into the red, and Columbia execs less than impressed by what they'd heard. The tour schedule was intense: they arrived in Auckland on Tuesday, February 6 and left Sydney just over three weeks later, having played a total of 14 shows. And this time around, Buckley threw the budget out the window, insisting that The Grifters and The Dambuilders, the band featuring his girlfriend, Joan Wasser, on violin, come along for the ride.

With Johnson's imminent departure looming large over Buckley and the band, you would have expected a certain sombre mood to be in the air. But that certainly wasn't evident on their day of arrival in Australia, as Dave Shouse gleefully recalled: all that lingered in the air soon after touching down in Sydney was a thick cloud of pot smoke. 'We went to a topless beach the day we landed,' he recalled. 'We rolled up a fat joint and went, "This is the shit". [We were] in this magical land where the seasons are inverted.'

Johnson had stayed tight-lipped about his resignation, because the rest of the touring party only learned about it when they reached Perth, in Western Australia, the most geographically isolated major city on the planet. According to Shouse, 'He said he was leaving the band and we went: "What the fuck?" [Jeff] was pushing in a new direction and Matt was sensing that he wasn't the kind of drummer that Jeff was envisaging for his music,' Shouse figured. 'Jeff was looking for something, maybe more anarchy, maybe a different kind of drummer, I guess. But Matt was a great drummer; he felt Jeff's intuitive, dynamic range, really well. We were shocked. [But Matt] said he never really got to know who Jeff really was. Jeff could be such a ham and a comedian, he could kick into impersonations and be really entertaining, but you could never be really sure – not to say he was disingenuous at all – but he was protective.'

Tour manager Jon Pope was back on board for Buckley's second lap of Australia, and this time he found that things were a little looser, a little more ragged and wild than their first visit, both on- and off-stage. 'They were definitely more worn out than the first tour,' he said, 'but songs would still change from night to night.' He, too, was initially unaware of Johnson's decision to jump ship, but sensed that something was amiss. 'I do remember Matt not being as happy as everyone else; maybe he'd made a decision to go,' he recalled. 'I had the feeling they were all breaking up at the end of that and the future was unknown.' Pope also noticed that the Buckley 'vibe' had changed: the so-called 'star-making machinery' had begun to play its part in his career, whether he liked it or not. 'A lot of people around them, by the time of the second tour, were hoping they were the next big thing,' he said.

Nonetheless, Buckley still found the time for some rest-and-recreation. When the tour reached Melbourne, he learned that Pope's birthday had just passed, and he had neglected to tell him about it. Buckley decided that Pope was a 'dickhead', in the local parlance, and decided to do something about it. Mid-way through their set at The Palais Theatre, Buckley stopped the show and nodded to the wings, where one of the crew brought out a penis-shaped cake to celebrate Pope's birthday. 'The birthday cake was a good example of that side of him; he understood a good gag,' Pope said.*

The joke, however, was somewhat lost on much of the crowd at The Palais, whose numbers included Led Zeppelin guitarist Jimmy Page. He spent the entire set standing next to the mixing desk, absorbed in the playing of Buckley and the band. Sound engineer Mark Naficy, a huge Led Zep fan himself, found the presence of the great man more than a little disturbing. 'I got the impression he was totally into what Jeff was doing,' Naficy said. Afterwards, Page went backstage and spent some time with Buckley, offering him an opening slot on an upcoming leg of the Page/Plant tour. 'That was a big moment for Jeff,' said guitarist Michael Tighe.[11] (No less than five tracks from this show ended up on 2000's *Mystery White Boy* CD, ample proof that Buckley was inspired.) As thrilled as he was – Page and Plant, after all, were two of his biggest musical heroes – Buckley passed on

---

* Several years later, Pope met up again with Buckley's co-manager Dave Lory. Lory gave him a photo of Buckley presenting the cake to him on stage; it was one of the few possessions he had with him in Memphis when he died. 'I thought I got through it OK, I wasn't emotionally scarred, but when Dave told me that I was shattered,' Pope said, looking back on his friendship with Buckley. 'It was one of those eerie things, just when I thought I'd gotten through the time OK.'

the offer. He knew that his second studio album was his biggest priority right now, although it must have been an incredibly tough call. According to Jon Pope, the presence of Page typified events on this tour. 'Everyone wanted to meet Jeff, it was Dylan-esque. Every night it was a case of "who's on the list tonight?" He knew that he carried weight. If people don't think you're famous enough they'll just turn up, they won't ask for an audience, but they weren't doing that.'

Like the new music he was hearing in his head, the relationship between Buckley and Joan Wasser had now blossomed into something exciting and more than a little dangerous. 'She was the new girlfriend,' Pope surmised. 'If someone swings on a pendulum from good to bad, he was swinging wider from good to bad when she was around. [But] she was nice and obviously loved him.' Wasser also tapped into Buckley's wilder side. One night, Pope had to referee a shouting match between Johnson and Buckley (Johnson, admittedly, did most of the shouting). The drummer was sharing a room with Buckley, but on returning late one night found that Buckley and Wasser had very clearly had frenzied sex in both beds, and pretty much trashed the room, as well. 'I was in the room, I remember the racket,' Pope recalled. 'Both of the beds had been fucked up, they were wrecked. Joan and Jeff were drunk as skunks and lying in one of them, when the other band member came back to his room – he'd been out clubbing – he couldn't even sleep in [the bed]. That's when the yelling and the drama started. It was the only incident I ever witnessed. I remember that being a sore point, if you will. You never knew from day to day what position on the temperament clock that Jeff chose to put the big hand.'

While on Queensland's Gold Coast, Pope pleaded with Buckley and Wasser not to take a midnight swim at the famously unpredictable Coolangatta Beach, known for its deadly tides. 'I was shitting myself,' admitted Pope. 'I wasn't going to go down to the beach in the middle of the night and follow him and Joan, but I really had to warn him that it was dangerous. And he didn't care, he still had to go.' In hindsight, Buckley and Wasser's swim couldn't have been any more portentous: if Buckley had a reckless streak, it was on full display that night in Coolangatta. 'He's exactly the kind of guy who I could imagine being careless to the fullest,' Pope added. 'He lived his life to the fullest.' On another occasion, Buckley helped out with the lights at a Dambuilders sideshow, at Sydney's Annandale Hotel. He also assisted with some stage-trashing at the end of the set, according to local legend, although Dave Shouse had trouble picturing the band actually wrecking their gear. 'I could see Joan trashing a set, though, she is impulsive,' he said. 'I don't know about it, but I like the story.'

'Joan was great,' said local singer/songwriter Ben Mullins, who played on several dates of the Hard Luck Tour. 'She was very outgoing and boisterous and life of the party. There was a big party backstage at [Brisbane's] Festival Hall, we all got onto it.' As on their previous tour, there was a bevy of beautiful women at each show. 'Women were drooling; they couldn't wait to meet him,' said Mullins. 'I even had a lot of female interest, because I was supporting Jeff Buckley. "Can we come backstage?", that kind of thing.' Mullins also noticed how Buckley came to life on-stage; elsewhere he almost blended into the scenery. 'I was standing side stage with my girl-friend watching The Dambuilders and she said, "Who's the guy next to you?" I looked and here was this scruffy guy, singlet, jeans, hair unwashed, skinny little bloke, and I said, "That's Jeff." She said, "Really? He looks like he needs a clean-up." I told her to wait until he walked onstage and started singing.'

On-stage, Buckley and the band were now playing harder, faster and louder than ever before, transforming *Grace's* slowburning epics – 'Last Goodbye', 'So Real', 'Eternal Life' and the title track – into rock and roll firestorms that bordered on the metallic. 'Mojo Pin' circa 1996 was almost unrecognisable: Buckley screamed so hard as the song built to its thunder-ous climax that you feared he'd cough up a vocal cord. Behind him, Johnson hit the drums with the ferocity and power of a woodchopper; it seemed as though he was taking out his anxiety and frustration on his helpless (and by tour's end, useless) kit. And Buckley continued to introduce his songs in strange and unusual ways, hinting at his slightly frantic state of mind – 'Last Goodbye' was dedicated to 'two lesbian lovers who broke up', 'Lilac Wine' was 'a song I find myself singing to myself a lot', and Buckley lost himself in what was described as some wild 'classroom-rape-fantasy' during 'Eternal Life'. And finally, they were also playing new songs-under-development, including the then-instrumental 'Vancouver', a Tighe/Buckley/Grondahl co-write, built around a chunky New Wave-ish groove and some Roger McGuinn-worthy burst of raga-rock guitar from Buckley. They also intro-duced the raw, bluesy 'Mood Swing Whisky'; and 'All Flowers In Time Bend Towards The Sun', the ballad Buckley had recorded with former lover Elizabeth Fraser. The lurching, bluesy dirge 'Edna Frau' was now in the set, with Mick Grondahl taking over on vocals.

Another new track added to the playlist was 'I Woke Up In A Strange Place', a surging, urgent slice of modern guitar rock. '[That's a] song about being caught out there – do you know what that means?,' Buckley asked, when he spoke on Triple J during the tour. 'Say you're a traveller, you're not home in your mind, you're sleepwalking through everything, and that's a freedom in a way from certain trivial responsibilities, reality. It leads more into intoxication, introspection, daydreaming, sex, maybe, with whom it doesn't matter. You're free sort of, though not really. Things happen and you get caught out there, maybe you meet the wrong stranger or you give too much away, maybe you wake up with someone that you can't believe; maybe it's yourself.'[12]

In the same interview, Buckley confessed that he was not the most prolific songwriter, hinting at his 'creative inertia'. 'I wish I had a real reservoir [of songs], but I don't,' he said. 'It just sort of comes. Thoughts lead into each other and gain momentum and then BOOM! Some weird gibberish will come into my mind and I'll go, "That's the one." Dreams, too.' When asked about the progress, and the direction, of his second LP, Buckley was vague. 'The album is somewhere in between,' he said, 'but lately it's been coming from a lower, sweeter spot, which I've been waiting on for a long time. I want to work on stuff between gigs, see how they work, get stoned with the other bands, don't get in trouble. Right now the new music is in my head and that's what I want to focus on.' Buckley seemed more comfortable discussing pot, or 'the benevolent giver', as he described it. 'Nobody can get in trouble with pot. I love pot. You got some?' he asked the startled announcer, just as he'd done during a previous Triple J interview.[13]

Grondahl admitted that the shows on this second Australian tour weren't as consistently 'great' as those from 1995, and most local critics agreed. The same writers who'd searched for superlatives a few months before were now questioning whether Buckley was 'sick of the same old songs'. 'One wondered about halfway through this tedious performance,' noted the *Sydney Morning Herald*, 'what's happened in the past six months? Did the gambler run out of luck? Whatever the reason, this was not a great concert.'[14] There was no shutting down of cash registers this time around to 'maintain the vibe'. Even in interviews, Buckley sounded out of sorts, sometimes defensive. 'I've accepted that this is my life,' he told a writer from *The Age*. 'Lots of bad things have happened and lots of irreparable damage has been done. It's the agony of learning all over again.'[15]

'I'm used to being a fool,' Buckley admitted to Triple J. 'I'm a horrible clown, doing the funny shit that falls flat. I'm the poster boy for saying the wrong thing at the wrong time. Look up faux pas in the dictionary. Anyone who performs for a living will tell you that a lot of strength comes from having a commitment to what you do; you really have nothing to lose. You're already ridiculous for getting up there in the first place so you have nothing left to lose. That's the way I live my life. What could possibly happen? All fools are brave, I suppose. It's just comfortable for me.'[16]

'We were starting to get more modern rock, you could say,' said Mick Grondahl, when I asked what had changed on-stage. 'Jeff was interested in doing harder stuff, not grunge, but something more punky, while keeping that interesting voice,' he added. 'It wasn't like hardcore punk, you know, "You suck! You suck!"' Grondahl believed it was very clear where Buckley was drawing inspiration: another credible group of indie rockers, Shudder To Think. (Just before the tour, Buckley and STT had cut an almost note-perfect Stax soul tribute, 'I Want Someone Badly', for the soundtrack of the film *First Love, Last Rites*.) 'Craig [Wedren] used his voice in an almost operatic way, with this dissonant, hard rock sound. I think that was one thing Jeff was interested in. Jeff was always interested in a variety of sounds: he'd want to do that and a French waltz. There was always a variety of idioms.'

'At first the new songs bothered me,' admitted Mark Naficy, 'but then they grew on me and I thought they were great. I think deep down he was a hard rocker and that's what he was chasing. I think by the time of that second Australian tour he had some new influences, some new songs, and was gearing up for some change of direction.'

At the same time, Buckley hadn't completely lost touch with his past, especially his love of prog rock. He'd bonded with Tripp Lamkins, The Grifters' bassist, over Genesis, Yes and King Crimson, prog's 'holy trinity in our eyes', according to Lamkins. Innocently, Lamkins mentioned to Buckley that he'd always wanted to record a cover of 'Back In NYC', a typically complicated slice of Peter Gabriel-era Genesis, from their *Lamb Lies Down On Broadway* set. During some downtime in Australia, Buckley astounded Lamkins and the entire entourage by sitting on the steps outside a venue and playing the complete song. 'Once again Jeff blew my mind by launching right into it on guitar,' said Lamkins. 'It wasn't perfect but considering he'd just pulled it out of his ass it was damn close.' (Buckley would continue working on the song, in private, when he returned to USA.)

Even if the shows were less consistent than the year before, the 'cult of Buckley' was possibly even more extreme in 1996. Dave Shouse witnessed this first-hand. 'We saw it in record stores,' he said. 'People would come to our in-stores with poetry to get to Jeff. That was the closest they could get; the shows were sold out, they didn't know where he was staying, so they'd come to us. And I'm talking about several dozen people at a time. We were just freaked out.'

The tour's final show, and Johnson's last gig with the band, was a hastily arranged extra date at Selinas, an ugly beer barn directly across the street from Coogee Beach, a haven for backpackers visiting Sydney. It had none of the ambience of The Metro, where Buckley had made his Oz debut six months earlier, but it could accommodate somewhere near 2,000 people, a sign of Buckley's increasing market value. It was his fourth Sydney show on this tour alone, a remarkable achievement for a city of just under four million, and for a man whose music was still only being played on 'alternative' radio. But the evening didn't start well for Buckley, thanks, indirectly, to Ben Mullins, who was again on the bill. Mullins had scored a backstage pass for a friend, which turned out to be a very bad move. 'He was a boozer, and I wasn't far off, and I said, "You have to behave yourself." He comes back later and he's off his face and he tells me he's taken all this acid. He wandered into someone's dressing room and [tour manager] Pope caught him and threw him out. Then he lets down the tyres on the Tarago [van] outside with Jeff still in the van.'

Soon after, Mullins spotted Buckley, who'd escaped the van and was sitting alone, at the rear of the venue, playing the guitar by himself. 'I got the feeling that something was amiss. I remember Jeff being alone a lot on that tour.' The set Buckley and band played that night bordered on the ferocious; Mullins, looking on from side stage, felt that they 'sounded exhausted at that Selinas show, like they were rushing through it, getting it over with.' Buckley made his feelings clear when he altered the lyrics of 'Eternal Life' to a lewd 'and all you want to do is FUCK EVERYONE!' At the end of the song, amidst a wail of feedback that would have done Sonic Youth proud, Buckley stopped and announced Johnson's decision.

'This is Matt Johnson,' said Buckley. 'Matt decided that this will be the last show he plays with us. It's been two fucking years of outstanding service and musical inspiration, from the man who brought you "K-K-K-Kangaroo". I want you to wish him a fond farewell.' Johnson mumbled a gentle, 'I'd like to say goodbye and thank you', and led the band into an impassioned, furious 'What Will You Say'. At set's end, after a final crash-and-burn through 'Kanga-Roo', as Buckley suggested that everyone 'go and get drunk', Johnson got up from his kit, walked through the crowd and went straight to the beach across the road, burying his head in his hands. (A rumour that he left before the set ended, and that Buckley drummed for the remainder, are untrue, although Buckley did ask, 'Where's Matty?' when he returned for the encore.) As the rest of team Buckley packed their gear and headed back to the US – soon after returning, Grondahl broke up with a girlfriend he'd managed to keep while on the road, an irony that wasn't lost on him – Johnson stayed behind for another three weeks, hiding out at the Sydney home of 'den mother' Kristina Karasulas. As far as he was concerned, he hadn't just quit the band, he'd quit music altogether.

Notes

1. Fine, Antony: *Jeff Buckley Drowns* (unpublished)
2. Browne, David: Dream Brother: *The Lives And Music Of Jeff And Tim Buckley*, Fourth Estate 2001
3. www.jeffbuckley.com
4. Creswell, Toby: Grace Under Fire, *Juice*, February 1996
5. Elder, Bruce: Forging Old Rock Sounds Into New, *Sydney Morning Herald*, August 30, 1995
6. Kingsmill, Richard: Jeff Buckley's High 5, *Triple J FM* August 29, 1995, transcript
7. See note 6
8. See note 6
9. See note 1
10. See note 3
11. Engleheart, Murray: Last Goodbye, *Hobart Mercury*, May 11, 2000
12. Catterns, Angela: Interview With Jeff Buckley, *Triple J FM*, December 18, 1996, transcript
13. See note 12
14. Elder, Bruce: Gambler Runs Out Of Luck, *Sydney Morning Herald*, February 19, 1996
15. Jellie, Dugald: Buckley's Burden, *The Age*, February 23, 1996
16. See note 12

Chapter Ten

'Jeff wasn't supposed to come to Memphis – *and fucking die!*'

When Buckley returned from Australia in March 1996, he should finally have been able to turn his attention to his much-discussed second album. But, as it turned out, he seemed more interested in catching up on a couple of years' missed sleep. A road trip was planned for Buckley and Steve Berkowitz, with Mike Webb at the wheel, ostensibly to see Columbia label-mate Branford Marsalis perform at the Rhode Island School Of Design, but more importantly to discuss Buckley's plans for *Grace's* successor. 'Steve needed some time with him,' Webb recalled, 'but Jeff just seemed beat.' Buckley slept all the way up to Rhode Island, but, according to Webb, 'was very animated on the way back. That was supposed to be one of the first conversations about the next album but it was just Jeff hanging out with the A&R guy, making fun of the chick from the Cranberries and Chris Cornell – note for note, he had the sound in his head and could do it. It was amazing.'

The sessions that had been aborted just prior to The Hard Luck Tour recommenced not long after, with Eric Eidel again in the drummer's seat. A dozen, maybe more, songs-in-progress were laid down during these sessions: they included a storming cover of 'When The Levee Breaks', a song that Led Zep co-opted for their fourth album from the Memphis Minnie original, plus a handful of songs that would make Buckley's next 'proper' album, including 'Opened Once', and some tunes Buckley would only finish as four-track demos, such as 'I Know We Could Be So Happy Baby', and obscurities like 'River Of Dope' and 'When My Love Comes Down'.* It

---

* Many of these songs have been assembled on the easily traceable bootleg *Rarities From NYC*.

was pretty obvious that the bulk of these cuts were in their early stages: you can actually hear Buckley talking the band through 'I Know We Could Be So Happy Baby', yelling out 'Gimme A, A, A, A, A ... '

Despite Columbia's uncertainty regarding Buckley's choice of producer – Dave Shouse remains convinced that 'the whole boardroom at Sony must have like shit themselves' – Verlaine and Buckley adjourned to Manhattan's Sorcerer Studios on June 15 to begin recording. Buckley's manager George Stein insisted that the sessions were purely an 'experiment'; it seemed that no-one close to Buckley was quite ready to accept that he was intent on making an album with Verlaine. 'They knew they had an amazing talent, but you kind of knew they were flipping out, you know?' said Shouse. Amongst this first batch of recordings was 'Morning Theft', 'Vancouver' and 'The Sky Is A Landfill', a Buckley/Tighe co-write with a lyric that was atypical Buckley: this song was far more political than personal, as he railed against the state of the environment, politics and 'the system'. It's possible that the lyric was influenced by discussions Buckley had with his LA-based friend John Humphrey; they often referred to 'those forces of power and commerce that feed off the spirit', according to Humphrey, who had a name for these forces: 'The Squashing Machine'.

But the Sorcerer Studios sessions, like the Sag Harbour jams before them, were not a success. Verlaine wasn't satisfied with the drumming of Eidel, nor was he convinced that the songs were ready for recording. With Buckley a further $10,000-and-a-bit out of pocket, the sessions were shut down and a planned EP was shelved. The idea of recording an album of covers, which several people had suggested to Buckley, must have seemed tempting.

As was his habit, Buckley searched out a safe haven, an escape from the building commercial and creative pressure. That came in the form of a gig as bassist, helping out Mind Science Of The Mind, a side project of Shudder To Think's guitarist Nathan Larson. Buckley would play four dates with the band, who were pushing their self-titled album, beginning on May 2 in Washington, DC and winding up in Cambridge, Massachusetts, a few days later.*

---

* Larson, to his credit, has resisted saying much about his relationship with Buckley, although he did email me the following: 'I've had some very bad encounters with the media regarding my friend Jeff. I've watched his record company suck his memory dry, and I've watched as his mythology has been built up and poked at by fans and journalists and "former friends" whom I've never heard of. We all know it's very, very fucked up when somebody dies,' Larson continued, 'and it's doubly strange if they were people who had a cult profile and mysterious persona like Jeff, which stemmed more from desire for privacy than some sort of mystical force. If I thought I could say something that would somehow further clear the cobwebs, I would, but I think at this point I'd rather steer clear of speaking about him at all in a public way.'

Another escape for Buckley was a stab at journalism. A few months earlier, *Interview* magazine ran a lengthy interview with Nusrat Fateh Ali Khan, conducted by Buckley. He'd also written liner notes for the qawwali master's album, *The Supreme Collection Volume One*, which was in turn dedicated to Buckley. This time around, Buckley accepted a commission from *Mojo* magazine to interview bed-ridden 'space age septuagenarian' Esquivel, the king of lounge music. It was the kind of conversation that only musicians could really enjoy, as Buckley quizzed Esquivel – who'd recently broken his hip – about his unusual studio techniques, his experiences in Hollywood, a possible Duke Ellington influence on his work, and whether or not he was the kind of man to sweat. All the while, though, Buckley knew that eventually he'd have to return to work.

At the same time, Grifter Dave Shouse had been whispering in Buckley's ear, talking up Easley Studios, a very unassuming recording facility located in the southeast corner of Memphis, just around the corner from a Walgreen's supermarket. 'We'd worked on a lot of people to come down here: Sonic Youth, Sebadoh, Jon Spencer Blues Explosion, just because the studio here was so fabulous and the people were so cool,' said Shouse. (The Grifters used Easley for their highly-regarded 1994 album, *Crappin' You Negative*.) Easley was also a steal at $650 a day, which had some appeal to Buckley, who was haemorrhaging major-label money at this point. On September 4, 1996, Buckley and Berkowitz flew to Memphis to check out Easley. Buckley, at least, was sold on the idea, and told Shouse of his plans. 'We were just hoping that he'd come, at first, to visit and chill out, maybe get a place and write and then go back to New York,' said Shouse. 'But we were real surprised when he said that he'd booked sessions, and with Tom Verlaine. It was such a crazy thing that he even came down here.' (Although a massive fan of Television's *Marquee Moon*, Shouse knew little of Verlaine, apart from the fact that he was a chain smoker.)

Buckley still had to address the Spinal Tap-worthy problem of finding the right drummer. When he and the band ran through a selection of their new songs at Sony's New York studio for Berkowitz, in September, it was clear that Eidel wasn't the right man for the job. Soon after, he was out of the band. Buckley, meanwhile, had some personal problems to address: while driving in New Jersey with his friend Inger Lorre, of the punk band The Nymphs – a woman notorious for once pissing on the desk of a record company exec – he was busted for possessing a solitary joint. As ever, he arrived late for the hearing, where he pleaded guilty and was told that his record would be expunged if he went conviction-free for the next six months. It was hardly Keith Richards circa 1977, getting busted for a hefty amount of smack in Toronto and facing a lengthy jail term, but Buckley certainly didn't need the distraction.

On October 25, Buckley went on-line, announcing some upcoming low-key solo shows, and his ever-evolving plans for album number two. His posting contained the usual mixture of good humour, bitter cynicism and out-there oddness. First off, Buckley excused himself for his recent silence, but explained that 'I don't really get excited about calling people or making any kind of social contact through computers or phones. I'm just a lazy bastard. [But] I'm doing pretty nicely.' He then announced his upcoming 'phantom' solo tour in December, yet another attempt to recapture the simplicity of Sin-E. 'I'll be wandering around in an ugly rented car,' he wrote, 'and dropping by some undesignated venues, maybe in your town if you're in the northeast.' And then he moved on to the key issue at hand, studio album number two. 'The new record will be out supposedly in late spring '97,' he said, without any real certainty. 'It's called *My Sweetheart The Drunk*' – a line taken from an unpublished Buckley poem – 'but you don't have to call it anything. Watch it get destroyed.'

His description of his new songs may have started optimistically, but a sarcastic tone soon took over, as if Buckley was having a not-so-subtle dig at the business in which he was now well and truly immersed. 'Every song,' he wrote, 'will have a quiet part and then a loud part... and the lyrics will totally open up new pathways in the human mind, allowing both sexes to fling themselves into the path of modern boredom and sloth like an oncoming PATH train.' But then came the change of tone: 'There will only be Coca-Cola and Disney [in the songs]. And hooks, lots and lots of hooks for the kids at summer break. For the employees of the year who suddenly crack under pressure and ascend to the clock towers with their candy bars and automatic rifles, or anyone who has finally come to the answers of life. And lots of songs about chicks, I almost forgot... life. Chicks. Hooks... Click. Click. Bang.' *I love you. Take care. Jeff.* [1] Within days of this posting, he headed back to the west coast, briefly, for a family reunion. It was the last time he would see, or talk at any length, with his mother Mary Guibert.

In November, Buckley turned up at New York's KGB Theatre, ostensibly to watch a performance of *The Last Will And Testament Of Quentin Crisp*. But when the sound system failed, Buckley the roadie came to the rescue. Danny Fields had witnessed Buckley's eagerness to lend a hand at a 'wake' for the still-living Taylor Mead, a former Warhol 'star'. (Rufus Wainwright, whom Fields contends 'envied Jeffy's voice', was also performing.) Once again, when an amp stopped working, Buckley leapt up and did his bit to fix the problem and keep the show moving along, even though, as one person told me, he wasn't necessarily the most technically minded guy in the world. But he just wanted to help.

November 17 marked Buckley's 30th birthday. For a man who spent his first 20-odd years trying to find himself, personally, geographically, romantically, musically and in many other ways, the past few years had flashed by in a blur of shows and songs and miles and kudos (if not quite sales). He and Wasser planned to celebrate by going to a Soundgarden gig, but when that was cancelled, they spent the night dancing to the jukebox at New York's Daydream Café. It wasn't a bad birthday, all things considered. 'Jeff... was always in the moment of the music and that's the way he was in life, too,' Wasser told a colleague of mine. 'He loved life more than anyone maybe I've ever known. Following it where it took him.'[2]

Matters continued to improve when Mick Grondahl told Buckley that he may have found the right drummer for the band, a friend and one-time bandmate of his, a scrawny powerhouse named Parker Kindred. He was 24 years old, and as inexperienced as Grondahl and Tighe – he'd played mainly with punk bands – but the New Jersey native's father was a jazz musician, so he certainly had the right bloodline. (Amongst his myriad musical influences, Kindred was into Billie Holiday, Nusrat Fateh Ali Khan, Miles Davis, Led Zeppelin and John Coltrane, all artists that rated highly with Buckley.) Kindred threw himself into jams with the band at a couple of different New York rehearsal spaces, just before Buckley hit the road to play his solo dates. According to Dave Shouse, Kindred believed he had some sort of understanding where Buckley was heading, musically-speaking. 'Parker was like, "I think I know what Jeff wants." Jeff definitely had something in mind, rhythmically, for the new stuff.' To his friend Grondahl, Kindred differed from Matt Johnson in that he was 'more, like, loyal, an in-for-the-long-run kind of guy.'

On December 6, with an entourage of one – Jack Bookbinder, Dave Lory's assistant, the designated driver – Buckley began his Phantom Solo Tour. The recently dismissed Eric Eidel had a theory about this guerrilla tour: he felt that Buckley needed to road test his new songs. 'He wanted to return to the [songwriting] process he'd used before,' Eidel said, 'working out the songs' arrangements in small settings, intimately, letting them take shape through performance.'[3] It was also clear to Buckley that by playing solo, with absolutely no fanfare, he might recapture a little of the magic that had made his café days at Sin-E so damned special. He also needed some time and space to make his decision about Kindred, although he had a feeling he'd 'found his man'.

Buckley didn't bother to fully explain his motivation for the Phantom tour until it was all over. In a posting, dated December 18, 1996, he revealed plenty: 'There was a time in my life not too long ago,' he wrote, 'when I would show up in a café and simply do what I do, make music, learn from performing, explore what it means to be me, i.e.: have fun while I irritate and/or entertain an audience who doesn't know me or what I am about. I worked very hard to get this kind of thing together,' he explained. 'I loved it then and missed it when it disappeared. All I am doing is reclaiming it. Don't worry about my phantom solo tours, they are simply my way of sur-vival and my own method of self-assessment and recreation.'[4]

He played eight shows on the tour, which began at a coffee-shop called Old Vienna in Westborough, Massachusetts, and came to an end nine days later at Soho in Washington, DC, and each was billed under a different name. Despite the pressure to deliver some new music, which was building day by day, Buckley obviously hadn't lost his sense of humour. On the first night he was 'The Crackrobats', the next night in Boston he was known as 'Possessed By Elves', then 'Father Demo' (in Buffalo, New York), 'Smackrobiotic' for a gig in Cleveland, Ohio, 'Crit-Club' in Manyunk, Pennsylvania, 'Topless America' (Baltimore, Maryland), and, respectively, 'Martha & The Nicotines' and 'A Puppet Show Named Julio', for two dates in Washington, DC.

Buckley's intentions were pure: he didn't do any advance press for the tour, and no members of the music industry, even writers who were mad for *Grace* and keen to see where he was heading next, weren't told about the shows. Buckley's cry for anonymity worked: at his Manyunk gig, at a cof-feehouse called La Taza, about 20 confused patrons looked on as he sang and played. Most of them had little idea who Jeff Buckley was, let alone some-one calling himself 'Crit-Club'.

That was also the case at the Spot Café, where Buckley rolled up to play on December 9. Most of the punters wondered why this skinny guy with the guitar was intruding upon their caffeine fix. Buckley was more relaxed than he'd been at any time on the Grace tour; this truly was like Monday nights at Sin-E. He chatted with those who bothered listening – at one point losing himself in an anti-smoking rant, moaning about how the 'world has become one big ashtray' – endlessly tuned up, and stopped songs midway through, searching for the right inflection, as cups and saucers rat-tled and people ordered coffees, shouting over the top of Buckley and his guitar. Clearly, though, he wasn't quite ready to plunge headfirst into a new setlist: 'Lover, You Should Have Come Over' stayed, even more beautiful in a stark solo arrangement, and he persevered with 'Mojo Pin' and 'Grace'. Buckley even dusted off 'Dink's Song', the bluesy raver he'd played with Gary Lucas. His new songs included 'Vancouver' and 'The Sky Is A Landfill', while he also strummed a cover of 'Yard Of Blonde Girls', a song he'd been introduced to by Inger Lorre.*

On December 18, Buckley got back on-line. 'The question is,' he wrote, 'why did he tour and not tell us where he was playing? Why, why, why?' After offering the explanation detailed earlier, he signed off with this worrying coda: 'I'm in the middle of some wild shit now... please be patient. I'm coming soon to a cardboard display case near you and I'm coming out of my hole and we'll make bonfires out of ticket stubs come the summer. Merry Christmas all and a kiss for your New Year's headache. *Bye, Jeff.*'[5] That would be his second-to-last posting; before the year ended, he chided his mother for addressing fans' questions on-line. His scepticism towards this relatively new form of communication was increasing.

As a new year dawned, there was a perceptible change in the mood of Buckley's beloved East Village. It was no longer a refuge for 'illegals' and drunken Irish musicians, or bohemians who didn't fit in elsewhere. Sin-E had closed in late November; regular Tom Clark stated that when Shane Doyle sold the place, 'the vibe went with him'. (The new owners still owed Doyle money from the sale when the venue closed.) NYU had acquired a lot of housing in the Village and it was now awash with students, rather than painters and songwriters and dreamers. What was once a comparatively under-populated part of Manhattan was now as crowded and lively as anywhere else in the city. It was around this time that Buckley started, in the words of one close friend, to consider going 'somewhere to live a life that wasn't available in New York anymore.' His Big Apple dream was fast fading; he needed to get away, just as he'd fled LA for New York many years earlier.

Speaking on the BBC's *Everybody Here Wants You*, Parker Kindred talked about the changes he saw in Buckley. 'I knew that he had to get out of here [New York]; he was going insane,' said Kindred. 'On a good day the city's an incredible place to be, on a bad day the city can eat your soul. He needed to write some music and he couldn't do it here, there was just a lot of temptation, I think. He was just trying to isolate himself.'[6]

Memphis was an obvious choice for Buckley. Thanks, mainly, to the number of bands dragging their gear through the raggedy foyer of Easley Studios – stopping briefly to admire the Elvis shrine – this sleepy southern

---

* Buckley would go to great lengths to point out, at various times, 'This is Inger's song, not mine'. They'd met at a session for a Jack Kerouac tribute, entitled *Kicks Joy Darkness*; Buckley played guitar, sitar and what he called 'mouth sax' while Lorre read Kerouac's 'Angel Mine'.

city had become a sort of indie-rock Mecca in the early 1990s. If he was going to record there, Buckley figured, why not try living in Memphis as well? Mick Grondahl, however, wasn't totally sold on his band leader's plan. 'I think it was rather uncalled for, to tell you the truth,' Grondahl said to me. 'It came about so quickly. I think in some ways it suited him very well, because it's a type of cultural centre, with a real legacy, a history, but it's also like where he grew up: big highways, houses with lawns, that type of scenery, so I think he felt at home in that way. He also had a connection to interesting things that were happening there; there was a kind of funky scene there, musicians playing out in the square during summer. I think he felt quite at home there, but I don't think he would have stayed. I wouldn't live there myself.'

But before he could relocate, Buckley had commitments. On January 2, 1997, he tried out more new songs on an audience at New York's Daydream Café, with Grondahl and Tighe sitting in. On January 24, drummer Kindred made his recording debut with Buckley and the band at Sorcerer Studios, during the second set of sessions with Tom Verlaine. Again, the results were relatively underwhelming.

Buckley wasn't quite ready to admit that his dream of recording with Verlaine was turning into a nightmare; 10 years later, Grondahl, however, would come clean. 'In hindsight, no, it would have worked out better working with someone else but we needed to find that out,' he admitted. 'We couldn't turn back at a certain point. I would imagine [Buckley] felt that there was a lack of the flow that's needed to occur in a creative situation. I think he would have sensed some of the things that I sensed.' It was decided that, once again, his second album would be put on ice, and sessions would recommence in mid-February at Easley Studios.

Buckley bumped into his buddy Mark Geary around this time, just around the corner from the site of Sin-E. 'He was doing that thing that we're all guilty of: he was walking around what I call Amnesia Lane. He was going back to the places he knew: clocking in at Sin-E and wherever. He said he was heading off [to Memphis] and he said, "I hear that you're doing great." The two of us were buzzing; things were obviously a little insane with him. So we said goodbye and see you soon, and that was it.'

Everything that Buckley did in those early weeks of February 1997 positively reeked of farewell. On February 4, he put in a cameo at the Knitting Factory, as part of the venue's 10th anniversary. 'Do I smell some pot happening there?' Buckley asked as soon as he walked on stage. 'Are people getting stoned?' St Ann's may have been the site of Buckley's New York debut, but it was the Knitting Factory where he and Gary Lucas had, for a moment, sensed the beginnings of a beautiful musical friendship. Buckley knew this, too, and, with Lou Reed looking on, invited Lucas on stage for an impassioned version of 'Grace', coyly asking: 'If Gary Lucas isn't too mad with me, would he like to play a song?' Even though earlier in the night they'd had an uncomfortable reunion, Lucas admitted that he still felt a deep connection with Buckley. 'Playing with him again gave me shivers,' he said.[7] Buckley ended his set with a quote from Smashing Pumpkin Billy Corgan that some read as a sign of his current frustrations. 'Despite all my rage,' Buckley announced as he left the stage, 'I'm just a rat in a cage.'

The next day, Buckley and the band reconvened with Verlaine – and engineer Michael Clouse, Buckley's old 'X Factor' partner – at a studio at 135 West 26th Street, where they completed a version of 'Haven't You Heard'. This time, finally, there was a sense that the tunes, and the possibilities with Verlaine, were on the improve. A few days later, Kindred made his public debut with Buckley at a 'secret' gig at Arlene's Grocery, the new downtown venue operated by Shane Doyle.

Buckley took the stage in a foul mood, confronting a bootlegger – 'you fucking dick; what are you going to do, study it?' – before launching into 'Nightmares By The Sea'. Aside from yet another anti-smoking rant from Buckley, and a fair-to-middling Tom Waits impression, the gig was notable for its bevy of new tunes: 'Witches Rave', 'Haven't You Heard', 'Morning Theft', 'Landfill' and something called 'Snail Drop-D Explosion' were all attempted on the night. It may have been the first gig with Kindred behind the drums, but the band seemed in great shape; the songs were sharper, faster and punkier than anything on *Grace*. Shane Doyle recalled that Buckley was in a typically livewire mood. 'He was bouncing around, talking here, talking there,' Doyle said. The next day, a scraggly-looking Buckley appeared at yet another New York studio for yet another tribute, this one in honour of the popular writer Edgar Allan Poe, best known for his tales of mystery and the macabre. With the help of Allen Ginsberg, legendary Beat poet, and former Dylan and Jack Kerouac sidekick, Buckley read 'Ulalume', a dream-like poem of love and death, with a strong and undeniably eerie connection to what lay ahead in Memphis. Ginsberg himself would die of liver cancer, aged 70, a month later.

Also at the session was ageing chanteuse, and former lover of Mick Jagger, Marianne Faithfull. She'd befriended Buckley in 1995, when they shared a stage at Lyon, in France, but before then she'd been spellbound by one of his Sin-E sets, which she'd attended at the urging of Hal Willner. 'Of course, like everybody,' she told *Interview* magazine, 'I just completely fell in love with him.'[8] By the time of the Poe reading, it had been a year since

Faithfull had seen Buckley, and she was concerned about her 'great, great friend. He just looked so tired and thin, you know?' she said. 'He needed a good meal and a bit of a rest and maybe someone to take care of him.'[9]

Faithfull was also friends with Penny Arcade, on whose doorstep Buckley turned up in tears later that night, his final evening in New York before heading to Memphis. The platonic pair had spent a considerable amount of time together in these previous few months; even though she didn't drink, Arcade was quite prepared to hold up whatever bar he nominated, as he spilled his guts on his career, his life, even his love of The Grifters. He'd even started to consider the idea of hiring her team of dancers to open his next Australian tour.

Arcade had seen him in some distress a week or so earlier, when they learned that the analyst that they both saw, an African/American woman named Mrs Williams, wasn't just out of town, but had actually suffered a heart attack while holidaying in the Caribbean. This time, though, he was 'inconsolable'. It took Arcade several hours of comforting to get him back to some kind of coherent state, and not until early the next morning, the day of his departure for Memphis, did he seem to have regained some of his composure. The feeling is that his meltdown was related to 'coming to terms with his analysis and his father'. Buckley may have also been trying to extricate himself from his relationship with Wasser.

Within days of arriving in Memphis, Buckley found himself a residency at a tiny venue called Barrister's, hidden away in an alley just off Jefferson Avenue in a part of town frequented by the legal profession, hence the name*. Just like his Phantom solo road trip, it was yet another attempt by Buckley to reclaim the anonymity and freedom of his pre-Columbia days. Dave Shouse, who, along with his wife Tammy, would become Buckley's de facto hosts in Memphis, was stunned by these early sets. 'Those shows were so intense,' he recalled. 'Jeff just got up and hypnotised people. Originally it was a small group; he chose a Monday night [a la Sin-E], the weakest night of the week. Originally there might have been a couple of dozen people. We'd round people up and take them down there.'

Buckley and band's ongoing sessions with Verlaine began in Easley soon after his first Barrister's gig. One of the first songs they nailed was the smoky soul ballad, 'Everybody Here Wants You', which Mick Grondahl felt was one of their more satisfying moments in the studio. 'Tom Verlaine told Parker to really beat the shit out of those drums, really hard on the snare, at the start,'

---

* Buckley began playing there on February 12 and began his residency in March.

he said. 'That was one of the good things he did; he wanted a good signal on the board, something strong to work with.' Soon after, Grondahl would have trouble convincing people that 'Everybody' was actually cut at Easley, indie-rock's ground zero. '[They] said that we must have doctored the shit out of it, which we didn't. So apparently the sound on that song isn't typical of what they'd get there.' Still, Grondahl, like Buckley, was a fan of the studio. 'I thought the room sounded really good, the vibe had a lot of character, they were very nice people. The sound worked out really well.'

Yet their progress with Verlaine was stop-start at best. It was becoming apparent that Buckley had chosen the wrong guy; he may have admired Verlaine as a player, but they simply weren't gelling as musician and producer. Nevertheless, his second album had now progressed to a stage where it was almost impossible to pull out. Mick Grondahl agreed with this, yet as much as he respected Verlaine he felt the record simply wasn't happening. 'Tom Verlaine: great guitar player, great album, but in terms of being a producer with us it wasn't working. We had to learn that. It was difficult because we so much wanted to believe it could work but it didn't.' To add to the general confusion, Verlaine wasn't even sure that these were album sessions – he thought it was just another 'run through' of the songs. Buckley, however, felt otherwise. When Chris Dowd and Buckley spoke on the phone, Dowd told him that he should hire Daniel Lanois, the French-Canadian who'd worked alongside Brian Eno with U2 and also who'd produced great albums with Bob Dylan, Peter Gabriel and Emmylou Harris. 'I think he would have been perfect,' said Dowd. 'I don't think Steve Berkowitz was into it, but I told Jeff to work with Lanois and stop fucking around, or produce it himself. But he wanted it so bad because he really admired Verlaine. He was one of these people who was loyal to a fault, until it hurts.'

The Shouses, meanwhile, were proving to be the perfect southern hosts. Buckley would drop by their house for what Shouse described as 'big vegetarian dinners'; they'd eat, drink some wine and, according to Shouse, talk about 'anything but music and family'. (The Shouses figured that Mary Guibert and Tim Buckley were all no-go zones.) Often their conversations would turn to the Memphis Zoo, which was fast becoming a favourite hang-out of Buckley's. 'Looking back on it we tried to hopefully take his mind off everything,' said Shouse. 'It was like Alice and the rabbit hole: "Come on down and it'll be a dream world, a sane dream world". On our part there was kind of a nurturing thing; you couldn't help it, he put out some strong vibes and people responded strongly to him, whether it was nurturing or affection or infatuation – there was a lot of that.'

213

The only false move that Shouse made was attempting to jam with Buckley. A little sheepishly, he admitted that the temptation to play with such a great musician, and hope something would rub off, was just too great. 'It was the worst thing I've ever done,' Shouse said. 'It was awkward to the point where we just stopped. I came in with a huge set of expectations; basically I'd planned to stop and watch him play, you know, "Knock me out, Jeff, knock me out!" I should have known just to pick up something and start playing, and not say anything, don't predicate it, just do. And that's all Jeff wanted: to be in the moment and let it go, not attach anything to it.'

Shouse's bandmate, Tripp Lamkins, who had bonded with Buckley over a shared love of Yes, did have a more successful jam with Buckley during his Memphis days. Lamkins lived in a building nicknamed 'Rockopolis', due to the many bands who lived and rehearsed there. (Andria Lisle, a writer, who'd also become close with Buckley in 1997, lived across the hall. Buckley would sometimes stop by and listen to old blues records with her.) Buckley would also drop in and jam with Lamkins and Roy Baker, The Grifters' drummer and a room-mate of Lamkins. One afternoon, after 'smoking way too much weed', according to Lamkins, the trio attempted to play Rush's complex album *2112*, in its entirety. Buckley may have been able to pull Genesis' 'Back In NYC' 'out of his ass', in Lamkins' words, but this prog-rock epic was beyond even him.

In early March, Steve Berkowitz and Dave Lory arrived in Memphis to check on the progress of *My Sweetheart The Drunk*. It was during this visit that Shouse witnessed the change that came over Buckley when the 'business people' were in town. He got a call from Buckley, asking him to dinner. This was very peculiar, because Buckley always went to the Shouse home for meals; they never went out. 'But his A&R guy was coming into town and he wanted someone else to talk to at dinner,' Shouse said. 'There were moments like that where you felt he was nervous.'

While Berkowitz was in Memphis, he and Buckley took a walk, and Buckley admitted that Verlaine simply wasn't working out. He was now more than $350,000 in the red to his label, for the second album alone. 'I think there was a lot of chaos going on in his life and we were trying to record,' Parker Kindred said in *Everybody Here Wants You*. 'At times it ended up being like that and sounding like that. Then the pressure started and all started to back up, you know, and everybody got really tense.'[10] According to Shouse, 'The Verlaine thing didn't work, obviously; and I guess Jeff took it upon himself to fix the problem.'

By the middle of the month, after some final recordings with Verlaine, the sessions were again shut down, and Verlaine was effectively fired. Just before he flew back to New York, Verlaine had some final words for Buckley. 'This stuff sounds really good to me,' he said. 'If you feel dissatisfied maybe you want to take it a little easier on yourself, because there's nothing wrong with this.' Half joking, Verlaine added: 'I know you probably want to change everything.'[11]

Buckley then dropped another bombshell on his entourage; he was staying on in Memphis. He quickly found a house at 91 North Rembert Street, which he rented for a mere $450 a month. He tinkered away at some new songs on a four-track recorder, one of his few possessions, while Kindred, Tighe and Grondahl returned to New York. (The ever-helpful Shouses supplied the few items of furniture in Buckley's house.) Pat O'Brien, his landlady, lived a few doors down the street, and was a little startled on first meeting Buckley. 'He came and wanted to rent a place; he was ready to move in right then and there. He scared me at first but when I met him he was a really nice guy. He didn't have much: a chair, his phone and a phonebook. When he first came, he wanted to be left alone. You know when you've had too much, and you want to be left alone?'[12] Andria Lisle, Tripp Lamkins' neighbour, would come by to visit and she'd find Buckley lying face down in the overgrown lawn. 'He hid in the grass in his yard and no-one could see him for days. He could be Jeff – or whatever Jeff he wanted to be,' she told the BBC.[13]

Buckley found a local Vietnamese restaurant, the Saigon Lee, which was much to his liking – for one thing, he could ride there on his bicycle, his preferred mode of transport while in Memphis. 'The folks at Saigon Lee immediately adopted him; the girls there loved him and gave him a Saigon Lee T-shirt, which he immediately put on,' said Shouse. 'Jeff threw his old shirt into a sack, grabbed his food and rode off wearing the T-shirt. Then there were these rumours going around that he was just trying to be a normal guy and blend into Memphis, delivering food for Saigon Lee.'*

Buckley's chance of maintaining some sort of anonymity with his Barrister's residency soon started to fade. Word began to spread on-line that Jeff Buckley – *the* Jeff Buckley, the guy who made *Grace* – was playing low-key sets there every Monday night, and the 'uber fans', as Shouse called them, began to roll up to the venue. 'People would start coming in from Nashville, or Little Rock, Arkansas, which is about 120 miles away, and from small college communities around here,' Shouse recalled. 'Within two or

---

* The restaurant is now one of several must-visit locations for Buckley-spotters who make the pilgrimage to Memphis.

three months the place was full and suddenly he'd have to deal with those requests: *"Play Hallelujah!"* I think he really enjoyed the intimacy of those early shows, but then it became an event and he got a little wary of even going and playing sometimes.'

Tammy Shouse, who'd collect Buckley and drive him to the shows, knew when he was feeling the strain of being Jeff Buckley, star: he'd sit beside her, scribbling in his notebook, keeping well and truly to himself. It was as though his 'secret place' had been discovered and his cover had been blown. 'The immediacy of the Internet, even then, annoyed him,' said Andria Lisle, 'fans posting online what he wore, and what his setlists were at his Monday gigs. His mom could read about them before he could even get home from downtown. He loved going unrecognised, and here he could do that.' While hanging out with Lisle at a 'ridiculous' karaoke bar, Buckley mentioned to a friend of hers that he 'worked from home'. She asked if he did telephone work. 'He loved that,' Lisle recalled.

During one night at Barrister's, well before his actual set, Buckley decided to take a stab at 'Back In NYC'. Tripp Lamkins was looking on. 'I was hanging by the bar when Jeff announced he was going to do a cover,' said Lamkins. Buckley asked Lamkins – a bassist by trade – to join him on drums, but he backed out. 'I'm an OK drummer,' he said, 'but there's some crazy time signatures going on in that song. Anyway, he played the whole thing and it was great. Definitely, nobody enjoyed it more than I did; he even made fun of the lyrics while he was singing it.' When Buckley reached the lines: 'Held my heart, deep in hair, time to shave, shave it off, it off', he stopped and spoke to the audience. 'I'm not kidding,' he chuckled, 'these are the actual lyrics.' No-one, at this point, not even Lamkins, knew that Buckley was home-recording the song, with a view to including it on his album-under-development.

Buckley had other escapes. Joan Wasser would come and stay with him for one week out of every four, and he once rode the bus to Atlanta to see her perform. He also played a show at Hendrix College in Arkansas, with Shouse acting as chauffeur. A discovery soon after this one-off gig proved just how little Buckley cared about money. 'They paid him with a cheque,' said Shouse, 'and maybe a week later I went over to his place and it was laying there, with a footprint on it, coffee spilled over it. He didn't worry about making or having money. He was just more interested in checking Memphis out, hanging out.'

Buckley did receive a rude financial awakening when he started to make enquiries about buying the house on North Rembert, which was as close to a home as he'd ever had. Despite the sold-out shows and improving sales of *Grace*, there simply wasn't enough money in the bank to cover the purchase. He spoke about this with Kathryn Grimm. 'After all those months of touring he didn't have the $40,000 to buy the house. I think he was very bitter about that,' she told me. 'And this was a guy who spent his money on guitars and CDs; he wasn't very materialistic. Something was screwy with the accounting. That's when he started noticing something was rotten.' It certainly didn't improve his increasingly tense relationship with Columbia. 'At a certain point the label was keeping him afloat,' Leah Reid countered. 'He needed money to live and they gave it to him. I think when he said that he wanted to buy the house they said no. Then there was the Tom Verlaine stuff. Money was being thrown in all directions.' Buckley found an outlet for his stress; when he checked in on a Grifters' album session at Easley, he yelled advice to the band from the control room. 'He'd be in the studio screaming, "Don't let them Sony-ize your work!" ' Shouse laughed.

At home on North Rembert, Buckley was making steady progress with his new music, when he wasn't hanging out at the zoo – the butterfly enclosure was a particular favourite – cycling around town in his Saigon Lee T-shirt, or taking in the services at Al Green's church with Andria Lisle. In an act of retribution in which he clearly revelled, he recorded his new songs on pre-recorded cassettes of Michael Bolton albums, which he'd picked up cheap in downtown Memphis.

Berkowitz returned to Memphis in late April, and sensed that Buckley's mood towards the album, and the songs, was definitely improving. Berkowitz proposed that *Grace's* producer Andy Wallace be hired to work on *My Sweetheart The Drunk* (he also floated the idea of using Steve Fisk, a Seattle-based producer, who'd worked with Soundgarden, indie moodists Low and Soul Coughing). Buckley agreed on Wallace, and plans were put in place for the producer to visit Buckley in mid May, and then begin work at Easley on June 23 and continue until the middle of August.

Buckley had clearly emerged from his creative dry spell. While living in Memphis he recorded rough drafts of numerous songs: the bizarrely titled 'Murder Suicide Meteor Slave', plus 'Demon John', 'Jewel Box', the positively lascivious 'Your Flesh Is So Nice' and his surprise cover of Genesis' 'Back In NYC', which he'd given an avant-garde makeover. After meeting with Andy Wallace, Buckley spoke with his mother on the phone, for the final time. They hadn't spoken at any length since the family reunion in October 1996. Guibert, like many others who talked with Buckley in the spring of 1997, felt that he was upbeat about the future. 'He had been through a period where he was trying to sort some things out in his life,' she said. 'There were all of these expectations and he felt under pressure. But he had come through that and into the light. He was ebullient and full of life.'[12] Michael Tighe sensed this, too, when they spoke around this time. Buckley, to him, seemed 'relaxed and confident, [as if he was] going through a metamorphosis.'[13]

Back in New York, Grondahl, Tighe and Kindred received a parcel in the post, a cassette entitled *My Sweetheart The Drunk – Sketches For My Boys*, which contained rough drafts of his new tunes. Grondahl spoke for the entire band when he said that he was relieved and comforted by the tape. 'The demos that he sent us, I thought of those as blueprints, as sketches, they informed me as to exactly what I had to work with and how I was to approach the songs from a bass player's point of view,' he said. 'He'd done a lot of work and had fleshed out the arrangements quite well.' According to Grondahl, it was very similar to the time Buckley presented him with the demos for *Grace*. 'He had the guitar and voice part down, and what he needed was a band arrangement, a bass part, a drum part, a second guitar part and whatever arrangement was needed. We had our work cut out for us, but I felt there was little doubt; all the songs were good and worth recording. We were really ready to go.'

Yet for every upbeat conversation Buckley had with his band or his mother, there was any number of unsettling reports. Chris Dowd, who was about to leave the country, called Buckley, his old friend, who didn't even recognise his voice at first. 'I knew there was something wrong. He wasn't suicidal or any crazy shit like that, but something was wrong.' John Humphrey, his pal from LA, also had an unnerving conversation with Buckley, during which he frequently mentioned Satan (although, in hindsight, it's worth noting that Buckley was reading Salman Rushdie's *The Satanic Verses* at the time). Humphrey felt that Buckley was 'under a lot of stress'.

In Dublin, Glen Hansard, Buckley's buddy from the days of The Commitments touring band, came home and received a strange message from his flatmate. 'Fucking Jeff Buckley just called you,' he was informed. 'He said he was ringing to see how you were.' 'I was overjoyed,' Hansard recalled, 'and my flatmate [a big fan] was blown away. Jeff had never called me; it's the weirdest thing, the wackiest thing. I would have loved to have spoken with him. I missed his call by about 15 minutes.'

Buckley also placed unexpected, and occasionally unhinged calls to Rebecca Moore; his ex-drummer Eric Eidel; Tom Clark, a singing/ songwriting peer from Sin-E (Buckley told him that he was over his writer's block), and Daniella Sapriel, his father's old friend. He also spoke for several hours on the phone with Penny Arcade, who felt that he was 'freaked out'. There was a suggestion that Buckley's concern was, in part, due to a business move of Gene Bowen, his tour manager. He was managing a singer by the name of Jimmy Gnecco, soon to front a band called Ours, who was a huge Buckley fan, and was very clearly influenced by him. It was as though a clone was taking Buckley's place. And the lack of money in the bank also clearly upset Buckley; he may have treated money with little or no respect, but he was acutely aware when it was in short supply and he felt he'd been misinformed in this regard.

At Barrister's on May 26, Buckley shocked the crowd when he walked on stage and announced: 'Dead, dead, dead, dead, dead, he's fucking dead, the guy from Brainiac is fucking dead. I want this to mean something to every fucking one of you.' He then launched into Brainiac's 'Terminal Cancer', as a mark of respect to the lead singer of the punk band, Tim Taylor, who'd just died in a car wreck. Buckley then segued into 'Hallelujah' as the final part of his tribute. He was clearly in an unusual mood, fluctuating between anger and overwhelming largesse – he even bought red wine for the entire bar. 'Free,' he said, 'that's spelled f-r-e-e.' He also performed 'Corpus Christi Carol', the ethereal ballad he'd dropped from his set almost two years back. 'Is that how you like your rock heroes – dead?' he demanded at one point. Afterwards, he was just as volatile; when a fan requested an autograph, and innocently asked how Taylor had died, he exploded, shouting: 'He blew up!' and hurled a beer bottle away in disgust. Gayle Kelemen, who ran Buckley's unofficial web page, approached him. 'Are you upset about one of your favourite musicians dying?,' he snapped at her. 'I hope you are, I hope you are because that's why I create music.'[14]

Two days later, Bowen and his assistant, Keith Foti, flew in and began to set up a rehearsal space for Buckley and the band, in preparation for the sessions with Andy Wallace. One of the first things Buckley asked of Bowen was to find him a new analyst; he also asked again, without luck, about the possibility of buying the house on North Rembert Street. Grondahl, Tighe and Parker were due to arrive in Memphis the following day and stay until late July. In New York, the word had started to circulate that Buckley hadn't just asked the band down to record; they were about to undertake a ceremony, according to Glen Hansard. 'The stories I'd heard was that he was bringing the band to Memphis to burn the tapes of the record he did with Tom Verlaine. I was getting that from his friends in New York. He was gathering the band up to have a ceremonial burning of the masters. He was really unhappy with it.'

Grondahl, Tighe and Kindred were scheduled to arrive at Memphis airport late on the afternoon of May 29. Not too long before they landed, Andria

Lisle strolled over to Buckley's home on North Rembert, where she found him with Gene Bowen and Keith Foti. Lisle asked Buckley if he was up for a trip to the local casino; he said no, he had to see the band and get ready for their recording sessions. With a shrug, Lisle agreed to check in with him later, and report on how she fared. With the arrival time of the band fast approaching, it was agreed that Bowen would collect them from the airport, while Buckley and Foti would drive to his new rehearsal space. It was obvious that Buckley wanted to launch himself straight into the sessions with Andy Wallace. This time, for sure, they'd get the damn album recorded.

While Bowen headed to the airport, Buckley and Foti realised that neither could remember the actual location of the space. They weren't too far from the Wolf River, the site of a tourist site, reached by monorail, called Mud Island. Buckley knew the spot; he'd actually swum there before, ignoring the signs warning of the potential dangers. He suggested to Foti that they stop there and hang out, while they tried to remember the route to the rehearsal room. Foti shrugged, 'Sure, why not?' The weather was good, Buckley seemed in an upbeat frame of mind, so what harm could it do? They had an acoustic guitar and a ghetto blaster in the car, and when they pulled up, Buckley grabbed them both and walked down to the riverbank. He was wearing a bulky pair of Doc Martens, jeans and a black-and-white T-shirt, with the word 'Altamont' printed on the front.*

Foti sat down on the riverbank and started strumming the guitar; he thought that Buckley would sit alongside him. But, no, he said he was going for a swim. Foti said that wasn't such a great idea, but Buckley either didn't hear him or didn't pay any attention. He eased himself into the shallows, all the while wailing the lyrics to Led Zeppelin's 'Whole Lotta Love': 'You need cooling, baby/I'm not fooling,' Buckley crooned, 'I'm gonna send ya back to schoolin'.' The water felt cool, soothing, so Buckley flipped onto his back and swam a little farther out, still singing. Dusk was starting to fall. The occasional boat motored by. It was another mellow Memphis evening.

Buckley had been swimming for maybe 15 minutes when Foti noticed that a large tugboat was about to pass. He looked out and saw that Buckley had also spotted the tug, and was heading back towards shore, trying to beat the heavy wake created by the boat. Concerned that the wash might reach the shore and drench their ghetto blaster, Foti briefly turned his back on

---

* Altamont was the site of the infamous outdoor Rolling Stones concert in 1969 at a racetrack near Livermore in northern California, where Hell's Angels ran wild and an armed audience member was stabbed to death. Buckley's obsession with rock history was at work again.

Buckley to ensure it was safe. Reassured, he turned around, and saw that Buckley was gone. At first, Foti thought Buckley was fooling around; the guy was fond of a joke. He called out for him, hesitantly at first, and then in an increasingly louder voice. Foti considered jumping in and trying to locate Buckley, but had no idea where to begin. A passer-by heard Foti's yells, and called the cops. It was 9.22 pm.

Within a half-hour, a full-scale search was in full operation, involving scuba divers and a high-tech police helicopter. The band, meanwhile, had landed in Memphis, and when they didn't find Buckley and Foti at the rehearsal space, headed over to his house. There was a strange, somewhat desperate message on the answering machine from Foti, who mumbled something about 'Jeff's missing'. Soon enough, they, too, were standing on the riverbank of the Wolf River. 'It was traumatic,' Mick Grondahl under-stated. 'When I talked to the coast guard, who was this big, burly guy, I asked him what was going on and he said there was no news. He said, "I swim very well and I would never go down there" – and he pointed to where Jeff went in. It doesn't look that bad but it was dug very deep so that the big boats could pass through, so it went down quite a few metres even in that tributary.'

After a futile three hours, at around 1am, the search for Buckley was called off for the night. Andria Lisle, meanwhile, was walking her dog, and stopped by the house on Rembert Street to report on her night at the casino. She knocked on the door. 'Who's there?' asked a voice from inside. The door remained shut. When Lisle replied, she was told to go away. 'I didn't think another thing of it,' Lisle wrote in 2000, 'and I went home and went to sleep.'[15] When Lisle went into work that next day, she was pulled aside by her boss, who asked whether she'd been with Buckley the night before. Then her phone rang: it was a reporter, asking for a comment about his death. She had absolutely no idea what to say.

Official statements soon appeared, from Columbia Records, and from Mary Guibert. By now it was clear that Jeff Buckley had drowned. 'It has become apparent to me,' Guibert said, 'that my son will not be walking out of the river. I ask people who cared about Jeff to please be honourable and faithful to his memory, to send their best wishes to Jeff and to all of us who are mourning his passing.'[16] As maligned as Guibert was, and still is, by Buckley fans and friends, the tragic loss of her son, coupled with the OD death of her husband Tim 22 years earlier, was almost unimaginable.

A Jeff Buckley shrine, complete with flowers, cards and CDs, began to grow outside the site of the original Sin-E in the East Village. Mike Webb, Steve Berkowitz's right-hand man, had by now left Columbia, but he called his former boss as soon as he heard the news. 'Steve told me that he didn't want anyone to find the body, that way he could believe Jeff just got fed up and disappeared.'

As the news hit the wires, those close to Buckley began to re-assess his recent behaviour, and his occasional recklessness. Taking a dip in a treacherous body of water wasn't out of character; he and Wasser had done the same in Australia. 'I'd say he was quite free-spirited in the way of Jim Morrison, or other loonies like him,' admitted Grondahl. 'I'd seen him do screwy stuff but never thought he'd take it to that level. I don't think he committed suicide but what he did was suicidal. He had a lot to live for. It was just bad decision-making and it cost him his life.'

Merri Cyr, who'd fallen out with Buckley over the botched-up 'Last Goodbye' video, was angered by the news. 'I felt sometimes he really could be suicidal; there were times when I wasn't sure he was going to be OK, and he said, "No, I'm going to survive this." So I felt OK, he was going to make it. When he died, whether it was an accident or not, I was so angry that he'd checked out. Who knows what he was thinking that day; maybe he'd had enough of this planet. I think people are on this planet as long as they want to be. To me, it was like, "You chicken".' Yet to even whisper the word 'suicide' to Buckley's west coast ally Chris Dowd, despite their bizarre final conversation, brought out what he referred to as the 'South Central side of me that wants to knock someone the fuck out. He had too much of an ego towards things like living, a healthy respect for life,' Dowd snapped. 'There was no fucking romantic shit; it was a horrible accident and that's it.'

The abundance of watery images in Buckley's songs, however, did nothing to dispel rumours that he had some weird premonition of what would occur in Memphis. But the idea of suicide – by drowning, no less – seems very hard to accept. Despite his obvious creative struggles, there were too many good things happening in Buckley's life – a new record and a new city, for starters – to suggest that he had a death wish.

The Grifters, Buckley's closest musical compadres in Memphis, were on the road, in Green Bay, Wisconsin, when they heard that Buckley was missing. According to Dave Shouse, 'I remember the van was parked at the hotel and the hotel was adjacent to Packer Stadium. We were sitting there on the back fender of the van, looking out at the stadium, just thinking, "This is so weird." There was all sorts of talk about what happened. But we knew that he went in with these combat boots, Doc Martens, and so maybe he was trying to get out of the way of the boat and his boots filled up with water and he got leg cramps. We're not talking about a guy who swam a lot. We were all kind of family and Jeff was the bright shining star of the family.'

Shouse added. 'We were going, "Why? Why? What the fuck?" Jeff wasn't supposed to come to Memphis – *and fucking die!'*

Danny Fields, friend to both Jeff and Tim Buckley, was 'opening' up his summer house in the Hamptons, when his phone rang. To his surprise, it was Linda McCartney, calling from her home in the UK. Point blank, she asked: 'Is Jeff Buckley dead?' 'What are you talking about?', Fields replied. 'I've never heard such a stupid thing from such a smart girl.' Yet McCartney persevered. 'No, seriously, is he dead?,' she insisted. 'I think he's dead.' Fields agreed to place a call to Sony and see what he could find out, and then he'd call her straight back. 'I just knew from the way the phone was answered; you knew that something tragic had happened, it just goes through the wires,' Fields said. 'I was told that they think he was dead, that he was washed away by a wave. "Rivers don't have waves," I said. "This must be some drunken prank." And he sure could drink, you know. But it was true. And I had to call Linda back and tell her.'*

Still deep in shock, Fields' phone ran again. It was Rufus Wainwright, another young, pretty associate of his, whose path had intersected with Buckley during the early 1990s in New York. Fields and Penny Arcade were their mutual friends. 'Oh Rufus, I guess you heard the news?' Fields asked. 'What news?' replied Wainwright. When Fields told him about Buckley, the line went silent, just for a minute. 'I thought this was the reason for the call and his silence was him accumulating the appropriate amount of grief,' Fields recalled. 'Then he said, "Oh wow, he's dead... but listen the reason I called is that you've got to hear my record – *it's great!*" That's why he called; he wanted to prepare me for the arrival of his new album. I thought it was a sweet and telling irony. I think he got more than his 85 cents-worth for his call.' In New York, Gary Lucas sobbed at hearing the news.

As the days passed since Buckley took his fateful and fatal dip, memorials and tributes began all around the world, with a fervour that almost matched that of John Lennon's senseless death in 1980. On stage, R.E.M. and Bush dedicated songs to Buckley; during a massive stadium show in New Jersey, U2's Bono stopped and did likewise. 'Jeff Buckley was a pure drop in an ocean of noise,' Bono announced, high praise from one of the biggest stars of the past 20-odd years. Yet it wasn't until June 2, four days after Buckley went missing, that news reports actually intimated that he was dead. It seemed as though the media, not just his fans, friends and family, were

---

* Marianne Faithfull's response on hearing about Buckley's death almost echoed that of Fields. 'Didn't he read Huck Finn?' she asked out loud.

hoping, somehow, that he'd emerge from the Wolf River, thereby pulling off a miracle to match the wonders he could perform on-stage.

Steve Berkowitz's wish, however, that Buckley had simply ran away, was derailed on June 4, when, at around 4.40pm, a passenger on the *American Queen* riverboat noticed something unusual in the water. The boat's first mate, Dave Williamson, climbed into a dinghy, pushed his way through clumps of bushes and debris, and made the grisly discovery. It was the body of Jeff Buckley. His bloated corpse had washed up at the foot of Beale Street, the musical and spiritual heartland of Memphis. Even in death, it was all about the music.

An autopsy conducted at Memphis' University Of Tennessee showed that Buckley was sober at the time of his drowning. He tested negative for drugs, while only a miniscule trace of alcohol – 0.04 milligrams, which equated to roughly one glass of beer or wine – was found in his system. 'Death was [due] to drowning,' read the report. 'No other evidence of injuries is seen.' Before his body was cremated, his family asked that a DNA sample be taken, in order to negate any 'bogus paternity suits'. Buckley readily admitted that he was a lover, so this was an understandable reaction from Guibert.

Apart from the Sin-E vigil, several memorial services were held for Buckley. At Brooklyn's St Ann's church, where he'd made his New York 'debut' in 1991, Elvis Costello performed a musical tribute, as did several members of Buckley's band. Nusrat Fateh Ali Khan's 'Aag Daman Lag Jai' was used as the processional music, and the 'So Real' video was aired. Buckley's lean, spare reading of The Weavers' country ballad 'Satisfied Mind', recorded on Nicholas Hill's *The Music Faucet* in 1992, was played as the mourners left the church. In the program for the service, Guibert included several excerpts from Buckley's diary. 'The thing is that I want it all next week, right now, this millisecond,' it read. 'Life should sparkle and rush, burn with fire hot like melting steel, like freeze-burn from a comet.'[17] It was as though he'd written his own eulogy.

This service took place on a steamy summer's day, but not everyone who attended was especially comfortable with the way it was handled by Buckley's family, or the behaviour of some of the mourners. One attendee reported that Keith Foti, who'd been with Buckley when he took his fateful plunge into the Wolf River, came in wearing shades 'and dressed like a rock star'. Tense words were exchanged between Penny Arcade and Inger Lorre, who sang a tribute to Buckley during the ceremony. 'It just seemed that there were a bunch of people there talking shit who didn't know anything about him,' said Tom Chang, who was at the service. 'It was like this industry thing, which made me sick. Then there was this special service afterwards, and that was just a bunch of jive, too. There were postcards of Jeff wearing Calvin Klein underwear. I just thought, "What the fuck?" That was the last thing this guy was about. That wouldn't have been what he wanted.' One of the more bizarre moments was when Buckley's dentist approached Mary Guibert on the reception line. He told her how Buckley had always insisted on metal fillings, telling him: 'I want them until they fall out when I am an old man.' Guibert was touched; she felt it was very much 'the spirit in which Jeff lived his life... gain wisdom as if you were going to live forever.'[18]

Danny Fields was quietly walking around the grounds of St Ann's when he was approached and asked to say something at the service. Although renowned for his public speaking, Fields was unprepared, and a little insulted that he hadn't been asked earlier. 'I was resentful for that, and I was also resentful at Jeffy for dying,' Fields recalled. 'And I needed someone to curse under my breath as I ran for the bus stop. It was so hot, so horrible. The whole thing was horrible, and that he was dead was horrible. They were putting chairs around in a circle like an AA meeting, I mean, Jesus Christ, what are they going to do, pass the speech bucket around? Count me out. I fled.'

The memorial service held on the west coast, at the Anaheim chapel where Guibert and Tim Buckley had been married, was equally uncomfortable for some who attended. A few days earlier, Kathryn Grimm, Buckley's bandmate from Group Therapy, received a call from Guibert, asking her to sing at the service. When Grimm asked Guibert what song she thought was appropriate, she was taken aback: Guibert requested the theme from the turgid drama *The Rose*, a soggy ballad that opens with the lines: 'Some say love/It is a river/That drowns the tender reed.' Given the nature of Buckley's death, it seemed wildly inappropriate. 'Are you sure?' Grimm asked. Guibert replied that it was one of his favourite movies and he loved it as a young kid, and it really touched him in a deep way. 'I was surprised by that, really kind of stunned.' Reluctantly, Grimm sang the song. 'I was really choked up,' she said. 'That was the first loss that I really, really felt deeply. It was such a shock. I found myself wanting to talk, talk, talk about Jeff, so it was incredible, really helpful, but I've felt sad ever since.' Ron Moorhead, Buckley's stepfather, played a selection of classic rock numbers on the church organ, while Rebecca Moore also sang. 'The memorial was odd,' observed a friend of Buckley's. 'The emotions were still so raw.' Some of Buckley's closer friends, including Carla Azar, his one-time band mate, weren't even advised about the service.

As difficult as it was for those close to Buckley to deal with his sudden, tragic departure, what lay ahead presented almost as much discomfort: in death, just like his father Tim, Jeff Buckley was set to become a far bigger star. As Chris Dowd told me, there was no way Buckley would have chosen to have been remembered as some sort of tragic, doomed, James Dean-like figure. 'If he had any idea that anything was going to happen to him, he wouldn't have left his legacy to [his mother]. He would probably given every-fucking-thing with his name on it away. That's how he was. He was a truly selfless person.'

Notes

1. www.jeffbuckley.com
2. Dwyer, Michael: Out Of The Shadows, *The Age*, September 29, 2006
3. Fine, Antony: *Jeff Buckley Drowns* (unpublished)
4. See note 1
5. See note 1
6. BBC2: *Everybody Here Wants You* documentary
7. Bambarger, Bradley: Fans, Friends Mourn Passing Of Jeff Buckley, *Billboard*, June 14, 1997
8. Sischy, Ingrid: *I Never Asked To Be Your Mountain*, Interview, August 1, 1997
9. See note 8
10. See note 6
11. Flanagan, Bill: *Sketches For My Sweetheart The Drunk*, liner notes, Columbia Records 1997
12. See note 6
13. Engleheart, Murray: Last Goodbye, *Hobart Mercury*, May 11, 2000
14. Arcade, Penny: Jeff Buckley: *Mannish Boy, Setting Sun*, www.pennyarcade.tv/friends/jeff_buckley.html
15. Lisle, Andria: One Glorious Spring, *The Oxford American*, summer 2000
16. Irvin, Jim: It's Never Over, *Mojo*, August 1997
17. See note 3
18. Somerville, Colin: Mother Of A Job, *Scotland On Sunday*, May 7, 2000

Coda

It's a bitter irony that the success Jeff Buckley sought while alive only really came his way after his death. In the decade that's passed since he took that fateful dip in the Wolf River, he has joined the 'pantheon of the posthumous', alongside such acts as downbeat folkie Nick Drake, ethereal songbird Eva Cassidy, politicised hip-hopper Tupac Shakur, and, yes, Tim Buckley, who've all become far better known – and far more commercially successful – in the years after they died.

The two records that Buckley actually completed in his lifetime, *Live At Sin-E* and *Grace*, have both continued to sell in reasonable numbers since his death, and his timeless songs are constantly drawing new followers: everyone from Hollywood heartthrob Brad Pitt to squillion-selling soft-rockers Coldplay have talked him up with due reverence. Buckley is no longer merely the favourite of '50-year-old rockers' as he half-joked when he was alive. His version of 'Hallelujah' has redefined the term ubiquitous, while the steady stream of posthumous Buckley releases, including various live albums, DVDs and documentaries, plus the Legacy re-issues of *Grace* and *Live At Sin-E*, have established a profile that Buckley failed to achieve while he was alive. There's no doubting that the irony wouldn't be lost on the man himself.

The high regard with which Buckley was, and still is, held by his fellow singers and strummers is evident by the remarkable number of songs that have either been inspired by Buckley, or quite clearly been written as a tribute to the man with the golden voice. Buckley has been celebrated in song even more than Beatles John Lennon and George Harrison, a telltale sign of what a singular talent he was (and quite possibly an indicator of the rather dire musical climate from which he emerged). The list runs from the obvious – Amy Fairchild's 'Jeff Buckley Song', Thomas Dybdahl's 'From Grace', Badly Drawn Boy's 'Fall In A River' – to the deeply personal: Buckley's lover Joan Wasser has written several songs about him; Rebecca Moore recorded 'Live In Blue Sparks' for her former beau, while Chris Cornell, who became actively involved in Buckley's legacy, cut 'Wave Goodbye' in his honour. There are also heavy-hearted musical tributes from Aimee Mann ('Just Like Anyone'), Elysian Fields, a band featuring Mick Grondahl and Michael Tighe ('Cities Will Fall'), PJ Harvey ('Memphis'), Rufus Wainwright ('Mississippi Skyline'), The Frames (' 'Neath the Beeches'), Juliana Hatfield ('Trying Not To Think About It') and many, many others whose paths crossed, or whose music was touched by Buckley. The band Ours, whose singer, Jimmy Gnecco, would play a role in Buckley's musical after-life, also recorded a couple of songs that honoured Buckley, including 'As I Wander' and 'Bleed'.

Possibly the best and most Buckley-like tribute was recorded by Duncan Sheik, who'd almost given up songwriting after witnessing a devastating Buckley in-store. The elegiac, Eastern-flavoured 'A Body Goes Down' appeared on his 1998 album *Humming*, and was used for the 2004 Buckley documentary *Amazing Grace*.* The song also marked the return of drummer Matt Johnson, whom Sheik lured out of his self-imposed exile in Texas, where he'd landed after that final Sydney show in 1996, to work on the song. 'To all intents and purposes,' said Sheik, '[he'd] quit the music business. Matt, who's one of the healthiest people on the planet, was teaching yoga, and my manager called him and said, "You really should come back to New York, I have an artist that would love to record with you." He'd sent him a couple of songs and I guess he was excited enough to jump in his car and drive back to New York and start working with me. When it came to recording "A Body Goes Down", I had a few conversations with Matt as to whether he thought it was respectful,' Sheik added. 'Matt was game. I don't think he needed to mythologise Jeff.' They'd work together for several years, a move that kick-started Johnson's now enviable career CV; he's currently drumming for Rufus Wainwright, and returned to the studio with Sheik in late 2007.

'I think it's a kind of way of placating ourselves,' said Sheik, when I asked why he wrote 'A Body' and why so many Buckley tributes exist. 'It's one of those mysteries of life that we can't answer, but it feels better to think that he came here to do this one amazing thing and bring this deep beauty to the world and that process was finished and he needed to go back, as Buddhists say, to that state of neither existence or non-existence, another place, another

---

* Sheik recalled how Mary Guibert dropped him 'a really nice note' thanking him for the use of the song.

existence. I don't really believe in fate, but there are things like that that make me start to think that certain fates are written in the stars, that there are people, like Jeff, with a strong tendency for something like that to happen. I mean, his body washed up on the same street as a statue of Elvis.'

It's hard to pass judgment on the intentions of the dozens of Buckley tribute songs, nor would it be fair to criticise the many high-profile bands – Starsailor, Coldplay, Radiohead, amongst many others – whose music was clearly touched by the man. But there's much disquiet and heated debate within the Buckley community regarding the way his musical legacy has been handled by Mary Guibert and Columbia. The almost-unanimous belief amongst those close to Buckley is that much of the music that has emerged in his name since 1997 not only runs contrary to his perfectionist streak but would never have seen the light of day had he stayed alive. It's no accident that the word 'Sketches' was added to his first posthumous release, *Sketches For My Sweetheart The Drunk*: even in death, Buckley wanted it known that these songs were nothing but rough drafts.*

Mick Grondahl cut through the crap when I asked him what Buckley would have thought of the situation. 'I can speak for Jeff when I say that he wouldn't be happy with the live albums that have come out. But if it introduces people to our music, and that's how it happens, that's the way it is. But I have nothing to do with it.'

Glen Hansard was equally forthright. 'I've never listened to *My Sweetheart The Drunk* and this mate of mine didn't want it released, so why should I listen to it? I've always had a weird relationship with that idea. A bunch of records have been released on Jeff's behalf, but he was really against bootleggers. He'd go into the audience and argue with people, pull tape recorders out of their hands. I've seen him do it. My theory is that if this guy wasn't into it, then leave it the fuck alone.' Hundreds of pristine quality live recordings of Buckley and the band exist from the *Grace* era, but steps have been taken to ensure that most of these tapes are never heard, mainly because they were recorded purely for the band to review on the day after their shows. They were never intended to become public property.

The lively and profitable Jeff Buckley cottage industry kicked into gear within months of his death. In August 1997, Mary Guibert hired her own

---

* Admittedly, it could be worse: the mother of Layne Staley, the Alice In Chains singer who OD'd and died in 2002, actually sings his songs at the annual memorial for her son.

lawyers, effectively displacing George Stein and Dave Lory, and preventing the planned September 1997 release of a single album of Buckley's final studio recordings with Tom Verlaine, which had been mixed by Andy Wallace and Steve Berkowitz. Guibert, with the support of the remaining band members, was able to delay the release until early 1998, even though Sony owned the masters. She called the label's plans 'exploitive and premature'[1] Guibert reached out to Michael Clouse, Buckley's partner from the X Factor days, and they began sifting through the four-track demos that Buckley had been cutting in his Rembert Street house in Memphis, with a view to also releasing the pick of these, and spreading the album over two discs. This would become known as *Sketches For My Sweetheart The Drunk*.

With the various memorials done and dusted, some of Buckley's musical cronies now started to pay their own respects. In late 1997, The Grifters, who'd been on the road when they heard about Buckley's death, reached New York, where they got together with Michael Tighe, Grondahl, Parker Kindred, Joan Wasser and others, to raise a glass to Buckley. 'That was an intense night and I don't remember too much about it because I was really drunk,' said Dave Shouse. 'We pretty much had to be.' Tighe and Wasser would briefly become lovers, while members of Buckley's band, along with such people as Shouse and Wasser, would subsequently work together in Black Beetle, The AM and Those Bastard Souls, plus various other projects.

'You can't deny that it hit everybody so hard that you kind of collapse into a heap together,' said Shouse, who played with Wasser in Those Bastard Souls. 'There was a lot of unspoken things; it wasn't like when the Souls were touring that I'd grab Joan and say, "I just had a Jeff moment in the bathroom!" But it felt good to be with everybody and hope that it was doing some good and help people get over things.'*

Mick Grondahl felt Buckley's death particularly hard. Glen Hansard witnessed the bassist's deterioration first hand, when he booked Grondahl and another friend of Buckley's, Jack McKeever, to play a show in Dublin. 'I got them a place at a friend's B&B; she was a huge friend of Jeff's and Jack's and Mick's. My friend was really embarrassed because she fancied Mickey and loved Jeff's music, but ended up having to clean up this toilet bowl that he'd smashed. It was embarrassing. It was a B&B in Dublin, it wasn't the Chateau Marmont. All the money we made on the gig was spent fixing the hotel

---

* Buckley's death inflicted a crushing financial blow on Memphis' Easley Studio, which struggled to fill the two-month block that he'd booked for the proposed 1997 sessions with Andy Wallace. The studio burned down in 2005.

room. It was a sad end to the whole Jeff story for me. Those guys were so fresh when I first met them.'

Penny Arcade, meanwhile, was also mourning Buckley's passing. She'd heard about Jimmy Gnecco, the Buckley soundalike who was actually managed by Gene Bowen. (There was a wild rumour also doing the rounds that Gnecco was being considered as a vocal 'replacement' for Buckley, stepping in to complete the *My Sweetheart The Drunk* album.) Arcade was up for a fight soon after Buckley's death when she learned that Gnecco was playing a gig at Arlene's Grocery, Shane Doyle's new club, which was considered hallowed Buckley turf, being the site of his last New York show. A few songs into his set, Arcade stood up and yelled: 'Dead man on stage. Jeff Buckley lives!' and was thrown out of club. Bowen called Arcade the next day and abused her, but as far as she was concerned, she was doing Gnecco a favour. Bowen and Arcade haven't talked since.*

In February 1998, in anticipation of the release of *Sketches*, an official Jeff Buckley web site (www.jeffbuckley.com) was established. At around this time, Mike Webb, who'd left Columbia, was hired by Steve Berkowitz to log 'everything Buckley' that could be found in the A&R man's office: cassettes, DATs, videos, the works. Berkowitz also invited Webb to his house to hear the *Sketches* recordings and revealed to his former assistant 'the problems of making the record'. When Webb heard the sultry ballad 'Everybody Here Wants You', he almost asked for his job back: he felt that he could have broken the song at 'black radio', which would have tapped a whole new audience for Buckley. Berkowitz agreed with him.

By April, the *Sketches* album was being streamed at Buckley's web site, in advance of a May release for the LP, which would combine the 'finished' album of Verlaine-produced, Wallace-mixed tracks with an assortment of Memphis home demos, plus the radio recording of 'Satisfied Mind' that was played at Buckley's memorial service. In a *Billboard* article from May 4, Guibert appeared on the defensive, as if anticipating disapproval from certain quarters. 'This album may not be what Jeff would have wanted to release in his lifetime,' she admitted, 'but his lifetime is over.' She insisted, tellingly, that the album was compiled 'with more love than commerce in our hearts', something her many detractors would question.[2] Producer Andy Wallace added: 'I know Jeff wanted another go at these songs, but I think the material he recorded with Tom stands up to anything around. As

---

* Jimmy Gnecco failed to respond to a request to speak for this book.

far as the demos, they're unsweetened and a harder listen. Jeff is very unguarded on those four-tracks – listening to them is like reading his diary.'[3] (Interestingly, there are several home recordings still unreleased, including 'Let's Bomb The Moonlight' and 'Peace Offering', songs as strong as any others on that second disc.)

Sketches remains a challenging listen, which is understandable, given the emotional baggage and the musical expectations that are attached to it. It's clear from the Verlaine-produced tracks – with the exception of the stark, beautiful 'Everybody Here Wants You', which would receive a Grammy nomination in 1999, and the hypnotic 'New Year's Prayer' – that he was searching for a much more raw, aggressive sound than could be heard on *Grace*. One writer likened *Sketches* to the idea of 'Nick Drake fronting a grunge band'. And the 'flying Buckleys' were nowhere to be found; an Australian musicologist, who wrote a dissertation on Buckley's remarkable voice, noted that the highest note he attempted on the album was during a track entitled 'Gunshot Glitter', which was only included with an international release of the record. 'He loved to wail in "head" voice' – his show-stopper note, as it were – 'on half the songs on *Grace* but mysteriously stopped doing them on *Sketches*,' she observed.[4] As contrary as ever, it seemed as though Buckley was striving to escape the restraints of being known simply for his crystal-shattering voice. And the lyric of 'Nightmares By The Sea' – 'stay with me under these waves tonight' – was bound to haunt anyone who listened to the record. It was ample proof for those who suspected that Buckley had some sense of his limited time on the planet, even if it's a stretch to believe he actually knew how he was going to die.

Reviews of *Sketches*, which was released in North America on May 26, and packaged in some countries with Buckley's written apology to Bob Dylan, were mixed. The first disc was generally well received – 'it has moments of astonishing beauty', noted one critic, 'it often approaches brilliance', said another – but the second CD, the home demos from Memphis, was a harder sell. *The Observer* felt that it was 'almost unlistenable'; an Australian critic called it 'a waste of time'. Most reviewers agreed that the *Sketches* part of the title summed up the album neatly: this was Buckley's 'last incomplete hurrah'. Well, not quite.

In June 1999, Dave Lory sent Mary Guibert a box containing almost 100 live recordings, from shows between 1994 and 1997. Assisted by Michael Tighe, she began sorting through them with a view to compiling a live album. The original plan was to release one live show in full but this was scrapped for an album of individual recordings. The 12-track *Mystery White*

Boy album, much of which was taken from the 1996 show at the Melbourne Palais, with Jimmy Page looking on, was released in early May 2000. A few days later, *Live In Chicago*, a May 1995 show from the Cabaret Metro, and possibly the only Buckley concert to be professionally filmed in its entirety, was released on DVD and VHS. Again, Guibert acted as spokesperson for these releases, describing how she pieced the projects together with a box of Kleenex nearby, and stressing that the releases were a response to fan demand, rather than an attempt to raid the Buckley vaults. 'I feel a responsibility to his legacy and fans,' she said.[5]

To the credit of Guibert and Tighe, there was enough on *Mystery White Boy* to make it more than purely a must-have for grieving Buckley true believers. The inclusion of 'Lilac Wine' and Judy Garland's 'The Man That Got Away' paid due tribute to Buckley as a song interpreter – likewise the snippet of The Smiths' comi-tragic 'I Know It's Over' – while 'What Will You Say' was the enticing 'bonus track', a hitherto unreleased gem. As with *Sketches*, the reviews were balanced, the verdict being, in the words of Australia's *Sunday Herald*, that it was 'a pretty fair summation of Jeff Buckley live'.[6] Some reviews read as if it was a relief to go back to the source, as it were: since Buckley's death, the charts had been clogged by the likes of David Gray, whose *White Ladder* had an unmistakable Buckley influence, and Coldplay, whose runaway hit 'Yellow' and its parent album, *Parachutes*, tapped into the same strain of emotional frankness and sonic grandeur that powered *Grace*. The rise of other Buckley-wannabes such as Keane, Travis, James Blunt and Snow Patrol, none of them worthy enough even to re-string Jeff's guitar, loomed in the near future.

Subsequent posthumous releases appeared at regular intervals over the next few years. Another in-concert set, *Live At L'Olympia*, which captured French Buckley hysteria at its peak, dropped in July 2001. It was another good-enough document of Buckley and band live, notable for his credible attempts to connect with the locals – sometimes he dropped into serviceable French, to their delight – and his reading of Edith Piaf's 'Je N'En Connais Pas La Fin'. The 'bonus' track was a recording of Buckley and revered Azerbaijani singer Alim Qasmiov jamming 'What Will You Say' at the Festival Of Sacred Music, held at Saint-Florent-Le-Vieil on July 18, 1995.

L'Olympia was again compiled by Guibert and Tighe, with the 10 L'Olympia recordings – including a balls-out version of 'Kick Out The Jams' and a surprise cover of Led Zep's 'Kashmir', often described by Robert Plant as 'the pride of Led Zeppelin' – taken from a cassette tape found amongst Buckley's few possessions in Memphis. Mark Naficy nominated *L'Olympia* as his favourite Buckley recording. 'He was so much better live; I could never listen to *Grace*, it just doesn't do it for me,' the soundman admitted. 'They're not his best vocal performances; it's like listening to a covers band. But I think *Live At L'Olympia* is great, I listen to that a lot. That's one of his best performances.'

Mystery White Boy and *Live At L'Olympia* were treated with due reverence; it was agreed that these were documents of a rare talent, and were both worthwhile releases. But the next Buckley release, 2002's *Songs To No-One (1991-1992),* an indie-label release of New York-recorded oddities from Buckley's time with Gary Lucas, wasn't greeted so favourably. 'The Gary Lucas thing [*Songs To No-One*], well, I don't even want to begin, so I have no comment on that,' snapped Mick Grondahl, when I asked him about it. The response from Buckley fans has been mixed: '*Songs To No-One* is hard to stomach,' wrote one devotee at www.amazon.com. 'Why listen to crappy versions of ['Grace' and 'Mojo Pin'] when you could just listen to them on *Grace*?' According to Gary Lucas, 'A lot of disappointed fans were expecting more from it.'

Once again, it was a record touched by the hand of Mary Guibert, as Gary Lucas outlined in an email to me. 'I came up with the idea for that album after Jeff's death, but it did not quite turn out like I envisioned, to say the least,' he wrote. The album was essentially a document of the time Lucas and Buckley had worked together, both with Gods And Monsters and as a duo. The 11 tracks were taken either from their few live shows or from demos recorded at Lucas' New York apartment. But a strange decision was made to rework two tracks, 'She Is Free' and 'Satisfied Mind', the first with additional backing from the well-regarded jazz ensemble (and Knitting Factory regulars) Sex Mob, the latter featuring guitar overdubs from esteemed picker Bill Frisell. And a handful of hitherto unheard Buckley/Lucas collaborations were left off the record. 'Normally,' Mary Guibert observed in the liner notes, 'I'm resistant to the notion that anything of a historical nature should be overdubbed in any way. However, their subtle contributions... add a particularly enjoyable dimension otherwise absent from the original recordings.'[7] However, Hal Willner, who was also involved with the project, summed up *Songs To No-One* in his own liner notes, when he wrote, amongst many personal observations: 'These tracks were originally recorded for demo purposes and never intended for release.'[8] That's probably how they should have remained.

The album may have seemed like the final dredging of the Buckley archive, but Columbia and Guibert had other plans: so-called 'Legacy' editions of *Live At Sin-E* and *Grace* followed, in 2003 and 2004, respectively. While both were noteworthy snapshots of an artist under development, neither were essential: the original *Sin-E* release was culled down to four great live tracks, while this sprawling 2 CD monster featured 34 songs, monologues, asides and oddities, and was packaged with a DVD, and essays from, amongst others, Mary Guibert. It may have been pieced together with all due respect for Buckley's café days, but it was simply too much.

As for *Grace*, this was another epic: 22 tracks were collected over two discs, including the now highly acclaimed original album, plus alternate takes of 'Dream Brother' and 'Eternal Life', covers of Screamin' Jay Hawkins' 'Alligator Wine' and Big Star's 'Kanga-Roo', amongst others, the track cut with Shudder To Think ('I Want Someone Badly') and a remix of 'Dream Brother', named for Buckley's favourite brand of incense, Nag Champa. But wait, there was more: the *Making Of Grace* DVD was also included, along with the various videos that Buckley had either contributed to, or that had been pieced together by Columbia after his death. There were also lengthy liner notes and the obligatory tasteful selection of photos and ephemera, but this was Buckley overkill, a document designed purely for rabid collectors. It even included the old chestnut 'Strawberry Street', a track his one-time bandmate Andrew Goodsight dismissed as 'crappy'. He was certain that Buckley, ever the perfectionist, wouldn't have wanted the track released, yet here it was in all its hair-metal ugliness. *Grace: The Legacy Edition* wasn't much of a musical epitaph, and its release seemed odd in the light of the fact that the original album continues to sell well in the USA – up to 1000 copies a week, even now – and internationally. Indeed, the chances are that *Grace* will soon recoup its substantial production and promotional costs, estimated to be in the neighbourhood of one million dollars. Guibert has stated that the album has now just about 'broken even'.

All was relatively quiet on the re-release front, until 2007, when *So Real: Songs From Jeff Buckley* appeared. Once again, it was a beautifully packaged, well documented tribute to Buckley, which featured the odd rarity – a cover of The Smiths' 'I Know It's Over', a live rip through 'Eternal Life', recorded for the Columbia Records Radio Hour show in 1995 – but it was hardly essential. Dave Shouse summed up the general response to *So Real* when I asked him how he thought Buckley might have reacted to its release. 'I think he'd be pretty uneasy about it, something coming out on the 10th anniversary of his death; he'd be totally creeped out by that. Reissuing stuff that people pretty much already have, slapping a new picture on the cover: he wouldn't be real happy, I don't think.' Mick Grondahl agreed. 'It's just too much,' he said.

It's unlikely that *So Real* is the last gasp of Jeff Buckley Inc, because high quality recordings exist of dozens of live shows, including Australian gigs from his 1995 and 1996 tours, plus sets from Glastonbury 1995, the Elvis Costello-curated Meltdown Festival, Japanese concerts, even his final New York dates, both solo (at the Knitting Factory) and with his band at Arlene's Grocery. And somewhere in the thriving world of Buckley bootlegs there are bound to be recordings from his last gigs at Memphis venue Barrister's, which would make for fascinating curiosity pieces. If nothing else, a further series of Guibert-and-Columbia authorised releases would stem this lively illegal trade.

Of course, no tragic life is complete without a Hollywood bio-pic, and in late 2006, after much speculation, it was announced in the *LA Times* that a film entitled *Mystery White Boy* was in development, with the full, if somewhat reluctant support, of Guibert. Hollywood player Brad Pitt had earlier sought out Guibert's blessing for a film, sweetening the offer by helping her establish an archive of her son's music and writings. In a bizarre twist, he'd hired British writer Emma Forrest to work on a screenplay, insisting that she use *The Rose* – the turgid Bette Midler vehicle, loosely based on the life of Janis Joplin, that Buckley allegedly loved as a child – as the inspiration. Guibert rejected the screenplay, in part over a scene that might have been lifted from Oliver Stone's *The Doors* where Buckley, on LSD, hallucinated a meeting with his long-dead father. Despite the statements made by Buckley's friends in this book and elsewhere, Guibert has denied that her son took drugs or suffered from depression. Guibert, allegedly, also blocked efforts from fledgling screenwriter Train Houston to turn David Browne's excellent 2001 biography of both Buckleys, *Dream Brother: The Lives And Music Of Jeff And Tim Buckley*, into a film. When Houston's one-year option on the book lapsed, it wasn't renewed. 'He thought he was running into too much resistance from her,' Browne wrote in an email.

Guibert softened her stance when she met producer Michelle Sy, a former director of development at Miramax Films, who'd worked on the Johnny Depp film *Finding Neverland*. Sy hired a 20-something screenwriter/director, Brian Jun, to develop the Buckley screenplay. Guibert will be credited as producer if the film eventually gets made. Curiously, Guibert has said that she was drawn to Jun because he had no intention of sugarcoating her son's story, even though she'd rejected the earlier screenplay because of the drug-related scenes. 'I've looked into his eyes and I know that he's a straight shooter,' she told the *LA Times*. 'He has the courage and skill to do this the way it should be done.'[9]

One night recently at Memphis' Saigon Lee, Dave Shouse and some friends were having dinner, when they noticed that fingers were being pointed in their direction. 'They were movie people,' Shouse said, 'in town to check out his place, and the girls there went, "They knew Jeff personally," and we said, "Don't tell them that!" ' His wary reaction pretty much sums up the response that Buckley's friends and peers have towards both the proposed film and the seemingly endless stream of 'new' releases. Enough is enough. 'I felt like I'd lost my brother or someone that deeply connected to me and we were all like that, he was so special,' said Dave Shouse. 'It was like a tornado had come to town and it produces these beautiful water spouts and rainbows and all this damage and when it leaves, you don't know what to say.' The only thing that could be said for certain is that while Jeff Buckley may be 10 years dead, the world hasn't heard the last of him, not by a long shot.

Notes

1. Williamson, John: Touched By Amazing Grace, *The Herald*, April 21, 2000
2. Bambarger, Bradley: Columbia Readies Buckley Release, *Billboard*, May 4, 1998
3. See note 2
4. www.jeffbuckley.com
5. See note 1
6. Didcock, Barry: In Praise Of Broken Dreams, *Sunday Herald*, May 7, 2000
7. Guibert, Mary/Willner, Hal: *Songs To No-One 1991–1992*, liner notes, Knitting Factory records, 2002
8. See note 7
9. Brown, Kimberly: Hollywood's Knocking But Mum Guards The Door, *LA times*, October 29, 2006

Jeff Buckley
Selected Discography

Live At Sin-E
Columbia August 1993
Mojo Pin/Eternal Life/J N'en Connais Pas La Fin/The Way Young Lovers Do.

Grace
Columbia August 1994
Mojo Pin/Grace/Last Goodbye/Lilac Wine/So Real/Hallelujah/Lover, You Should've Come Over/Corpus Christi Carol/Eternal Life/Dream Brother.

Sketches For My Sweetheart The Drunk
Columbia May 1998
CD1: The Sky Is A Landfill/Everybody Here Wants You/Opened Once/Nightmares By The Sea/Yard Of Blonde Girls/Witches' Rave/New Year's Prayer/Morning Theft/Vancouver/You & I
CD2: Nightmares By The Sea/New Year's Prayer/Haven't You Heard/I Know We Could Be So Happy Baby (If We Wanted To Be)/Murder Suicide Meteor Slave/Back In N.Y.C./Demon John/Your Flesh Is So Nice/Jewel Box/Satisfied Mind.
* Australian version included bonus track 'Gunshot Glitter'.

Mystery White Boy: Live '95–'96
Columbia May 2000
CD: Dream Brother/I Woke Up In A Strange Place/Mojo Pin/Lilac Wine/What Will You Say/Last Goodbye/Eternal Life/Grace/Mood Swing Whiskey/The Man That Got Away/Kanga Roo/Hallelujah – I Know It's Over (medley).

DVD: Dream Brother/Lover,You Should Have Come Over/Mojo Pin/So Real/Last Goodbye/Eternal Life/Kick Out The Jams/Lilac Wine/What Will You Say/Grace/Vancouver/Kanga Roo/Hallelujah.
Bonus tracks: So Real (acoustic)/Last Goodbye (acoustic).

Live At L'Olympia
Sony International July 2001
Lover,You Should Have Come Over/Dream Brother/Eternal Life/Kick Out The Jams/Lilac Wine/Grace/That's All I Ask/Kashmir/J N'en Connais Pas la Fin/Hallelujah/What Will You Say (featuring Alim Qasimov).

Songs To No-One 1991–1992 (with Gary Lucas)
Knitting Factory Records October 2002
Hymne A l'Amour/How Long Will It Take/Mojo Pin/Song To No One/Grace (studio demo)/Satisfied Mind/Cruel/She Is Free/Harem Man/Malign Fiesta (No Soul)/Grace (live).

Live At Sin-E (Legacy Edition)
Columbia September 2003
Disc 1: Be Your Husband/Lover,You Should Have Come Over/Mojo Pin/Monologue/Grace/Monologue/Strange Fruit/Night Flight/If You Knew/Monologue/Unforgiven (Last Goodbye)/Twelfth Of Never/Monologue/Monologue/Eternal Life/Just Like A Woman/Monologue/Calling You
Disc 2: Monologue/Yeh Jo Halka Halka Saroor Hai/Monologue/If You See Her, Say Hello/Monologue/Dink's Song/Monologue/Drown In My Own Tears/Monologue/The Way Young Lovers Do/Monologue/J N'en Connais Pas la Fin/I Shall Be Released/Sweet Thing/Monologue/Hallelujah.
DVD: Interview/The Way Young Lovers Do/Kick Out The Jams/New Year's Eve Prayer.

Grace (Legacy Edition)
Columbia August 2004
Disc 1: Mojo Pin/Grace/Last Goodbye/Lilac Wine/So Real/Hallelujah/Lover,You Should've Come Over/Corpus Christi Carol/Eternal Life/Dream Brother
Disc 2: Forget Her/Dream Brother (alternate take)/Lost Highway/Alligator Wine/Mama,You've Been On My Mind/Parchman Farm Blues/The Other Woman/Kanga-Roo/I Want Someone Badly (with Shudder To Think)/Eternal Life (road version)/Kick Out The Jams (live)/Dream Brother (Nag Champa mix)

DVD: The Making Of Grace plus videos: Grace/Last Goodbye/So Real/Eternal Life/Forget Her.

So Real: Songs From Jeff Buckley
Columbia May 2007
Last Goodbye/Lover, You Should've Come Over/Forget Her/Eternal Life (road version)/Dream Brother (alternate take)/The Sky Is A Landfill/ Everybody Here Wants You/So Real (live)/Mojo Pin (*Live At Sin-E*)/ Vancouver/J N'en Connais Pas la Fin (*Live At Sin-E*)/Grace/ Hallelujah/ I Know It's Over.

Jeff Buckley also appears on the following recordings:
John Zorn's Cobra Live At The Knitting Factory (1992)
Jazz Passengers: *In Love* (1994)
Brenda Kahn: *King Of Cairo* (1994)
Rebecca Moore: *Admiral Charcoal's Song* (1996)
Brenda Khan: *Destination Anywhere* (1996)
Patti Smith: *Gone Again* (1996)
Various Artists: *Closed On Account Of Rabies: Tales Of Edgar Allan Poe* (1997)
Various Artists: *Kerouac: Kicks Joy Darkness* (1997)
Seedy Arkhestra: *Puzzle* (1997)
Nusrat Fateh Ali Khan: *Supreme Collection Volume 1* (1997)
Shudder To Think: *First Love, Last Rites* (1997)
Various Artists: *Modern Day Storytellers* (1998)
Various Artists: *Rare On Air, Volume 4* (1998)
Morley: *Sun Machine* (1998)
Inger Lorre: *Transcendental Medication* (1999)
Various Artists: *Coded* (2000)
Thinking Out Loud: *Install Rebel Government Here* (2001)
Original Soundtrack: *Vanilla Sky* (2001)
Tom Clark/The High Action Boys: *Cross-Eyed And Bow-Legged* (2002)
Patti Smith: *Land* (1975-2002)
Original Soundtrack: *Feast Of Love* (2007)
Various Artists: *For New Orleans: Benefit For The Musician's Village Ne* (2007)

For a complete discography, and a full list of DVDs, go to: *www.allmusic.com and/or www.jeffbuckley.com*.
For a reasonably comprehensive list of bootlegs, see
www.jeffbuckley.com/rfuller/buckley/discography/bootlegs.html

Acknowledgements

As most Oscar winners declare, I have many people to thank for the existence of this book. My thanks go out to Pippa Masson, of Curtis Brown, a literary agent who knows how to knock both a deal and an author into shape; Chris Charlesworth and Norm Lurie at Omnibus Press, for their continued support and boundless enthusiasm; my wife Diana and our ever-expanding family – my daughter Elizabeth Asha and son Christian Jai – for their ability to deal with a temperamental author (who's also a dedicated father and husband, I hasten to add). I can't emphasise just how important David Browne's excellent tale of two Buckleys, *Dream Brother: The Lives And Music Of Jeff And Tim Buckley*, was in guiding me through the tricky emotional and historical terrain of what he refers to as 'Buckleyland'. He was right, incidentally; it wasn't easy, but it was definitely rewarding. I should also thank Lee Underwood, both for his advice and observations and for his own fine memoir, *Blue Melody: Tim Buckley Remembered*, another incredibly useful guide for my own book.

And due props to the many – and I mean many – people who gave their time, thoughts, opinions, emotions and insights freely and generously for this book. I've done my best to list them all below, but if there's anyone whom I've accidentally left off the checklist, feel free to write and illustrate my oversight. I'm sure you will.

They are Steve Addabbo; Eric Andersen; Penny Arcade; John Barry; JD Beauvallet; Todd Berhorst; Jack Bookbinder; Jen Brennen; Drew Carolan; Tom Chang; Gary Comenas; Merri Cyr; Helene DelleChiaie; Florian Diguet; Peter Doggett; Chris Dowd; Shane Doyle; Michael Dwyer; Peter Fenton; Danny Fields; Kate Foster-Lomas; Mark Geary; Andrew Goodsight; Kathryn Grimm; Mick Grondahl; Mary Guibert; Glen Hansard; Daniel Harnett; Nicholas Hill; John Humphrey; Sharon Jeskey; Kristina Karasulas;

Richard Kingsmill; Tripp Lamkins; Nathan Larson; Claire Leadbitter; Andria Lisle; Gary Lucas;Val MacIver;Tony Maimone; Steve Matthews;Jack McKeever; Rebecca Moore; Ben Mullins; Mark Naficy; Janine Nicholls; Don Nino; Clif Norrell; Zoran Orlic; Jon Pope; Deborah Reed; Leah Reid; Sylvia Rochonnat; Carol Rothman; Mark Sariban; Michael Schwartz; Iain Shedden; Duncan Sheik; Dave Shouse; GE Smith; Rhianne Smith; Randall Stoll; Peggy Bryan Thompson; Mike Webb; Jerrod Wilkins; Howard Wuelfing.

Index

243